MERCER ISLAND

From haunted wilderness to coveted community

This King County Planning Commission map is from 1947.

MERCER ISLAND

From haunted wilderness to coveted community

Jane Meyer Brahm

based upon *Mercer Island—The First 100 Years*

and *Mercer Island Heritage*

by Judy Gellatly

Mercer Island Historical Society
Mercer Island, Washington

© 2013 by Mercer Island Historical Society

ISBN 978-0-615-49866-9

Published by the Mercer Island Historical Society
P.O. Box 111
Mercer Island, WA 98040
www.mihistory.org

Library of Congress: 2013932895

All rights reserved. No part of this publication may be reproduced or transmitted in any form or by any means—graphic, electronic or mechanical, including photocopying, recording, taping or information storage and retrieval systems—without permission in writing from the publisher, except in the case of brief quotations embodied in articles and reviews.

Design by Jenny O'Brien
Composition by Jane Meyer Brahm
Copyediting and indexing by Miriam Bulmer
Maps by Vince Gonska
Printing and binding by Leo Paper Group
Printed in China

Cover Photo:
A view of Mercer Island from Seattle on July 2, 1940, when the first Lake Washington floating bridge opened, finally connecting Mercer Island to Seattle.
Museum of History and Industry

To the people of Mercer Island,

especially the community volunteers,

for their commitment

to the traditions of yesterday

and the vision of tomorrow

Foreword

When Phil Flash, president of the Mercer Island Historical Society, approached me about updating the history book of Mercer Island, I said "Sure, why not!"

I had no idea what I was getting myself into. In the writing world, I was a sprinter, not a long-distance runner. I didn't realize the amount of work I was committing to, nor the amount of discovery, camaraderie and just plain fun that was ahead.

I assembled an editorial board—Sally Brown, Susan Blake, Dick Decker, Nancy Gould-Hilliard and Laurie McHale—to help research, edit and proofread the chapters. We met monthly to discuss the book, to identify photos and wrangle over editorial decisions. None of us is a historian, but we are all interested in history and share a love of Mercer Island. Three of us also shared journalism backgrounds and years working together at the *Mercer Island Reporter*. That was fitting, since it is said, "Newspapers are the first draft of history."

This book is based on two previous editions, *Mercer Island: The First 100 Years,* published in 1977 and *Mercer Island Heritage*, published in 1989. Both were written by the late Judy Gellatly, with the contributions of a host of community volunteers who are acknowledged in those volumes.

We have attempted to build on the work of the past, making changes as necessary and adding photos and sidebars to appeal to today's readers.

It was the vision and foresight of the Mercer Island Historical Society Board that enabled this project to move forward. They are: Phil Flash, Susan Blake, Virginia Anderson, Kisi Goode, Sally Brown, Rand Ginn, Ed Rice, Dick Decker, Bob Lewis and the late Hu Riley, Sam Lake, Ed Maloof, Walt Rogers and Dave Harris.

This new edition would not have been possible without the encouragement and help of the *Mercer Island Reporter* and its editor, Mary Grady. The *Reporter* generously opened its archives for research and its files for numerous photos in the book. We are most grateful.

Special thanks to Terry Moreman, Nancy Lee and Kris Kelsay for marketing, and to Roger and Nancy Page for distribution, to the Mercer Island Library and University of Washington Library for their help in research.

We are grateful to Matt Brashears, Chad Coleman and Owen Blauman for their photography skills, and a number of people whose names are under the personal photos that they allowed us to use in the book.

Acknowledgements

It takes a community to produce a community history such as this. We would like to thank the following people for help in researching, fact-checking or providing content for the book:

Virginia Anderson, Bill Bailey, Bill Barnes, Bob Bersos, Owen Blauman, Pat Braman, Larry R. Brown, Camille Chrysler, Nile Clarke, Ruth Mary Close, Rich Conrad, Duke Coonrad, Richard Curry, David Dykstra, Dick Eichler, Roy Ellingsen, Jean Enerson, Bob Ewing, Myrtle E. Ford, David Garrison, Jerry Gropp, Don Gulliford, Trudy Webster Hanson, Ted Heaton, Dave Henderson and others on city staff, Peggy Follmer Hiatt, Chick Hodge, Jim Horn, John and Heather Hunt, Terri and Paul Jackson, Carolee Jones, Rich Kraft, Jan LaFountaine, Dr. Bob Lewis, Joe and Lynn Lightfoot, Andrea Lorig, Tove Winkler Lund, Emmett and Sandy Erchinger Maloof, Barbara A. Marcouiller, John Marsluff, Jeff and Eve Martine, Matt McCauley, Joel McHale, Sandra Kusak McLeod, Rita Moore, Dick Nicholl, Angelina Odievich, Marilyn Close O'Neill, Diane Oliver, Craig Olson, Kelly Panelli, Ed Pepple, Gary Plano, Harry Poole, Dorothy Reeck, Charlotte Riley, Judy Roan, Dave Ross, Gerry Scalzo, Mick Schreck, Dr. Al Skinner, Virginia Smyth, Ali Speitz, Marguerite Sutherland, Alyce Stroh, Connie Strope, Jack Swanson, Dorothy Swarts, Michael R. Terry, Robert and Linda Tjossem, Chris Tubbs, Joel Wachs, Chip and Barbara Wall, Marcus and Kirsten Ward, Kendall Watson and The Patch, William L. Webster, Robert and Kay Wiley, Susan Wineke, Ginny Wortman, Michael B. Wright and Milt Yanicks.

Finally, I want to thank my family, especially my husband, Bob, for their patience and understanding during this process.

We hope some day to put this book online together with a searchable web site for the Mercer Island Historical Society. Proceeds from the sale of this book will help with that process. So, if you find a reference you can correct or amplify, or if you have memories of Mercer Island that you think should be included in its history, please contact the Mercer Island Historical Society, www.mihistory.org.

Jane Meyer Brahm

Contents

Forword/Acknowledgements.............................vi

Sponsors...viii

Introduction...I

1   From Legends to Loggers.................................13

2   Getting Settled...19

3   The Island's First Tycoon................................25

4   East Seattle, Mercer Island.............................29

5   Early Transportation....................................37

6   Building a Community...................................43

7   The Schools...47

8   The North End..69

9   The South End..83

10 The Depression, World War II........................91

11 At Last, a Bridge..95

12 The '40s and '50s.......................................101

13 The '60s and the Birth of a City.....................111

14 The '70s and '80s......................................121

15 The Ties that Bind.....................................139

16 Communities of Faith.................................149

17 The '90s..157

18 Wild Things in the 'Hood............................177

19 Neighborhoods and Homes..........................181

20 The Sporting Life......................................191

21 2000 to the Future....................................203

22 Then and Now...223

    Appendix...233

    Index...245

| vii

Sponsors

Our sincere thanks to those who have donated to make this book possible

Robert W. "Spike" Anderson
Virginia Moss Anderson and Fred Anderson
Ina Bahner, Windermere Real Estate
Nancy and John Bates
Frank D. Black
Susan Botkin Blake and sons Christopher, Andrew and Matthew
Marilyn and Keith Blue
Mark and Carolyn Boatsman
Glenn Boettcher
Scott Bowman, MIHS '58
Bob and Polly Bragg
Bob and Jane Brahm
Dan and Pat Braman
Larry R. Brown and Sally J. Brown
Bryan and Suzanne Cairns
The Cero family: Mike, Suzie, Olivia, Sophia and Will
William R. Coffin
Coldwell Banker Bain
Covenant Shores Retirement Community
Foster S. and Patricia J. Cronyn
Richard R. Decker
Maggie McKee Dorsey
Eastside Heritage Center
Ewing & Clark Real Estate
First Church of Christ, Scientist, Mercer Island
Philip N. Flash
Sam Fry
Lloyd and Elizabeth Gilman
Rand and Judy Ginn
Kisi Goode
The Gould-Hilliard family
Dan Grausz and Clare Meeker
Don M. Gulliford
Harlow D. Hardinge
Rich and Dee Hitch
Jean Hunt
Island Books Etc, Inc.
Linda and Eric Jackman
Ron and Lori Kaufman
The Keeler family: Travis, Suzy, Allison, Rochelle and Julie
Kris and Todd Kelsay
Gwen Kuhn
Aron and Stephanie Kornblum
Nancy LaVallee
Donna M. Lenox
Dr. Bob Lewis and Dr. Chris Lewis
Marylyn C. and Joseph F. Lightfoot
Bruce and Andrea Lorig
Tove Winkler Lund
Natalie and Bob Malin
Emmett and Sandy Maloof
Ted and Mary Ann Mandelkorn
Gordon and Marilyn Mathis
Voni McCormick
Jack and Laurie McHale
Mercer Island Chamber of Commerce
Mercer Island City Council, 2013
Mercer Island Kiwanis Club
Mercer Island Lions Club
Mercer Island Lodge 297, Free and Accepted Masons of Washington

Mercer Island Presbyterian Church
Mercer Island Women's Club
Lynn G. Meyer
Stephen Monohan and Katherine North Monohan
Buddy and Terry Moreman
Barbara and Larry Morris
James and Susan Ogilvie
Roger and Nancy Page
David N. and Gail D. Parrish
Irene V. Pennell
Gene A. and Edyth Phillips
Barry Potashnick
Jane Potashnick
Leigh Potashnick
Max Potashnick
Rob Potashnick
Olivia Potashnick
Alan D. Quigley
Dean and Donna Quigley
Mrs. Ted Rand
Dorothy Reeck and The Roanoke Inn, LLC
Betty and Ed Rice
Charlotte F. Riley
Kris Robbs
Paul W. and Bettie S. Romppanen
Greg Rosenwald, Coldwell Banker Bain
Jeffrey Ross
Rotary Club of Mercer Island
Lynn Sparrow Saxey
Bobette and Kevin Scheid
Seattle Children's Hospital Guild/Mercer Island Directory
Senior Foundation of Mercer Island
Tana Senn
Dale and Barbara Showalter
Bharat Shyam and Sarah Ford
Alfred L. Skinner, M.D., Mercer Island Pediatric Associates, est. 1955
Allen Smith
Matthew Hunt Smith and Pamela Fricke Smith
Diane and Ed Spaunhurst
Katrina Spaunhurst, M.D.
Glen Thomas Sparrow
Margaret Adele Sparrow
James and Ingrid Stipes
Stroum Jewish Community Center
The Tourtillotte family
Mary Ann Trombold
Linda Tsang
Cindy Hertel Verschueren
Veterans of Foreign Wars Post 5760, Mercer Island
Donald Vollimer
Lindy and Thomas Weathers
Dr. and Mrs. Robert L. Welsh
Mary Ann and Robert Wiley, Jr.
Carrie York Williams, Mark, Elisabeth and Braden Williams
Windermere Real Estate/Mercer Island
Dr. Charles Wischman
Benson Wong and Terry Mark
Michael B. Wright
Brice York, Megan Nichols York and Chase York
Carrie York, D.D.S. and Rebecca Zerngast, D.D.S.
Shelly Zhou

x

Welcome to Mercer Island

When I moved to Mercer Island in 1976, I was struck by how it felt like a small town. I'd see familiar faces in the grocery store. People on the street would say hi. Thirty-seven years later, it still feels like a small town.

Over the years, I've heard people describe Mercer Island as unique, a jewel, as they try to articulate why it feels so special.

I'm convinced it has to do with its "island-ness." Even though Mercer Island is closer to downtown Seattle than most parts of Seattle are and even though one can get to the heart of Bellevue from Mercer Island more quickly than most Bellevue residents can—still, Mercer Island is separate. It's in the center of things, but its shores are boundaries.

The most populous island in a lake in the United States, Mercer Island is a city, with its own police force and fire department. It is the only place in the state where the city and school district boundaries are identical. Residents call themselves Islanders and refer to others as off-Islanders. Mercer Island has limits; it's surrounded by water. All this makes for a strong sense of identity and a feeling of community.

The Island's shared values are easy to identify. Because Islanders value education, they want good schools for their children. Because they value the beauty of a natural environment, they treasure the Island's parks and open spaces. Because they seek to take care of each other, they want the streets to be safe and they support social programs for residents of all ages.

This book opens with a series of photos of Mercer Island today. It then traces the community's development through the decades, from the 1850s to 2013. This work is not intended for the academic or the serious historian. Rather, it's meant for the average person who is curious about the people, places and events of the Island.

It's not easy to capture the soul of a place. But we hope that, through its framework of historic events, this book provides a sense of what this special Island community is like.

Jane Meyer Brahm
Mercer Island Historical Society Editorial Committee
July 2013

This 2006 view looking west shows the Olympic Mountains and the Seattle skyline in the distance, with I-90 curving across the north end of Mercer Island. The East Channel Bridge is at the lower right. When the original Mercer Island floating bridge was built in 1940, it was an engineering marvel, the world's first concrete floating bridge. When the I-90 corridor project across Mercer Island was completed in 1989, it was one of the largest, most complex, most expensive and most controversial highway projects in the world.

Peter Yates / The New York Times / Redux

Mercer Island Report

Above: A sailboat and a paddleboarder ply the waters of Lake Washington along the shores of Mercer Island. Right: A trillium blooms in Pioneer Park.

Mercer Island Report

Mercer Island, Washington 98040

"Once you've lived on an island, you'll never be quite the same."

—Ruth Mary Close
longtime Island resident

Mercer Island Reporter
Left: A home in The Lakes, a development on the south end of the Island.
Below: Kayakers are a familiar sight along the shores of Mercer Island.

Introduction | 5

Poet Jack Prelutsky entertains Mercer Island schoolchildren, right. Buses line up for the afternoon pickup, below.

Mercer Island Reporter

Led by the Seattle Seahawks' mascot, above, kids line up at the starting line of the Kids' Dash, one of the events associated with the of the Mercer Island Rotary Half Marathon. Thousands of runners, left, participate in the annual half marathon and other races and walks held that day, raising money for colon cancer research and other Rotary Club charities. The event marked its 40th anniversary in 2012.

Mercer Island Reporter

Chad Coleman / Mercer Island Reporter

Above: The Mercer Island High School marching band takes to the streets of the Town Center during the 2009 Homecoming Parade. Nearly 300 strong, the marching band has won numerous awards through the years. It played in the Rose Bowl Parade in 1993, 2006 and 2012, and in the New Year's Parade in London in 2011. Far right: Members of the Mercer Island High School drill team drum up some school spirit during a school assembly. Right: Three boys sit on the sidelines watching a basketball practice.

Mercer Island Reporter

The Sunday Mercer Island Farmers Market is a popular weekly event that runs from early June to the end of November.

Chad Coleman / Mercer Island Reporter

Summer Celebration, Mercer Island's annual summer festival and Seattle Seafair event, includes a parade, an arts-and-crafts street fair, an art show, a fun run, three-on-three basketball, a car show, boat rides on Lake Washington and a fireworks display. The two-day festival is held in July. Tricyclists, above, join the parade in pirate attire, to correspond with that year's theme.

10 | Introduction

Chad Coleman/Mercer Island Reporter

Seniors clap to the music during a class at the Stroum Jewish Community Center. Seniors can choose from a wide range of activities offered there as well as through the Mercer Island Parks and Recreation Department. Below, a gardener waters his flowers in the community pea patch near the Mercer Island Community and Event Center.

Introduction | 11

Rowers on Lake Washington head back to the Mount Baker crew house at sunset.

Museum of History and Industry, Seattle.
The Duwamish people paddled this type of canoe around Lake Washington, though they never settled on Mercer Island.

From Legends to Logging

Tales were told of an island that sank into Lake Washington each night

Mercer Island was a late bloomer in regional history. While Seattle had developed into a rough-and-tumble town by the late 1800s, Mercer Island was generally uninhabited, thick with berries, fir trees, wild game, birds and summer encampments of the Duwamish Tribe.

The Duwamish left their coastal villages on food-gathering migrations, drawn to Mercer Island for its blackberries, thimbleberries, salmonberries, salal, Oregon grape, blackcaps, huckleberries and strawberries. They were known to hunt deer and raccoons and trap muskrats and weasels on the lush island.

Legend says that the Duwamish believed an evil spirit dwelt atop the Island, so none would venture near it. Other lore was that the Island sank into the lake each night and rose again in the morning. Possibly the sunken forests found in three places off the Island's shore—one near the south point, one near the west-central shore, and the third at the north end—gave rise to that legend.

No kitchen middens have been found to indicate long-term Indian habitation, but circles of smoke-blackened stones, probably from fires for cooking and berry-drying, were found when the lake was lowered in 1916 as part of the locks project.

Other artifacts have surfaced: an item resembling a candleholder found on a westside beach in 1920; a small, white, quartz-like arrowhead on an eastside beach in 1937; an arrowhead near Ferncroft on East Mercer Way in 1953, later identified by the University of Washington Department of Archaeology as a 2,000-year-old spearhead.

The Indians called the East Seattle area "The Place Where Gooseberry Bushes Grow."

The Indians called the East Seattle area "The Place Where Gooseberry Bushes Grow," according to the late Northwest journalist and historian Lucille McDonald. The southernmost point was called "Stripping" because of a legendary old man who came by canoe to gather bark from dead trees. Fabled earth beings lived in the old stumps, and when he removed the bark it left them naked. The creatures drove the old man crazy and thus the Indians feared the place.

Chapter 1: From Legends to Logging | 13

At least one Indian was born on the Island, according to Loretta Slater, a Seattle social worker who in 1944 interviewed an elderly Sammamish woman. Asked the date and place of her birth, the woman told this story: Her people had once traveled by canoe from their home on Lake Sammamish, by way of the Sammamish Slough, to the lake and "its island where they hunted and picked berries." They had planned to return home before nightfall, but a strong wind and heavy rain came up. So they made a shelter near the beach and stayed overnight.

The Sammamish woman's mother gave birth to a baby that wet and stormy night, on the Island where Indians allegedly feared to stay because of the spirits. That Sammamish baby may have been the first person known to be born on Mercer Island, circa 1870s.

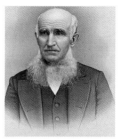

Mercer Island is named for Thomas Mercer, one of three famous Mercer brothers who moved to the Puget Sound region in the mid-1800s. His namesake island was thick with old-growth forests of Douglas fir, western hemlock and red cedars, and madronas and maples.

Museum of History and Industry
Mercer Island Historical Society

1849 Mercer Island becomes part of Oregon Territory.

1854 Judge Thomas Mercer names Lake Washington and Lake Union. His friends name Mercer Island after him.

1859 Washington Territory separates from Oregon Territory.

1860 First survey of Mercer Island.

1869 Seattle's population: 1,107

1876 Vitus Schmid builds a cabin on the Island but doesn't stay.

1879 East Seattle School District begins.

1884 Gardiner Proctor and his Indian wife, Ellen, settle on the Island.

Island's namesake

Thomas Mercer, who came to Seattle in 1852, was friendly with the native tribes. He often had an Indian row him to "Klut-Use" (translation: the Island) in the morning and return at evening in time to row him back. Mercer enjoyed exploring the quiet, wooded Island. He picked berries and walked along the shoreline.

On one such occasion, when the Duwamish Indian returned, Mercer was not waiting. When it began to get dark, the man left. When he returned in the morning, Mercer was waiting. The Indian stepped ashore and carefully felt Mercer's clothes. They were not soaking wet and he concluded that Mercer had supernatural powers, since he had survived the island's nightly sinking.

It's likely that Mercer Island was named after Thomas Mercer, who led a wagon train from Illinois over the Oregon Trail in 1852 with his wife, Nancy, four daughters and younger brother, Aaron. His wife fell ill on the journey and died before crossing the Cascades.

Of the three Mercer brothers, the most famous was the youngest, Asa, who is best remembered for his efforts to solve the shortage of marriageable women in the Puget Sound region. He recruited the "Mercer Girls" from the East Coast.

At just 22 years of age, Asa

Legacy from the Ice Age: Island of blue clay

Indian lore of Mercer Island's mystical beginnings—that it submerged by night and arose each morning as a berry-picking playground—is partially right. The natives' circumstantial evidence: the underwater forests offshore from what's now Forest Avenue and Clarke Beach and on the Island's northern tip. Carbon tests show that these sunken forests are about 1,100 years old.

More recently, geologists' scientific evidence (from studying glacial sediments and tertiary rocks in massive submarine slides in Lake Washington) supports the theory that slope failures probably were triggered by large earthquakes along the Seattle Fault, or even stronger ones elsewhere in Cascadia. Such submarine slope failures occurred more than once in the last 11,000 years—probably every 300 to 500 years in the Puget Sound region, say geologists.

Could it be that the coastal Salish/Duwamish, who were thought to have come to the region 5,000 —9,000 years ago, witnessed some of those massive sloughs, or at least heard of them?

While portions of Mercer Island were submerged by ancient landslides, today the trend continues with an average of six to 15 slides per winter, according to the city, which has mapped areas of weak ground and potential hazards.

Mercer Island sits squarely in the Seattle fault zone, which further heightens earthquake hazards. The winter rainy season is the most problematic, when saturated and unstable soil causes slumps of clay and unbound gravel to sheer off the slopes.

However, 12,000-plus years ago, the Island's bedrock was ocean bottom, as seen from archaeological fossils and other findings. There is evidence of an ancient shoreline approximately 40 feet below lake surface, where the waves cut into the rock.

Mercer Island Reporter

In a typical year, Mercer Island has from six to 15 landslides, with damages ranging from a few thousand dollars to hundreds of thousands. The "landslide season" is from late winter to early spring, with January being the peak month. The landslides are triggered by excess precipitation and discharges from roof drains and excavations in high-risk areas. This 1977 photo in the 8400 block of West Mercer Way shows one of the more destructive slides in recent years.

Once late-Pleistocene glaciers advanced from the north, much of the earth's crust was bulldozed by nature and reshaped into present configurations. Prior to Lake Washington, a master Lake Russell drained southward during initial glacial retreat, its melt filling the spaces from Seattle to Chehalis. The Duwamish tribe called it Xacuabš (Lushootseed for "great amount of water"), until it drained and reformed into Lake Washington and other recessional lakes.

As you sit atop Mercer Island's highest outlooks, such as Upper Shorewood and Lakeview Highlands, you see Lake Washington, the handiwork of the Ice Age stretching from Renton to Kenmore. This 20-mile-long ribbon lake was glacially carved to 210 feet at its deepest, leaving gravelly till from the Vashon Glacier, familiar to many local gardeners.

Mercer Island is one of five islands in Lake Washington; the others are Foster, Marsh, Ohler's and Pritchard. They were results of glacial moraines, or deposits of gravel, volcanic ash, blue-gray clay and silt. (This glacial clay is of such a fine texture it now is used by potters.)

Under the thousands of pounds of glacial weight, Mercer Island took its contemporary shape—similar to a miniature South America. Other natural forces, such as nearby volcanic ash deposits and uprisings, and more glacial floods and water lowerings, also had their way with the Island.

The last water-lowering was man-made in 1916, and caused Mercer Island to gain substantial real estate on its perimeter. The Lake Washington Ship Canal and its Hiram Chittendon Locks were built to connect Lake Union to the salty Puget Sound to enable ships' passage. After the Montlake Cut connected the waterway to Lake Washington, the lake became 9 to14 feet lower, and Mercer Island was but one of the lake's land masses to gain larger waterfront lots.

became the first president of the new Territorial University of Washington in Seattle, which became the University of Washington.

Aaron Mercer built a home for his family on a meandering waterway later named for him, the Mercer Slough. He later settled in the South Park area of Seattle, where he lived until his death in 1902.

The eldest Mercer, Thomas, filed a claim for land in Seattle in 1852 and built his home near what is now the intersection of Taylor Avenue and Roy Streets. He was the area's first probate judge, a post he held for 10 years.

It started at a party

The story goes that Mercer Island was named at a party that Judge Thomas Mercer hosted at his Seattle home on the Fourth of July, 1854. He transported most of the settlers by horse-drawn team, making many trips to assemble the crowd for the gala picnic.

After dinner at noon, a meeting was called for the purpose of naming two local lakes. Mercer proposed naming the large lake after George Washington, the first president of the United States, and the smaller one Union, expressing his patriotism. He also predicted that one day a canal would connect Lake Washington to a bay (Shilshole, also named that day) along the Puget Sound, with Lake Union as the connecting link.

A prominent citizen at the picnic suggested that the large island in the lake be named after their host, Thomas Mercer himself. The partiers heartily agreed.

Although none of the Mercer brothers ever lived on the Island, it is named for the one who loved to walk its shores.

Mercer Island Historical Society

This view of the west-side waterfront of Mercer Island circa 1910 evokes the days when the Duwamish Indians would come to the Island to hunt for game and gather berries and roots.

16 | Chapter 1: From Legends to Logging

Museum of History and Industry

At least one steam-driven donkey engine like this one was set up on Mercer Island to aid in logging the Island. In only two decdes of intensive logging, nearly all of the old-growth timber was harvested.

Logging fever hits in the 1880s

Before its settlement, the entire Island was heavily wooded. The evergreens probably grew to great heights in their long lives, sheltered from winds by the east and west ridges and by Lucas Hill. When logging fever hit in the 1880s, it took only 20 years to harvest the stands of centuries-old cedar, Douglas fir and western hemlock that covered the Island.

Yarding, a process of hauling logs to a central loading area, began in earnest in the 1880s when steam engines replaced animal teams to yard logs. These donkey engines were fueled by ever-plentiful wood. A long cable was attached to a log, then the donkey engine reeled it in.

A steam donkey was set up near 80th Avenue Southeast and Southeast 29th Street. Logs were yarded and sent down the skid roads, bumping along down 84th Avenue Southeast to the Luther Burbank beach.

Ernest Person retold his father's stories of how he would walk to what is now 76th Avenue Southeast and Southeast 32nd Street and watch the donkey engine at work.

"The skid road was left for years, from the vicinity of 32nd and 80th, north along the ridge, then to the northeast following the slope to what is now the swimming beach at Luther Burbank Park," he recalled. "Horses and oxen were used to skid logs to the lake from the donkey engine. Logs were then boomed and towed to sawmills on the lake."

When an area had been logged off, the logging camp—with temporary structures such as bunkhouses, a cookhouse and sheds for horses—was moved on large scows.

Florence Guitteau Storey remembered finding remnants of skid roads, rotting and overgrown, when she lived on the north end of the Island in 1901.

Chapter 1: From Legends to Logging | 17

Mercer Island 1909

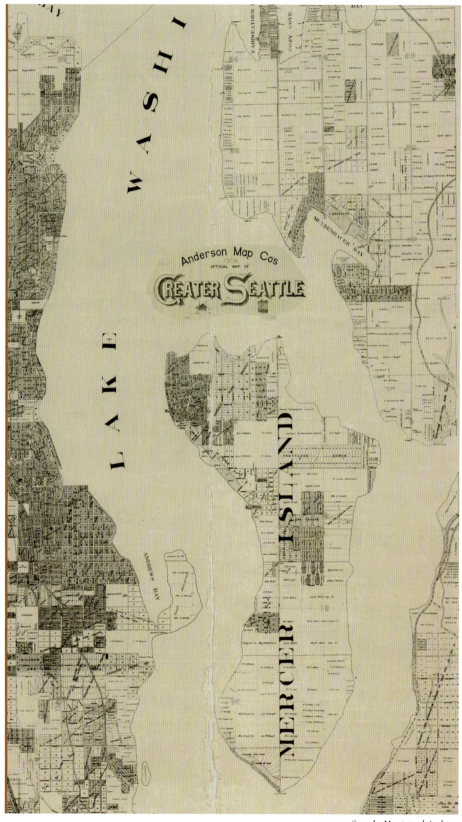

Seattle Municipal Archives

Getting Settled

A hearty few braved the rigors of early Island life

First settlers

The Island was slow to attract settlers and for years was known only to hunters, trappers and berry-pickers. Its rocky and wooded hills were daunting for would-be farmers. But the Homestead Act and the transcontinental railroad generated a mighty wave of westward movement in the 1870s and 1880s. A few European immigrants settled on Mercer Island.

Schmid's bad luck

Vitus Schmid, a wagon-maker from Hohenzollern, Germany, came to the U.S. at age 16 after serving his apprenticeship. He worked his way west, building snow sheds for the Northern Pacific Railroad.

Schmid is thought to have built the first wagon in Seattle in 1872, for teamster David Morris. Schmid and John Wenzler, a cobbler from Chicago, filed a 160-acre claim on the central part of Mercer Island, and built a log cabin in 1876. After a windstorm toppled a large fir tree onto their house, completely demolishing it, they abandoned their claim. Wenzler went back to his cobbler's bench and Schmid returned to Chicago.

Two years later, Schmid returned to the area to make a fresh start, now with his wife, Sarah, and their sons, Conrad and Victor. Three weeks after their arrival, a daughter, Theresa, was born in a shack on the Tacoma waterfront. Schmid opened a tavern, patronized largely by German immigrants. Another daughter, Caroline, was born. Wife Sarah died in 1885 at age 29.

Schmid filed another claim on Mercer Island in 1878 and built another cabin.

Luck was still against him.

A lumber company challenged his right to the claim and the case was in the courts for 11 years. Schmid won and finally received clear title. He sold his tavern, married Ida Dreyer from Chicago and moved his family to Newcastle in 1891 and then into the cabin in 1900. Later he built a new home on the hill above the cabin.

But bad fortune was still his lot.

A daughter, born to Ida and Vitus in the

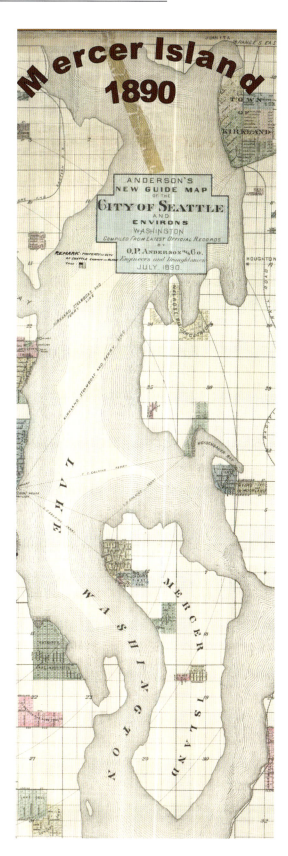

This 1890 map, "Anderson's New Guide Map of the City of Seattle and Environs," was compiled "from the latest official records" by O.P. Anderson and Company in July 1890. It shows only three areas were platted on the Island: East Seattle, the green area on the west side identified as "Harry White's Plot," and the "Olivet" and "Lindley" plots in the mid-central part of the Island.

Seattle Municipal Archives

Chapter 2: Getting Settled | 19

early 1900s on Mercer Island, died in infancy. His two sons, Conrad and Victor, lured to the gold fields of Alaska and the Yukon, died in 1898 when their ship capsized and sank. This sorrow, so close to the death of her infant half-sister, was too much for his daughter, Caroline, who left home at age 18.

Schmid donated an acre of land for a school, and in 1890 the Allview Heights School opened. It was closed five years later for lack of students. Today the Mercer Island Library stands in its place on part of Vitus Schmid's 160 acres.

The original Schmid cabin, located just above Island Crest Way west of the area now known as Maple Lane, was torn down in 1954 to make way for new homes.

Vitus Schmid's descendants show up in plat maps of his "East Seattle Acre Tracts:" Theresa, Caroline, Conrad and Victor Avenues, all named after his children. These names were removed when, in the 1930s, King County changed Mercer Island street names to numbers.

More settlers arrive

While Vitus Schmid was waiting out litigation over his claim, other settlers moved to the Island.

Gardiner Proctor and his Native American wife, Ellen, homesteaded 160 acres, the area from the floating bridge south to what is now Southeast 34th Street, and from West Mercer Way to the lakeshore. He built a log cabin with a dirt floor, planted an orchard and made other improvements.

On June 22, 1873, Proctor sighted a bear near his property and gave chase, according to a story in the June 26, 1873, *Puget Sound Dispatch*.

The bear "took to the lake" and Proctor followed in a skiff, shot and killed the animal and towed it ashore. Proctor didn't know the weight of the bear, but said it was more than 7 feet long. He presented the bear's foot, which measured 8 inches long and 4 inches wide, to Beriah Brown, editor of *Puget Sound Dispatch*. Proctor believed it was "the largest black bear ever seen in this section."

Vitus Schmid and his second wife, Ida, lived in a house they built west of Maple Lane, on part of his original 160-acre claim. Schmid called himself a farmer in most censuses, and a saloon-keeper in others, although he was trained as a wagon-maker.

Mercer Island Historical Society

This photo, taken in about 1910, shows Vitus Schmid, age 61 (right) and his wife, Ida, 48, (second from left) with their daughter and son-in-law, Theresa Schmid McMahon and Edward McMahon, around the dining room table in their Mercer Island home.

Mercer Island Historical Society

20 | Chapter 2: Getting Settled

Mercer Island Historical Society
Agnes and Charles Olds, from a tintype taken in 1868 soon after their marriage in Illinois. In 1885 they settled in the Appleton area on the east side of the Island.

1885 Charles Olds, his wife, Agnes, and children Alla and David settle on Mercer Island.

1886 Bellevue's population is 52.

1887 C.C. Calkins lands in Seattle with $300 in his pocket.

1889 First school is held in a warehouse on the ferry dock on the Island's north end.

1889 C.C. Calkins builds a lavish resort on the northwest corner of the Island, in the area between Calkins Landing and Slater Park.

1889 Swan Person starts a dairy farm on Mercer Island.

1889 Washington Territory becomes a state on Nov. 11.

1890 A school is built in East Seattle, east of the present West Mercer Way, near 27th, and is dubbed "the little white schoolhouse." Eleven students attend.

Gardiner Proctor died in 1889, and Ellen returned to her relatives on the Black River.

The log cabin deteriorated and was bulldozed sometime in the 1940s. Now Proctor's Landing and Proctor Lane are the only memorials to that early pioneer couple.

First family

The legacy of Charles and Agnes Olds, dubbed Mercer Island's "first family," was more enduring.

They were married in 1868 in Illinois and moved to Missouri, where a daughter, Alla, was born in 1875, followed by a son, David, two years later. Prompted by a letter from Henry Yesler describing the wonders and opportunities in the Puget Sound country, Olds packed up his family and moved west.

They traveled to San Francisco by train, then up the coast by ship, reaching Seattle in 1883. Olds built a house in Seattle and worked in Yesler's lumber mill. An accident there almost cost him his life, and did cost him an eye.

Seeking a change of livelihood after his recovery, Olds looked for farmland. In 1884 he filed a claim on property with a good stream about midway on the east shore of Mercer Island. He paid $1.25 an acre for 123 acres of land, including more than 1,200 feet of waterfront. The total price was $156.43; his receipt is dated January 26, 1885.

He finalized his claim just before Washington became a state in 1889, and his deed was signed by President Benjamin Harrison.

Olds built a cabin—one room plus loft—up from the waterfront near the stream. In November 1885, the family loaded its possessions, including a goat, onto a barge at Leschi and towed it by rowboat around the north end of the Island and down the East Channel to their claim.

Charles Olds paid $1.25 an acre for 123 acres of land, including more than 1,200 feet of waterfront.

The next spring they cleared more land and planted 12 acres with a variety of apple and other fruit trees. Olds named his place Appleton. The name survives today, along with a few fruit trees.

In the mid-1880s, isolated by lake and forest, Charles and Agnes Olds were creating a home and raising a family. At first, they had no neighbors, no school, post office, telephone, roads or communication with other parts of the Island. Occasionally, tramp steamers would drop off sacks of feed and other necessities too large for rowboats. To reach civilization, the Oldses needed to row around the north end of the Island and across the lake to Leschi, where they would beach their boat and, climbing over fallen timber, make their way to a wagon road to the foot of Yesler Way.

For a long row and a long walk, the reward was mail from home, their weekly *Seattle Gazette* (later the daily *Post-Intelligencer*), the *Ladies' Home Journal*, *Youth's Companion*, the *Firemen's Fireside Journal* and the excitement of the

Mercer Island Historical Society
Henry E. Kelsey, a young teacher from New York, was hired by Charles Olds and his friend, George Miller, to teach their children in a makeshift cabin on the northeast corner of the Island.

big city. The Yesler cable railroad had not yet been built, Washington was still a territory and the Seattle fire had not yet ravished the waterfront.

First teacher

Although he had chosen to build his home in the wilderness, Charles Olds believed in elementary schooling for his children. He and George Miller, who lived in Enatai and had four children, worked out a plan to start a school in a cabin owned by Miller's son. It was on the northeast shore of the Island in an area called Briarwood, near what was to become the Island end of the East Channel Bridge.

A one-room cabin was refurbished with boxes for seats and black oilcloth for a blackboard. The plan was to hold school on the Island for four months, then for four months at Enatai in Bellevue, where a squatter's cabin was repaired for the purpose.

Charles and Agnes' daughter, Alla Olds Garrison Luckenbill, recalled in 1955, "We lived a long

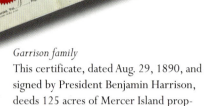

Garrison family
This certificate, dated Aug. 29, 1890, and signed by President Benjamin Harrison, deeds 125 acres of Mercer Island property to Charles L. Olds.

way from that Briarwood shanty, with heavy timber between it and us. The teacher, Henry E. Kelsey, recently arrived from New York, proposed that he board at our house and row David and me back and forth.

"It turned out that he didn't know much about rowing, and one November day the boat swamped. We were soaked, and father had to rescue us. Mother, who feared the water, was so worried she wouldn't let us go by boat anymore in bad weather, so the teacher moved to the school and 'batched it.'

"During the second month the four Miller children were his only pupils. The water was calm between their house and the school, and they didn't mind rowing. When school was held on the Enatai side, we didn't go. Mother taught us for five years. Sometimes we had a tutor. Henry Kelsey went to Hawaii, became a well-known educator and lived the rest of his life there."

After the Schmid family came in 1889, Charles Olds and his daughter, Alla, hiked across the backbone of the Island to visit the new family. Alla was 14; Theresa Schmid was 11. Theresa later re-

Mercer Island Historical Society
This photo of Barnabie Point on the northeast shore of the Island, taken in about 1916, shows the Cedarhurst ferry stop. The view looks east toward Enatai, where the I-90 bridge now crosses. The makeshift cabin where the Olds and Miller children had classes under the tutelage of Henry Kelsey was nearby.

22 | Chapter 2: Getting Settled

called that Alla was leading a goat on a string. Alla remembered that they had 25 goats, and she was the herder and trainer. She sold two goats to a Seattle man who wanted them for a goat-cart team, and received a $10 gold piece, the first money she ever earned.

The pioneering life

Walking or horseback riding were the only ways to get around, via trails cut through the thick forest. In 1886, the first road was built. Charles Olds gathered a number of lumberjacks who needed to work out their poll taxes, and with their help began creating a cart road from his East Mercer farm to the west side of the Island.

From the top near the present intersection of Southeast 47th Street and 92nd Avenue Southeast, the road wound down to County Dock. King County preceded statehood, and road district No. 64 was formed, with Charles Olds as supervisor.

The second official road on the Island began in 1890, five months after Washington became the 42nd state in the Union on Nov. 11, 1889.

Charles Olds, like Judge Thomas Mercer, was friendly and fair to the Native tribes. Alla told about a time when her father, visiting a Native settlement at the mouth of the Black River, saw a woman with a broken arm, the bone protruding. Alla believed this was Ellen, widow of Gardiner Proctor. Olds took her to a doctor and had the arm set and splinted. After that, salmon would appear frequently and unexpectedly on the Oldses' doorstep.

It seems that Olds was something of a domestic despot. Alla wanted to go to the Territorial University. Her father thought higher education was "wasted on females," so refused to let her go.

But Alla had a will of her own. She went anyway, supporting herself by working as a domestic in private homes. As part of her punishment, her father sold her horse so when she taught at the Island's East Seattle School in 1897-1898, she had to walk about 10 miles daily, from Appleton to school and back.

Her brother, David, was more submissive. He wanted to ship out with the Schmid boys when they left for the gold fields of the North. His father flatly forebade it, and David did not go. He escaped death by drowning when the *Jane Gray* went down.

Seattle Times
Appleton, the Olds homestead on East Mercer Way, in the 1890s. Charles Olds is left front; Alla Olds, wearing the brimmed hat, stands behind her mother, Agnes.

Garrison family
Agnes Olds feeds the pigs in about 1915 with her granddaughter, Myrta, in the foreground and grandson George on the fence.

Mercer Island Historical Society
Haying in Appleton, circa 1914.

Garrison family
Agnes Olds at the family graveyard in Appleton, about 1917. The five graves of the Olds family were later moved to a cemetery.

Garrison family

Alla May Olds came to Mercer Island as a child with her parents, Charles L. and Agnes Olds. Alla married Harry Lee Garrison in 1906; this is their wedding photo.

Garrison family

This photo, circa 1917, shows Alla Olds and her children, Myrta and Harry. The back of the photo reads: "At cemetery following Grandma's (Agnes Olds') funeral, 1917."

Olds-Garrison legacy

Charles Olds' first cabin burned. The second also burned. Part of the third may still exist, as it was one of two cabins put together after the fire in 1914; it has been enlarged and remodeled so the original is hardly recognizable.

Olds continued to farm and build roads, living out his life on the homestead. He died of meningitis in 1898 and was buried on his own land, on a knoll above his cabin.

Alla May became the sole support of the family. Two years later, when her younger brother, David, had an attack of acute appendicitis, she rowed around the Island to Leschi in Seattle to get help. Capt. John Anderson fired up the steamer, went to the Appleton dock and transported David to the hospital in Seattle.

But peritonitis had already set in, and David died at age 21. The second marker in the family graveyard was David's.

Alla taught in 1900 at Meydenbauer Bay, Bellevue. She also taught in Factoria and Renton and again in East Seattle for two years.

Harry Garrison, who worked on the steamer *Quickstep*, asked Alla to tutor him in algebra, and that led to their marriage in 1906. They had three children; the first died and was buried in the family plot.

Harry and Alla separated in 1909, so again she was the head of the family—her mother, daughter, Myrta, and son, Harry Jr. She managed by farming and selling eggs, fruit and milk. Her mother, Agnes Olds, died in 1917. Three years later, Alla married George Luckenbill.

Alla Olds Garrison Luckenbill remained active in Mercer Island affairs almost to the end of her 80 years. She was an excellent raconteur and enjoyed speaking to club groups, individuals and reporters. She evoked a sense of pride in the Island's beginning and inspired admiration for her pioneer efforts.

She died in December 1955 and was buried on the knoll—the last of Mercer Island's pioneers.

The knoll was not to be the last resting place of the family, as inevitably the freedoms of frontier life ended along with the isolation and hardships.

The five caskets were eventually moved to a cemetery, the grave markers were placed closer to the Olds-Garrison house, and the original grave site went into other ownership.

As of 2012, a descendant of Charles Olds, great-great-granddaughter Dorothy Swarts, still lives on Mercer Island.

24 | *Chapter 2: Getting Settled*

Museum of History and Industry

The hotel built by entrepreneur and developer Charles Cicero Calkins was a fashionable resort visited by the region's elite—and even U.S. President Benjamin Harrison.

The Island's First Tycoon

In less than a decade, C.C. Calkins won and lost a fortune

Mercer Island would look very different today if the dream of its first visionary and entrepreneur, Charles Cicero Calkins, had not gone up in smoke.

"C.C.," as he preferred to be called, was a native of Wisconsin, a lawyer, a trader and a speculator—and, by all accounts, a wheeler dealer. At age 34, he had made and lost a fortune by the time he landed in Seattle in September 1887 with $300 in his pocket. He was described in the December 1890 issue of *Pacific Magazine* as "one of the most progressive and thoroughly active men of Puget Sound."

Within about 10 days of arriving in Seattle, he was the owner of 21,000 acres of land and was in debt by $19,000.

In a few more days, he disposed of 700 acres of this land, and, after wiping out his indebtedness, had $170,000 worth of property left. About 16,000 acres of land passed through his hands in less than four months.

He purchased Gardiner Proctor's homestead of 160 acres, plus some adjoining land, and made plans for a great resort in East Seattle.

The grand hotel

The centerpiece of his dream was a grand hotel, an ornate structure of three floors, with wide verandas and storybook towers, designed by John Parkinson, an English-born architect who came to Seattle in 1889.

The first floor contained an immense reception room or ballroom, a big hall with a grand staircase, a fine kitchen, a very large dining room and several small parlors.

The two upper floors contained large parlors and 24 rooms for guests. There were tiled floors, elaborate hearths and mantels, handsome wall decorations, state-of-the art appliances and fixtures, an electrical system of lighting from a powerhouse generating direct current, good wells and an observatory.

Surrounding the hotel were parklike gardens containing hundreds of varieties of flowers, a maze and lovely rippling fountains. The boathouse held 100 boats and had 28 dressing rooms plus Turkish baths.

C.C. Calkins

Calkins spent $131,000 in East Seattle and was planning to add a fine church and a college. To make it easy for Seattleites to visit Mercer Island, a new 78-foot steamer, the

Museum of History and Industry

The posh Calkins Hotel had a large arboretum, a dock and a boathouse for 100 boats. It was located on 60th Avenue Southeast (Navy Yard Road) at about Southeast 28th Street.

Mercer Island Historical Society

This 1890 letter from Calkins to the Customs Office at Port Townsend requests that a "collector" be sent at once to approve his new steamer so that it could begin its runs on Lake Washington.

C.C. Calkins, ran 13 round-trips each day from East Seattle to Leschi.

In 1891, Mercer Islanders thrilled to the sight of decorated boats steaming across the lake on the occasion of President Benjamin Harrison's visit to the Calkins Hotel. Other celebrities visited; the Calkins enterprises thrived.

"Everything money, taste and industry can do will be done to promote the beauty and comfort of East Seattle," gushed the *Pacific Magazine* article. "When Calkins has fully matured plans, East Seattle will be THE place to live. . . An electric railway is to girdle the island, steamboats are constantly plying to and from points on Lake Washington and the magnificent steamer, *C.C. Calkins*, is being run for the special accommodation of the residents and visitors to East Seattle . . ."

William Putnam Guitteau built Mercer Island's first real road for Calkins. It was a mile-and-a-half-long road from East Seattle to Calkins Point, in the present Luther Burbank Park, which Calkins had purchased for his own home.

There Calkins built a big brick house and a large barn with towers and gables for himself and his wife, Nellie. Behind the mansion was a six-sided building with a reservoir on the upper floor and a potting shed below. Attached to this was a long greenhouse. Beyond stood a large, ornate birdhouse—almost a replica of the big hotel—with verandas and balconies. Gravel walks and lawns surrounded the mansion. Orchards, pastures, berry patches, grapevines, rosebushes, shrubs and trees completed the estate.

Thus Calkins promoted gracious living on an island of log cabins, pioneer settlers and a formerly simple existence.

Calkins' dream dies

Misfortune ended Calkins' grand scheme for East Seattle. The Great Fire of 1889 destroyed his real estate office in Seattle. Compounded by financial troubles brought on by a slowing economy, personal problems piled upon each other.

A second child died soon after birth. When his wife and 3-year-

old daughter, Ruby, were traveling back East, Ruby fell from an open Atlanta hotel window and was killed. Before Nellie Calkins could rejoin her husband after the tragedy, their mansion on Mercer Island's north shore burned to the ground. After returning from the East, Nellie moved into a hotel in Seattle, perhaps trying to escape the memory of her life on Mercer Island.

In the summer of 1891, C.C. filed for divorce from his wife of 10 years, claiming abandonment. According to J. Kingston Pierce in *Eccentric Seattle*, "The passing of their two daughters had wrenched a gap between them that they were unable or unwilling to bridge."

With the financial crash of 1893, Calkins was forced to mortgage all of his holdings on Mercer Island for $120,000 – only a few years after the opening of his grand hotel. Even the steamer named after him, the *C.C. Calkins*, met an unfortunate demise; it was partially destroyed by fire in 1898, and later its hull was scavenged for a new boat.

In about 1894, Calkins left the area, never to return. He died in 1948 in Los Angeles at age 98.

The fate of the hotel

The hotel was taken over for a time by Dan Olden, owner of a Seattle furniture store, but it stood empty for years.

Florence Guitteau, whose father had worked for Calkins, recalled visiting the abandoned hotel.

"We knew a window we could push up and climb through every chance we had," she wrote. "We visited every room again and again. All furnishings had been removed. The walls echoed our footsteps. The ceilings of all rooms except the kitchen were plastered in fancy ways with cupids, baby angels and flowers in scrolls and curley-cues and all painted in colors.

"The walls were covered with wonderful paper, the panels with pictures of landscapes and people. The grand staircase was a sight to see. One could imagine fine gentlemen and ladies parading the verandas and balconies, going up and down the wide stairs."

The Calkins Hotel and Calkins' other holdings were purchased in 1902 by Eugene Lawson, and the hotel was leased to Major Cicero Newell, to be used as a school for delinquent boys.

The residents of East Seattle objected to some of the school's disciplinary techniques, especially chaining boys to the fence. So Lawson leased Major Newell the property that had contained Calkins' home, which later became known as the Luther Burbank Parental School for Boys.

Mercer Island Historical Society
A 1905 ad for the Seattle Sanitarium, located in the former Calkins Hotel.

The hotel was next sold to a group of doctors who equipped it as a sanitarium and alcoholic treatment facility. Known as the Seattle Sanitarium, it was operated until 1905 by a Dr. Murray.

One story described one of the doctors as a former narcotics addict, and the sanitarium as a narcotics treatment facility. A

A fine resort with 'all the comforts'

The following is a description of the Calkins Hotel from Seattle Illustrated, a Chamber of Commerce publication of 1890:

"The hotel is beautifully furnished, and was laid out adopting the latest improvements which are so pleasing and necessary in hotel appointments. Tile flooring, costly hearths and mantels, handsome wall decorations, perfect sanitary appliances, electric system of lighting, and wells, and to crown all, an observatory for the grandest mountain and water scenery in America.

"Upon the grounds over $50,000 have been spent. Walks, mazes, flowers are in profusion. Over 12,000 trees, Monterey and Italian cypress, arbor vitae and shade trees are on the ground. A greenhouse 20 x 160 contains the finest collection of flowers outside of California, there being 635 varieties of roses alone.

"The waterfront has been boulevarded and is a delightful strolling and boating resort. On the grounds are twenty-five fountains, one with a sixty-foot bowl.

"At an elevation of 165 feet above the hotel is a reservoir holding 1,500,000 gallons of water and fed from eight large springs of pure, fresh, soft water. Twenty-five arc lights of 2,000 candle power, mounted on eighty-foot towers, illuminate the surroundings. A bathhouse holds 100 boats and twenty-eight dressing rooms for bathers, also a complete system of Turkish baths.

"A fine church and college are to be located, and within a short time the conveniences of old established cities will afford to the residents all the comforts that can be wished for."

turn-of-the-century Seattle directory listed "Hagy Institute—Bichloride of Gold cure—Most pleasant resort—electric lights—steam heat."

After Dr. Murray's death in 1905, the property was leased to a Mrs. Garkins, a Seattle First Hill boarding house operator. She moved her boarders over and operated a boarding house in the hotel for two years. In 1907, a Dr. J.J. Leiser operated it again as a summer hotel, renaming it Hotel Mercer.

At the beginning of the 1908 season, on July 2, the building burned—dramatically and completely.

There were rumors that a Japanese houseboy employed by Dr. Leiser had resented a scolding. To get even, he had plugged a chimney with greasy rags to make, as he said, "big smoke."

Nevertheless, Fire Marshall Gardner Kellogg, who lived near the hotel, had noticed that the kitchen chimney was in a state of disrepair. He had commented on it, but the comment went unnoticed.

At 5 p.m. on Thursday, July 2, Mr. and Mrs. John Peterson, who also lived nearby, saw sparks flying from the chimney and roof, and rushed to the hotel to give the alarm. Cries of fire aroused everyone in the building. Dr. Leiser and some servants hustled to carry out personal belongings.

The blaze attracted nearby residents, who worked hard rescuing furniture and bedding. Most of the guests' personal belongings were saved, but little furniture.

Soon the fight became useless, as the fire gained momentum and spread to the whole building. There was nothing to do but watch it burn.

Some bedding that had been carried into the small post office contained sparks that started a fire there. Roofs of some houses in the neighborhood, the nearest only 200 feet away, were smoking badly, but with wet blankets and

Seattle Times
This photo is from the newspaper account of the fire that destroyed the Mercer Island landmark on July 2, 1908.

garden hoses, they were saved.

The hotel was a total loss, without a cent of insurance. The newspaper account reported: "Fire Destroys Lake Landmark—Wipes Out the East Seattle Sanitarium with Loss of $28,000."

The burning of the hotel marked the end of Calkins' dream but left the East Seattle settlement, where some of the Island's earliest homes still stand today.

Calkins' vision of a nonindustrial, noncommercial, almost purely residential Island was adopted by subsequent settlers who added to the summer rental cottages, permanent residences, ferry dock, schoolhouse, store, fuel yard and water system.

East Seattle was the Island's first and for many years the only center of community activity and the birthplace of many of today's ongoing activities and traditions.

The first church, library, post office, telephone system, the longest surviving elementary school, community organizations, nursery school, cultural happenings—all had their beginnings in this most historic community.

Ernie Person

This 1918 photo shows the Island's first business center, built around 1900 at Southeast 28th Street at 60th Avenue Southeast, just upland from Calkins Landing. On the far left is Hap Lightfoot, who purchased the building with his brother George (at right). Left of George are J.B. Brown and Elsie Person, who later married Hap Lightfoot.

East Seattle, Mercer Island

The Island's oldest community

While Calkins' grand dream came true for only a few years and his hotel ultimately went up in smoke, he planted the seeds of the East Seattle community.

The Island's first store

The first real store on the Islans was built along the west side waterfront on 60th Avenue Southeast south of Southeast 28th Street, near the East Seattle Dock (now Calkins Landing). Around the turn of the century, Frank Sandell owned the store. Ownership changed several times until the Lightfoot brothers, George and Hap, purchased it in 1918.

The East Seattle Grocery was a country general store, selling everything from hams to harnesses, large tins of cookies and penny candy to garden produce, shovels and tools. If a needed item was not in stock, it could be ordered.

The post office and a bakery-restaurant occupied part of the building. Upstairs, the huge hall was the first community center, where meetings, work parties, dances, movies and social events occurred. It was the only large gathering place on the Island until the Episcopal Church built the Guild Hall just south of Secret Park at Southeast 28th Street and West Mercer Way.

For the earliest settlers on the heavily wooded Island, rowboat or barge were the easiest ways to get goods. Islanders had to plan ahead carefully to obtain groceries and supplies that could be hand-carried to rowboats. Heavy items like sacks of feed or furniture could be delivered on non-scheduled tramp steamers. The floating grocery store, the *Grubstake*, stopped at many isolated docks on a fairly regular schedule.

The advent of car ferries in the 1920s changed some of the Islanders' shopping habits. Commuters did weekly marketing in Seattle, often with heavily laden cars on Friday's trip to the Island.

East Seattle was the center of activity on the Island for nearly 50 years. Besides the general store, such enterprises sprouted as Peggy Greene's Dance Studio, a Standard Supply store, a farrier, and fuel and lumber dealers. One home-kitchen business in East Seattle, the Canterbury Candy Company, eventually grew into a major candy manufacturer in Seattle.

As the Depression hit hard in the 1930s, charge accounts ran long overdue. During the 1940s, the original East Seattle Grocery closed; eventually the building was torn down and the great old beams were used to build the Dunden home at Roanoke.

The Standard Supply store went out of business and the building, on Southeast 28th Street and 61st Avenue Southeast, was remodeled into apartments.

Chapter 4: East Seattle, Mercer Island | 29

The Lightfoot family

Taken about 1925, this photo shows one of the Lightfoot brothers' grocery delivery trucks, with Hap alongside it, headed west in front of their house on Southeast 27th Street, in what is now downtown Mercer Island.

Sally York Brown

In 1889, C.C. Calkins built a Victorian-style water tower to provide water to his hotel and adjacent area. A longtime landmark of East Seattle, it was located near "the Castle," the D.B. McMahon home built in 1910 at 2740 West Mercer Way. This photo was taken in 1962. Neglected and vandalized, the tower burned down in 1975.

Mercer Island Historical Society

The Island's few roads were dirt and full of ruts. This was taken on what is now Southeast 32nd Street, looking east from Proctor's Landing. The intersection in the distance is West Mercer Way.

The Post Office

Until 1920, the mailing address for everyone on Mercer Island was East Seattle, Washington. No records can be found to indicate an established mail service during the years of the Calkins enterprises, but the developing community had enough residents by 1904 to quality for a post office. It opened on March 1, 1904, in a small building at 61st Avenue Southeast and Southeast 30th Street.

Frank Sandell was the first postmaster. Mail came three times a week by steamer from Seattle to East Seattle Dock (Calkins Landing). On some schedules the mail was off-loaded at Roanoke Dock and carried to the post office.

By 1913 mail came and went daily on the steamer *Dawn*, in a pouch that sometimes contained only a handful of letters. In 1918 the post office was moved to the East Seattle Grocery on the corner of present-day Southeast 28th Street and 60th Avenue S.E.

Not until George Lightfoot became postmaster in 1920 was a rural route laid out. Daily mail delivery began in 1921, the same year that the horse and wagon were replaced by a car.

The post office moved to the Boyd Building in the new Central Business District in 1948, then to its present building on 78th Avenue Southeast in 1961.

Early water system

In 1887 when the Calkins Hotel was being planned, a good water supply was assured by the discovery of a spring on First Hill, north of Southeast 28th Street.

Calkins built a water tower of Victorian design compatible with the hotel to provide a holding tank for the water piped from the spring. He built living quarters inside, possibly for an early water commissioner. The volume of water was sufficient to supply the early homes in the immediate area.

After the hotel burned down in 1908, the D.B. McMahons built a large home at Southeast 28th and West Mercer Way near the water tower. Dubbed "the Castle," it had an indoor swimming pool, an innovation in 1908. After a succession of owners, it became a parsonage for vicars of the Emmanuel Episcopal Church, which was then nearby. The house stands today, privately owned.

The old water tower, neglected, vandalized, and disintegrating through the years, was being con-

I plainly visualize East Seattle as it was during the 1904-1907 era. It was laid out with dirt streets and sidewalks made of 2-inch by 12-inch planks laid end-to-end. There were some houses of similar architecture, beautiful lakefront estates, small farms, woodsy dells where trilliums and violets grew in profusion, and a large hotel that seemed to be unoccupied most of the time.

As a boy, I enjoyed riding to East Seattle to visit on the Peterson farm, or to hike along various roads looking for wildflowers, hazelnuts or Christmas trees. Leschi Park was exciting in those bygone days, with boats ever coming and going, band concerts, dances, and crowds of people.

But the countryside was also interesting, in a different way. It was delightful, mantled as it was in quietness and rural atmosphere and a remoteness that the lake seemed to accentuate.

—Quoted from a letter by Howard Hallgren
to Virginia Ogden Elliott, May 6, 1961

sidered for restoration in 1974, when fire damaged it beyond repair.

Another spring on the west ridge of First Hill was developed by the Crystal Springs Water Company. It had an even greater capacity and could serve both East Seattle and the newer McGilvra area, north of the current downtown.

As early as 1908, 75 customers paid $1 per month for 100 metered gallons of water. In 1912, August Meerscheidt became owner of the renamed Meerscheidt Water System with a daily capacity of 6,000 gallons. The two water systems had a combined capacity to serve 400 families and constituted the first community water supply on the Island.

In 1923 and 1924, problems arose with equipment replacement. As a result of a study by the Mercer Island Community Club, the Mercer Island Cooperative Water Association was formed and acquired title to the system in September 1925.

Over the next 14 years, the original plant was entirely replaced. Membership increased from 102 members in 1925 to 180 in 1940.

As a nonprofit cooperative, the group set its own rates, free from state regulation. A board of nine members and one full-time employee operated the system.

According to an article in the *Mercer Island Journal* of 1928, the cooperative had assets of more than $12,000 and net annual revenue of $300.

The system lasted until the 1960s, when Seattle's Cedar River supply became available on the Island, and a completely new system was installed.

East Seattle farming

Among the earliest inhabitants of the East Seattle area were Swan Person and his wife, Helena Olivia Bjorklund. Person had left his homeland in Sweden at 17 and

1890 The steamer *C.C. Calkins* is launched, making regular trips across Lake Washington.

1890 Allview Heights School is constructed on property donated by Vitus Schmid.

1891 President Benjamin Harrison visits the Calkins Hotel.

1891 Eleven students are enrolled in East Seattle School.

1893 A nationwide financial depression hits — the Panic of 1893.

1898 Swan Person starts a dairy farm on Mercer Island.

1900 The first business center is built, along the westside waterfront at present-day 28th Street.

1903 The Calkins property in East Seattle is leased to Major Cicero Newell for a parental school.

1903 A couple buys five acres of land in Mercer Park for $33 at a tax title sale and establishes the Alexander farm, with a hay barn, horse and cow barn, orchards and a windmill.

1904 The first Mercer Island post office opens March 1 at present-day 61st Avenue Southeast and Southeast 30th Street.

1905 Allview Heights School closes for lack of students.

1908 The Calkins Hotel burns down July 2.

1909 Emmanuel Episcopal Church congregation meets in private homes in East Seattle.

1911 Frank Nolan starts the Island's first newspaper, *Mercer Island News*.

1912 The Good Roads Association District 8 is formed.

1913 The first autos arrive on the Island but have to return to Seattle because there are no passable roads.

1913 The March 13 issue of *Mercer Island News* advertises 2 ½ acres of land in the Fruitland area for $750 cash.

1913 The Island has 200 registered voters.

1913 The assessed valuation of the entire Island is $1.27 million.

1913 Barnabie School, a one-room schoolhouse, opens on the northeast side of the Island.

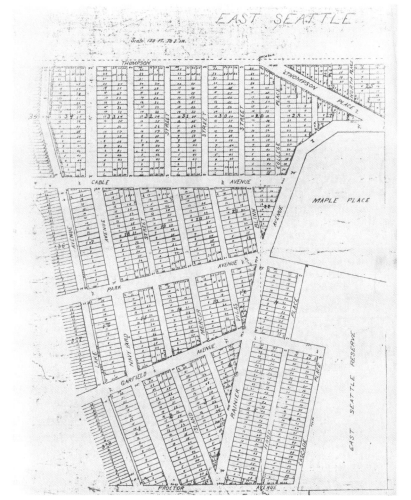

Mercer Island Historical Society

This early plat map of East Seattle shows original street names: Southeast 24th Street was Thompson Avenue; Southeast 27th was Cable Avenue; Southeast 28th was Park Avenue; Southeast 30th was Garfield Avenue; Southeast 32nd was Proctor Avenue. Running north-south, 60th Avenue Southeast was Navy Yard; 61st Avenue Southeast was Island Street; 62nd Avenue Southeast was Mercer Street; 63rd Avenue Southeast was Vilas Street; and West Mercer Way was Rainier Avenue.

been petitioned by more than 100 property owners in the northwest end of Mercer Island to establish a herd law which shall make it unlawful to permit any livestock to run at large in a specified area: ¼ mile east of Parental School south to road leading from Allview Schoolhouse to County Dock. Violators will be subject to fines."

After the herd law was enacted, the blackberries and weeds re-

Elsie Person Lightfoot remembered seeing cows grazing all over East Seattle, keeping down weeds and blackberry bushes, as well as the flowers and vegetables in people's gardens.

claimed the vacant spaces in East Seattle, and householders had to do their own mowing.

Ernie Person, born in 1911, shared some of his early memories, before his death in 2001:

"Sometimes Pop would hitch Jumbo, the delivery horse, to the buggy and drive out to see how construction was coming on the new boulevard (West Mercer Way). I was all eyes to see so many teamsters, workhorses and wheel scrapers.

"Then came the flu epidemic in 1918. Harold and I wore masks as long as they were required. By then, we were delivering the milk in East Seattle, with Jumbo and the cart. Harold was the teamster, I was the swamper and Foxie was the escort. He was a long-haired dog about the size of a fox terrier. He would lead the way, right down the center of the road. When the mud was too deep, he might use the boardwalk for a short distance, then back to the middle."

Pedestrian traffic was better accommodated than today, Person said. "Where it was heavy, there was a two-plank walkway; where it was light, one plank. Those walkways crossed the roads, of course, so when we came along with Jumbo

eventually came to Seattle early in 1889. He sent to St. Paul, Minn. for his fiancée. They were married in Seattle in 1889 and moved to Mercer Island in 1890.

East Seattle was having its troubles—a recession, a vacant resort hotel, no steamer service and few residents. A mortgage for $730 was foreclosed on the August Workman home at what is now 3049 68th Avenue SE; the Persons bought it for $350.

Swan found work in Seattle and would row to Leschi each day, take the cable car to Third and Yesler, then take a streetcar. When the first Person baby was born in 1900, Swan rowed to Seattle to get a doctor, but the baby arrived before the doctor did. That baby was August, the first of eight children (August, Esther, Elsie, Alice, Harold, Ernest, Richard and Robert).

In 1908, Swan Person bought 12 cows. Though still working in Seattle, he made daily milk deliveries—two daily in summer, because there was no refrigeration. There was no home-grown hay, so barge-loads of hay were offloaded at East Seattle Dock and hauled up Garfield (Southeast 30th Street) to the farm.

Elsie Person Lightfoot, Swan and Helena's third child, remembered seeing, as a little girl, circa 1910, cows grazing along the muddy, rutted hillside roads. They grazed all over East Seattle, keeping down the weeds and blackberry bushes, as well as the flowers and vegetables in people's gardens. They mowed (and fertilized) lawn grass erratically, and frightened little children.

In the May 1, 1913, edition of the *Mercer Island News,* the following notice appeared:

"County Commissioners have

32 | Chapter 4: East Seattle, Mercer Island

Emmanuel Episcopal Church
The Island's first church, Emmanuel Episcopal Church, was built in 1914 on Southeast 27th Street and West Mercer Way.

and the cart, it was up and over and back into the mud. Occasionally some fool motorist would try to tour East Seattle in the winter, and he would bog down to the running boards. John Peterson, the local teamster, would come to the rescue with his horses.

"Charlie Fruehauf, the blacksmith, was buying up old wagons in Seattle and storing them on the Island, so he would have the wagons when the public gave up on autos and trucks."

In 1914, a *Seattle Times* article stated flatly that autos would *never* replace horses!

The Person dairy farm moved in 1923 to the then-developing area platted as Mercer Park, on the hillside east of the present business district.

The Person farm had two barns, an ice plant and the family home. Both barns burned down and were replaced. The dairy was expanded to 70 cows, and a number of milk wagons. Later, trucks could go aboard the ferries.

Ernie Person drove a milk truck in East Seattle from 1927, when he was 16, until 1946, when the dairy business was sold. Before school he would deliver to 30 customers. The last of the dairy cows were sold in 1949. Swan Person died at home in 1952, his wife in 1954. The last barn was burned in 1963 after the land was purchased for a gas station. Ernie Person continued to live on the family property until the early 1980s. By that time the hillside site of the original farm was filling with apartments and houses where cows once grazed.

In 2012, the last of the Persons' estate was sold, by grandson Carl.

The first church

For many of the Island's early residents, spiritual and moral guidance, and much of their social life, was generated from one small, yet influential institution: Emmanuel Episcopal Church.

The church began as a mission in 1909, when a small community of worshipers, not all of whom were Episcopalian, met with the Rev. Thomas A. Hilton, rector of St. Clement's Church in Seattle. The group met first in a home in East Seattle, then in the little white schoolhouse. After the schoolhouse burned down in 1914, the church occupied a store near the East Seattle Dock. The Rev. Hilton arrived by steamer once a month to lead the worship services.

By 1911, a group was eager to found a Women's Guild to enlighten the women of the Island spiritually, to provide social communication and, ultimately, to raise funds for the building of Mercer Island's first church. The Women's Guild held potluck suppers, socials, sewing projects and a Grand Masquerade Ball on Nov. 23, 1912, which provided lively entertainment and a profit of $21.

A church building was realized in 1914 on a donated lot at West Mercer Way and present-day Southeast 27th Street. Charles Meyer, Island resident and builder, constructed a small, rustic church for $1,760. The pews and altar cost an additional $80. Mercer Island had its first church.

By 1921, the many activities of the church required more space. A new goal was set: construction of a Guild Hall. This endeavor also inspired non-church members. Funds were raised bit by bit, labor was donated, and the Guild Hall was built west of the church, adjacent to East Seattle School.

The building was the center of the Island's activities for many

The Emmanuel Episcopal Church's Guild Hall, built in 1922, served as the community activity center for the Island for many years. The sign over the door in the bottom photo reads, "Mercer Island Library," for it housed the library from 1945 until 1955. The Guild Hall was sold to the school district in 1961, and was torn down in 1976.

Mercer Island Historical Society

years, housing Emmanuel's Sunday school, choir practices, Women's Auxiliary functions, the Mercer Island library, Girl Scouts, Boy Scouts and Camp Fire Girls. When play equipment and a fence were added in 1933, the Mercer Island Co-op Preschool was held there for nearly 20 years.

The Mercer Island Straw Hat Summer Theatre, a highlight of local summer entertainment for several years, performed in the Guild Hall. The Badminton Club played there regularly, and young ladies learned to dance there in the 1940s.

The Guild Hall's outstanding ecumenical effort helped the church meet a mortgage payment due in 1929. A smash-hit opera was directed by Miss Virginia Richards, a sixth-grade teacher who also taught music at Luther Burbank School.

She recalled, in an interview for *The Seattle Times,* that she had "the most troublesome cast ever, before or since, assembled." Her many cue cards, her tolerance of the high-jinks at rehearsals, and her willingness to fill in for a missing actress at the last minute all paid off. *The Bells of Capistrano* ran for two nights, April 26 and 27, with all-out community participation and the *Dawn* making special runs from Leschi to East Seattle. The effort brought in $200.

When the mortgage was paid off completely on October 2, 1940, Islanders of all denominations celebrated. As an old-timer explained, "Everyone was an Episcopalian in those days."

After the completion of the Mercer Island floating bridge in 1940, the Island's population grew, and so did Emmanuel's. A full-time minister was necessary, so a "prefab" cottage served as the vicarage until 1951, when the congregation purchased "the Castle" across West Mercer Way from the Guild Hall. The church sold the home in 1957.

In July 1955, when the Rev. Matthew Paul Bigliardi arrived, Emmanuel was still a mission church in the Diocese of Olympia. "Father B," as he was known, and the leaders of Emmanuel decided to seek parish status. One of the requirements was the ownership of three acres of land, not available at the current location.

An important decision was made: the church and Guild Hall were sold to the school district for $16,800. In 1956, Emmanuel purchased five acres at Southeast 44th Street and 86th Avenue Southeast, part of the original Schmid homestead, for $25,000. Until the new church was ready, the school district leased the old property back to Emmanuel for $1 a month for three years.

At the beginning of 1961, the old church served briefly as city hall for the newly incorporated City of Mercer Island. Later, the church was burned as a practice for volunteer firefighters. The Guild Hall was used by the schools until 1976, when it was torn down.

Mercer Island Historical Society

Mail delivery by horse and wagon was replaced by the car in 1921, the same year daily delivery began on the Island.

Tale of the first mail carrier on the Island

Frederik S. Nielsen was Mercer Island's first and, for nearly 30 years, only mail carrier. Born in Denmark in 1889, he came to Puget Sound in 1912 and bought a small chicken farm on Mercer Island, where he lived for the rest of his life.

When he began his postal career in 1920 he earned $66 per month—a lot of money in those days. He was able to build a house with two bedrooms and a full basement for $500.

Three times a week Nielsen carried mail the 13.7 mile route around the Island. Reminiscing at age 81, Nielsen said about those early years:

"Mail transport was by wagon, pulled by a horse named Bill who was part Arabian and part stubborn. Wagon harnesses were bought at George Lightfoot's store. A light buggy was bought from the local blacksmith, Charles Fruehauf. A top was rigged to protect the mail. There were two mailboxes on the first day of delivery. Mail increased during 1921, so daily delivery was needed. That year the horse was replaced by a 1919 Ford, but when road conditions were bad or car trouble was worse, I borrowed Swan Person's milk delivery rig.

"Everyone came to the post office. It was a friendly place, you knew everyone and all the news just naturally seemed to clear through the lobby—about weddings, births, parties, funerals—as friends met and talked. They discussed politics and problems, national and local.

"During World War I the post office sold war bonds, and handled War Department telegrams. After the East Channel Bridge was built, in 1924, the mail kept coming by the steamer *Dawn* to the East Seattle Dock, or sometimes on the *Triton* to the Roanoke Dock.

"Then in 1928 the contract was changed to the Trailways Stage Line, and for the next 10 years mail came in twice a day. Later a private contractor delivered mail to Mercer Island, Bellevue, Fall City and North Bend."

Here is Nielsen's list of the rural carrier's duties:

"Furnish own car for delivering mail.

"Sort and deliver all mail, including parcel post, c.o.d., registered and insured mail. Collect letters.

"Sell stamps and supplies.

"Collect and rate up parcel post.

"Accept money orders and registered mail, giving receipts.

"Deliver live chickens and beehives.

"Take census for U.S. Dept. of Agriculture, listing farm acreage, numbers of cows, hogs, etc.

"During Christmas rush my days were 14 to 16 hours long. My longest day was 22 hours straight, and I had to be back on the job in two hours," he said.

Nielsen carried Island mail until he retired in 1949. Until the route was divided in 1948, Nielsen carried all the mail. The Mercer Island route had become the shortest but heaviest rural route in the United States.

Frederik S. Nielsen was 84 years old when he died, in July 1973.

Chapter 4: East Seattle, Mercer Island | 35

Mercer Island Historic Sites and Early Streets

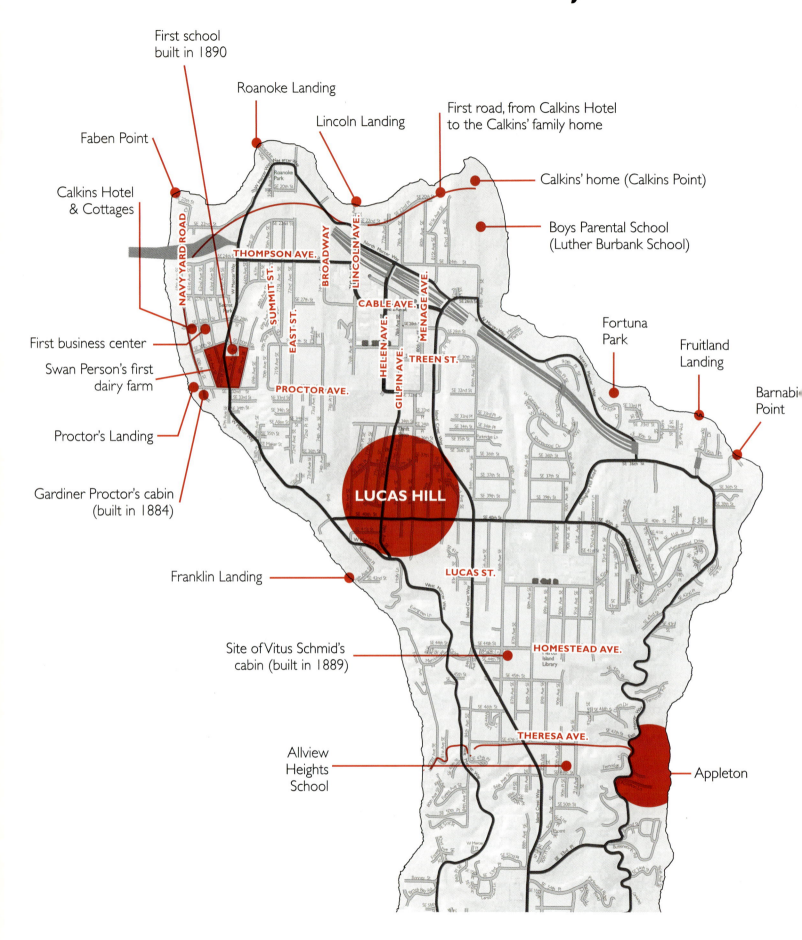

36 | Chapter 4: East Seattle, Mercer Island

Mercer Island Historical Society
Girls swim from a dock in 1923 or 1924, with the ferry *Dawn* in the background.

Early Transportation
Before bridges, ferries were the Island's lifeline

Truly an island for 50 years after its first settlers arrived, Mercer Island could be reached only by water. Boats—first canoes, then rowboats, steamboats, naphtha- or gas-powered boats—were the sole means of transportation between the mainland and the Island.

Long before there were any houses on Mercer Island, Capt. John Anderson operated public boats on Lake Washington—but he bypassed the Island until some docks were built. Later, Anderson-built boats and ferries became the most popular boats on the lake for Mercer Island residents.

Island ferrying

Scheduled boat service to Mercer Island probably began when the steamer *C.C. Calkins* transported people from Leschi to the East Seattle resort in the early 1890s.

Ferries were not only crucial to Island transit in the early days, but the locus of community news and debates.

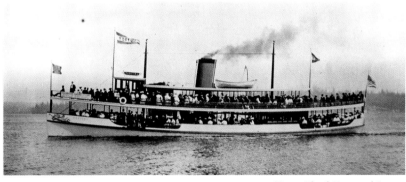

Mercer Island Historical Society
The *Fortuna* was a popular boat with Mercer Islanders. Launched in 1906, it was part of the fleet of Capt. John Anderson, on the around–Mercer Island run.

Mercer Island Historical Society
The Roanoke Dock, at the northwest tip of the Island, in the 1930s.

Chapter 5: Early Transportation | 37

The *Dawn* was replaced by the steamer *Mercer*, above, in 1938. At left is the ferry, *L.T. Haas*, appearing to list with the weight of its passengers, most of whom are decked out in their Sunday finery. At right are numerous boats on Lake Washington, with a hot-air balloon on the left.
Mercer Island Historical Society

A few steamers were particularly popular with Islanders, who could tell by their whistles which was coming, even in fog or dark of night. One popular ferry was the *Fortuna*, launched in 1906.

"For many years she served on the around–Mercer Island run, which was quite a treat in the early days," wrote one Islander. "She used to zigzag from Island to mainland, stopping at many docks—Roanoke, McGilvra, Parental School, Killarney, Beaux Arts, Fortuna Park, Fruitland, Cedarhurst, Hertford (or Enatai), Factoria (or Southview), Newport, Ackerson, Adams, Appleton, and a few others before reaching Kennydale. From there she made a non-stop run to Leschi along the southwest shore of the Island. After being rebuilt into a ferry boat, she followed that route as far as Adams (or Ferncroft) Landing, where she turned around."

The *Issaquah* was built in 1914 for the Leschi to Roanoke (Mercer Island) to Newport (Bellevue) run. She was a 288-ton ferry, 114 feet long, powered by a 250-horsepower engine. She had a revolutionary new double-ended design, so that cars and teams of horses could load and unload at either end. She had a hardwood dance floor, and in summertime made moonlight-dance excursions around the lake. On regular runs to Newport, a connection could be made with a coach to Issaquah, Fall City, North Bend and Snoqualmie. With the construction of the state highway in 1915, Seattle and Mercer Island drivers could ferry, then drive to the east.

The *Vasten* was a 42-foot launch built in 1911 by Capt. Charles Gilbert. He operated an early-morning and late-evening schedule from Leschi to Roanoke, McGilvra, the Parental School, Fruitland, Beaux Arts, Briarwood, Cedarhurst, Enatai, Southview, Newport, Appleton and Adams.

The *L.T. Haas*, one of the so-called tramp steamers, operated as a freight boat to all landings on the east side of the lake and on Mercer Island between 1902 and 1909. One of its jobs was ice

Of all the boats on the lake, the steamer *Dawn,* built in 1914, was best known by before-the-bridge residents of the Island. She was called the "Queen of the Lake," because when other ferries had to tie up for bad weather, the *Dawn* kept chugging along, going about her business as though the lake were as flat as glass. "She's a seaworthy old girl," said Captain Frank Gilbert.
Mercer Island Historical Society

"**Most of the affairs on the Island were settled in that warm, oil-smelling, smoke-filled little room. It was both transportation and city hall."**

–Virginia Ogden Elliott
Writing about her memories of the Dawn

delivery. Jimmy Miles was the ice man for Mercer Island, off-loading chunks of ice from the Leschi ice house on order from Island waterfront residents. Sunday papers were delivered too; they sometimes missed the dock and needed to be fished out of the lake.

The *Grubstake* motor launch was actually a waterborne grocery store that stopped all around the lake, serving the isolated settlers in the early 1900s.

"Seen through the eyes of a small child who was lifted down into its good-smelling interior, the little *Grubstake* has lived in memory for lo these many years," wrote Virginia Ogden Elliott in 1961.

"It was a small, huffy little gas boat—this floating store so aptly named. Memory preserves the dim cabin intact, with shelves of groceries around the sides, bins of grain and flour. We were dependent on that little *Grubstake* making its rounds from dock to dock. We children watched for her and gave our elders no peace until she was properly welcomed, whether they wanted groceries or not."

The beloved *Dawn*

Of all the boats on the lake, the steamer *Dawn* was the best loved, as she was Mercer Island's "own" steamer, serving the west side commuters. Capt. Anderson built the *Dawn* after a design he had seen while traveling in Europe in 1913 and thought suitable for the increasing traffic on the Mercer Island run.

Although she could carry 250 passengers, the vessel was only 65 feet long, short enough so lifeboats were not required. With her squared-off stern she was built for economy and utility, not for beauty. The *Dawn* was, by many accounts, a fine little boat, very seaworthy and very reliable.

Frank Gilbert was the longtime skipper of the *Dawn*. As a young man in 1914, he helped build the *Dawn* in the Lake Washington Shipyards at Houghton, now part of Kirkland.

In an interview for a *Seattle Times* article in 1957, Capt. Gilbert said, "Back in 1919 I was going to help a fellow out on the *Dawn* for a few days. I stayed 22 years. Her home port was Leschi. She called at landings all along the west side of Mercer Island: Thompson's (east end of the old floating bridge), East Seattle (now called Calkins Landing), Proctor's, Tennent's, Zimmerman's, Ogden's, Island Park, Franklin, County, Merrimount, Lott's, Miller's and Michael's. The fare was 25 cents a round trip; commuter's 10-trip ticket was $1. School children got 20 trips for $1. The passengers were wonderful. I knew them all as friends."

Chapter 5: Early Transportation | 39

Gilbert was pilot, conductor and roustabout, working the 5:30 p.m. to 1:30 a.m. shift. After the bridge replaced the *Dawn*, Capt. Gilbert continued steamboating as captain of the side-wheeler *Leschi*, which made her final landing at Kirkland in January 1950. After a total of 55 years of steamboating, Gilbert retired in 1955.

Islanders remember

Memories of the *Dawn's* days include Dorothy Brant Brazier's in *The Seattle Times* in 1973: "As a little girl, I lost my new Easter hat overboard one Sunday morning as I leaned over the ship's rail looking for fish. . .

"I remember empty coffee cups stashed in the shrubbery near the docks as commuters finished their breakfasts, waiting for the *Dawn*. Some of the passengers barely made it on time, though they lived close to the lakeshore. . .

"A rumor was that on cold mornings and evenings when commuters clustered around the old boiler, Democrats ranged on one side and Republicans on the other. That lone feller outside in the cold and dark could be a third-party member, or just a fresh-air fiend."

Virginia Ogden Elliott wrote these memories of the 1920s: "Inside, the *Dawn* was divided, like all Gaul, into three parts. The inside cabin for the women, children, and transient travelers; the outside and upper decks for the teenagers, and the engine room for the men. The engine room, which was on the way to the cabin, had benches around both sides of the engine, and behind the boxed-in warm boiler. These seats were the men's property and smoking section—no woman was bold enough to smoke on the boat in those days.

"Most of the affairs on the Island were settled in that warm, oil-smelling, smoke-filled little room. It was transportation and city hall.

"Our fathers sat in a certain irrevocable order on the long benches, and we remember with amusement one of them standing reading his paper, glancing up—perhaps glaring—until the offender took the hint and moved to another seat. They were there in the same seats every day—Higday, Clarke, Ogden, Lane, Albin, Kellogg and so on. Newer Islanders or summer folk sat on the other side of the boiler, as did a few bold women

> **"When something brings to mind that stubby little steamer and the blast of her whistle calling the laggards down to the next dock, some of us wish the calendar would roll back for just one day."**
>
> —An oldtimer recalling the *Dawn*

who did not know better.

"Behind the hooded boiler in the warmest spot crowded the teenagers, all giggles, scuffling, and chewing gum. They took the *Dawn* to Franklin High School first, then later to Garfield High School."

A woman remembers the shoe rack. On the way to the dock, Mercer mud would ruin city shoes, so mud shoes were worn, and city shoes were carried. On the steamer, the mud shoes were stashed behind the life preservers mounted on the cabin walls. There they remained all day, until the wearer claimed them on the homeward trip.

Commuters running for the *Dawn* were sometimes in varying stages of undress and completed their dressing on board. Their wives would later go—often down a steep bank—to the docks to collect articles of clothing—coffee cups, breakfast dishes and anything else left behind by the streakers.

The *Dawn* faithfully made her appointed rounds for 24 years, until 1938, when a steamer named *Mercer* replaced her.

After her retirement, the *Dawn* sank at her moorings at a Rainier Beach dock, almost disappearing beneath the water. The Seattle City Council requested that she be sunk.

William Gilbert, Island resident and son of the *Vasten*'s Charlie Gilbert, was given the contract. She was towed out and sunk in the depths of the south basin of the lake.

In early 1989, divers found her between Rainier Beach and the Island she served for so long.

Ferry system fades

Nostalgia aside, the entire ferry system had been losing money for years. King County, of necessity, had taken over the operation in 1918. Capt. John Anderson managed it. During the Depression, the number of passengers riding the ferries decreased even as the deficit increased.

Islanders were vocal in both their

The first East Channel Bridge, below, opened in 1923; the building on the right later became Rochester's Garage.
The wooden East Channel Bridge served the Island from 1923 until 1939 when the next bridge was built (left). The lower photo shows the old and new bridges on June 1, 1940.

Museum of History and Industry

complaints about the ferries and their requests for improved service. In 1915, the McGilvra Improvement Club requested that the *Fortuna* and the *Triton* be sure to whistle when they left the Parental School Dock before McGilvra Dock.

In 1923, the South End Club requested a schedule change to accommodate the 7:30 a.m. workers. In 1932, a request for lower fares, 10 cents one way, was turned down.

Such proprietary requests indicate the attitude that ferry service belonged to the Islanders, and it was their right and duty to praise it or to blame it, but always seek improvements according to their needs. At the same time, Islanders' desire for a bridge was growing.

The first bridge

For years Islanders pleaded for a bridge to connect them to the mainland. They wrote letters to Washington, D.C., to Olympia and to King County commissioners asking that a bridge be built.

The Mercer Island Improvement Club sent this letter to the Army Corps of Engineers in Seattle in 1922:

"Mercer Island, with a population of 2,500, situated 10 minutes by water from Seattle, is in great need of better transportation fa-

Mercer Island Historical Society

cilities. The one hope is to build a bridge to connect Mercer Island with the mainland.

"This bridge will be the means of building up this Island of 5,000 acres, one of the finest residential sections in the state."

It was signed by Frank Sandin, president of the Mercer Island Improvement Club.

Finally, Mercer Island's first bridge, across the East Channel to Bellevue, opened on November 10, 1923. The wooden bridge was 1,200 feet long, from Enatai in Bellevue to Barnabie Point on northeast Mercer Island.

The opening celebration included speeches by notables followed by a luncheon party at Fortuna Park.

Now the public could drive to Mercer Island, 22 miles from Seattle by way of Renton.

The construction of the East Channel Bridge was a turning point in Mercer Island's history, the first physical link to the mainland, marking its end as a true island set apart and unconnected.

By the 1930s the old bridge was so rickety that the driver busing children to Bellevue for school would instruct the students to get out and walk across. Then he drove across and picked up the students.

In 1939, the Works Progress Administration built a second East Channel Bridge next to the first one, then demolished the old bridge in 1940. The second bridge was in use until 1983, when the current bridge replaced it.

Chapter 5: Early Transportation | 41

42 | Chapter 5: Early Transportation

Mercer Island Historical Society

In the summer of 1922, north-end neighbors purchased land and built the Keewaydin Clubhouse (now the VFW Hall) as a gathering place for meetings and social events. Volunteers cleared the land and designed and built the structure themselves. The clubhouse became a community center and civic center for the Island. It was later called the Mercer Island Community Club. It was purchased by VFW Post 5760 in 1966. The post raised $150,000 in 2012 for a new roof and new siding on the building.

Building a Community

Before city government, Islanders organized themselves into community clubs

From the 1880s until Mercer Island's incorporation in 1960, the Island's governing body was King County. During many of those 80 years, the Island was hardly unified. It was a group of isolated neighborhoods, some grown from summer colonies, separated by rough roads, differing opinions and varying dreams for the Island's future.

Residents banded together into improvement clubs, developing the grassroots government of Mercer Island that endured for many decades. Interacting with the clubs, county commissioners could get a consensus of public opinion and find a sounding board for county proposals.

Roads associations

The first community club of record was reported in Nolan's *Mercer Island News*. On Sept. 1, 1912, in the hall above the general store in East Seattle, an improvement club met for the first time.

Club president C.H. Horton gave the opening address:

"Ladies and gentlemen, we live on the most beautiful Island in the Northwest, containing 5,000 acres of beautiful natural parks, and if a proper means of transportation was secured, all these acres could and would be improved with homes, built by our best and most desirable citizens. Roads, yes, we people of the Island have heard of them. But ours are on paper. What few we have start at some inaccessible point and end nowhere. A ferry, yes, that is as necessary as good roads, and the two combined would bring the extreme South End of the Island within 30 minutes of Pioneer Square (Seattle).

"An engineer, C.M. Anderson, has outlined a boulevard around the Island that takes none of our waterfronts from us, but opens up our hillsides and viewpoints. Now, a few of us got together and decided to form an organization that would cover the whole Island, and would get for the people their just dues. Ride over the macadam road to Snoqualmie Falls, and we'll show you where your money has been expended. Roads are being

Chapter 6: Building a Community | 43

Mercer Island Historical Society

The poor condition of Island roads prompted the formation of various community clubs to lobby the county commissioners for improvements. The first community club of record was the Good Roads Association District 8, formed in 1912. Above, a road crew works at Merrimount and West Mercer Way between 1914 and 1916.

built, with our money, but not on our Island."

Only by forming a legal entity that could sue, be sued and contract debts could an apportionment of $50,000 from a $3 million King County road-bond issue be made available for Mercer Island.

Thus, Good Roads Association District 8 was formed in the fall of 1912.

But the notion of one organization representing the ideas of all Islanders was far from reality.

For reasons of its own—maybe because after six years of annual road tax levy the south part of the Island had no roads—Allview Heights Good Roads Association District 8 also was organized.

That same fall, on Nov. 23, 1912, a meeting was held at Allview Heights schoolhouse to try for agreement between the two rival groups.

Sure enough, hot controversy followed. Each group filed names of candidates for Island road supervisor.

A letter to the editor of the *Mercer Island News* of March 1913

The first recorded civic controversy on the Island was in 1912, a fight between two neighborhood groups over road development.

stated, "Good Roads District 8 will be sorry if it keeps up wrangling...." One club's trustee said, 'There's no compromise. They began the trouble, and must come over to our side, unconditional-surrender-like.' The other club's trustee says, 'We were there first. They started the fight. Let them come to us. We're right anyway!'"

The wrangling was resolved when a King County Superior Court judge directed county commissioners to appoint a Mercer Island road supervisor, at $4 per day.

Scores of controversies and thousands of letters to the editor have followed this first recorded civic brouhaha.

The Island developed in spite of differing opinions and confron-

tations. Whether over a road, a school, a shopping center, a dog park, a golf course, a tree ordinance, a greenbelt—the controversies have been lively, sometimes dangerously libelous and even comical.

Other clubs

The next community club of record was the McGilvra Improvement Club, founded Oct. 10, 1914, by 21 women concerned about the quality of life on the Island. The McGilvra area was platted in 1905, and by 1914 had several year-round homes along the waterfront between present-day 72nd and 80th Avenues Southeast, around what was called Serena Cove. The plat extended from the lakefront to present-day Mercerdale Park, and included farms and upland residences.

Club members made window curtains for the ferry-dock shelter. They raised money for a tennis net when a member donated land for a court. They threw a dance at Fortuna Park, and raised $6.90. A

44 | *Chapter 6: Building a Community*

The Keewaydin Club—later called the Mercer Island Club—was the center of Island life for decades. The photo upper right shows its construction, by volunteers, in the summer of 1922. The building was used for meetings, socials, dances, religious services and all manner of gatherings. It is now owned by Mercer Island VFW Post 5760.

Mercer Island Historical Society

petition requesting a rural free delivery (RFD) system was circulated in 1915 because McGilvra people had to make the trek to the East Seattle Post Office for their mail.

During the winter of the big snow in 1916, club members collected money to pay for snow removal ($6.75) and for repair of the roof of the McGilvra School.

They hung signs on East Street (now 72nd Avenue Southeast) and on the dock asking residents to please keep the weeds cut around the plank walks. When World War I came, the members voted to gather every Friday to sew for the Red Cross.

This same type of community-minded people became active members of the Mercer Island Community Club in the 1920s.

Keewaydin Club

On Nov. 29, 1921, the Keewaydin Club was organized among the members of the Mercer Island Community Club. They purchased property at present-day North Mercer Way and 72nd Avenue Southeast, and in May 1922 began constructing a clubhouse. Club members cleared the land in one day and completed excavating and concrete work in June.

The club report of July 1, 1922 noted, "A feat equal to an old-fashioned log-rolling was performed. Twenty-seven people moved 60,000 feet of lumber and 58,000 shingles from a barge on the lake up a stiff grade to the club building site."

The Keewaydin Clubhouse (now the VFW Hall) became a community center and almost a center of government for the Island. Meetings were held once a month. The other new group, the South End Improvement Club, attended when large issues arose.

A growing number of Islanders expressed their opinions about the quality of Island life. Transportation was a primary concern—roads on the Island and ferry service to Seattle—as well as fire fighting, water supply and sanitation control.

One big item of discussion for the club was a bridge across Lake Washington to connect Mercer Island with Seattle. An early pro-

> Transportation was a primary concern—roads on the Island and ferry service to Seattle—as well as fire fighting, water supply and sanitation control.

Chapter 6: Building a Community | 45

This is a stock certificate for one share in the Mercer Island Golf and Country Club, proposed in the 1920s for the south end of the Island. It was not the last proposal for a golf course on Mercer Island.

Mercer Island Historical Society

posed route was off West Mercer Way across the narrow part of the lake between Seward Park and the midsection of the Island, including connecting roads on both sides.

Eventually, the Keewaydin Club faded as a social club, but it grew in influence and participation as the Mercer Island Community Club.

The local community clubs joined with other clubs around Lake Washington through the Federated Clubs to promote the common good and give the clubs greater political influence with county and state governments. A spirit of friendship and cooperation prevailed among club members and their elected leaders.

The South End Improvement Club

In 1920, south end residents formed a club to improve road conditions and bring in electricity and telephone service. The first meeting was held at the Lakeview School in September 1920, with 10 members present.

The Ladies Auxiliary was formed that same evening, and became the Pleasant Hour Club.

The club was a social-action group and sounding board for public opinion to communicate with King County government. Everyone walked to the meetings.

In 1921, 44 members sent a request to the telephone company for phone service at the south end. In 1922, the club asked for and received from Northern Pacific Railway permission for free camping and berry picking on the railroad's south-end property, the current site of the Mercer Island Beach Club. The club lobbied Puget Power for electricity; it finally came to the south end in 1923.

The Roanoke Transportation Company offered bus service in return for investment in bonds by individuals. County commissioners assured the club that winter road maintenance would be sufficient for bus travel. Plans were for 15 regular daily passengers and 25 weekenders to and from the Roanoke ferry landing and South Mercer. The service operated for a year or two.

South End Club members favored a proposed golf course in the Lakeview neighborhood. By December 1928, the golf club had 34 members, owned the site and had $452 in the bank. It looked as if a golf course was close to reality.

South-end residents made an agreement with owners of two boats, *Valdez* and *Naomi*, that they be guaranteed transportation to Rainier Beach by paying $75 each in cash, the money to be used to keep the boats in repair. The fare was 6 cents each way.

The decade of the 1920s ended in some frustration for south Mercer Islanders, as expressed by John N. Todd, charter member of the South End Improvement Club:

"We at the South End of Mercer Island are left without any means of transportation—bus, boat, or ferry. For two years we have been told not to expect any new road development, for the BRIDGE would mean a new road map for the Island...

"Seattle seems to think that dirt roads and slow-moving ferries with long waiting intervals are good enough for Mercer Island. You know we are willing to do our part and see Seattle go forward, but we have reached the limit of our endurance and must fight to protect ourselves.

"We will open headquarters in Seattle and fight the bond issues that are coming up, and fight every man on the ticket who is responsible for delaying the Mercer Island Bridge."

That Mercer Island spirit—citizen concern, willingness to spend many hours and much effort, and the urge to take direct action—has been part of the Island's cultural heritage since the beginning.

46 | Chapter 6: Building a Community

Mercer Island Reporter

Mercer Island elementary school students line up for the bus one foggy morning in 1987.

Mercer Island Schools

A source of community pride, schools are one of the Island's greatest assets

Mercer Island public schools have been likened to private education for more than seven decades. Local real estate agents agree schools are the Island's number-one attraction. They provide enriched curricula and learning resources, personalized teaching and a community willing to go the extra mile to pass levies, bond issues and other private support to "bridge the gap" of state funding.

Pat Braman, a school board member and former teacher who moved to the Island in 1977, echoes countless parents who moved to the Island primarily because of the schools. "I recognized the quality of teaching and wanted my kids to be exposed to that," she said. "We also moved here for the music and art programs, which were being cut in other districts. I feel my kids got a private-school education in a public school."

She has seen firsthand the parents volunteering in the classroom and on field trips. Although class sizes cannot compete with private

"Our students will thrive in the cognitive, digital, and global worlds while sustaining their passion and inspiration for learning."

- Mercer Island School District vision statement, 2012

schools', the district has worked to keep them as small as possible.

"We have been a public school of firsts—with computers in the classrooms, tech training for staff, the largest marching band in the Northwest, the first district/community recycling center and all schools moving up their green levels in recycling and energy consumption," said Braman.

"Our graduates compete at the best universities in the country and tend to maintain their high-school grade point at college. Our numerous national and state recognitions of teaching, our consistently high state test scores, our fine arts, our counselors in each school—all are unheard of in other public schools and are supported by the city as well."

In 2011, the Mercer Island School District celebrated its 70-year anniversary as an official unified school district. As of 2013, the district has one high school, one middle school and three elementary schools serving 4,000 students. Facing growing enrollment and aging schools, the district is in a planning process for the 21st century.

Mercer Island is also rich in its private-school offerings, including a French-immersion school, a Catholic school, a Jewish high school and numerous preschools and a school for special needs.

The early years

Quality schools have been paramount to Mercer Island since 1884, when the Island's first family, Charles and Agnes Olds, hired a teacher to instruct their two children. However short his tenure, Henry E. Kelsey (for

This postcard depicts the first East Seattle School, often called "the little white schoolhouse," built in 1890 on the site of what is now Secret Park. The building burned to the ground in November 1914.

Mercer Island Historical Society

(2) MERCER ISLAND SCHOOL HOUSE, East Seattle

whom Kelsey Creek in Bellevue is named) will go down in Mercer Island history as the Island's first teacher.

In 1889 concerned parents started East Seattle's first school in the ferry dock warehouse on what is now the area of Calkins Landing. Miss Clarissa Colman, daughter of pioneer James Manning Colman, was the first teacher of eight or nine pupils. School District 28 was organized.

East Seattle was the center of Island education for many years. As the Calkins enterprises flourished and the number of pupils increased, a regular school building was built in 1890 on land donated by C.C. Calkins off West Mercer Way at Southeast 27th Street.

Often referred to as the "little white schoolhouse," this was the first East Seattle School. Part of that school site is now Secret Park, purchased by the city from the school district.

From Florence Guitteau Storey's memoirs of 1894: "The building had three rooms, a large entry or cloakroom, one large classroom, and a supply room. The teacher stoked the wood stove, and was the janitor and wood gatherer. I was 9 and in the fourth grade; I can't remember any children older than me. Wall maps and pictures and descriptions of birds, flowers and animals adorned the walls. We sat at low tables on little chairs and used colored sticks, balls, and blocks for seatwork.

"Our attendance was poor. The mile and a half we had to walk from home was too far for my sister Ollie and me in bad weather.

"One of the teachers was Alla Olds, who rode horseback from her home at Appleton. After her father sold her horse, she walked to school. Alla taught in 1897, 1898 and again in 1905.

"All eight grades were in one room, and for a few years an alcove in the classroom also housed a kindergarten.

"Difficulties of hiring teachers, inclement weather, long walks to school, all shortened the school year. In 1891, there were 11 pupils enrolled, one teacher who received $50 per month, and 78 school days, or four months total. By 1905, there were 18 pupils and 173 school days; the teacher's salary was still $50 per month."

The little white schoolhouse served the Island for 24 years.

More Schools

Meanwhile, a school was built at Allview Heights in 1890, on the donated Schmid acre where the library now stands. The county

Allview Heights School, built on the property where the library now stands, was almost identical in design to the original East Seattle School.

Mercer Island Historical Society

48 | Chapter 7: Mercer Island Schools

East Seattle School had four classrooms and a play space at ground level below the classrooms. The main entrance to the school, built in 1914, was originally on the west side, as shown below.
Museum of History and Industry

Mercer Island Reporter

Mercer Island Reporter

Lakeview School—currently Sunnybeam School—was built in 1918 for the children who lived on the south end of the Island. It also served as home to the South End Community Club.

commissioners appropriated funds since a school in the center of the Island was needed because of lack of roads and other transportation problems. The building's design was similar to the first East Seattle School.

Allview Heights School was closed in 1895 for lack of students. In 1915, the school was used briefly, but it was again closed in early 1916. The structure remained and was put to occasional community use, then was torn down in 1938 for lumber to build a gymnasium in East Seattle.

Also early in the 1900s, McGilvra School, a one-room school for grades one to four was built across from Hap's service Station. It was located near where Interstate 90 currently passes under 76th Avenue Southeast.

Barnabie School, built in 1912 at Southeast 40th Street and East Mercer Way, served the children on the northeast side of the Island, with one room and one teacher.

East Seattle School

By 1914, Mercer Island had almost 100 pupils, most of them in East Seattle, and a new school building was constructed. The exterior was terracotta, with maroon tile trim around the doorways. Hope D. Stewart was the builder. Miss Laura Hicks, teacher at the little white schoolhouse, was the first principal.

Eighty-one pupils in nine grades started school in the new building in September, 1914. The building, much remodeled, served as a school until the mid-1970s, when it became the home of Mercer Island Boys & Girls Club.

In November 1914, the little white schoolhouse at Secret Park burned to the ground, after having served as a community center, church meeting place, dance hall, prize-fight arena and polling place, as well as a school. On election night, after the 200 ballots had been counted and people had gone home, the fire left burning in the stove caused the conflagration, ending

Chapter 7: Mercer Island Schools | 49

School Days

Students at Allview Heights School, at the location of the current library.

Students at the first East Seattle School in 1923.

Students attending the first East Seattle School in 1921 or 1922.

East Seattle School, 1937.

Students at Lakeview School (now Sunnybeam School) in 1937-1938, with Mrs. Peterson, teacher, and Mrs. Gregory, custodian.

This 1931 photo shows the "bus" for Lakeview School.

Mercer Island Historical Society photos

Students at East Seattle School in 1922.

Mercer Island Historical Society

Mercer Island Historical Society

Lakeview School, date unknown. During the 1930s, students in grades one to eight were taught in one room by one teacher. The building became Sunnybeam School and is listed on the U.S. Register of Historic Places.

Sally York Brown

Mercer Island High School class of 1958, the school's first graduating class. In the fall of 1959, the school added 119 new students, bringing the total enrollment to 489. By 1961 MIHS had 660 students and 50 staff members.

Chapter 7: Mercer Island Schools | 51

'The children are coming! Hurry! Get ready!'

The late Virginia Nygren, former principal of Island Park, Lakeridge and Mercer Crest schools, captured in her breathless prose the mood of the 1950s as the school population was booming:

"The children are coming! The children are coming! Prepare! Get neighborhood school sites! Buy now! Pay later! Sell bonds!

"The children came! They kept coming! ...The building during the '50s, and '60s never stopped! Homes were being built in the center of the Island. 'Give us a neighborhood school!' cried those taxpayers. Once again bulldozers moved in, trees fell, more concrete blocks and cement! Another school was born and dedicated in the fall of 1957: Island Park Elementary School. And in 1958 a Mercer Island Junior High [later Islander Middle Schoo] was opened at the South End of the Island...

"A North End junior high was built. What was it to be called? 'Don't bother us with details!' said the board. 'Call it North Mercer Junior High, change the one on the South End from Mercer Island Junior High to South Mercer Junior High, name the elementary school being built on West Mercer, West Mercer Elementary. That should just about take care of that. Next item on the agenda.'

"The next item on the agenda was what to do with the administration. It was housed in a creaky building, the old Episcopal Church Guild Hall, across from East Seattle School. The citizens were always helpful in telling the administration what to do and where to go. This time it was a new building. In 1966, the administration building was built.

"From then on the 'building age' became less interesting. It was additions, renovations, and portables. Another high school was much discussed, but with fewer homes being built, the school population leveled off."

the building's 24 years of service.

On the South End, students attended classes in a little shack on the southwest side of the Island, the first schoolhouse of King County District 191. In 1918, the local school district issued local improvement bonds to build a schoolhouse for all the grades: Lakeview School. The original building still stands today, known as Sunnybeam School.

The Barnabie and McGilvra schools were closed, and by 1930 all children attended East Seattle or Lakeview School. Students walked, rode horseback, bicycled or later rode the first school bus, driven by Charles Claringbould of Bellevue.

In 1938, a federal grant was obtained by School District 28 to add a gymnasium and auditorium to the East Seattle School. The Works Progress Administration provided labor worth $14,000, and a special school district levy, which passed despite the Great Depression, brought $2,550. Materials included recycled lumber from the Barnabie and Allview Heights schools.

By September 1941, with improved roads and diminished enrollment at the south end's Lakeview School, all students were bused to the remodeled, enlarged East Seattle School. School Districts 28 and 191 merged to form District 400.

East Seattle School remained the center of education until 1950, when the first of the "modern" schools was built at Mercer Crest, at Southeast 40th Street and 86th Avenue Southeast.

Seattle Post-Intelligencer Collection, Museum of Science and History
Lakeridge Elementary was used in the fall of 1954 as a temporary junior high school.

Enrollment boom

The school population burgeoned with the opening of the floating bridge in 1940 and the Island's first multifamily development, Shorewood Apartments, in 1949. The school enrollment doubled every year for several years, then tripled and quadrupled for several years through the mid-1950s.

The district began constructing schools at a frantic pace. Between 1950 and 1960, six schools were built: four elementary schools (Mercer Crest, Mercer View, Lakeridge and Island Park), a junior high and a high school.

The Citizens Advisory Committee was organized in 1947 as volunteer advisers to the school board and to help wage campaigns for school funding. It took an active part in school planning until it

Mercer Island Public Schools

Allview Heights School
4400 88th Ave. SE
Opened: 1890
Closed in 1895; torn down in 1938

Barnabie School
Southeast 40th Street and East Mercer Way
Opened: 1912
Closed by 1930, exact date unknown

Crest Learning Center
4150 86th Ave. SE
Opened: 1971 as the **Contract High School** in East Seattle building, then East Seattle School; moved to library of former Mercer Crest Elementary in 1987; renamed **Crest Learning Center** in 1987; remodeled in 1998. Operating as of 2013

East Seattle School
Calkins Landing
Opened: 1889
Burned down in 1914

East Seattle School
West Mercer Way at Southeast 28th Street
Opened: 1914
Closed as a school in 1982; leased to Boys & Girls Club until 1984, when school district donated it to the club. Property sold in 2007; main building essentially unused as of 2013

Island Park Elementary
5437 Island Crest Way
Opened: 1957
Remodeled in 1995; operating as of 2013

Islander Middle School
8225 S.E. 72nd St.
Opened: 1958 as Mercer Island Junior High; renamed **South Mercer Junior High** in 1961; became **Islander Middle School** in 1982. Remodeled in 1994, 2000; operating as of 2013

Lakeridge Elementary
8215 SE 78th St.
Opened: 1954 as Lakeview Elementary; name changed to Lakeridge in the late '50s Remodeled 1995; operating as of 2013

Lakeview Elementary School
8635 SE 68th St.
Opened: 1918
Closed as a public school in 1941; home of the South End Improvement Club until the 1950s; operating as Sunybeam School as of 2013

McGilvra School
76th Avenue Southeast and Sunset Highway
Opened: Early 1900s
Closed by 1930; exact date unknown

Mercer Crest Elementary School
4140 86th Ave. SE
Opened: 1950
Closed in 1983; rented until 1986, when all but the library was torn down

Mercer View Elementary School
8236 SE 24th St.
Opened: 1960
Closed 1980; leased to the city until 1990; purchased by the city, then torn down for new community center, which opened in 2005

Mercer Island High School
9100 SE 42nd St.
Opened: 1955
Remodeled in 1998; operating as of 2013

North Mercer Junior High
88th Avenue Southeast and Southeast 40th Street
Opened: 1961
Closed in 1982; as of 2013 houses Youth Theatre Northwest, various preschools and CHILD School

West Mercer Elementary
4141 81st Ave. SE
Opened: 1962
Remodeled 1995; operating as of 2013

Chapter 7: Mercer Island Schools | 53

Ted Heaton

Mercer Island High School opened in 1955. The "Mushroom," the futuristic-looking cafeteris building, shown under construction in the photos above, was added later. It was torn down in 1997 and replaced with the "Commons" as part of the renovation completed in the fall of 1998.

> **In the mid-1960s, the school district had six elementary schools, two junior high schools and one high school. There was talk of building a second high school.**

Mercer Island Reporter

When North Mercer Island Junior High opened in 1961 it was the second junior high school on the Island. With its distinctive roofs, it was sometimes called "the pygmy village." Currently housing Youth Theatre Northwest and several preschools, it is now part of what is referred to as "North Campus."

Mercer Island Reporter

Tom Potter, school psychologist, surveys the panoramic lake view at Mercer View Elementary School. Built in 1960, Mercer View was closed as a school in 1980 and leased to the city of Mercer Island for use as a community center.

dissolved around 1980, and eventually was replaced by the Committee for Mercer Island Public Schools (CMIPS).

In 1953, the school district's 1,016 pupils were housed in two buildings, East Seattle School (eight rooms) and Mercer Crest Elementary (20 rooms), plus two kindergarten rooms rented at the South End Club. The 210 high school students were transported to Bellevue; 12 others went to Seattle schools at their own expense. Four school buses transported all elementary students.

Lakeview Elementary School (the name was changed to Lakeridge in the late '50s) won a prestigious design award for the work of architect Fred Bassetti. It was built on the 10-acre tract at the south end acquired in a land swap with the South End Club. The school served as a temporary junior high at one point.

Community participation grew through the Parent Teacher Stu-

Mercer Island Reporter

Mercer Crest Elementary School (top) served the school district from 1950 to 1983. The photo above shows children on the last day of school before the school closed permanently in June 1983.

Mercer Island Reporter

During the 1960s, Tarywood was the home of Mercer Island High School's Humanities Block program. After district budget cuts, the district sold the property and "Block" was forced to relinquish the "splendid isolation" of a separate off-campus classroom. The property is now Tarywood Estates development.

> "We had a peacock, a rooster and a wounded fawn. People even came to school on their horses. It was very rural and charming."
>
> **Sherry Savage Broman,**
> **former kindergarten teacher**
> *recalling her years teaching at Island Park Elementary in the late '50s and early '60s*

dent Associations, the Preschool Association and other civic groups. Citizens had an important influence on the management of the school system.

The schools' fine reputation spread, attracting more families to the Island and creating more pressure on the schools.

Islanders voted by a 5-to-1 margin in favor of building a high school, and the million-dollar Mercer Island High School opened in September 1955, under the supervision of Superintendent Robert Studebaker.

MIHS was dedicated May 20, 1956, its first phase consisting of 23 classrooms, a library, administration section, gymnasium, music room and boiler building. The cost was about $800,000. The Mushroom (cafeteria), auditorium and additional classrooms were added later.

School enrollment increased from 800 in 1950 to 4,300 in 1960, a faster rate than the population increase.

In the mid-1960s, there were nine public schools on the Island: six elementary schools (East Seattle School, Island Park, Lakeridge, West Mercer, Mercer View, Mercer Crest), two junior high schools (North Mercer Junior High and South Mercer Junior High) and one high school (Mercer Island High School).

The increasing sophistication of the school program that was to accompany this growth of the school system can perhaps best be assessed by the fact that in 1950 there were no school libraries, no special education programs, no

Chapter 7: Mercer Island Schools | 55

Sally York Brown

Mercer Island High School graduated its first class in 1958, when traditions like the Chile-Chowder Bowl began. The school colors of maroon and silver changed to maroon and white in the fall of 1956. Top right are cheerleaders and song queens in 1958 (from upper left, clockwise, Toni Bordeau, Sue Wheeler, Maureen Renshaw, Kay Wallace, Alice Guthrie and Vickie Black). At bottom right is a 1958 graduation party held on a boat, with a luau theme.

developmental reading programs, no organized or documented curriculum—all facets of the school program taken for granted in later years.

In the midst of the enrollment boom, there was some thought of adding a second high school on the 40-acre tract owned by the district immediately west of South Mercer Junior High School (now The Lakes), and perhaps another elementary school on the Tarywood site.

Then the bust

After two decades of rapid growth, enrollment in Mercer Island schools began to decline, due in no small part to the "Boeing Bust" of 1970-1972, when 60,000 employees were laid off. Many Islanders remember the big billboard south of Seattle, which read, "Will the last person leaving Seattle turn out the lights."

At the beginning of the 1976-1977 school year, 5,236 students were registered in Mercer Island schools. In the 1987-1988 school year, 3,172 students represented a loss of nearly 40 percent.

The district had to live within a diminished budget since state support, the greatest part of the revenue, is based on student enrollment. Furthermore, a state levy lid severely limited the funds the community could additionally supply its schools via a special property-tax levy. It was a painful time of RIFs (reductions in force) and budget cuts. Yet even as programs were honed, the technology boom required the introduction of computers, software, computer training, and closed-circuit and broadcast educational TV.

The precipitous drop in enrollment required decisions on school facilities and land holdings, since it appeared that the number of students was not going to increase in the foreseeable future. It also meant a district-wide reorganization, moving to the K-5, middle school (6-8) and four-year high school configuration.

Property values on Mercer Island would continue to increase, minimizing the influx of young home buyers; zoning regulations would not be amended to allow for smaller, lower-cost home sites; and the amount of still-buildable land on Mercer Island diminished. In fact, the school district's sales of its own undeveloped property created the largest increase in new home construction.

Swaps and sales

The district decided to sell the "South Forty" and Tarywood for residential development, to sell Secret Park to the city; and to trade Mercerdale Park to the city for the 9611 Building on the frontage road of I-90. (Later the district sold the 9611 Building back to the city for the new city hall.)

When Mercer View Elementary School closed in June 1980, it was leased to the city of Mercer Island as a community center until the city finally took it over in 1997.

East Seattle School was leased to the Boys & Girls Club in 1982 and later sold to the club.

North Mercer Junior High was closed as a junior high in 1982 and South Mercer became Islander Middle School, with the ninth grade moving to the high school. North Mercer became North Campus, housing the overflow from the high school, the Contract High School, and the Special Services Department.

When Mercer Crest closed in 1983, it became rental property and housed the district's half-day activity program and some overflow from the senior high until 1986.

Mercer Crest was vacated in 1987 with the exception of the office building, which became Maintenance and Operations. Its library was refurbished to house the Contract High School. The remainder of the schools were demolished.

The Administration Building was remodeled to house the Special Services Department. North Mercer was leased to City University, Country Village Day School, Northwest Children's Academy, Classical Music Supporters, and Youth Theatre Northwest, and the gym to the city of Mercer Island for community use.

After City University departed, its space was taken over by CHILD (Children's Institute for Learning Differences).

Mercer Island Reporter

For years the Mercer Island Schools Foundation's sole fundraiser was its annual fall Phone-a-Thon. Pictured above "dialing for dollars" in this 1980s photo, counterclockwise from center bottom, are Richard Weinman, Cathy Oshiro, Lindy Weathers, Laura Karl, Jenifer Malakoff, Carol Gregg and Marianne Wolff.

Schools Foundation funds excellence in public schools

When the Mercer Island Schools Foundation was started in 1981 it was a novel idea: a privately funded organization to raise money for the public schools to enhance teaching and learning experiences for students.

Since then it has become a model for other cities eager to support their schools with additional instructional materials and programs beyond what the state provides.

Two factors have made the Mercer Island Schools Foundation one of the nation's fundraising powerhouses: the careful planning of the campaigns and the energy and size of its enthusiastic volunteer organization.

In the early years, the focus was on one large fundraising event, the annual fall Phone-a-Thon. The foundation's goal, in consultation with the school administration, was to fund a small number of major items each year. Hundreds of volunteers staffed the phones for two evenings, kept records and provided follow-up for donations. Decals of the foundation logo, a red apple, appeared on computers, electronic equipment and textbooks funded through foundation donations.

Over the years, donations to the Mercer Island Schools Foundation have continued to grow and the organization has become more sophisticated. It has increased participation to more than 50 percent of families in the district.

Since 2004, the foundation also has put on an annual Community and Business Leaders Breakfast, "Breakfast of Champions," to benefit the schools. The 2011 breakfast raised a record $644,000. In 2012 the Schools Foundation and PTA "Bridge the Gap" campaign raised $1.2 million.

The foundation board matches the top academic needs with the resources made available from dedicated donors, the business community and volunteers.

Because of the efforts of the Mercer Island Schools Foundation, more than $13 million has been donated to the schools since 1981.

The success of the organization reveals how much the community supports quality education.

In the classroom

At right, Mary Margaret Welch conducts a science experiment with some middle school students. Below, three Mercer Island High School students work on the computer together in a science classroom in 1989. Below right, longtime band director Gene Ferguson watches as a student onducts a band practice. Bottom left, Lakeridge fifth-grade teacher teacher Tarry Lindquist teaches an art class on Native American art. Bottom right, Michael Delgado, NASA astronaut in training, gives a talk to elementary students at Island Park School in 1989.

Mercer Island Reporter photos

58 | *Chapter 7: Mercer Island Schools*

Artist Karen Stocker of the artist-in-residence program sculpts the head of mayor Ben Werner during an art class at Lakeridge Elementary School in March, 1989.

First lady Nancy Reagan visits with Island Park Elementary School students in 1987, as principal John Evans and teacher Susan Gilson look on.

Lakeridge second-graders participate in the all-school musical, *Celebrate Our World* in 1994.

Mercer Island High School principal Larry Smith hands out diplomas to the class of 1987. He retired the same year.

Teacher John Kummen helps West Mercer students launch a hot-air balloon in the 1990s.

Mercer Island Reporter photoss

Chapter 7: Mercer Island Schools 59

The aging schools made up-to-date technology difficult in the 1980s and 1990s. Mercer Island High School students in Wendy Sauer's American Studies class work on computers in a classroom that was never designed for them, with ceiling plugs and extension cords, as evidenced in this 1995 photo.

Mercer Island Reporter

Mercer Island Reporter

Making signs to publicize the Islander Middle School Ski Swap in 1994 are Mandy Mulally, Jessica Myre and Stephanie Curry (left to right). The IMS Ski Swap has been an annual PTA fundraiser for decades.

Developing traditions

Despite enrollment declines in the 1980s, neither the caliber of the district's instructional program nor the level of achievement suffered. It was during this time that the schools developed many of their unique programs and annual traditions, some of which continue.

Lakeridge had its annual all-school musical, an annual retreat for fifth-graders and the ice cream social and open house, as well as the fall spaghetti dinner and family barbecue. West Mercer had an annual PTA musical, recycling activities, Great Books program and tuition foreign-language classes. Island Park, which was organized into "clusters" containing students of varying grade levels, had an annual Veterans Day assembly, monthly musicals for each cluster and a country fair.

The elementary school PTAs organized an annual fundraiser for all three schools, Metrathon, in which students gathered pledges for the number of kilometers they walked on courses around the school.

The extracurricular offerings ranged from science clubs and chess clubs to art clubs and "fit kids" groups. A before-school foreign language program for French and Spanish began in the late 1980s for elementary and middle school students.

Islander Middle School has always had a high level of participation in after-school clubs like Natural Helpers and the Science Olympiad Club, and sports of all kinds. The highly popular band and orchestra programs, beginning at the fifth grade level, were long credited with being the foundation of the strong music programs at Mercer Island High School.

To augment arts programs, a group of parent volunteers formed the Visual Arts Advisory Committee, which later became the Fine Arts Advisory Committee.

60 | Chapter 7: Mercer Island Schools

It brought art-docent programs and artists in residence into the classrooms.

District traditions include All Island Band Night, when all band students, from fifth to 12th grades, play at halftime during a Mercer Island High School football game.

Fine Arts Showcase, started in 1980 and fueled by hundreds of volunteers, became an arts extravaganza that has grown to involve nearly every student in the district in a two-evening celebration of visual and performing arts.

Crisis of confidence

A number of upheavals rocked the school community in the 1990s. In February 1990, Mercer Island voters turned down a $49.5 million bond issue that would have remodeled four of the district's five schools and replaced Lakeridge Elementary with a new school.

The issue sharply divided the community. Proponents said the remodels were sorely needed and packaging them together would actually save the district money. But opponents said the bond was simply too much money and they wanted the project to be done in phases.

The result—63 percent vote against measure—was a resounding defeat for the schools, which had not failed to pass a school tax measure in more than 20 years. It pointed to a change in demographics on the Island: Only one-third of residents had children in the schools.

In the summer of 1990, Corey Wentzell, former superintendent in Abbotsford, Canada, was hired as school superintendent to replace Wilma Smith, who resigned after a five-year tenure.

Less than two years later, the superintendent search process and the decision to hire Wentzell were scrutinized as a major budget crisis unfolded. In February 1992, Wentzell was put on leave. He subsequently resigned after the School Board learned of an unexpected budget deficit of $758,000; the shortfall represented 5.5 percent of the district's $18 million budget. An investigation showed no malfeasance; the shortfall resulted largely from overstaffing and overspending.

But the budget crisis resulted in a crisis of confidence in the community. The school board president, Nancy Clancy, resigned, saying her credibility had been damaged beyond repair; board member Liz Warner resigned shortly after.

Mercer Island Reporter

Despite state funding cuts and pressure on the budget, the Mercer Island School District managed to maintain its excellent arts programs. Top, teacher Tom Cox directs the high school's jazz choir. Above, West Mercer students in 1995 watch artist-in-residence Luc Fiedler show them how to make clay tiles. The artist-in-residence program is funded by the PTA and the Schools Foundation.

Beyond the classroom

At left, kindergarteners enjoy playground time at Island Park School in 1996. Below left, Peter Donaldson, longtime art educator, teaches an art enrichment program in 1976. At lower right, a parent volunteer leads the 1992 Walk Against Drugs, an annual event of the "Just Say No" clubs and Mercer Island Youth Services. At bottom, the Mercer Island High School cheerleaders whip up enthusiasm for Homecoming 1988, despite the rain.

62 | Chapter 7: Mercer Island Schools

Numerous STEP (Science and Technology Education Program) clubs cropped up on Mercer Island in the 1980s and 1990s. The after-school clubs for elementary and middle school students, run by parent volunteers, encouraged students to make a connection between science and everyday life.

Elementary school students (above left) participate in the PTSA's annual Metrathon in 1994. Students solicited pledges for the number of kilometers walked to raise funds for PTSA activities. At right, Mercer Island High School students tend the Homecoming bonfire in 1994.

"Fantasy Islanders" is the theme of Homecoming 1979, as the Mercer Island High School Band stands in formation during the halftime festivities.

Mercer Island Reporter photos

Chapter 7: Mercer Island Schools | 63

Mercer Island Reporter

Mercer Island High School class of 1994 gathers in front of the Mushroom. It was torn down in 1997 and replaced with the Commons in 1998 as part of the high school renovation.

Back on track

Dick Giger, hired as interim superintendent, had the job of getting the budget back on track and helping to repair the relationship between the School Board and the community. The district launched a major cost-savings effort; teachers helped by reusing paper, cutting back on copying and other austerity schemes. The following September, Giger was hired as permanent superintendent.

In the summer of 1993, after studying the reasons for the defeat of the 1990 capital bond issue, the School Board decided to put an $11 million measure on the November ballot to renovate Islander Middle School. The measure passed easily.

In February 1994, the district hired architects to come up with plans to remodel the three elementary schools. That October, the bond for the renovations was set at $16.4 million.

In November the measure was the only school issue in King County to pass. Construction began in December 1995, with the projects planned so that the students wouldn't have to be relocated. The remodels were disruptive, noisy and dusty, to be sure, but most of the work was done after school hours and during the summer.

With four successful remodels completed, the district began holding meetings in late 1995 about whether to build a new high school or remodel the existing one. More than 150 people showed up at the first meeting in December.

In February 1996, the School Board voted unanimously to remodel the high school, at

Within a four-year span, the district renovated three elementary schools, the middle school and the high school.

an estimated cost of $41 million. Target for completion was September 1998.

The board voted to put forward a $26.7 million school bond to remodel Mercer Island High School. The additional $10.5 million was to come from the capital projects fund.

Despite opposition organized by "Citizens for Common Sense," the measure passed in May 1996 by 2 to 1. Demolition began in February 1997, and that summer the project moved into high gear, with up to 120 workers on site every day. The project was completed on time, without displacing students.

In the span of just four years, the community had remodeled all five of its schools.

64 | Chapter 7: Mercer Island Schools

Mercer Island voters are accustomed to seeing signs like this at election time. Voters have a reputation for supporting school bonds and levies.

Mercer Island Reporter

The annual Career Day brought hundreds of parent volunteers into the schools to give students a peek into different walks of life. In 1994, well-known musician and Island resident Frad Radke gives a presentation on being a musician, by "playing" the hose before an audience of Lakeridge students.

Focus on curriculum

The district's foreign-language program came under the microscope in the mid-1990s. Foreign languages were offered only at the high school level, and there was a tuition-based, optional language program offered before school. But many parents felt the district was falling behind in not offering more language classes.

In January 1996, more than 100 people squeezed into Island Park for a meeting on the future of world-languages program. Eventually the School Board voted to offer Mandarin Chinese at Mercer Island High School and eliminate the German program. Spanish and eventually French were offered at the middle school, and Chinese at Island Park.

During the mid-1990s, the district adopted a new strategic plan; decided on an Internet policy; adopted a new "closed campus" policy for high school freshmen, requiring that they remain on campus all day; established a new "block" system at MIHS, changing the daily schedule to allow for larger blocks of time each week for classes; and made MIHS a new beat for a police officer (Officer Ed Holmes became the first school resource officer). A new schedule for Islander Middle School included more fine-arts electives and foreign language in the school day.

The 2000s

The new decade ushered in a new crisis: the sudden resignation of Superintendent Paula Butterfield. After only seven months on the job, she left with a $197,000 settlement, and the only explanation by the School Board was that "it was not a good fit." Hundreds of Islanders turned out for a public meeting, filled with expressions of anger and distrust. The *Mercer Island Reporter* and *Seattle Times* made public records requests for documents.

Chapter 7: Mercer Island Schools | 65

Mercer Island Enrollment Trend 1972 - 2016

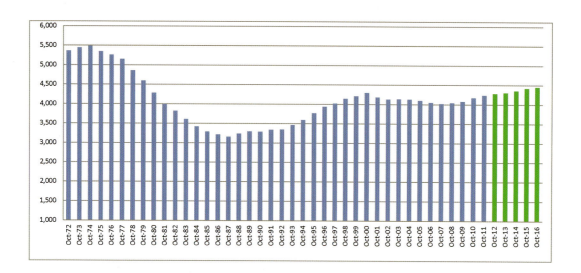

1991-2010 October P223 Enrollment
1972-1990 P105 State of Washington

Mercer Island School District

This chart demonstrates how the school population has varied since 1972. The enrollment peak in the district was in 1969, when the district had 5,963 students. The school population in 2012 was approximatly 4,100.

Ultimately, after a lawsuit was filed, the judge ordered the district to release most of the documents, cluding a mid-year performance review that portrayed Butterfield in a negative light. After the state auditor issued a report criticizing the School Board, the board president, Terry Pottmeyer, resigned.

A year later, the Office of the Superintendent of Public Instruction cleared the School District of any wrongdoing in the way it handled the Butterfield case. After an extensive search, the School Board hired Bill Keim from Oregon to be the new superintendent.

Enrollment continued to concern the school district. After more than a decade of precipitous decline, to its nadir in 1988, the number of students in the district began to grow slightly—and then more substantially.

In 1996, the district had the largest percentage enrollment increase of any Eastside district—5.3 percent over the previous year. Then, in 2000, the schools opened with 121 fewer students than the year before, the first decline in student population in more than a decade.

In 1996, the Mercer Island school district had the largest percentage enrollment increase of any Eastside district.

A decade of changes

Change—and the pace of it —became an issue early in the 2000s as the district adopted a controversial strategic plan and a new high school improvement plan, which increased the number of Advanced Placement offerings. Some felt the high school plan didn't trust teachers to make curriculum decisions; others said proposed changes were too drastic and too fast. Parents, staff members, students and administrators at times bitterly wrangled over issues facing the district.

Mercer Island High School principal Paul Highsmith surprised everyone by resigning in March 2002; more than 60 people packed the School Board meeting demanding that the board not accept his resignation, and hundreds of students walked out of classes in protest. A week later he agreed to assume a co-principal position with Donna Zickuhr.

Meanwhile, after two years on the job, Superintendent Bill Keim shocked the community with his resignation in June, 2002. When Cyndy Simms was selected to be superintendent in April 2003, she was the fifth person to hold the top job in four years.

Simms' top priority was to heal the wounds in the school community; she brought in a facilitator for a major three-day workshop where district officials and board members came up with an agreement on how they would work together. In 2004, 70

66 | *Chapter 7: Mercer Island Schools*

A tradition of excellent schools

- Measured by test performance, Mercer Island is consistently one of the top districts in Washington state. This has been true over the years and regardless of the test: the ITBS (Iowa Test of Basic Skills) administered until 1997; the WASL (Washington Assessment of Student Learning), from 1997 to 2009; and MSP (Measurement of Student Progress) and HSPE (High School Proficiency Exam), administered since 2009.

- On state exams, the elementary students consistently place among the top 4 percent of schools in the state, and the middle and high school students score among the top 10 schools in the state.

- The on-time graduation rate for Mercer Island High School is consistently high. In 2012 it was 96 percent.

- In 2010, Forbes magazine rated the Mercer Island School District among America's 25 best school districts for one's housing dollar, and one of the top 10 districts in small cities across the country.

- Mercer Island High School was awarded the Silver Medal of Distinction in U.S. News and World Report magazine's Best High Schools 2009 Search for the top-achieving high schools in the nation.

- Islander Middle School (2003) and Mercer Island High School (2006) were designated Blue Ribbon Schools by the U.S. Department of Education.

- The Council of Chief State School Officers and Standard & Poors have identified Mercer Island as an "Outperforming District" for performing at a level that significantly exceeds statistical expectations.

- The Seattle Times School Guide rated Mercer Island High school the number-one public high school in Washington for quality preparation of students.

- In 2009, district students achieved the second-highest average score on the state's Measurement of Student Progress and High School Proficiency Exam proficiency tests.

- In 2012, 29 Mercer Island School District teachers achieved National Board Teacher Certification.

people attended a conflict-resolution workshop for the school district to learn how to mend divisiveness over how to run the schools.

The district put a new emphasis on the arts, relationships and community. It put into place anti-harassment and anti-bullying programs in the schools. In 2004, Mercer Island High School began Bridges, a program in which students meet in groups for an hour each week to discuss social and academic issues, with the goal of creating in the students a sense of belonging.

The next year, the school established a new mentoring program, the Connections Committee, which matched juniors and seniors with incoming students, with a goal of improving the school climate.

In the mid-2000s, the curricula in all schools in the district emphasized emotional as well as academic growth. In addition, the federally mandated Wellness Policy was phased in, designed to fight childhood obesity. Soft drinks in schools were replaced by juice or water.

In 2004, parents, teachers and community members were buzzing about a new book published by elementary school teacher Joby McGowan. A "tell-all" expose entitled Teaching on Poverty Rock, it dished about demanding "helicopter" parents and micromanaging administrators.

When Superintendent Simms left the district in 2008, Gary Plano, assistant superintendenent, stepped in, first as an interim superintendent and then as a permanent replacement, ushering in a period of calm and stability.

Cooperation between the school district and the city grew in the 2000s on such issues as Mary Wayte Pool, the availability and maintenance of athletic fields and the funding of non-academic counselors to work in Mercer Island schools.

Enrollment rises again

Student enrollment in Mercer Island schools ebbed from 4,147 in 2000 to 3,842 in 2009. It was forecast to continue declining, causing worry over the outlook for school funding. A committee of Islanders explored ways to find more tax dollars, and out-of-district students were accepted—31 in 2007 and 100 in 2008—to offset the loss in per-student revenue.

But that changed in 2010 as enrollment began to rise again. By 2011, 600 students were housed in elementary portables, enough for a whole new school. The 21st Century Facilities Planning Committee, a group of 20 residents representing a cross-section of the community and 13 Island organizations, was formed in August 2010 to formulate master plans for the public schools for the next 50 years. It presented its recommendations to the School Board in September 2011.

After community input and debate, the School Board voted to put a $196.3 million bond measure on the ballot in April 2012.

The bond was to replace the elementary schools and middle school, buy land for school use, mod-

Chapter 7: Mercer Island Schools | 67

Private School options

Numerous private schools and tutoring operations have been part of the Island community. Some that have had enduring impact include:

Children's Institute for Learning Differences (CHILD) was founded by Trina Westerlund in 1977 to help students and parents dealing with learning disabilities and behavioral challenges. About 10 years later it moved to North Campus on the Island. CHILD serves about 50 students ages 3 to 17.

Country Village Day School opened with a handful of students in 1971 in a room at United Methodist Church, and it's grown to more than 200 students and 42 staff in the current location on the North Campus.

French American School of Puget Sound was founded in 1995 with two teachers and a dozen students in a building at East Mercer Way alongside I-90. Since then it has grown to more than 380 students in kindergarten through 8th grade, with a faculty of 55. It is an immersion-style school teaching in both French and English, with the aim that students excel and thrive in French, American and international cultures. The head of school is Eric Thuau.

Northwest Yeshiva High School, established in Seattle in 1974, purchased the former Baptist Church property in the middle of Mercer Island above Island Crest Way in September 1992. The school opened the following year, with a student body that ranges from 70 to 100. It is the only full-time college prep Jewish high school in the state. The orthodox school offers a standard high school curriculum coupled with Judaic studies. Rabbi Bernie Fox is dean.

Privett Academy, founded in 1995, is a nonprofit, state-accredited private middle and high school that offers flexible schedules and course offerings as well as personalized instruction not available in a traditional school setting. Carol Meyer is director of the school, located in the Ogden Building on Southeast 36th Street.

St. Monica Parish School is a co-ed Catholic school for grades pre-kindergarten through eighth grades. Located adjacent to St. Monica Church, the 10-room school opened in 1960 with 186 students. The school has been remodeled several times over the years. The school teaches Christ-like values in addition to emphasizing academic excellence. The principal is Anca Wilson.

Yellow Wood Academy, formerly known as Education Tutoring and Consulting (ETC Preparatory Academy) was started in 1981 by two Island educators, Jan Bleakney and Sheila Scates. It became a state-approved private school in 1992. It is a non-profit organization that offers instruction and academic credit in all disciplines kindergarten through grade 12.

---

ernize Mary Wayte Pool and the high school stadium and make improvements/additions to Mercer Island High School.

Overcrowding in the schools and the current favorable financing and building climate were the key sales points.

The Committee for Mercer Island Public Schools sprang into action, launching a campaign to support the bond measure. But soon a campaign against the bond emerged, with websites and yard signs, evidence of a level of dissension over the bond not often seen on the Island.

Meanwhile, after the death of longtime Islander Lewis Stevenson, his heirs decided to sell their property, a 4.89-acre parcel of land off Island Crest Way south of Island Crest Park. The school district entered into negotiations to purchase the property. This added fuel to the debate over whether it was best to add a fourth elementary school rather than simply expand the three elementary schools. And it confused the issue for voters.

The bond measure needed 60 percent approval for passage, but it was soundly rejected by nearly that amount, 59.67 percent. Fifty-four percent of registered voters took part in the special election, 9,208 voters of a possible 16,953.

The overwhelming no vote was a blow to the district. But it also was a strong impetus to bring opponents and proponents together to forge a new solution.

The first step was a survey conducted in May 2012 to determine the key reasons for the failure of the bond. The "no" voters believed the amount of money ($196 million) was too much, that buildings could be expanded rather than replaced, and that the planning was over-ambitious.

By the end of 2012, the school district was continuing to study and gather community input on various options for future school facilities. The most likely first project would be construction of a new elementary school on the North Mercer campus. Funding for an addition to Islander Middle School and the addition of science classrooms at Mercer Island High School could also be on the ballot in 2013 or 2014.

Meanwhile, the City Council and the School Board pledged to work together to help find the best solutions for school facilities.

And Islanders again stepped up to continue the supportive tradition begun by its pioneers. Within weeks of the bond failure, the district announced that the Schools Foundation's Bridge the Gap campaign had succeeded in raising $1.2 million to help fund additional teacher salaries.

Marie Blanche Lucas milks a cow on the family dairy farm. The original 80-acre farm included the present-day Mercerdale Park. Eventually, the family owned more than 140 acres at the top of the Island.

Mercer Island Historical Society

The North End

There were dairy farms on the hillsides and a swamp where the Town Center is today

In the early days, Mercer Island was a place for hardy folk, as there were no roads, no cars, no electricity and only one store.

Gordon McGilvra platted the area from the waterfront to present-day Southeast 32nd Street as McGilvra. The eastern part was platted as Mercer Park. To the south were the Lucas and Kristoferson farms, where Holy Trinity Lutheran Church, Homestead Field and many homes are today.

Waterfront docks were built first, to give steamers access to the area. The East Seattle Water System extended its network of wooden water mains and promised an adequate supply of spring water.

Waterfront homes sold readily around Serena Cove, as the first residents called the waterfront from present-day 72nd to 80th Avenues Southeast. Owners built summer houses first, then homes for year-round living, and all had their front doors facing the water. There were no roads to access the inland sides of the houses.

Even without roads, a few upland homes were built. One owner was a 50-year resident, Ralph Beddow, who wrote in *The Seattle Times* of Sept. 15, 1957, about those early days:

"I bought a lot near Roanoke Dock in 1908. My friend, George McGuire, and I pitched a tent and began camping out in March, 1911. Nobody lived around here then. The next year my dad helped me build the house. We carried lumber on our backs up the trail from Roanoke Dock.

> 'There was just one thing—when the autos reached the Island, the trail was so bad they couldn't go anywhere except back on the boat to Seattle.'
>
> **Ralph Beddow**
> *remembering the early days —1913 or 1914—when cars first came to the Island*

There were a few hundred persons on the Island—all seemed to be pioneers, and all liked the outdoors.

"Automobiles first appeared in 1913 or 1914, put aboard the *Fortuna* in Seattle (carpenters had widened the gangplanks for them). There was just one thing—when the autos reached the Island, the trail was so bad they couldn't go anywhere except back on the boat to Seattle.

"When the boats were running, we knew everybody who lived on the Island, because we met them aboard ship. You felt like a different person getting on the boat at Leschi in the evening and coming back to a different world.

"A couple of boardwalks for passengers to get in and out of Roanoke Dock ran past our house. We used to hear the ferry or steamer whistle, grab our coats and a last piece of toast, and run for it."

Later, the East Seattle area was accessed by a two-plank boardwalk built by Clarance Larson to provide a safer path for his children to walk from their home near 40th Street along West Mercer Way to the school at East Seattle. Many Island youngsters recall walking "on the boardwalk," according to Ruth Mary Larson Close.

First impressions

Newcomers continued to arrive, some eagerly and others reluctantly. Mimi Sandin gave a bride's view of Mercer Island in 1917:

"We were married in 1916, and lived in a Seattle apartment. My husband, Frank, didn't like apartment living because he felt like a caged lion. He wanted to follow his brother to Mercer Island, where his brother had bought an acre and built a house a few years earlier.

"I was not keen about crossing that treacherous lake every time I went to Seattle. I said to my husband, 'Well, let's go over there and buy the half acre from your brother for an investment.' Acreage was cheap then.

"One blustery March day, we started out, taking the cable car to Leschi Park. There I saw the lake with waves rolling high. I saw the big launch, the only means of transportation to the North End of the Island, run by Charlie Gilbert. When I looked at those waves, I said, 'I won't go!' But he persuaded me to get into the boat. Halfway across, water was coming into the boat. I saw one of the men put on a life preserver, and I was fit to be tied! We finally got safely to Roanoke Dock.

"As we walked up from the dock, I said, 'Frank, I'll never, never live on Mercer Island. I mean it.'

"Well, when we got up there, we saw two lovely deer right on this property. The trilliums were in bloom, and the dogwood, and other shrubs. A great virgin forest, 40 acres of it, spread from the present toll plaza over to where the shopping center is now. It was so beautiful! It was like a miracle to me. My heart melted right then and there. Just such a paradise. I said to Frank, 'I feel like Eve — you're Adam.' How we loved it.

"We bought the property that same day, and started right in to clear, because we planned to camp here, whether we ever lived here or not. Oh, my, it was fun. We came over here every weekend, regardless of weather.

"The next spring, in 1918, we came back and cleared some more. One lovely day when the bird-chorus was singing as beautifully as a symphony orchestra, Frank said, 'Mimi, how would you like it if I fixed this place real snug, added some rooms, so we could live here next winter?' I couldn't refuse.

"He added a kitchen, dining, bath, bedroom. We came over here to live, and we were very happy. I had to eat those words about not ever living on Mercer Island! My goodness, I wouldn't want to live anywhere else. That

Mercer Island Historical Society

After the Island was logged, most of the land was cleared for pasture. The Kristoferson's homestead, now Homestead Field, was one of the early dairy farms. The Lucas farm, pictured above, was in the Mercerdale area. The photo below shows Josephine Lucas with her daughter, Marie Blanche, and a dog.

A waterfront resident surveys her new front yard after the lowering of Lake Washington in 1916. In the background are docks left high and dry.

Virginia Ogden Elliott

was 58 wonderful happy years ago. Great years."

These are the words of Mrs. Frank Sandin, recorded in February 1976 after her husband had died. The house was in the path of the proposed I-90 freeway. She did not live to see the coming of the freeway or the end of her cozy home.

Lowering the lake

Mercer Island literally grew in size after the construction of the Chittenden Locks in 1916. After decades of planning, the saltwater connection between Lake Washington and Puget Sound finally became a reality. Since the level of Lake Washington was higher than Lake Union, a cofferdam was built at the Montlake Cut so the canal could be built.

When that coffer was blown out, Lake Washington rushed into Lake Union and its level dropped 9 feet, adding land to many parts of the Island and remodeling the shoreline. Some steep shores remained, like sides of a rugged mountaintop. Residents complained about the mucky mess and the need to rebuild docks that in many cases were left high and dry.

Later those who had complained realized that they had reaped an unexpected bonanza, a gift from the lake in their front yards. The shallow north end of the Island gained from 80 feet in most areas to more than 700 feet in the coves near Luther Burbank Park.

The inlet and outlet of the lake also changed. The Black River had been the outlet, flowing into the Cedar River below Renton, then into the Duwamish. The Black River dried up, and the Cedar River was diverted into Lake Washington to diminish flood danger and provide water at the Chittenden Locks to raise and lower boats with a controllable water level.

Dairy farms

Before 1900, August Kristoferson's homestead, now the site of Homestead Field, was one of the early dairy farms. After the logging of the 1890s, settlers cleared the land for pasture.

Farmers carried milk and cheese down to Franklin Dock (at the west end of present-day Southeast 40th Street) to be taken by rowboat to Leschi Dock in Seattle. It was a much longer row than from Person's Dairy in East Seattle to Seattle.

The story of the Lucas farm, dating from 1889, appeared in the *Mercer Island Reporter* on July 4, 1974:

"It was the tale of a French governess turned farmer's wife, and her struggle from atop Lucas Hill that brought the turn-of-the-century Island life alive.

"Mademoiselle Josephine Pachoud had traveled throughout Europe with the family of a Russian countess before she came to Seattle. W. J. Stimson, a local lumber baron, engaged her to tutor his daughter, Dorothy. (Later Dorothy Bullitt founded KING Broadcasting.)

"It was at a social given by the French Consul that the red-haired governess met her future husband, Eugene Lucas, Sr. Together they farmed the original 80 acres (now Mercerdale) Eugene had bought when he came to the Island in 1889. Pheasant under glass wasn't served before her anymore; instead she was tending leaf lettuce and cabbage under cold frames. There were potatoes and strawberries to hoe and harvest in the fields of 'gravel topsoil.'

"There were fires for them (and other settlers, too) to fight. Hay fields and logging slash caught like tinder from lightning, land clearing and burning, and logging.

"Three children were born—Joseph, Gene, and Marie Blanche—who, in time, helped milk the cows. They competed for customers with Person's Dairy. Then the family became more prosperous, hired 20 Japanese to work the gardens, bought up more land and got a motor-driven scow.

"'Dad's scow was big enough to put two teams aboard and run across to Mount Baker. He'd drop a ramp on the beach and go peddle his vegetables,' Gene said.

"'In 1907 the scow was found floating, unmanned, near the Merrimount Dock, and shortly after a teamster in East Seattle found Eugene's body, apparently the victim of drowning. My mother was left a widow with us three kids and a mortgage,' Gene said."

Chapter 8: The North End | 71

Mercer Island Reporter

Built in 1914, the Roanoke Inn, "the Rowy," is the oldest business on the Island.

The Roanoke Inn—beloved Island landmark

When automobile traffic was off-loaded at Roanoke Dock beginning in 1914, there was nowhere to drive, nothing to do except return to Seattle. When Island roads improved, brave tourists went exploring. To appeal to visitors and serve the community, George McGuire built the Roanoke Inn, a chicken-dinner restaurant, not far from the ferry dock on 72nd Avenue. "The Rowy" stands today, well preserved, more popular than ever and looking much the same as when it was built.

At first, business was not exactly brisk, and McGuire lost the inn because of debts. A Mr. Green took over and operated it as a hotel. Subsequently it was sold several times, sometimes falling into ill repute, rumored to be a brothel and a purveyor of illegal booze served in coffee mugs during Prohibition.

In the years after Prohibition when the Roanoke was a tavern, groceries, ice cream and pop were sold. But minors were not allowed inside, so a window to the right of the door provided access where children could buy ice cream cones or complete their shopping errands.

In 1943, Edwin and Laura Reeck purchased the Inn, and it has been in their family ever since. Ed and Laura made it a true inn, with meal service as well as beer and wine. A gathering place for Islanders and off-Islanders, the inn developed a friendly, homey atmosphere, with a working fireplace and the Reecks as friendly hosts.

The grocery store continued into the 1940s and 1950s. The Reecks drove their Model T Ford to Seattle once a week to buy supplies. Other small grocery stores in the same area had come and gone through the years. A big store, the Roanoke Grocery and Meat Market, located in a long white building on the north side of the Roanoke Dock, burned around 1930. During World War II, the Roanoke had the Island's only store other than Standard Supply in East Seattle.

After Ed Reeck died, Laura married Bill Bice in 1953, and they carried on the old traditions, but without the grocery store. Fifteen years later, after the death of Bill Bice, Laura's son, Hal Reeck, joined his mother as coproprietor until she died in 1982. Hal Reeck married Dorothy Farrill and since his death she has been the matriarch of the business, continuing the family tradition of running the Roanoke Inn.

Many important issues of city governance have been hashed out at informal gatherings at the beloved watering hole over the years, and "The Rowy" has become *the* place for Friday nights and countless Mercer Island High School reunions.

The Roanoke Inn is the oldest business enterprise on the Island. And it has lived up to its slogan, "A place where friends meet friends."

After World War II, the Lucases subdivided some of their property, which included Lucas Hill, Mercerdale, part of Homestead Field and 140 acres at the top of the Island that now includes St. Monica Church and Mercer Island High School. Josephine Lucas kept working a small truck farm until her death in 1949.

The Flats

While activity increased along the waterfront, The Flats, south of the newly built Boulevard (North Mercer Way), remained a place of swamps, upended tree stumps and low grassy hollows where wild strawberries grew.

A favorite place for Island children to play in 1918, it was described by Virginia Ogden Elliott in her *Mercer Island Reporter* column in 1961: "Our Flats were indeed a magic land, our own private country, mapped, charted and named. And here we grew up—quite a gang, with four Hemions, two Clarkes, three Ogdens, three Higdays, two Balches, and in summer, two Vinals.

"Each of us had our special camps, trails, and haunts in the little valley. There was the Tree House, the Queen's Highway, the hollow stump where we tied up one girl as a hostage in some 'war' and went off and forgot her.

"From the West Boulevard, we entered the Flats along a skid road overgrown and rotting away so that one had to hop from mossy log to log, often missing and coming down ankle deep in swamp ooze. Wild huckleberry bushes overhead, and trilliums grew in profusion all along the road.

"Deep mossy pools reflected in their black surfaces the contorted tree branches covered with moss and licorice fern. High firs reached up into the sunlight. Great 10-foot high stumps had cuts in their sides made by the springboard logging of a more hasty and wasteful era. Most of the stumps were fire-charred by the forest fires that ravaged parts of the Island in an earlier time.

"The Flats had another name, 'Devil's Hollow.' The Flats were littered with the bleached bones of dead cattle. The whitened ribs made excellent weapons when the 'Fighting Five' clashed in one of their periodic wars with the 'Kingdom of Tigers.' But most prized of all were the bleached skulls. For many years they could still be found, moss-covered and hidden in the bracken ferns. They were the grim mementoes of a wild, snowy winter when the Lucas herd was killed after the snow caved in the cowshed roof.

"Down the hill from the Lucas farm, past the big madronas, where the sheds were, there we could find skulls to wear. We remember being gratifyingly terrified by the sight of whitened skulls walking around with legs under them. It was those same skulls, worn by most of us, that gave Devil's Hollow its name. We can personally attest to the devils that inhabited it, wearing the old skulls of the doomed cows. We kept silent when our children told us of apparitions that had been seen in years gone by. For we ourselves had been devil's heads with legs underneath."

Jenna Lee Easter recounted how her father came to live at the east side of The Flats: "My father, J.B. Brown, came west from Missouri in 1906 to die. He was a relatively young man, but the doctors had told him his days were numbered because he had a serious case of incurable ulcers.

"On the Island, he first lived on the waterfront near McGilvra Dock, but a heavy snowfall one winter (1916) made him decide to move inland. He gave away his waterfront and bought property where the Bank of America now

In 1914, proudly showing off his new auto, August Kristoferson drove toward the Olds-Garrison farm, slid into a ditch on the old 1893 wagon road and was rescued by a team of horses. The car was towed to Appleton Dock and hoisted aboard the ferry *Fortuna*. Kristoferson is at left, with young Harry and Myrta Garrison on front mudgards.

Myrta Garrison Baker

Mercer Island Historical Society
Three girls head to The Flats, with baskets for berrypicking, to spend the day.

stands, and south, up to Southeast 30th Street. Where the Union 76 gas station stood until recently he built his home and built a barn, planted an orchard, and built chicken houses. At one time there were 1,000 chickens in residence.

"I well remember hearing the story of the day I was born, Dec. 28, 1920. My father was away. My expectant mother began to have labor pains. She sent her son down to the only telephone in the neighborhood, at Hap's Service Station. He was to call the doctor in Seattle to find out what to do. When Hap heard about the problem, he came to the rescue and took my mother to Leschi Landing in his outboard boat. I can just imagine what a ride *that* was! Mother and daughter made it to the hospital on time. And here I am."

The Flats of yesteryear are the Town Center of today, the central business district.

Roadside businesses

Automobile-carrying ferries stopped at Roanoke Dock as early as 1914, but the driving was uncertain, especially in muddy seasons when an unlucky or unwise driver needed rescue by a team of horses. Other services were also needed as traffic increased.

In 1918, Hap Lightfoot opened the first service station on the Island, located at present-day 76th Avenue Southeast and Southeast 24th Street. Across the street was the small McGilvra School. With a small grocery store and a hall for meetings, plus the only telephone in the area, Hap's served as a north-end community center.

Notes in the Historical Society files written by an old-timer state, "About 1921 or 1922, there were movies on the Island. Admission was 10 cents. One night the pictures would be shown at East Seattle in the building where the post office used to be, and the next night at McGilvra at Hap's meeting hall. The music used was a phonograph, and young boys would change records, taking them at random. The movies were run for about a year and then discontinued."

In 1930, the road from Roanoke Dock to the East Channel Bridge was paved, and the occasion was marked by a celebration, with speeches by dignitaries and great rejoicing by the increasing number of automobile drivers.

Longtime north-ender Huston Riley was born in 1921 in the small waterfront house his parent built, and lived there until his death in 2011. He remembered the small grocery store that operated for a time on Roanoke

1914 A new school is built at East Seattle, for grades 1 to 8.

1914 The McGilvra Improvement Club is founded Oct. 10.

1914 The Roanoke Inn opens.

1914-1916 North Mercer Way is built.

1916-17 The size and shape of Mercer Island changes when the Chittenden Locks are completed, lowering Lake Washington by 9 feet.

1917 The Mercer Island Improvement Club combines several earlier improvement clubs.

1918 The post office moves to the back of a grocery store on the corner of present-day Southeast 28th Street and 60th Avenue Southeast.

1918 Lakeview School opens on the south end. It has one classroom and an open, covered play area..

1918 The flu epidemic spreads; Islanders don masks.

1919 Boy Scouting begins on Mercer Island, with a troop at East Seattle School led by scoutmaster J.K. Carr, manual training teacher at East Seattle School.

1920 The first telephones come to the Island.

1920 The South End Improvement Club forms.

1920 Allview Heights School is torn down for lack of students.

1920 George Lightfoot becomes postmaster, with a salary of $66 per month. Mercer Island's first rural mail route is laid out.

1921 Oct. 1, Homer Hadley formally proposes a concrete pontoon floating bridge across Lake Washington.

1921 The first group of Camp Fire Girls begins on the Island.

John Dunney: Island's first real estate agent

John Dunney opened the first real estate office near the Roanoke Dock. His long involvement with Island affairs began in 1914, when he was an engineer with King County's Road Engineering Department, assigned to right-of-way procurement for the boulevard around the Island.

He was born in Seattle in 1890, worked his way through Seattle College to become a civil engineer, served with the U.S. Army Engineers in World War I, returned to Mercer Island and bought property for his home on West Mercer Way.

He used to tell how, as a boy, he built and sailed his boat named *Gooey Duck* around the lake, camping sometimes at Bellevue. He got to know the shoreline and the thickly forested, thinly populated Island well.

He cleared his own land, built his own home and helped build the Keewaydin Clubhouse in 1922. In 1924, he lost his eyesight in a hunting accident. He started to sell insurance in Seattle, but soon decided to move to his Mercer Island home, which he had finished except for the fireplace mantel, when he lost his sight. There he and his wife, Grace, lived for the rest of their lives.

In 1937 Dunney received his new "eyes," a Seeing Eye dog named Teddy. They became a familiar sight as they strode along Island roads, fields and paths.

Dunney was the only Island real estate agent for 15 years.

In a *Mercer Island Reporter* interview in 1974, he said, "When we started advertising property in 1924, we never mentioned Mercer Island in our ads because Seattleites didn't know where it was. They thought it was in the San Juans or Aleutians. On the phone, we'd tell people it was only 10 minutes from Leschi Park."

In 1954, he relocated his office to what became the Island's business center. He had an unquenchable faith in Mercer Island as a residential district even when times were tough, the roads were rough, vacant houses were falling into disrepair and land was being lost for taxes. Dunney advised owners to hang on and not sell at sacrifice prices.

Dunney's community participation included many committees, the Community Club, the Chamber of Commerce and many kindnesses to individuals, especially the blind. He died in 1974, after more than 60 years on the Island. His memory is honored with the John Dunney Trail, which leads from the former Flats up the hillside where the old skid road took logs down past the site of his office in the business center.

Dunney Realty Company
John Dunney clearing his land in the early 1920s.

John Dunney with his Seeing Eye dog, Teddy.

John Dunney

The Lightfoot family and their enterprises

When Fred Lightfoot and his family came to Mercer Island in 1914, they built a small white house facing south on present-day Southeast 27th Street, where they raised their two sons, George (Speed) and Ewart (Hap), and their daughter, Mary. In the mid 1920s, Mary was married in the house, and shortly after that the living room was converted into a grocery store. By the early 1930s, they quit selling groceries there and moved to another house on the north end. In the early 1950s, when this photo was taken, you could see a Shell station and the U.S. Highway 10 in the background. Today this is the site of The Mercer apartments.

The Lightfoots built the first service station on the Island, in 1919, at the northeast corner of what is now 76th Avenue Southeast and Southeast 24th Street. It burned down in 1928 and was replaced with a brick station. The sign on the top front reads "Speed's Garage"; the sign on the front fascia reads "General Repairing."

In the early 1940s, a new "lube" room was added to the old brick service station. Before that, there was a grease pit behind the station. The grease pit was made of concrete, with two elevated wheel ways and a trench to go down into for servicing. This 1945 photo shows the one remaining hand pump on the right.

Lightfoot family photos

76 | Chapter 8: The North End

> **"I am convinced that the Island will become the most desirable residential district near Seattle, but I hope the Islanders will realize, before it is too late, the need for parks. Mercer Island is 4,000 acres of the Evergreen Playground forever set apart from the smoke, bustle and noise of the city, ready for people who value good things to build good homes. Mercer Island has, indeed, a bright future."**
>
> — John Dunney
> writing in *The Livewire Mercer Island News* in 1942

Dock, owned by neighbor Harry Hawkins. In addition to groceries, it had a soda fountain and chairs, and one gas pump.

As a young boy, Riley sold newspapers to ferry riders at the Roanoke dock; the *Seattle Post-Intelligencer* sold for 5 cents a copy.

In 1928, Hap's Service Station and the meeting-hall building and grocery store burned to the ground. Only the service station was rebuilt. In 1939, the state Highway Department bought the site of the McGilvra School for the new Sunset Highway and built an overpass at 76th Avenue Southeast where the school had been.

Another early business establishment was Moore's Lumber Yard, located southeast of Hap's Service Station. Moore carried a small stock of lumber and would order materials and deliver to do-it-yourself Islanders. The meadow around his little white house, where he kept his lumber piles, is now paved over in the business district.

The north end became a throughway when the first East Channel Bridge opened in November 1923. Drivers from Seattle could embark at Leschi, cross the lake by ferry, drive off at Roanoke, drive across the north end on the boulevard, across the wooden bridge to Enatai and take off for Issaquah, Snoqualmie, Renton or elsewhere on the Eastside. The increased accessibility of the Island triggered growth.

Luther Burbank

After the state Legislature passed a bill in 1903 authorizing larger cities to establish "parental," or truant, schools, the Seattle School District purchased 16 acres of the old Calkins property on the east shore of the Island for its Industrial School.

Major Cicero Newell, who had been operating the school in Seattle and then in the vacant Calkins Hotel in East Seattle, took the children to the Calkins property to tent-camp during the summer of 1904.

During that time the first two school buildings were built, with the second floors used as dormitories. In 1905, Major Newell resigned, reporting in his memoirs, "I have accomplished what I had been seeking for years, a home for boys and girls who had no one to care for them."

The name was changed from Industrial School to Parental School to avoid the stigma of a correctional institution.

After a year under the superintendency of William Baker, Willis Rand, who had been associated with the school as a teacher and house parent, was appointed superintendent.

In 1912, Rand bought 80 acres for the Seattle School District for $15,000. All except 16 acres, the original purchase, had been leased. In 1914, a hospital, laundry and a large barn were built. In the same year, the girls were transferred to a school of their own, Martha Washington School, south of Seward Park. The Mercer Island campus was renamed Boys Parental School.

Rand pursued his idea of developing a farm. Boys went to classes half a day, then spent the rest of the day working on the farm. They gardened, fed the stock, picked apples, milked cows and developed a prize Holstein herd. In 1915, Rand hired an agriculturist to supervise farm activities.

In 1929, a central heating plant and a brick dormitory known as Lake Cottage were built. Today all the wooden farm buildings, schoolhouses and dormitories are gone. Only the brick cottage and central heating plant remain.

The name of the school was changed in 1931 to Luther Burbank School, after the horticulturist and American pioneer in agricultural sciences, in line with the Seattle School District's policy of naming schools for famous persons. The farm program continued, and the students came from county juvenile courts all over the state.

In a 1944 interview, Rand recalled, "Some of the city boys are pretty awkward, especially those who never saw a cow up close before. But they all like a farm, and all want to take care of the horses. I make them work up to it through poultry, which few like, through truck gardening, pig-feeding and milking. We raised 500 chickens and 20 hogs per year, had seven acres of truck gardens, 10 acres of orchards, and 35 acres of pasture for 12 cows."

By the time the agriculturist retired in 1944, the farm was more than self-supporting. Production had increased, and many boys had learned not only about farming, but about coping with daily problems

Mercer Island Historical Society

Nestled in a neighborhood of million dollar homes, the Craft Guild remains as it has since 1940.

The Craft Guild is a vestige of bygone years

In the late 1930s, some neighbors on the north end wanted to pool their resources and share power tools for woodworking and boat building.

That was the genesis of the Mercer Island Craft Guild, a still-thriving private nonprofit cooperative in the East Seattle neighborhood.

According to records kept by the late Harry Slater, 10 men from the East Seattle neighborhood got together on April 4, 1940, and formed a co-op.

They bought an undersized, 30-by-90-foot lot at 2832 61st. Ave. S.E. for $50 at a tax sale. And they set about building a wood shop.

They salvaged most of the wood for their building from the construction of the I-90 floating bridge, and hunted up secondhand power tools.

They installed a 55-gallon chip-burning barrel, which is still the only source of heat for the 1,000-square-foot clubhouse. There's still no plumbing. In fact, inside the place looks pretty much as it must have looked some 70 years ago—except for some of the high-tech, computer-controlled tools and the power vac.

Membership dues pay the bills, and members receive a key to the clubhouse and access to its tools. The number of members has ranged from 30 to 70 members through the years, with men—and occasionally women—from all walks of life and ranging in age from their 20s to their 80s. The guild is strictly for hobbyists and is not to be used for commercial purposes.

Over the years, members have gathered as needed for work parties and to maintain the building. Members volunteer to cut the grass in the summer, oil the machines and do odd jobs.

Safety rules and bylaws are posted inside the shop, along with reminders to clean up after oneself and return tools to their original places. There's just one official gathering per year, the annual business meeting in February, usually accompanied by strong drink. It's the only time most members ever see each other.

Nobody knows how many tables or bookcases or boxes or boats have been built in the Mercer Island Craft Guild over the years.

But one thing is sure: The Mercer Island Craft Guild is a rare vestige of the old days on Mercer Island. And it's likely to remain proudly, even defiantly, the same for many years to come.

Barto family

This aerial photo, circa 1950, was taken looking east, with the campus of Luther Burbank School at the top. The road parallel to the lake in the middle of the photo is 82nd Avenue Southeast.

in their lives.

During Rand's 40 years of service, he supervised the expansion and development of the campus, and contributed to the educational and social needs of the children.

Rand had married a teacher named Martha who had attended the school in 1904. Their son, Ted, born and raised on the campus, became a well-known artist and children's book illustrator, and lived out his years on Mercer Island.

Ted Rand recalled that "for many years that very valuable waterfront which costs so much per front foot now, was occupied solely by pigs! That's where the pigpens were."

In 1942, Willis Rand retired. The program continued until 1957, when a change in state law required that the state of Washington operate all parental schools. The farm at Luther Burbank was discontinued.

The number of students increased, and the old wooden buildings were falling into disrepair. Two possible solutions were discussed.

One was a complete rebuilding of the Mercer Island campus; the alternative was to relocate both the boys school and the girls school to a tract of state-owned land near North Bend. Either would be financed by a statewide bond issue. Public hearings were held.

Many Mercer Islanders had spent numerous hours volunteering for the Burbank School—organizing clubs and Boy Scout troops, taking carloads of kids to Snoqualmie for sledding and providing refreshments for birthday parties. Such people spoke in favor of rebuilding the existing campus.

Other residents felt that the school had become a pox on the community and should be removed. The runaways were a nuisance and the presence of so-called riffraff was inappropriate, they said.

Debate continued for about five years, until Sen. Albert Thompson of Bellevue promoted passage of two bills in the 1963 Legislature: one authorizing moving the school to Preston, the other placing a $4,600,000 bond issue on the 1964 ballot.

Both measures passed and the new Echo Glen campus was built; Luther Burbank Boys School moved out in December 1966.

The future of Luther Burbank remained in question. Some wanted it to be a golf course, others wanted a park, still others wanted development. Debate and discussion about the property continued until 1968, when King County bought the 77-acre park for $2 million as part of the Forward Thrust bond program.

Chapter 8: The North End | 79

A boy's life at the Luther Burbank School

Mercer Island Parental School became an all-boys school in 1928, and in 1931 the name was changed to Luther Burbank School. Enrollment peaked at 137 students in 1944; the average stay was nine months. At top, boys ages 9 to 17 went to classes in the morning and worked on the farm in the afternoon, but had time for play, photo above. Above left is the administration building, and above right are members of the school staff. The photo at left shows the administration building and the tower.
Mercer Island Historical Society

80 | Chapter 8: The North End

Each boy tended his own garden and helped in the fruit orchard. At one time the school had 500 chickens, 20 hogs, 10 acres of orchards and 35 acres of pasture for 12 cows.

Mercer Island Historical Society

Mercer Island Historical Society

In addition to farm duties, boys could participate in the school's marching band, among other activities.

The farm program at Luther Burbank School provided new experiences for many urban children who had never milked a cow or even seen one before.

Mercer Island Historical Society

Chapter 8: The North End | 81

Fortuna Park was the site of the annual all-Island family picnic. The park included a dance hall, swimming beach, boats to rent and food booths. It was a popular weekend destination for Seattle residents.

Mercer Island Historical Society

The dilapidated buildings were torn down, and the brick dormitory was repaired, refurbished and leased to the City of Mercer Island Parks and Recreation Department. Later, the King County Parks Department was located there.

King County owned and operated Luther Burbank until 2001, when a budget shortfall forced the closure of 20 parks throughout the county. In 2002, King County approved the transfer of ownership of the park to the city of Mercer Island.

Fortuna Park

When settlers were dependent on boat transportation, excursion boats offered a day's outing at Fortuna Park (named for the steamer) on the north shore.

The park was created in the early 1900s by Capt. John Anderson, boat builder, ferry owner and operator. He bought land, cleared it and laid out playfields. He built a dock and a large barn-like building for a dance hall, with an excellent hardwood floor. He had a swimming beach, rental boats, booths for food and beverages. This was a great way to increase his weekend and holiday ferry traffic.

Chartered by club groups from Seattle, the resort was not as much a part of Island life as were other gathering places. Some parents refused permission to their young to go down to "that place." Except, that is, for the annual all-Island bash. Steamers called at each dock to transport everyone to Fortuna for a great all-day family picnic, with something for everyone.

After Capt. Anderson's death, his widow put the property on the market. It was purchased by a hop grower from eastern Washington who planned a Bavarian-type village with small cottages to rent. But when he died, the planning ceased and the land was again on the market. The dance hall was leased and its operation continued.

The next owner was Charles Clise, a Seattle businessman. During the 1950s growth, he built eight buildings on the lakeshore, with a total of 116 apartments. The area was lower Shorewood.

Upper Shorewood was built next, with a total of 38 buildings and 568 apartments. Clise owned and operated Shorewood Apartments for 25 years. After his death, the complex was purchased by one developer who went bankrupt, then by a mortgage company and finally by the Covenant Retirement Communities.

They changed lower Shorewood into a retirement community and remodeled and updated the buildings. The old dance hall was transformed into Fortuna Lodge, a dining hall and community center for the residents of Covenant Shores Retirement Community. Later the Covenant Shores Health Center was built.

The greatest changes

The north end of the Island was never one entity like East Seattle. Waterfront residents formed one grouping, inland farmers another and business owners yet another.

When the boulevard, North Mercer Way, was built in 1914–16, it became a boundary line further underscored by the Sunset Highway, constructed in 1939.

North of that line, the development is residential, as from the earliest days. To the south, the pastoral scenes of 1900 to 1945 disappeared, transformed from gardens, farms, orchards, dairies and pastures to apartment buildings, gas stations, fast-food and other eating places, offices, post office, banks and a bustle of activity.

The heart of the Island's commerce and services, the north-end area and the Town Center have experienced more changes than any other part of the Island.

Shantell Wallace and Andrea Holland ride horses in Pioneer Park in 1990. The 120-acre urban forest on the south end is a reminder of early Mercer Island.

Mercer Island Reporter

The South End

Isolated, woodsy and slower to develop

In the early days, "the south end" meant any area south of Southeast 40th Street, and even today it is still a vague geographic area. Like other parts of the Island, its development progressed from waterfront camps to farms and homes. Dense woods became logged-off platted areas, from sparse to dense habitations, with parks, church, shopping center, community club, recreation clubs and schools. The difference was that the south end remained rural much longer than the rest of the Island.

The south end is relatively flat at the top, forming a wide plateau, then drops very steeply down to the lake. Many large firs and cedars remain, although logging took most of the virgin growth. Even though few vacant lots remain, the area retains the woodsy, blackberry-vine-bedecked appearance admired by nature lovers, conservationists, raccoons and residents. The three Pioneer Park quadrants are a reminder of early Mercer Island.

The first survey, in 1861, divided the Island into sections and quarter sections, with many acres allotted to the Northern Pacific Railroad. From the southernmost tip along the east shore up to present-day Southeast 50th Street, the land was all designated NPRR on old maps. When land fever struck because of the rush for timber, some quarter sections were sold. South-end names on a circa-1900 map were Sanders, Loomis, Thompson, Hyde, Ritz, Tarbell and Cushman.

The story goes that when a Seattle real estate agent took Frank Flood on a round-the-Island steamer excursion, the agent pointed out property just north of the present Clarke Beach Park as he pulled out an earnest money agreement. "There it is, Mr. Flood. Do you want to buy all that fine timber or not?" "I'll buy it," said Flood. After it was logged off, the land was platted as Flood's Lakeside Tracts.

Mercer Island Historical Society

This 1937 photo along 90th Avenue Southeast shows a previously logged area that was burned for clearing.

Chapter 9: The South End | 83

1921 The mail horse is replaced by an automobile—but the road conditions are so bad that the mailman often has to borrow a horse to make deliveries.

1921 A floating grocery store, the "Grubstake" begins calling at the various docks on the Island to sell food and provisions.

1921 On October 1, engineer Homer Hadley formally proposes a floating concrete pontoon bridge across Lake Washington at a meeting of the American Society of Civil Engineers.

1921 North-end neighbors build the Keewaydin Club.

1923 The wooden East Channel Bridge opens, connecting Mercer Island and the east shore of Lake Washington at Enatai.

1923 Electricity comes to the south end of the Island.

1923 The Mercer Island telephone directory lists 200 names.

1924 The town name "East Seattle" is changed to "Mercer Island" on April 14.

1928 The Mercer Island Orthopedic Guild organizes, with a membership of 15.

1928 The Mercer Island Golf Club has 34 members, owns its south-end property free and clear, and has $452 in the bank.

1929 The Christian Science Society is founded; services are held in the Keewaydin Club.

1929 Lake Cottage, a brick dormitory, is built at the Parental School for Boys.

1930 Mercer Island population is 1,069.

1930 The road from Roanoke Dock to the East Channel Bridge is paved.

1930s Island streets are given numbers instead of names.

1931 A phone directory published by Mercer Island Lumber Company lists 248.

In the 1920s, south-end residents sold shares to the Mercer Island Golf and Country Club. By 1928, the club had 34 members, owned the 120-acre site and had $452 in the bank.

Across the Island on the southwest side, a promoter named C.D. Hillman platted his Sea Shore Lakefront Garden of Eden addition to Seattle with 25-foot-wide lots along the waterfront, backed by 100-foot-wide upland lots.

One house was built on the shore, but the area was remote and land sales were slow. A sign, "Grocery Store," in huge letters, appeared on the house. From afloat in a launch, the real estate agent would assure prospective clients wondering about conveniences, that "right there" was the grocery. But never, to anyone's recollection, was there a grocery store inside. New owners, the Huffmans, who moved from East Mercer, painted over the sign, but it kept showing through successive coats of paint.

Getting provisions

Actually, those earliest southwest Islanders had easy access to shopping because a grocery boat, a meat boat and a beer boat, all from Rainier Beach's shopping center across the lake, made regular stops at the remote docks.

Many of the waterfront homes were at the foot of steep embankments that made access difficult from the land side. Residents of the southeast side of the Island shopped at Hazelwood or Kennydale across the East Channel.

One old-timer told how her husband swam over to the store, and swam back with a loaf of bread tied to the top of his head. Later, when the boulevard around the Island was passable for cars, the Standard Supply Store in East Seattle delivered groceries to the south end at least once a week.

The area was remote indeed in 1907, when Robert and Martha Rydeen purchased several acres of land north of Flood's Lakeside Tracts to build a home and raise a family. When the children were ready for school, there was no way to transport them to East Seattle School. When Robert Rydeen requested transportation, the school board suggested going by boat across the East Channel to Kennydale.

Throughout first and second grade, his daughter Thelma and her cousin Hank took a launch to the Kennydale dock and walked up the hill to the schoolhouse. When a few more children were ready for school, Rydeen petitioned for formation of a school district.

Lakeview School

The first schoolhouse of King County School District 191 was a little shack on the southwest side, and the first teacher was Miss Lucy Furness. Thelma Rydeen Glazounow remembered that the teacher wore a Gibson-girlish white blouse and a swishy black floor-length skirt. The great sport was to dip a pen in the inkwell,

84 | Chapter 9: The South End

Trudy Webster Hanson

A 1953 bird's-eye view of the south end of the Island. The cluster of docks at the very tip are in the Benotho neighborhood; the isolated dock at the end of the road at the right belonged to the Lions Club, which operated a camp at what is now Mercer Island Beach Club.

Thelma Rydeen Glazoumnow

The Rydeen family had a few cows and sold milk to their neighbors for 5 cents a quart. This 1915 photo shows cousins Hank and Thelma Rydeen delivering milk via rowboat.

and when that black skirt swished past, stab the pen toward it and propel a drop of black ink onto the black skirt.

In 1918, the local school district voted to build a schoolhouse by issuing local improvement bonds. Lakeview School's original building still stands today, known as Sunnybeam School. All grades were taught there.

Many south-enders kept chickens and a cow or two. Robert Rydeen had a few cows, and sold milk to the neighbors for 5 cents a quart.

In 1915, little cousins Thelma and Hank Rydeen delivered milk. Starting out neat and clean, with milk loaded in the rowboat, they rowed along the shore to neighbors' docks to unload their cargo. And then the oar dueling and water splashing began. After thwacking oars, they would return wet, muddy and bedraggled.

Utilities were not available at the south end for years after the northern sections of the Island had become quite civilized. The first telephone service began in 1920; electricity came in 1923. Because the roads were so bad for so long, there was little contact between the north and south ends except by water.

Chapter 9: The South End | 85

Unchanged hideaway: the North Star Lodge

It would be difficult to find a privately owned, seven-acre chunk of Mercer Island more unchanged from the old days than the North Star Lodge property. In the 6000 block of East Mercer Way, past the padlocked gate and the vintage "North Star" sign, you enter a place where time has stood still.

A narrow drive snakes down the wooded slope past 13 cabins built between 1926 and 1954, each one unique, some brightly colored with window boxes festooned with flowers, others with mossy roofs and fading paint. As the slope levels out to the 166 feet of waterfront, you see the white "pavilion," built in 1936.

The father of Roy Nelson, who remembers many summer vacations there, bought the property in 1913. Nelson was a happy, barefoot boy until September came and it was time to leave the fish and crayfish, climbing trees and swimming beach, put on shoes again and return to school.

One of Nelson's friends was a Mr. Landquist, president of the International Order of Good Templars in Seattle, a local temperance organization with deep roots in its Swedish heritage. In 1926, Nelson sold the property to the Templars for $5,000.

That year, North Star Lodge No. 2 began developing a *sommarhem* or summer home on Mercer Island. Members built summer cabins, and a pavilion for group activities, designed by Alex Haag and completed in 1938. The pavilion was used as a dance hall, theater, mess hall and activity center.

The park continues under the ownership of the nonprofit North Star Council for Alcohol and Drug Education. It provides a family-centered alcohol- and drug-free environment for its some 100 members. North Star runs summer camps and provides scholarships for youths dedicated to an alcohol- and drug-free life.

The late May Freeman told about summers at North Star: the days of wearing woolen swimsuits, taking the ferry from Seattle to Mercer Island, rowing down the lake to pick blackberries, taking marathon swims across the lake and looking for deer while driving the curves on East Mercer Way. One of her earliest memories occurred in 1930 at age 5: having a bonfire at night and looking across the lake to see only one or two other bonfires in an otherwise totally dark scene.

For more than 85 years, members have enjoyed vacations and daytime outings, meetings and picnics at North Star. Surrounded by fir trees, with no houses in sight, North Star looks just as it did in 1938.

The North Star Lodge was built on the Island's southeast waterfront in the late 1920s. Installing the sign are Alvin (left to right), Bert and Arnie Hagg.
At left, the pavilion in 1938.

North Star

Jane Meyer Brahm

The interior of the pavilion today (above) and one of the 13 cabins that dot the property.

Getting water

Before the bridge, south-end homes were almost all located along the shore, clustered around available water supplies. One of the large springs was on Flood's Lakeside Tracts. Wooden pipes carried water down to the waterfront and, during the upland development, to homes along the southeast slope.

John Wilhite succeeded Frank Flood as owner of the water system. South-enders of the '40s and '50s remember him striding through the forest like a latter-day Paul Bunyan, carrying over his shoulder not an axe, but a large Stilson wrench to shut off valves to remedy pipe problems.

The Wilhite water system supplied many south-enders until city water became available in the 1960s. The old pipes were so close to the surface that they froze occasionally.

One south-ender couldn't take her new baby home from the hospital because there was no water. Her husband went into the nearby forest and cautiously built fires to thaw the pipeline to get the necessary water so that his family could be reunited.

Remnants of that water system can still be seen off East Mercer Way just east of Pioneer Park, in an enclave of houses that were built in the early 1900s.

Five families of Scandinavian descent—the Olsons, the Johnsons, the Auras, the Gregorys and the Engstroms—came to the Pacific Northwest because the lake, trees and light reminded them of their homeland. The families knew each other in Seattle, and became neighbors on Mercer Island when they bought property and built summer cabins.

As the original families expanded, they built homes up the hillside. Young couples would live in the old cottage and later remodel it or build a new house elsewhere on the family property. Descendants of the families remain on the Island, connected by their long histories.

Connie Strope Schaeffer

The Johnson family bought about 20 acres of land at the south end in 1904, and built a cabin (above) in 1910. Painted a bright blue today, it is one of the few remaining original cabins on the Island.

Mercer Island Reporter

This 1980 photo shows one of the Groveland cottages. Located at Southeast 58th Street and 80th Avenue Southeast, the house was torn down in 1985.

Swimmers on the Johnson family dock, on the southeast shore of the Island, in the 1920s.

Connie Strope Schaeffer

1931 The name of the Parental School for Boys is changed to Luther Burbank School for Boys.

1933 The Girl Scout Council establishes Camp Tarywood on the south end of the Island.

1936 The Mercer Island Garden Club is organized, with 28 members.

1937 Mercer Island Preschool Association is founded.

1937 The first all-Island zoning ordinance meeting is held.

1938 The ferry *Dawn* is retired from duty.

1938 Mercer Island's first enclosed gymnasium is built at East Seattle School.

1938 Construction begins on Dec. 29 on the first floating bridge across Lake Washington.

1939 The "new," improved East Channel Bridge is built.

1939 Sunset Highway is built.

1940 The Lacey V. Murrow Floating Bridge, the largest floating bridge in the world, opens July 2. Gov. Clarence Martin pays the first toll.

The family of Knute Auguston bought acreage and built a house on the upland side of East Mercer Way, at about 69th Street. Directions to their home in 1950 were: "Turn from Sunset Highway (today's I-90) onto East Mercer and head south. We're the first house on the right." That actually meant almost four miles without a house on the right-hand side.

The 1920s were years of increasing summer campers and the construction of more beach cottages at the south end. Many Seattle residents had summer places on Mercer Island, a refuge from the city.

It was also during the 1920s that south-enders started an improvement club, the South End Club, which continued for more than 30 years.

Tarywood

Tarywood Camp was envisioned by a group of women who donated money to build an overnight camp. The women, whose group was an offshoot of the Rotary Club, took the last four letters of the word "Rotary" to create the name. They later sold it to the Totem Girl Scout Council, which established Camp Tarywood in 1933.

The main lodge and several tent platforms were built that year, and later open-air cabins. To the campers, it must have seemed like a true wilderness, with no electricity, telephone or conveniences.

In 1941, Tarywood became a day camp for the Brownies, the first such camp in the United States. The camp was sold in 1969 to the Mercer Island School District, and the shore area was purchased by the city to become part of Mabel Clarke Beach Park. The name remains on the upland tract, now a woodsy residential area, Tarywood Estates.

The Lions Camp

In the summer of 1930, the Central Seattle Chapter of the Lions Club bought eight acres of waterfront with 675 feet of shoreline on land granted earlier to the Northern Pacific Railroad.

The Lions built a camp for underprivileged city children that included a playground, dock, two dormitory buildings, kitchen shack and caretaker's cottage. The children were assembled at Leschi and ferried over to the camp by the Coast Guard Auxiliary.

The camp era ended with the coming of the Mercer Island floating bridge, then World War II. During and after the war, convalescing soldiers from Fort Lewis used the property.

At Lakeview School, built in 1918, students in grades one through eight were taught in the school's one classroom until 1941, when enrollment dropped and roads were improved enough to bus students to East Seattle School. Sunnybeam School, shown here in 1984, has operated in the historic building since 1957.

Mercer Island Historical Society

The Lions established a camp elsewhere, and the property was vacant. It went on the market with an asking price of $45,000, or $72 per front foot.

In 1952, members of the South End Club proposed formation of an all-Island-membership beach club to buy the property.

Led by Harold Oliver, who later became the Island's first mayor, they launched a membership drive, using a card table set up outside Art's Food Center. Memberships were sold to anyone who lived, worked or owned property on the Island.

The Mercer Island Beach Club was limited to 500 families; the initiation fee was $100; dues were $10 per year. Enough checks were received at the meeting for earnest money and a down payment.

On July 17, 1953, incorporation papers for the Mercer Island Beach Club were signed. It built a clubhouse, swimming pool, tennis courts, dock moorage and completed numerous other improvements. The remodeled caretaker's cottage is the only vestige of the Lions Camp of long ago.

Groveland

Another camp was established in the 1920s at Groveland, in what is now the 5700-5800 block of West Mercer Way. A Bible camp, it was originally a summertime gathering place for religious groups, mostly from off the Island. Most of the waterfront cabins on small lots have been torn down and replaced or remodeled to accommodate modern living.

The church camp property was purchased by the city in 1965 for a beach park. The Groveland neighborhood is home to Mercer Island's only one-way streets.

Childhood memories

After the war, the south end grew slowly. One person who moved there in 1945 recalls, "From the present Parkwood Estates all the way down 88th Avenue Southeast [now Island Crest Way], a dark forest loomed on either side of the narrow dirt road, with evergreen trees almost closing in overhead. South of Southeast 68th Street there were just two homes, Wilhites' and Harrises', and the Lakeview School. All else was forest down to the slopes just above the water. Houses were clustered around water systems."

The Anderson family built their home on the western waterfront just before World War II. Betsy Anderson wrote:

"Not long ago one of my sons said, 'Mercer Island was a wonderful place to grow up.' And indeed it was. There were acres and acres for children to explore. Across West Mercer Way from our eight acres (part of the old Denny estate), there was a lovely forest with huge fern-clad trees, and a stream that ran down through a ravine to the lake. The ravine is now lined with expensive homes, but then it had a wonderful bank of sand that made a slide to the bottom.

"I was invited to go along and try it one day. It was great fun, as was the swinging vine, an old flowering huckleberry vine hanging from an enormous tree. It made a small boy feel like Tarzan, and his mother, too! In the '40s and early '50s there were no water-skiers or power boats, only a few outboards and rowboats, so the lake and life in general were quiet and safe."

It wasn't until the early 1960s that the south-end business village developed. The south end today is no longer isolated, but does remain the more wooded part of the Island.

The Island according to Al Fleury

Alfred Fleury bought his south-end waterfront lot for $1,000 during the Depression, and rowed there from Rainier Beach to clear the land. He built an access road in 1933, and later a house and a floating dock. He raised goats, sold logs and became immersed in community volunteerism and Island politics.

When he died in 1993 at age 103, former *Mercer Island Reporter* publisher Peggy Reynolds wrote:

"For 44 years on Mercer Island, he got things done. With the fire district, which he served as secretary-treasurer. City incorporation, for which he worked tirelessly. The first city council, to which he was elected in 1960. The library, where he wasn't too proud to climb the roof and clear a gutter. His imprint can be found on virtually every Island civic betterment: roads, utilities, play fields, schools."

Fleury wrote a memoir that is intertwined with Mercer Island history. Here are some of his observations.

On city/county relations:

"Mercer Island was governed by the personal rule of three County Commissioners until 1960, when its citizens voted to manage their own affairs. Before this it had been necessary to appear before these overlords at a hearing in the County-City building in Seattle to plead for some road improvement, zoning change, public park or whatever was deemed desirable for the development of the Island."

On Lakeview School/Sunnybeam:

"It is interesting to note how the Club [The South End Improvement Club] became the owner of the old district 91 schoolhouse without knowing it for years. An old-timer had owned some 10 acres of cheap cutover land for many years. They were located far out in the inaccessible woods, hard to locate; he was unable to sell them.

"Tired of paying taxes on useless property he stated at a club meeting that, if the club would pay him $50 he would deed that property to the county as a public park. His generous offer was accepted, the money raised and transfer of title accomplished. My contribution was one dollar. Now we had a park far out in the boondocks, we thought.

"Time passed, the floating bridge was built, the Island's schools consolidated, our old one-room schoolhouse, now surplus, was only used for club meetings. The office of County treasurer had been held by a good politician whose antics kept him in office for a long time, even though his financial administration was poor.

"Only when the commodity called spondulics (cash) became scarce, the other politicians who depended on the regular supply of that kind of goods, were able to convince the voters that he should be replaced. It took the new County treasurer quite some time to get the real estate records in order.

"The club was surprised one day to receive from the County treasurer a nasty letter informing it that unless taxes were immediately paid, he would sell its property at public auction. Not knowing what this letter was all about, inquiry was made. It revealed the fact that at the time 10 acres were deeded as a County park, there had been no such park department to take possession of the property. The deed was an orphan without a home to go to. Therefore, to give it a foster home, some unknown official in the Treasurer's office registered the deed on the tax rolls as the property of the South End Improvement Club, and as the book had no such regulation, did not notify its lucky owners of this fact."

On the south end:

"The south end had a different identity. A lot of second-growth woods covered the top of the Island. The waterfront had scattered summer homes. Captain Anderson ran a boat from Kennydale to Rainier Beach, where we could take a street car to Renton or Seattle. The Island stop of his boat was at Benotho beach, a summer colony of Renton people. Next to it Avalon Park was subdivided. Its only inhabitant was a lawyer named Peterson, part owner, trying to sell lots. Farther north a lumberman named Ford had subdivided some of his holdings and established quite a settlement. On the west side Lakeview Highlands with beautiful waterfront homes was a restricted settlement where more affluent people kept to themselves.

"The south end was served by one 10-party line phone only."

The Depression, World War II

How the Island responded

The pioneering, rustic quality of life of the 1920s on Mercer Island gave way to the outside world's economic woes.

The nationwide Depression spread to Puget Sound, affecting many workers and their families. Still, life on Mercer Island was pleasantly rural, and people could live frugally. Within each neighborhood, friend would help friend-in-need when the economic crunch caused real hardship.

Farms flourished; the population increased little. People with gardens were generous and sharing. J.B. Brown would load his truck with vegetables from his farm (near the present Bank of America) and drive around the Island delivering produce to anyone who wanted it, whether they could pay or not. Swan Person's dairy made daily milk deliveries on the same basis.

In 1930, most of the 1,069 year-round residents lived on the north end. The Lakeview Precinct on the south end had only 89 residents.

By 1940, the Island's population was just over 1,200, so the increase during the decade was small.

But the population was on the move. Jobless young couples moved in with parents; some moved to the Island, and others moved away to find work. Some people became year-round residents in their cabins, camps and cottages when they were forced to sell or rent their Seattle homes. An unknown, uncounted number of squatters lived in shacks in the woods.

Land sales were virtually at

a standstill. King County auctions did a land-office business dealing in land whose owners had defaulted on their payments. Many Island tracts were sold for the taxes due. The upland areas of central and south Mercer Island, considered to be of little value because of the lack of water, were sold to investors for delinquent taxes.

Island businesses continued to include the store in East Seattle, the Roanoke Inn, Hap's Service Station on 76th, lumber and fuel yards, and a few other service businesses.

A new Island business of long standing was added in 1933 with the building of Rochester's Garage near the East Channel Bridge, at the top of the current I-90—East Mercer Way off-ramp. The service department, gas station and Chrysler-Plymouth dealership served the Island and traffic between the Roanoke Ferry Dock and the East Channel Bridge.

Prohibition was still in effect in the early 1930s, and the shenanigans of illegal trafficking in spirits livened up the Island—or sometimes just the opposite.

Postman Fred Nielson told of the time there were three Island bootleggers; one mailed a gun to a second one so he could kill off the third. He did just that, and Nielson was called to testify at the trial. Deep woods could be a hiding place for a still, as Al Fleury discovered when he stumbled across an abandoned one years later.

The Roanoke Inn was rumored to be serving spirits of a suspicious nature in coffee mugs. The stories were many, but with the repeal of Prohibition in 1933, the tales faded.

1940 Mercer Island's population is 1,200. The school population is 139 students in grades K-8.

1940 Mercer Island Free and Accepted Masons of Washington is established.

1940 Ten men form the Mercer Island Crafts Guild April 4.

1940 A total of 365 telephones serve the Island.

1941 Lakeview School closes. School opens again in 1945-46 for kindergarten classes.

1941 Mercer Island School District No. 400 is established.

1943 Mercer Island Orthopedic Guild produces its first Mercer Island Directory.

1944 The Mercer Island Fire District is established.

1944 Enrollment at Luther Burbank School for Boys peaks at 137 students.

1946 Mercer Island Volunteer Fire Department is organized.

1946 The Mercer Island Chamber of Commerce incorporates Dec. 11.

1946 Bellevue Square opens Aug. 20.

1946 Mercer Island has one dry cleaner, Mercer Island Dry Cleaners.

1947 Recreation Council forms to provide swimming lessons for kids.

1948 Holy Trinity Lutheran Church is organized.

1948 The post office moves to the Boyd Building on Southeast 27th Street.

1949 Lacey V. Murrow floating bridge becomes toll-free July 2.

Relief programs

When relief programs were available, they were handled at first by King County and the community clubs. In fact, the community clubs became more important than ever to Island life. As one old-timer put it: "There was nothing else to do—couldn't afford to go to the big city. So we went to the club."

The community club set up an unemployment committee to plan fund-raising projects. By December 1931, they had raised $20. State employees in Olympia took up a collection and distributed it statewide. That added $10 to the Island relief fund. By March 1932, $40 was on hand.

There was heated discussion about the use of the funds, with final agreement that recipients of the club's largesse should work on public projects, at the committee's discretion. Five school children needed hot lunches, so a collection was taken up.

By October 1932, King County Welfare was functioning, and it allotted $250 to Mercer Island. For the first time ever, Mercer Island was receiving outside funds, but the club continued to manage them. A welfare committee was set up and all other committees were discontinued, as state relief work began operating.

The WPA

As the Depression deepened, the federal Works Progress Administration (WPA) was established locally.

Al Fleury, who came to Mercer Island in 1933, remembered his days with the WPA. "Pay was $55 per month for a six-hour day, five days a week, with no fringe benefits except Social Security. I was assigned to build the Gallagher Hill road on the north end. I rode a borrowed bicycle to get there. Clearing brush there was a job I now could tell others how to do."

The highest number of families on the WPA program at any

Mercer Island Historical Society
A phone directory published by the Mercer Island Lumber Company in 1931 has 248 listings.

one time was 77. One record for March 8, 1933, reported 64 families on the WPA program at a cost of $900 a month. Fourteen families were rejected after investigation.

With winter's approach, the welfare committee was concerned about having funds and supplies available. Four hundred letters were sent out soliciting cash in amounts from 25 cents to $5 and supplies that included clothing, fruit, jellies, toys and standing timber for wood. Receipts were: pledges, $174.90; cash, $154.65; gifts of food and clothing, $37.61; for a total of $367.21.

Another activity of the WPA was the numbering of Mercer Island streets. All had names, usually designated on the plat by the original owner.

But names could cause confusion, and all north-south streets in Seattle were numbered. The plan was to extend that numbering and

This plaque installed by the Mercer Island Historical Society in the summer of 2009 marks the site of a U.S. Army anti-aircraft site at the southern tip of the Island.

Mercer Island Historical Society

make it continuous to the Eastside, and north and south of the lake also. The reasoning was that it was easier to locate addresses that way.

Joshua Vogel of the University of Washington, chairman of the Planning Department, explained to the members of the community club the Eastside Master Plan for street numbering. Because the members liked the street names, and because they protested mightily, the name of Gallagher Hill Road was kept; it was named after the foreman on the road-building job.

News improves

At the end of the 1930s news in general began to get better. The East Channel Bridge was being replanked. Lakeview School at the south end at last had a school bus to transport its 20 students. The county commissioners promised $75,000 to be spent on Island roads. In March 1938, 350 WPA workers arrived to clear roadsides and improve highways. The first street signs were installed. Additional road funds—$15,000—were allocated by the WPA. In May 1938 a committee from the clubs was authorized to open negotiations with the University of Washington for acquiring acreage above Groveland for a public park.

The community clubs had a flurry of heated debate over whether the Island should be annexed to Seattle. Finally, both clubs voted nay.

The best news was the bridge news. By 1936, the talk had changed from if to when there would be a bridge to Seattle. George Lightfoot reported that surveys of the lake were complete, and that surveyors were at work near Faben Point.

A test barge was anchored off Thompson Avenue (Southeast 24th Street) seeking moorings and anchorages for a floating bridge. At the end of the 1930s, Islanders realized that they had more togetherness than before, and that the inevitable bridge to Seattle would change Island life forever.

World War II

In 1940 and 1941, many of the permanent residents were summer people who had remodeled their cabins and cottages into year-round homes.

But the shadow of war brought curtailment of building supplies, so the expected home building boom did not occur. Then, 18 months after the Mercer Island floating bridge opened, Pearl Harbor was bombed and World War II was a reality.

Islanders turned away from their concerns about post-bridge development and plunged full force into civil defense. During the four war years, the Island's population increased by fewer than 1,000 new residents.

Pearl Harbor and the declaration of war shocked the world, and the frightening possibility of invasion by Japan shook the entire Puget Sound region.

Blackouts were immediately in effect on Mercer Island because of its proximity to Boeing, a potential target area. Blackout curtains were installed in many Island homes and businesses. The north-facing windows of the Keewaydin Club were boarded up with plywood—which wasn't removed until the 1990s!

Military officials set up guns and troops at strategic points to keep watch near large cities and defense contractors. The U.S. Army set up an antiaircraft unit on Mercer Island in the fall of 1942, at the Wasson farm on the south end. The land, at the very southern end of 79th Avenue Southeast, is at a high point on the Island overlooking Lake Washington. It was equipped with searchlights, listening devices and antiaircraft guns.

The location was considered a military secret, but the camp was in plain view and any Islander knew where it was. A historic marker, installed by the Mercer Island Historical Society on Oct. 15, 2009, commemorates the site.

Searchlights also were placed at the north end of the Island, with some 50 men to watch Lake Washington. The unit, Battery C, 260th Coast Artillery, included 200 men, four large 90 mm M1 guns, four machine guns, a radar installation and barracks for the soldiers. The installation at the north end was on the hill west of Luther Burbank Park, in the vicinity of 82nd Avenue Southeast and Southeast 20th Streets.

Civil defense efforts

Civil defense was organized statewide, divided into districts, areas and zones. Mercer Island

Chapter 10: The Depression, World War II | 93

was Zone 3 of Area 9, District 1. The local civil defense zone has its first practice in February 1942, with an emergency hospital set up at East Seattle School. Like the entire Puget Sound area, Mercer Island was on alert and aware of danger in the Pacific.

Many yacht-owning Islanders joined the Navy auxiliary fleet. Yachts were painted dark blue, and owners did patrol duty as wartime volunteers.

Red Cross first aid classes were held at the East Seattle School gym. Red Cross sewing groups turned out quantities of surgical dressings, as well as diapers, baby layettes, men's shirts, dresses and sweaters.

The call went out to "Get Your Scrap Metal into the Scrap." Island residents brought iron, bronze, steel, copper and aluminum to be resmelted for war use, to depots at East Seattle School or Rochester's Garage, which was civil defense headquarters.

The Victory Book Campaign collected magazines and books for Army camps and recreation centers, and a war bond department was set up in John Dunney's real estate office.

The women formed an auxiliary defense unit, a counterpart of the men's organization, with police, firefighters and ambulance drivers to be activated for emergencies only.

Many Islanders went off to war and returned to become active in the local posts of the American Legion and the Veterans of Foreign Wars.

During the remainder of the war years, community concerns joined national issues in the minds of the residents. For example, Jack Cassidy's editorial in the *Mercer Island News* echoed the thoughts of many Islanders:

"Every year at least one building on Mercer Island burns, and when a building catches on fire it burns to the ground. It's always the same procedure: save yourself and whatever else you can, and let the building burn. The latest fire destroyed the Lucas barn. There is no doubt about the need for fire protection. The civilian defense organization is a group whose duties are to fight fire in case of aerial attack, which may never come. But whether it occurs or not, why waste the organization? Why can't this group serve as a nucleus for a volunteer fire brigade to serve the Island after the war emergency is past? Mercer Island has public-spirited citizens and community groups who could initiate a unified plan on a long-range basis to work out our own fire protection." Before the war was over, that idea became a reality.

Another local problem concerned deer nibbling at victory garden vegetables. Deer had always roamed the Island, and were part of the natural beauty and woodsy atmosphere. When natural feeding for the deer decreased, war gardens became their food supply.

A petition was circulated to have the deer removed. The Garden Club opposed it. The newspaper suggested fencing, either of the gardens or of the deer. A resident declared that a glimpse of deer bounding across a road was one of the most pleasing surprises on the Island. He maintained he would rather see the deer than the gardens. The North End Community Club was asked to take action. Amos Wood volunteered to survey the entire Island by mail. The resulting replies favored the deer, so they remained.

The serious wartime stresses such as the rationing of food, liquor, shoes and gasoline; the trauma of crossing the new bridge in a blackout; the shortages of food that made victory gardens a must; the curtailment of activities like driving a car, building or remodeling—none of these could stop Islanders from engaging in a good hassle, even over the deer.

The war ended in the summer of 1945, and Islanders relaxed a bit, then braced for the period of the post-bridge, post-war changes to come.

1949 Shorewood Apartments opens with a total of 116 apartments ranging in rent from $77.50 to $125 per month.

1949 Mercer Island has its first permanent postmaster, Hal Riecks.

1950 Mercer Island's population is 4,500. Bellevue's population is 8,000.

1950 Mercer Island Cooperative Water Association has 825 members.

1950 The *Mercer Islander* advertises a case of 24 cans of beer for $2.99 at Art's Food Center.

1950 Mercer Crest Elementary School opens.

1950 Chick Tabit opens Chick's Shoes and Service.

1951 The population of the Island nears 8,000.

1952 The library board holds a "Literary Tea" May 22 to raise money to build a library.

94 | Chapter 10: The Depression, World War II

Washington State Department of Transportation

This photo, from October 1940, shows the Mercer Island floating bridge looking east, with the Cascade range in the background.

At Last, a Bridge to Seattle

The world's first concrete floating bridge is also the largest floating structure

The largest floating structure built by man was the Island's concrete lifeline to Seattle. Spectacular and widely acclaimed when it was completed, the bridge had a long and controversial history. Islanders had their own longtime dream of a bridge of some sort. But the actuality involved hundreds of off-Islanders, in Seattle, in Olympia and in Washington, D.C.

As with other developments, Islanders were actively involved in making their dream come true. In community club meetings, ferry forums and party-line telephone conversations, they discussed the bridge and everything about it. Bridge talk went on for a long time on the Island, but it wasn't until 1928 that the talk became official.

The Seattle City Council proposed a toll bridge be privately built and operated. The shortest, most protected route proposed was from Seward Park to the center of the Island, with a connecting road to the new East-

George Lightfoot

Channel Bridge.

For 10 years that route was under discussion. Protests against giving up any of Seward Park came from many quarters, even though environmental impact statements were unknown then.

Many Islanders were involved in bridge talks, but one of the most dedicated was George W. Lightfoot, often called "father of the bridge."

Lightfoot joined the fight in the early 1920s and stayed with it for nearly 20 years. A plaque at Roanoke Park honors him for his "untiring efforts resulting in the realization of the Lake Washington Floating Bridge."

In his *Personal History of the Bridge*, he recounted the numerous legal battles fought to make way for it. At first, the project was to be a private enterprise, but the crash of 1929 changed that. The type of bridge and proposed location changed a dozen times, but the earliest of all bridge plans called for a pontoon bridge to be built from old hulls of discarded boats left from World War I and

Museum of History and Industry photos

University of Washington

The Mercer Island floating bridge was an engineering marvel that attracted local, national and international attention. Construction was completed in just 18 months.

stored in Lake Union, he wrote. "This idea failed, but the final solution was a 'Pontoon Bridge.' However, instead of old hulls the accomplished fact is a 'Floating Concrete Bridge!'

"The project was then taken to Washington state and filed as docket No. 1 on the first Public Works Assistance program. It took five years to put it through, and early in 1937 announcement was made of a grant of $3,450,000 to King County to construct a bridge across Lake Washington.

"In spite of the effort of our commissioners, the County could not secure the necessary matching money and our bridge was on the verge of losing again," wrote Lightfoot.

Lightfoot made a hurried trip to Olympia and called on Gov. Clarence Martin to request the aid of the State Highway Department.

Lacey V. Murrow, director of state highways, agreed to investigate the matter further, and having been convinced that Homer Hadley's design for a floating concrete bridge was feasible, agreed to move the project forward to meet the Dec. 31, 1938, deadline for the federal grant.

Engineering marvel, huge challenges

Finally, the largest single road project in the state's history was under way, with the federal Public Works Administration financing 40 percent of the $8,854,000 cost.

The skeptics had asked, "Why a floating bridge?" A conventional bridge was impossible, or astronomically expensive, because of the depth of the lake, more than 200 feet at the deepest; the length of the crossing, more than one and a quarter miles; and the problems of the muddy lake bottom.

As for floating concrete, shipyards had built barges and ships of concrete cellular construction during World War I—and they floated just fine.

Museum of History and Industry

A crowd waits to cross the bridge on opening day, July 2, 1940. That first day, 11,611 vehicles crossed.

Research at Sand Point Naval Air Station in Seattle checked stresses by assuming a wave crest 6 feet in height and 6 feet from crest to crest. The bridge was engineered to be safe in a 90-mile-an-hour wind, even with 20-ton trucks bumper to bumper from shore to shore.

Still, no bridge like it had been built, so interest ran high.

The project involved a 6.5-mile-long highway, with a double tunnel through a high ridge to the west, bridge approaches, the floating bridge, a highway across Mercer Island and a bridge across the lake's East Channel to connect with the highway to the east.

More than 3,000 workers were employed for 18 months, including 1,200 on the job site.

The 25 floating concrete sections were constructed on Harbor Island in Seattle and towed through the locks and the ship canal to the bridge site.

The drawspan section was so large that it was brought through the locks in pieces. Each regular pontoon was 350 feet long by 59 feet wide, with 8-inch-thick reinforced concrete walls on the bottom, sides and top. Each had 96 watertight compartments 14 feet square, with walls 6 inches thick.

Pontoons were bolted together all the way across and at each shore were fastened to fixed approaches. Each pontoon was held in place by 65-ton anchors on either side, with cables 2.75 inches thick, coated with zinc, oil and waterproof paint.

The total length of the anchor cables was more than five miles. The pontoons were 14 feet high, and floated with 7 feet below the water.

Museum of History and Industry

This 1940 opening-day photo is of the Lake Washington Bridge Consulting Board, including Gov. Clarence D. Martin (fourth from left) and the bridge engineers.

Chapter 11: At Last, a Bridge to Seattle | 97

CONSTRUCTION OF FIRST LAKE WASHINGTON FLOATING BRIDGE

Early postcards of the Mercer Island floating bridge.

Mercer Island Historical Society

ONLY CONCRETE PONTOON BRIDGE IN THE WORLD.

When the lake level varied about 2 feet seasonally, the cells in the pontoons next to the fixed approaches were flooded or pumped out to control the flotation level. Anchor cable connections also had hydraulic adjustment mechanisms.

Near the Mercer Island side was a movable draw span, the largest of the floating sections. The moving part slid on tracks in and out of a 220-foot well—"the bulge"—with a forked roadway on either side, allowing ships to pass through the opening. Such a mechanism was reported to be the first of its kind in the world.

The grand opening

The daylong grand-opening celebration on July 2, 1940, began at 6 a.m. with a water carnival on the lake. Hundreds of boats made a colorful background for outboard and sailboat races, surfboarding, swimming and diving competitions, and a yacht parade.

All community clubs east of the lake were involved, with each one sending a queen and princesses.

At 11:15 a.m. on nationwide radio, Gov. Clarence D. Martin and other dignitaries held dedication ceremonies at the western end of the bridge. Then the governor's party drove to the Mercer Island toll plaza, where

98 | Chapter 11: At Last, a Bridge to Seattle

Museum of History and Industry

The Mercer Island floating bridge in 1940, above. Homer Hadley, above right. At lower right, then-Mayor Elliot Newman and Dr. Eleanor Hadley, daughter of Homer Hadley, listen to speakers at the dedication of the new I-90 bridge in 1993. The new bridge is dedicated to Hadley, the engineer who conceived of the world's first concrete floating bridge.

Mercer Island Reporter

Homer Hadley, (almost) forgotten engineer

The name of the genius behind the world's first concrete floating bridge was almost lost in history. Homer Hadley (1885–1967) wasn't recognized for his achievement until he was long dead and more than 50 years after the bridge—his bridge—connecting Mercer Island and Seattle was built.

It was a radically new idea in bridge building, and the largest floating structure ever built. But when Hadley, a young engineer working for the Seattle School District, came up with the idea of a concrete pontoon bridge, people scoffed and called it "Hadley's Folly." The story goes that Hadley had the revolutionary bridge-building idea one spring morning in 1920 when he was shaving in his home in the south end of Seattle overlooking Lake Washington.

His idea was a way to overcome the challenge of the extreme depth of Lake Washington, which makes building deep foundation pilings impracticable. And it utilized Hadley's experience of designing and building concrete ships during World War I.

He worked out the engineering problems inherent in the design. He found the best place to place the bridge and to bore a tunnel to Seattle. By 1921 he had completed a plan for the whole bridge. But the political and financial hurdles took much longer to overcome.

Hadley took a job that year with the Portland Cement Association, a trade organization promoting the use of concrete for large-scale projects.

In 1937, after federal Public Works Administration money became available during the Great Depression, Hadley took his idea to Lacey V. Murrow, then director the Washington Department of Highways.

Murrow approved Hadley's concept, but told Hadley he should distance himself from the project because of the perceived conflict of interest because of Hadley's association with the cement industry. Murrow assured Hadley he would get his proper recognition for the bridge after it was built.

But that never came to pass.

When the bridge was named in 1967, it was named the Lacey V. Murrow Memorial Bridge.

Homer Hadley might have been forgotten forever had it not been for Muriel Winterscheid, a Mercer Island resident who was a friend of Hadley's daughter, Eleanor. In 1992, Winterscheid and members of the University of Washington's Mortar Board alumni launched a statewide campaign to get Homer Hadley the recognition he deserved. The state Legislature unanimously approved the effort.

When the second bridge across Lake Washington was completed, a historic oversight was finally corrected: It was dedicated in July 1993 as the Homer M. Hadley Memorial Bridge.

Chapter 11: At Last, a Bridge to Seattle | 99

Museum of History and Industry
The bridge was named for Lacey V. Murrow, director of the Washington Department of Highways and brother of newsman Edward R. Murrow.

Martin paid the first toll. Millicent "Mimi" Moss, crowned Miss Floating Bridge, rode with the governor in the first car. Traffic was released from both ends simultaneously amid music and fireworks.

Perhaps prophetically, an over-enthusiastic motorist drove through the barricades on the new bridge two hours before the fanfare began. Not knowing that the draw span was partly open, he plunged his car into an 8-foot opening, wedging it there tightly until a wrecker cleared it away in time for the ribbon-cutting ceremonies.

Off-Islanders may have thought of the bridge as the gateway to all points east, but Islanders regarded it as their lifeline to Seattle. Every Islander knew that the end of an era had arrived, and that change for the Island was inevitable.

On that first day of the bridge, horses and teams were listed on the toll schedule, and paid a toll of 35 cents (50 cents for three or more horses).

The bridge was christened the Lake Washington Floating Bridge. In 1967, it was renamed the Lacey V. Murrow Memorial Bridge to honor the state highway director who was active in its realization.

However, it has almost always been called the Mercer Island floating bridge.

C.B. Blethen, publisher of the *The Seattle Times*, who had been one of the most vocal opponents of the floating bridge, became one of its biggest boosters.

He wrote, "The Lake Washington Floating Bridge is an unqualified success. In the beginning I opposed the pontoon bridge. What has changed my mind is that we have acquired something a hundred times more valuable than what we have lost. The beauty of the bridge is utterly amazing. It will be one of the half-dozen most important things to see in all America.

"The only objection I could possibly have is that more Seattle people will want to live on the eastern side of the lake the entire year around instead of just camping for the summer months.

"*The Seattle Times* is proud indeed of this beautiful new structure and sincerely admires the backbone of the men who thought it out and put it over in spite of all the opposition that was brought to bear. P.S. What sinks me is, the durned thing really does float!"

In an article in the *Seattle Post-Intelligencer*, Irene Loewenheim wrote that even though the Island had been connected to the eastern mainland, the residents considered themselves true islanders.

But now the Island as such would be no more. Residents would be able to come and go at will, just like city people. And the Island would have everything that big cities have—burglars and police, bright lights, wide streets and traffic accidents. People would need house keys and would have to use them. It had been a point of pride not to use a house key, or even to have one.

Islanders embraced the connection and convenience the bridge would bring, but at the same time mourned the loss of that special kind of individuality, that feeling of hardiness, of difference from mainland-based people. They cherished their "Islandish" attitude.

> "What sinks me is, the durned thing really does float!"
>
> —Gen. C. B. Blethen, publisher of *The Seattle Times*
> *a vocal opponent of the bridge who became one of the biggest bridge boosters*

Mercer Island Historical Society

Mercer Island Shopping Center was built in 1947 by Dick Anderson. It was on the site currently occupied by Island Square.

The '40s and '50s

After the war, after the bridge, a period of growth and change

The bridge was a reality and World War II was over. The Island had a population of 1,300 to 1,400 year-round residents who gradually realized that their island could no longer be a country area of disparate neighborhoods, but should pull together as one in order to determine its future.

The catalysts were the community clubs, which encouraged community planning, and the local businessmen who considered themselves progressive. But residents often were resistant to change and wanted the Island to remain as it was. At first, a small amount of unplanned progress was followed by a large amount of wheel spinning and procrastination on the part of the citizens.

The service businesses—always the heart of Island commerce—continued as before. Fordyce's Standard Supply in East Seattle sold groceries and supplies and housed the post office. Hap's Service Station had been on North Mercer Way since 1918, but now was tucked under the new highway overpass at 76th Avenue Southeast.

Rochester's Garage was near the new bridge over the East Channel. John Dunney's real estate office was located near the ferry dock, but there was no longer a ferry, and no ferry traffic passing by the Roanoke Tavern. The lumber dealer who lived in a little house on Southeast 27th Street still ran his backyard lumber business.

Local access from the highway was a west exit near the toll plaza, two center exits, and one East Channel exit. Owners of property near the new off-ramps began to predict the development of a business district there, rather than near the old ferry docks.

Still, traffic was so light on the early floating bridge that Islander Tom Callahan remembered that he and his high school pals would dance on the bridge without interfering traffic in the early 1940s. They would park their cars on the bridge and dance to the music of their car radios late into the night. Rarely were there more than one or two cars crossing the bridge while they cavorted, he recalled.

Business beginnings

Two real estate agents, John Dunney and Doug Smith, and three property owners in the central area, J.B. Brown, Dick Anderson and Harold Boyd, figured that the logical place for a business district was in "The Flats," near the two center highway exits. Lying between two ridges, the mostly vacant land appeared to be an ideal spot to serve Islanders en route to their homes or to Seattle.

The first to act was J.B. Brown, who returned to the chicken farm at Southeast 28th Street and Island Crest Way that he had abandoned during the Depression. He tore down his barns and chicken houses and recycled the lumber into six small homes in antici-

The Lightfoot family

Above is the home Frederick Lightfoot built in 1915, on present-day Southeast 27th Street, approximately where the drive-through Starbucks is in the Town Center today. The family turned it into a general store in the 1920s, and operated it until it was torn down in the 1950s.

At left, homes ranging from $23,000 to $40,000 dot the landscape in this 1955 photo of the Mercerwood development at the northeast part of the Island. Residents had beach privileges through the Mercerwood Shore Club. The East Channel Bridge is in the upper left.

Collection of Owen Blauman

pation of the postwar rush for housing, when building materials would be scarce and expensive. He used recycled trolley car windows, curved at the tops, in one of the houses. This became a retail complex best known after James Crosby took it over as a gift shop. It was demolished in the late 1970s to make way for Seafirst Bank's new building, now Bank of America.

Doug Smith, who had also left the Island during the Depression, returned in 1945 and went into the real estate business, having heard of the anticipated building boom. He set about buying land at tax-title auctions. One of his first purchases, for $100, was on Southeast 28th Street between the new highway and the site of the present Bank of America. The land was boggy, but the location had possibilities.

John Dunney also had purchased land near the highway, where his real estate office was located. Dick Anderson owned land to the west of Smith's lot, at the corner of 78th Avenue Southeast and Southeast 27th Street on a small hill. Smith and Anderson worked a miniature regrade project, pushing the Anderson hill into the Smith bog.

During this process, Smith eyed the land to the west, across 78th Avenue Southeast. He saw a meadow, a small white house where Moore had his lumberyard, a smaller building that was the Tabit family's summer place and the Lightfoot estate across Southeast 27th Street where the road curved. He decided to buy the meadow with the lumberyard house, and open his real estate office there. Thus, Smith became the first new businessman in what was to become the business center of Mercer Island.

Dick Anderson observed his land and Smith's land, and the increasing traffic. He had a dream of a coordinated, all-inclusive shopping center of white-trimmed colonial brick buildings with a covered pedestrian mall, perimeter parking and landscaping.

His architect's presentation to the community club brought applause. But at the hearing for business rezoning, other property owners proved unwilling to give up their individual lots and their own ideas for fragments of development. They outnumbered shopping center proponents. The King County commissioners were unwilling to rezone the entire area, preferring to retain spot zoning at East Seattle, East Channel, Roanoke Dock and other separate areas.

So the Anderson proposal, with its concept of a Carmel-like setting for businesses, was abandoned except for one building. On his own property, Anderson built structures that housed Art's Food Center, Gar Alm's drug store, and offices for Dr. Howard Eddy and Dr. Herbert Davidson, the first doctor and dentist to establish practices on the Island. The buildings were known as Mercer Island Shopping Center. It was later called Island Market Square, then, with later redevelopment, Island Square.

The remainder of the business district just grew, the flowering of free enterprise, with each businessman doing his own thing.

Harold Boyd owned property on Southeast 27th Street at 76th Avenue Southeast. Learning the post office was to be moved from East Seattle, he signed a lease with the government and built the business block to house the post office and a hardware store operated by his son. This building was later enlarged to include Look's Drug Store, with the first liquor store, and Croshaw's Food Store.

Chick Tabit's family owned a few acres on Southeast 27th Street with a small cabin that later became his shoe repair shop – and later Tabit Square.

Doug Smith shared his real estate office building with Lawrence White's Hair Styling Salon on the site of the present Walgreens.

In the 1940s and '50s this Mobilgas station was at the overpass at 76th Avenue Southeast and U.S. 10, which became Interstate 90.

Mercer Island Historical Society

Dick Anderson had a dream of a coordinated, all-inclusive shopping center.

Impending changes

The Island began to outgrow facilities that had been adequate before 1940. More homes meant more roads. More families meant more schools. Basic geology limited the use of septic tanks. Water supply would soon be insufficient. The Island needed to determine its own priorities, for eventually it would outgrow the Community Club—County Commissioner system of quasi-government.

A bold move was proposed: to incorporate into a city. The members of both the South End Club and the North End Community Club voted to petition the county commissioners to hold an election to incorporate the Island into a third-class city.

The pros and cons separated residents into two camps. A great battle of words and clash of opinions made the autumn of 1946 a lively time on the Island. Doug Smith organized a Chamber of Commerce among the few existing businessmen to boost incorporation. But it was too little and too late. In November 1946, Islanders voted down incorporation by a two-to-one margin. Cityhood would not be achieved for another 15 years.

As the Island population grew, so did the business district. The urgent need for planning prompted the clubs to sponsor a comprehensive plan that was drawn up

Hungry deer pose problems for gardeners

The deer continued to be a problem even after the World War II victory gardens had mostly been abandoned. Deer swam across the East Channel and established residence in the Island forests, emerging to dine on orchard greens, petunias, and other domestic plants.

Two letters of complaint were sent to the State Game Department in the 1940s protesting the marauders and requesting action. A reply stated, "We have in the past tried to have open deer season on Mercer Island to deplete the deer population thereon, but due to petitions circulated and signed by a large majority of property owners, the commissioners restricted any hunting or shooting of firearms on the Island. Therefore it has been difficult for the Game Department to cope with the deer situation."

Mary Douglas ran the Children's Educational Foundation for decades, until her death in 1944.
Barclay Stuart

Mercer Island Reporter

The Mercerwood Shore Club opened in 1953, on the site of what had formerly been a home for unwed mothers and, before that, the 80-acre Children's Educational Foundation, primarily for children from broken homes.

Before Mercerwood Shore Club, property was sanctuary for kids from broken homes

In 1913, the John Walter Ackerson Home for mothers and young children was built on 80 acres of prime waterfront property off East Mercer Way. The property was donated by Mrs. S. Louise Ackerson as a memorial to her husband.

Mothers could board their children there while they worked in Seattle, and orphans also were cared for there. The home had 14 rooms, and two large wards and sleeping porches; it was built at a cost of $6,000. When Barnabie School was opened nearby in 1916, the older children from Ackerson Home attended school there.

The Ackersons' will stipulated that the estate was to be used solely for the benefit of children. Anyone interested in an endeavor to benefit children was required to write a proposal and submit it to a board of regents.

In the late 1930s, Mrs. Mary Douglas sent a proposal to the Ackerson estate to use the building to house the Children's Educational Foundation (CEF), a coeducational school for students from first grade through high school who came from broken or abusive homes.

Mrs. Douglas was granted permission by the board of regents to operate the school, and she did so until her death in 1944. At its peak, about 45 students were enrolled; Douglas' grandson, Barclay Stuart, was one of them.

"She was a strict, no-nonsense disciplinarian," Stuart said of his grandmother. "Yet she was never a tyrant, always fair and solicitous, and a children's advocate."

Kids at CEF had duty shifts with such chores as shoveling coal, splitting kindling wood, peeling potatoes, setting formal dinner tables and cleaning up. Students dressed up for dinner, and ate at large round tables with white tablecloths and carefully placed dishes and silverware. There was a strict dress code and a flag salute every morning before school, outside around the flagpole. After school, there was a one-hour period of silent reading.

"But it wasn't all structure, duty and responsibility," wrote Stuart. "We had lots of room for fun. Summers we were down by and in the lake, swimming and diving off a raft. There were games of tag, relay races, picnic lunches and watermelon eating contests. Every Saturday, weather permitting, we gathered by the beachfront outdoor cooking facility and cooked up scores of pancakes. Evenings, we sang around the bonfire."

The school closed down during World War II after a fire destroyed the building. Subsequently a new brick building was constructed and the home reopened under the sponsorship of the Lutheran Churches, as a home for unwed mothers.

During the late 1940s, an Island resident, Russell C. Emrich, made plans to develop several acres west of the Ackerson House into an area to be known as Mercerwood Shore Club. The first of the postwar tract developers, he also purchased the brick building and remodeled it into a clubhouse with a swimming pool, tennis courts and other facilities for the use of Mercerwood residents.

The Mercerwood Shore Club opened in 1953. Now, 60 years later, the year-round club has a clubhouse, fitness center, 25-meter outdoor pool, four tennis courts and 500 feet of waterfront along the shore of Lake Washington. The club is in the planning process for a new construction project in the future.

in 1946 by Otto Risch, an Island resident, architect and city planner. His plan provided for basic zoning areas, a road network, minimum lot sizes and coordinated service areas. He suggested a road (where Island Crest Way later was built) to become a north-south arterial with feeder roads going into it. Many other aspects of this plan were implemented and formed a basis for today's development.

In 1948, Charles Clise proposed a 40-building, 700-family apartment complex. After numerous discussions, hearings and community club meetings, the majority of Islanders approved the project. In July 1949, Shorewood Apartments opened, located on 45 acres of the old Fortuna Park waterfront property and on 12 upland acres. Shorewood began the big population boom on the Island; individual home construction continued slowly.

While the business district began at the north end, the south end was pursuing its own course. The new bridge meant better transportation to Seattle at long last. New bus service began in September 1940, with fares of 10 rides for $2.15 on commuter tickets. The south end could grow because it now was accessible to the north end, although few houses existed between Southeast 44th and Southeast 68th streets.

The South Mercer Island Club continued to function as a quasi-governmental agency. For example, a resident asked the club's permission to raise muskrats, and was informed he could not, as it was contrary to the zoning ordinance.

The decade of the 1940s ended with proposals for an all-island planning commission to work with county commissioners. A comprehensive road and highway report was sent to the county engineers and to the State Legislature. The center road, now Island Crest Way, was made a secondary highway.

Big crowds turned out for the parade and ceremony celebrating the removal of tolls on the floating bridge on July 1, 1949. Some of the same Island princesses who were in the opening ceremony on July 1, 1940, were also in this happy parade.

In nine years, the $5 million bond issue, which partially financed the floating bridge, had been repaid from collected tolls, 21 years ahead of expectations.

This postcard from the 1940s is labeled "Mercer Island. Lake Washington. Seattle." The postcard rate was still 1 cent (it went up to 2 cents in January 1952).

Mercer Island Historical Society

1950s: growth and do-it-yourself spirit

As the wave of growth came to the Island, the pressures for change increased. Home building, business district expansion, parks, schools and library development, among others, made the 1950s some of the busiest years in Island history.

The Island's population boomed from 4,500 in 1950 to 12,000 in 1959. As more people moved to the Island, recalcitrant B.B. (before bridge) residents muttered against the concomitant problems. "We don't need a lot of people," they said. "Keep the city water out and you'll keep the builders out. Let's keep the roads in poor shape, then the people will stay away!"

The irresistible force of growth and the pleas of the progressives to annex to Seattle or, preferably, to incorporate as a city, met the immovable opposition of those who loved the Island so much as it was.

The 1950 membership in the South End Improvement Club reached a low. Interest was down and there weren't enough candidates for offices. The club voted against a proposal for a sewer district, refused to merge with the Center Island Club, opposed an underpass under Sunset Highway at Shorewood, but approved one at the north-end shopping center. King County refused to give the club permission to use Flood's Dock for recreational purposes. The club began investigation of a south-end fire station site and the possibility of acquiring a clubhouse.

But the South End Club came to life when it discovered, after receiving a bill for back taxes, that the club still owned a 10-acre tract of land that supposedly had been deeded to King County years before. The school board was interested in a school site, and accepted the club's proposal of an even exchange of the 10 acres for a 2.5-acre tract plus the outdated Lakeview School building. The deeds were signed on April 30, 1951. The building is now Sunnybeam School and is listed on the National Register of Historic Buildings.

On the 10-acre tract, the school district built Lakeridge Elementary and South Mercer Junior High. The club enclosed an open playroom of Lakeview School and rented it back to the district for a kindergarten. Cost of materials, $1,176, was contributed by the Preschool Association, parents of kindergartners in the south- and north-end clubs. Island residents donated many materials and all labor.

The do-it-yourself heritage came to the fore again, and the South End Club remained alive and well for 10 more years, becoming a community center for the slowly growing south end. In December 1952, the club had 218 members, an all-time high.

Both the south- and north-end clubs began to see the problems of water, sewer, roads, fire protection, zoning and planning. In 1953, when population had increased from 4,500 to 8,300 in just three years, representatives from the clubs organized a study group to analyze the critical situation.

The comprehensive report outlined three options: continue the status quo under King County government; incorporate as a third-class city, or become annexed to the city of Seattle.

The election was held in November 1953. What did the citizens do? They chose the status quo for more years to come. The irresistible force of growth had met immobility.

Mercer Island Reporter

James Crosby, a favorite gift shop, opened in the 1950s in one of six small houses built by J.B. Brown after World War II. They were torn down to make way for Seafirst Bank (now Bank of America).

Recreation

To fulfill the need for recreation facilities on the Island, a recreation council was formed in 1947 to provide swimming lessons for youngsters. Membership consisted of a representative from the churches, PTA, Scouts, Chamber of Commerce, community clubs and other organizations. By 1953, the group financed swimming instructors to give swimming lessons at the Lions Club Beach.

Except for a few street ends owned by the county, there were no parks until the county purchased a 40-acre tract near the planned Island Park School in 1953. Part of this was to be developed jointly with the school board, but development was hindered by lack of water.

Law enforcement

In the 1950s, police protection was improving, but was still handled by the East District of the King County Sheriff's office. Before any bridge, there had been

106 | Chapter 12: The '40s and '50s

Mercer Island Historical Society

This is the first Mercer Island fire station, circa 1948. Operated entirely by volunteers, it was located in the triangle-shaped property at 76th Avenue Southeast and Southeast 27th Street.

Fire Department has long legacy of helping

The tales of Mercer Island's earliest days are filled with stories of fires—from the Calkins Hotel to a variety of homes and barns. If something caught fire, it burned to the ground. Later, garden hoses and buckets provided the only fire protection.

During World War II, the Civil Defense group headquartered at Nelson Rochester's garage near the East Channel Bridge became the first organization of firefighters. Those volunteers used lightweight hand-pulled trailers and 5-gallon hand-pump cans of water.

Soon the Island population growth necessitated a higher level of fire protection. Islanders William Moore, Charley Landis and Nelson Rochester became a committee with a mission to create a fire district. These volunteers persuaded the people of Mercer Island to tax themselves for fire protection. On July 15, 1944, an election was held and Islanders voted 196 to 27 to create Fire District 21.

The first piece of fire apparatus was purchased in 1948—a GMC fire engine. Since there was no place to put it, local veterinarian and volunteer fireman William Green provided his garage as the storage location.

The first fire station, designed by the Island's first fire chief, Henry Borgendale, was built in the triangle lot at 76th Avenue Southeast and Southeast 27th Street at a cost of $12,000. It had a garage for two fire trucks, a night man's quarters and a meeting room for the firemen's club.

Every Thursday night, volunteers met there for three hours of drills, first-aid training and equipment maintenance. The club was a private organization that elected members and officers, took care of the station and equipment, and answered fire calls at any time.

Requests for the fire department's services were first provided via a telephone tree. Wives of volunteer firefighters would answer the home phone and pass on the request to other volunteers' wives.

By 195, a second truck was added, and a night man stayed at the station.

An emergency vehicle was needed, but space was limited. In 1955, a new, larger station was built at 3030 78th Ave. SE, the site of the current headquarters.

The south end was still without a fire station when the new north end station opened in July 1955.

In 1961, the City of Mercer Island took over fire protection and began building a professional department, while retaining the volunteers. That same year, a station housing two fire engines was built at the south end.

In 1962, Fire Chief Harry Slater resigned after 14 years. Gar Alm, owner of Alm's Drugs, was elected chief until a full-time paid fire chief was hired by the city, as provided in the 1962 budget. The first full-time firefighters were hired in 1967. Professional and volunteer (auxiliary) firefighters worked together until 2003, when the Mercer Island Volunteer Fire Department was disbanded.

In the 1980s, the Fire Department decided to phase in new fire trucks in an apple green color. But the color was never popular with citizens and by 2001 the department decided to go back to traditional bright red.

When the department outgrew the old station, the city of Mercer Island studied whether to rebuild on the old site or relocate the station. The one alternative site that was considered was a corner of Mercerdale Park.

After considerable community input in 1997 and 1998, the City Council voted to build a new station on the 78th Avenue Southeast site. The old station was demolished and a temporary one was set up on I-90 turn-back property near the Stroum Jewish Community Center.

The new, two-story fire station was completed in June 1999; with 16,400 square feet, it is more than twice the size of the old station. It was built without new taxes at a cost of $3.4 million, $34,000 under budget.

The station features bronze statues of a firefighter and a dog seeming to emerge from a fire on the façade of the building, and a bench commemorating Sgt. Steven Frink, who died in the line of duty in a motorcycle accident on Island Crest Way in 1993.

In 2012, Island voters approved a measure to replace the aging south-end fire station.

no protection, no enforcement and hardly any need.

After the East Channel Bridge opened, the patrol was infrequent and casual. With the floating bridge, the State Patrol assigned four men to the highway section between the bridge and Issaquah. A two-man prowler car was assigned nightly to Mercer Island.

But with increasing numbers came increasing theft, vandalism, speeding and other such crimes. The club study committee recommended eight patrolmen for the Island, but resigned themselves to the fact that the county sheriff would not heed their recommendation.

Business district

In the 1950s, the business district developed by leaps and bounds, continuing its haphazard arrangement of shops and customer services. In 1955 alone, 14 new businesses were added, including five gas stations, the Tradewell supermarket, Crosby's gift shop, a veterinary clinic, two real estate offices, two used car lots, a dry cleaner and a barbershop. By 1959, more than 41 businesses were scattered throughout the center.

The Chamber of Commerce's annual report for 1955 listed more than 85 members, almost double the number in the previous year. The chamber monitored zoning matters, opposed the reimposition of bridge tolls, promoted mercury lights in the business district and favored an underpass near the shopping center.

Another shopping-center proposal appeared in 1958, for the center of the Island near Island Park School. Arne Goedecke, developer of Maple Lane and of El Dorado Beach Club, presented plans for an 11-acre business center plus a large apartment complex, using fieldstone and cedar, and with covered

The Owen Blauman collection

On July, 1951, housewives and children demonstrated their opposition to the destruction of the old ferry dock at 28th Avenue Southeast and 60th Avenue Southeast. According to the news story, the picketers were disappointed because the county engineer's razing crew didn't show up as expected that day. But eventually, all the old county docks, deemed hazardous and a potential liability, were removed.

In 1955 alone, 14 new businesses were added in the business district, including five gas stations

walkways. An area for a fire station and a medical-dental unit was included.

But a rezone was necessary. A petition to rezone 11 residential acres between Southeast 50th Street and Southeast 53rd Place to permit the proposed shopping center and apartment complex was heard by the County Planning Commission Dec. 30, 1958. The South Mercer Island Club opposed it, and people packed the hearing room when the rezone was considered. The rezone was voted down and the plans went into the trash. A proposal for a retirement home in the same area met a similar fate.

One last rezoning proposal of the 1950s was for a motel with facilities to include a cocktail lounge to be located north of the highway. The local agreement on zoning specified no commercial development north of the highway. The hearing room was packed with citizens, and the King County commissioners refused the rezone request.

The largest all-Island community event came with the first MercerFair in 1959, sponsored by the Junior Chamber of Commerce. Robin Dunden won the first-ever Miss Mercer Island contest. A large float sponsored by the Chamber, shows, art exhibits, street dances, booths for games of chance and drill team performances were among the features. The Lions Club put on a 1,000-chicken barbecue.

The carnival atmosphere prevailed for two days in the roped-off street and parking-lot areas on Southeast 27th Street. MercerFair was repeated for several years.

The 1950s were years of tremendous changes for the Island. It was the end of an era of semi-rural living and relative simplicity of lifestyle; it was the beginning of the awareness of increasing complexities and new adventures as a densely populated suburb.

This 1990 photo shows Covenant Shores, formerly the lower Shorewood Apartments, with the historic Fortuna Lodge at the left.

Mercer Island Reporter

Shorewood, where the Island's boom began

The saying goes that everybody on Mercer Island lives at Shorewood at one time or another. As the vagaries of life dictate, it's the place for young singles and newlyweds; it's temporary housing for families remodeling their homes; it's the refuge when marriages don't work out; and it's home to a number of retirees.

The complex, built by Seattle businessman Charles Clise, opened in July 1949. Lower Shorewood comprised eight buildings on the lakeshore, with a total of 116 apartments. In 1949, rents ranged from $77.50 to $125 per month.

Upper Shorewood was built next, bringing the total to 38 buildings and 568 apartments. Since the highway bisected the two sections, an overpass and paths connected them. The marina and clubhouse—the old Fortuna Lodge—were available to all residents.

A "Children Welcome" sign was hung out. And the families came. In fact, Shorewood was credited with initiating the unprecedented population growth on the Island. School enrollment increased 287 percent from 1949 to 1951 as a result of Shorewood's opening. Like many families, that of Stanley Ann Dunham, mother of the future president Barack Obama, moved to Shorewood in 1956 so that she could attend Mercer Island High School.

With incorporation in 1960, the fledgling city needed a home. Shorewood housed Mercer Island's city hall and police department for 28 years, making Shorewood a hub of the Island. During the 1960s, it also housed a small convenience store known as The Rooster Tail, owned and operated by renowned hydroplane driver Bill Muncey. It closed circa 1970.

Charles Clise operated Shorewood for 25 years. After his death, the complex was owned by several entities until lower Shorewood was purchased by the North Pacific Conference of the Covenant Church in 1978 and was turned into a retirement community. In 1981, it became part of the national Covenant Retirement Community.

Covenant Shores has been extensively remodeled and updated, with several buildings demolished and replaced over the years. Assisted living was added in 1991 with the opening of a new building. A new 43-bed health center was built on vacant land within the property and opened in 1997. Four original buildings are still in use at Covenant Shores, as is Fortuna Lodge, which serves as the dining hall and community center. Covenant Shores has 208 residential apartments, 32 assisted-living apartments and 15 "memory care" units.

In 2009, Covenant Shores was recognized with the county's Emergency Preparedness and Response Award for its development of resident-led disaster drills.

Over the years, the 45-acre upper Shorewood property has change hands and expanded. When it was purchased in 1998 for $55 million by HAL Real Estate Investments, the transaction was the state's highest-priced apartment sale. HAL spent $23 million renovating the units and about $12.5 million constructing 78 new apartments and an activity center in 2002. The name was changed to Shorewood Heights, and it was recognized by the city for being the first to launch a multifamily recycling program, in 1990.

Security Properties and Principal Global Financial purchased Shorewood Heights for $141.3 million in December 2005; then, in the aftermath of the economic downturn, Goodman Real Estate and Pinnacle Investments purchased it in 2010 for $110 million. The 645-unit Shorewood Heights will continue to grow and improve in the future, as the new owners have permits ready to build 124 new units, a swimming pool and an expanded fitness center.

Rx: Remember the early days of medicine

There was no full-time doctor on Mercer Island until April 1948, when Dr. Howard Eddy established the first medical practice on the Island. He had fallen in love with the Pacific Northwest while stationed there during World War II and afterward decided to settle on Mercer Island.

Before long, he enticed his friend and classmate from Cleveland, Dr. Herbert Davidson, to set up the first dental practice on the Island.

"A decision was made to stay out west, and Mercer Island, an isolated community of about 1,000 people, looked like a good place to raise three boys," recounted Eddy's son, Roger. "Most Mercer Islanders lived modestly in those days. I recall we looked at a three-bedroom farmhouse with a barn, chicken house and 14 acres for $10,000. Some folks lived in Army tents or Quonset huts. Our house had been built out of Boeing packing crates. It was later remodeled several times."

In time, other medical practitioners joined Eddy and Davidson, hanging out shingles on the Island. Dr. Carl Stroud saw patients in a room in the basement of his home before he opened an office, with dentist Dr. Von Zanner, on Island Crest Way.

Doctors made house calls, patched up the cuts and scrapes of kids in the neighborhood, and knew not only their patients but their families as well.

Internist Dr. Chauncey "Chip" Paxson recalled that on one occasion while he was making a house call, an elderly, bed-ridden patient was unable to get out of bed to unlock the front door. Undaunted, Paxson shinnied up the drainpipe to an open window.

In the early 1950s, Dr. Harry Kettering, obstetrician and gynecologist, started working on Mercer Island part-time, using Dr. Howard Eddy's office on Eddy's days off.

"The big adjustment in Howard's office was the absence of an examining table," recalled Kettering. "Instead, he had a fancy chair like a barber chair for the patient. After taking her history and examining her chest, breasts, eyes, nose, throat, etc., you pulled a lever and zip! The patient reclined back and two stirrups flew out and there she was ready for the pelvic exam! I took great care to prepare the patient for this experience!"

Kettering and a dentist, Dr. Norman Strand, built an office at Island Crest Way and Southeast 30th Street, and were later was joined by Drs. David Wolter and Charles Flake. They rented offices in the lower level to pediatricians Al Skinner, Phil Deane, William Merritt, and, later, Bill Jaquette.

Doctors would rotate from one office to the next, starting out under the old Looks Pharmacy, moving to a space in the lower level of the real estate office on Sunset Highway, then moving into nicer, larger quarters.

Drs. Paxson, Bob Coe and Sam Davidson took over

Dr. Al Skinner

A number of doctors and dentists made their offices in this little building at 7705 Sunset Highway. It was eventually torn down to make way for I-90 construction.

the office in the real estate building, which was later sold to John L. Scott Real Estate.

In the early 1960s, Dr.s Skinner, Deane and Merritt joined with Paxson, Coe, Sam Davidson, Eva Gilbertson and dentist John Lind, to build the clinic building next to the Mercer Island Covenant Church: the Mercer Park Medical-Dental Center.

"The site was a peat bog at the toe of a hillside notorious for sliding," wrote Skinner. "We paid as much for site preparation as we did for the purchase, and the east foundation wall is as well-built as Grand Coulee Dam."

Later Drs. Ted Mandelkorn and Janice Woolley joined Skinner in Mercer Island Pediatrics. Other tenants included Drs. John Aberle, Bruce Bradley, Ernie Dunn and others.

In 1997, Skinner wrote to early medical practitioners on the Island, to collect their stories about the practicing medicine on the Island. One response holds true for them all, he said: "There is nothing ordinary about providing health care for, say, your neighbor or your grocer, who over decades share not only their health concerns but also their hobbies and friendship and family's care. Consider the privilege of caring for a colleague and two generations of his family."

Ellingsen family

Roy Ellingsen, who grew up on Mercer Island, remembers playing on the hill just east of downtown Mercer Island. This photo, taken by his father in 1958, shows him running along a construction site with his brother, Ken, following him. Island Crest Way is below them.

The '60s and the Birth of a City

The Island had two governments at the same time: the town and the city

One of the more bizarre chapters in the Island's history is the story of how it went from being an unincorporated backwater to an island with not just one government but two — a town and a city.

And it remained so for a decade.

In 1953, Islanders voted against incorporation and annexation, but by 1960 the Island's need for improved government was becoming evident to progressives and conservatives alike. Crime was increasing, water pressure was decreasing and sewage-disposal issues became more urgent.

The "no change" people so loved yesterday's Island and doubted the adequacy of the tax base that they wanted a predominantly residential area with minimal businesses. Newer, more progressive residents welcomed change, self-government and all the public amenities postwar America had to offer.

The status quo remained until 1960, when a determined developer named Glen Niquette became the catalyst for action.

The battle was a mighty one,

and when the dust cleared, two incorporated areas had come into being, a city of Mercer Island and a town of Mercer Island. It's a tale of lawsuits, countersuits, appeals, and a case that went all the way to the Washington State Supreme Court.

Niquette's request to rezone his property north of the highway for a motel and cocktail lounge was rejected, and King County would not grant him a liquor license. So, apparently deciding he needed a government he could control, he started a movement to create a fourth-class "town." He launched a petition to incorporate a 0.3-mile segment of land, then containing Person's dairy farm, a swamp and a few small businesses, into the "town of Mercer Island."

He filed the petition with King County in February 1960.

"We need to create a favorable tax climate to induce business to come to the Island," Niquette told a *Bellevue American* reporter, indicating that the town area should have a government to encourage commercial development.

Niquette's action raised concerns of many homeowners who valued their rural retreat. They

Chapter 13: The '60s and the Birth of a City | 111

1953 The Mercer Island Orthopedic Auxiliary celebrates its 25th anniversary. It produces 3,000 copies of the Mercer Island Directory.

1953 Mercer Island Beach Club is formed when Island families come together to purchase waterfront land at the south end of the Island.

1953 Lakeridge Elementary School is built.

1954 Fred Bassetti establishes the *Mercer Island Reporter*. A year's subscription is $1.50.

1954 Mercer Island Historical Society forms.

1954 Construction begins on Mercer Island High School. The $900,000 facility was referred to as "the million dollar high school."

1954 An ad in the *Mercer Island Reporter* lists tennis or play shoes from Chick's Shoe store for $5.25.

1954 Mercer Island Radio and Television advertises a 21-inch Pacific Mercury television for $169.95.

1954 Twenty-two students from Mercer Island graduate from Bellevue High School on June 10.

1954 The Roanoke Inn advertises T-bone steak dinners (with salad, cottage fries and toast) for $2.40. A hamburger dinner is 85 cents.

1954 DeCaro Menswear opens in September.

1955 Library Board breaks ground for new $15,000 library at Southeast 44th Street and 88th Avenue Southeast.

1955 Mercer Island High School opens

1955 James Crosby opens a gift shop in the lower level of his home on 80th Avenue Southeast.

1955 The Mercer Island Chamber of Commerce has 85 members.

Numerous community meetings were held to discuss the pros and cons of incorporation. This photo was was taken in the late 1950s.

Mercer Island Reporter

welcomed retail convenience stores, but generally were not interested in becoming a business center for cross-Island travelers. In May, an "all-Island" group presented the county with a counter-petition to Niquette's, to incorporate the entire Island.

George N. Prince, spokesman for this group, told *The Seattle Times*: "The Island is a geographic and economic unit. The shopping area and the rest of the Island must be considered together. If Mr. Niquette's petition carried, it would probably be by three dozen people, affecting the fortunes of all the 13,000 living on the Island. Equities and public policy require that the all-Island petition be heard."

Strategy dictated that an all-Island election should be held first, to provide a true vote of all residents. The town proponents sought to block that by a writ of prohibition. On May 10, 1960, the Superior Court ruled that the all-Island election was to consider incorporating everything *except* the proposed town area, the voting to be on July 5. The previously filed town incorporation voting date was to be Aug. 9.

Thirty-eight candidates filed for positions on the City Council, a fact that became a matter for comment and controversy.

The headline of the June 7, 1960, *Seattle Times* was "Inter-

For 10 years, there were two governments, the town of Mercer Island and the city of Mercer Island.

est High in Mercer Island Free-For-All," and stated, "Why are 30 Mercer Island residents running for seven City Council seats in a city which doesn't yet exist? The outpouring of candidates is credited to intense public interest in Mercer Island's community affairs and a widespread desire to help steer its development. Incorporation proposals have stirred controversy on the Island for several years."

The dreaded possibility was that the town would incorporate, the city would not, and the Island would become a patchwork of mini-incorporations, creating myriad problems with overlapping functions and loss of logical zoning and planning.

The *Reporter's* Letters to the Editor columns were filled with lively exchanges. It became a three-way battle when a few candidates for City Council announced both their candidacy and their opposition to incorporation.

On July 5, 1960, nearly 3,000 voters cast their ballots in the 20 Island precincts, exclusive of the town area. The final vote

112 | Chapter 13: The '60s and the Birth of a City

Mercer Island Reporter

Two legendary Islanders, Ernie Person, left, and John Dunney, talk together in this 1974 photo. Person was a member of the first Town Council; Dunney was Mercer Island's first real estate agent.

Annexation fight

The petition for annexation, filed by business and property owners, led to an election in January 1961, which favored annexation of part of the town area to the city.

In February 1961, the town brought suit in the State Supreme Court to declare null and void the Jan. 31 election on grounds that annexation of an area with a population of less than 2,000 was unconstitutional.

The next effort at forcing unity involved the state Legislature. A bill was introduced in the House of Representatives to the effect that "a fourth-class town which lies wholly within the limits of any city situated in a class AA county shall be deemed consolidated with and a part of such city." The House passed the bill. When it went before the Senate, it was labeled as "special legislation" since no such situation was known except for Mercer Island. The bill was defeated.

In March 1961, a petition for annexation also gathered an insufficient number of valid signatures. One last effort was made with a petition filed with the Town Council to hold an all-Island town and city election to have everyone vote on consolidation. The Town Council refused it.

For the next 10 years, Mercer Island had two governments. Peace was not truly achieved, but armed neutrality enabled the Island to live for a decade as a two-headed creature.

The city and town each set up an administration, the city in the Guild Hall building in East Seattle and the town in a little two-story structure in its northwest corner, just north of Sunset Highway. Soon the city leased a portion of the Shorewood Apartments for its administrative offices. The newly elected councils learned how to start a city and a town from scratch.

was 1,835 to 1,027 in favor of incorporation.

Meanwhile, another legal skirmish was under way.

A group of citizens filed a claim that there were fewer than 300 residents in the proposed town area. They sought in this way to block the town election, because 300 was the minimum number of residents needed to incorporate as a town. The plaintiffs said a "nose count" showed only 227 persons living in the area. But the judge determined the count was adequate, and the election schedule remained.

Campaigning for and against the Aug. 9 town election intensified, and there was a campaign to register more voters.

Many property owners within the town boundaries petitioned the new city of Mercer Island for annexation. This was blocked by legal action. A group of 81 people within the area circulated a flyer before the election urging residents of the town to vote against incorporating.

The final vote to incorporate the Town of Mercer Island was approved by a vote of 54 to 49. The first Town mayor was Henry Borgendale.

The residents of the town wanted to retain the final say on how the thriving business center was run. Some felt that the city wanted to gobble up the town largely because of its revenues. The town budget was $60,886. The assessed valuation of the town was $1.7 million.

Mercer Island, town of, and Mercer Island, city of, were occupying the same Island in Lake Washington, but there the togetherness ended. These two new entities battled on.

> "Why are 30 Mercer Island residents running for seven City Council seats in a city which doesn't yet exist?"
>
> —*Seattle Times,* June 7, 1960

Chapter 13: The '60s and the Birth of a City | 113

The Owen Blauman collection

The groundbreaking for the new $15,000 library, on property originally owned by pioneer Vitus Schmid, was on April 26, 1953. From left to right are Ray Ogden, Jr., building-committee chairman; Sherman Diamond, president of the Mercer Island Library Board, and Mrs. Al White, Ormond C. Nugent and Jesse Wilkins, building-committee members. A tea was held on May 20, 1953, at the Mercer Island Community Club to help raise funds for the project. Some $5,000 already had been raised through donations.

Library: Much more than a place for books

A library of its own was a long-sought addition to the Island: At the turn of the 20th century, book lovers faced challenges borrowing reading materials. They walked the Island's muddy trails to the ferry landing, crossed the lake to Seattle, rode the cable car to the Seattle Public Library and then made the long journey in reverse.

In 1942, the King County Library System (KCLS) was established, and each community desiring a library was asked to set up a library board and provide a site and staff.

The Mercer Island Library opened its doors in East Seattle on January 11, 1945, in a 12-feet-square room donated by Emmanuel Episcopal Church, with books provided by KCLS. Mrs. Geoffrey Lavender volunteered as librarian and Harry Slater served as the Island's representative to the county library system.

The tiny library in the church's Guild Hall was too small from the beginning, but it had the advantages of free rent and a convenient location across the street from the East Seattle School. Island organizations, including the PTA, the Preschool Association and the Mercer Island Community Club, provided support.

By the mid-1950s, the library was seeking a home of its own. A number of sites were proposed: in East Seattle, in the central business district and in the center of the Island.

Carolyn Park and Theresa MacMahon, daughters of Island pioneer Vitus Schmid, supported building the library on land that their father donated in 1891 as the site for a school. At the corner of present-day Southeast 44th Street and 88th Avenue Southeast, it was the highest point and the geographic center of the Island. The Allview Heights School was built on the site, but it was demolished by 1900.

Library board member Alla Olds Luckenbill, who moved to the Island in 1885 at age 10 and graduated from the school, also encouraged acquisition of the site for the library.

The school board gave a deed transferring the land to the library board, and a fundraising drive collected $8,000 for a new library building, along with $2,000 for materials. Island architect Jesse Wilkins volunteered his services to design the library and supervise construction. On Oct. 18, 1955, a new 1,200-square-foot building with space for 10,000 books opened, within walking distance of several schools.

Only a few years later, a larger library was needed to serve the Island's growing population. A $25,000 campaign funded a 1,920-square-foot addition, which was dedicated on Oct. 17, 1962. Library board president Mrs. Elias Solomon presented the deed to Tom Barto, mayor of the new city of Mercer Island, and the City Council voted to contract for library services from KCLS. A seven-member library advisory board succeeded the library board, which had represented 24 Island organizations.

King County Library System

By 1968, when this photo was taken, the Mercer Island Library was in need of expansion. It was renovated and expanded in 1969 and again in 1991.

By the end of the 1960s, the need for still more library space was evident. Fortuitously, the city was able to purchase two-thirds of an acre of land immediately south of the library. A building expansion to 5,422 square feet was completed in 1969, with a capacity for some 35,000 books.

The 1970s saw the establishment of the Friends of the Mercer Island Library, a volunteer organization that continues to support library programs and activities with funds generated by its popular sales of donated books and other media.

A popular bronze sculpture of a rabbit and boy reading, by artist Georgia Gerber, sits near the entry of the library.

By the mid-1980s, even the building's third expansion failed to serve Islanders' needs. The library possessed 54,000 volumes, and materials in electronic format as well as computers competed for space. Feelings were strong as Islanders were divided over whether to rebuild the library where it stood or move it to a civic center proposed for Mercerdale Field in the central business district.

In the end, the civic center proposal was defeated, and plans were drawn for a 14,600-square-foot library to replace the "three-piece building." A $2.18 million bond measure passed in November 1989 with a 66 percent majority.

The library moved to temporary quarters next to the liquor store during construction, and in April 1991 a new home for the library opened.

In 1993, voters approved a proposal to annex the city-owned library to the King County Library System.

The 1990s saw the introduction of many new technologies; Mercer Island was the first KCLS branch to have computers installed for public use.

In the new millennium, circulation continues to increase, and the library serves as a vital community resource for Islanders of all ages, from preschool story hours through senior computer lessons. Utilizing the KCLS website, library patrons reserve books, music CDs and videos from any library in the system and, increasingly, download electronic materials.

In 2009, the library received more than 200,000 visits and circulated more than 400,000 items.

In 2012, KCLS began planning a major remodel of the Mercer Island Library, to update the interior and acommodate the digital era.

In a recent survey, one patron wrote that the Mercer Island Library "is one of my most prized possessions, truly a home away from home."

1955 Mercer Island Lions Club is founded.

1955 A new Mercer Island Library opens on 88th Avenue Southeast on property donated for educational purposes by Island pioneer Vitus Schmid.

1955 Fourteen new businesses open in downtown Mercer Island.

1956 Mercer Island High School is dedicated May 20.

1956 Two hundred fifty new homes are built during the year.

1957 Island Park Elementary School is built.

1957 Eleanor Wolf and Marienne "Nuky" Fellows open the Mercer Island Nursery School Association. The school is renamed Sunnybeam in 1972.

1957 Mercer Island High School teachers Val Foubert and Clara Hayward start the Humanities Block. Jim Wichterman soon joins them.

1958 Winners of the Chamber of Commerce Christmas Decoration Contest are announced Jan. 1: first for exterior decorations goes to Brown's Floral & Nursery; first in window decorations goes to Chick's Shoe Emporium; first in interior decoration goes to Art's Food Center.

1958 Mercer Island High School graduates its first class of 78 students.

1958 The "ultra-modern" Mercer Park Day School opens at 3027 80th Ave. SE. Built by Jean and Ed Payne, it has a capacity of 80 children.

1958 Boyd's Hardware advertises sleeping bags for $8.95 in the Jan. 29 issue of the *Mercer Island Reporter*.

1958 The Mercer Island Recreational Council approves seven streets to be blocked off to allow skiing and sledding in the winter.

1958 Phone numbers change from six to seven digits. ADams numbers change to ADams 2.

The 1950s and '60s were a boom time in downtown Mercer Island, with the opening of scores of new businesses. In these photos from 1964, Seattle-First National Bank, above left, was on the corner of Southeast 28th Street and 80th Avenue Southeast. The Esther Marion Shop for women's sportswear was next door. Above right, Connie and Phil Schwarz owned and operated Mercer Island Travel for many years. At right, Dorothy Olson, owner of Mercer Island Stenographic Services, assists a Mercer Island Chamber of Commerce member in promoting the "Shop Mercer Isle" campaign.

Mercer Island Reporter

The South End Shopping Center

The last echo of the old system happened at the south end, which was still relatively rural. Before the city of Mercer Island planning department was established, a rezoning by the old method came about.

E.M. Greenwood, a property owner and developer, had a dream of homes, a club with tennis courts and swimming pool, as well as a shopping center on the south end of the Island. His architects presented plans to the South End Club when the petition to rezone was filed with the county commissioners. This shopping center development was on the site of the Golf and Country Club's proposed golf course in the 1920s.

The plan showed attractive buildings surrounding a mall. The club agreed to a 75-foot buffer strip around the property, which was a forest similar to and adjoining Pioneer Park. The center was to be an aesthetic addition to the community.

Thinking of other beautifully designed centers, south enders voted in favor of the rezoning, and the planning commission approved.

Then came disillusionment. All trees were removed. On the bare, bulldozed ground, stark buildings were built. A supermarket sported a huge revolving sign. When the developer was queried about the landscaping, he responded by planting a line of poplar trees and some flat junipers for ground cover. The neighbors petitioned for removal of the sign. It was taken down.

The South End Shopping Center opened in December 1961, the last rezone and development done under county jurisdiction. After that, planning and design were controlled by the Islanders' own governments, town and city.

Two governments

The City Council chose a council-manager form of government, and selected the mayor, Harold Oliver, from among the seven council members. Don Hitchman was the first city manager. The council appointed standing committees and boards: park board, road committee, planning commission, building board of appeals.

Among its first year's achievements the council maintained roads, cleaned ditches and started work on Island Crest Way; established a building department, which issued 301 permits in six months; moved city offices; created a parks and recreation depart-

116 | Chapter 13: The '60s and the Birth of a City

Mercer Island Reporter

Members of the Mercer Island City Council, in 1962, are, left to right, top row, John Day, Mayor Harold Oliver, Cleve Anschell; bottom row, Tom Barto, Red Howell, N.E. Boyce and Sheila LeClerq.

ment; adopted a comprehensive plan for land use; arranged for continuation of services of fire department and library; and ended 1960 operations with a cash balance of $57,703.

The town of Mercer Island established a mayor-council form of government, whose powers were expressly delegated to it by the state Legislature as a fourth-class city. The mayor appointed the town clerk, marshal, municipal court judge, attorney, engineer and police officers, who held office at the discretion of the mayor without confirmation by the council. The beautification committee was part of the Chamber of Commerce, and made recommendations to the council.

The population of the town was between 300 and 400. Chief administrative official was the clerk-treasurer, a position held for the life of the town by Norine Martin. She kept records of all council affairs, handled all financial matters, signed documents authorized by the council and was custodian of the town seal.

The Town Council went to work on land-use planning, which had been one of the issues in the incorporation controversy. Later in the 1960s, rezoning from single to multiple residences brought more apartment houses to the hillsides on either side of the valley of the business district. By 1966, five major apartment buildings had been constructed, and more were planned.

Throughout the 1960s, nobody in city government talked out loud about taking over the town, although the advantages to both sides became more and more obvious. And because they cooperated in important respects, the two governments functioned surprisingly well.

The town had a sheriff and three deputies, but contracted with the city for fire protection—in fact, the main fire station was within the town's jurisdiction. Separate districts provided water and sewer service to both jurisdictions. Town residents were required to pay $5 per year to use the library, which was owned by the city and operated by the King County Library District.

The city and town together contracted with a consultant for a study of land use and fiscal planning, completed in 1967. The city commissioned the John Graham Report of 1963, which dealt with such subjects as projected population, traffic circulation and recreation planning. The report was based on the following assumptions:

• Mercer Island will continue to be a residential community.
• Mercer Island will not allow industry.
• Commercial activities will be limited to the town, the South End Center, and a small commercial zone near the East Channel.
• The minimum lot size will be 8,400 square feet.
• The existing zoning ordinance will remain.
• Mercer Islanders will continue to preserve the rural atmosphere of the Island.

Promoting the Island

In the early 1960s, the Chamber of Commerce was busily promoting the Island and local businesses. A Shop Mercer Isle "SMILES" campaign in the summer of 1960 involved a roving committee of businessmen who would surprise smiling shoppers with a gift of merchandise.

The Island's first big public fireworks display was on the Fourth of July in 1962, financed by the Kiwanis' sale of "safe and sane" fireworks, in accordance with a new state law.

The grandest MercerFair, sponsored by the Kiwanis Club, was held in 1963, with the Miss Mercer Island competition, a horse show and Saddle Club parade through the business district, and a championship bicycle race sponsored by the Bicycle League of America.

> In 1959, there were 16 real estate agencies on the Island.

Chapter 13: The '60s and the Birth of a City | 117

Mercer Island Historical Society

This photo, taken in the '50s or '60s, shows Hesse's Restaurant, formerly the Floating Bridge Inn, at the intersection of Southeast 27th Street and 78th Avenue Southeast.

Other MercerFair attractions were the booths, including a Belgian waffle booth reminiscent of the 1962 Seattle World's Fair, games of chance, barbecues and street dancing. Live music drew teenagers from far and near.

The Chamber of Commerce sponsored a Concours d'Elegance on the high school field, displaying more than 100 antique automobiles and attracting more than 8,000 visitors in two days.

But as the turbulent '60s continued, interest in MercerFair began to lag.

By 1969, only the Kiwanians, Boy Scouts and Jaycees were involved, with a few booths and games, bike races, some parachutists and a tricycle parade. That year marked the end of MercerFair.

Metro saves the lake

By 1957, the water in Lake Washington had become almost brown in color and virtually opaque. Algae growth was profuse, stimulated by nutrients discharged into the lake from 10 sewage treatment plants.

Green scum collected on the windward shores. The odor of dying, decaying algae was strong, especially in late summer. Visibility for swimmers was only 2.5 feet; eight years earlier it had been 12 feet. Beach closures were frequent, and the lake was declared unsafe for swimmers.

A massive cleanup program became possible in 1957 when the State Legislature passed an act permitting the creation of an umbrella government for all communities around Lake Washington and on Puget Sound.

The Municipality of Metropolitan Seattle, known as Metro, had to be approved by voters in all communities concerned.

The first vote, asking for a spectrum of powers for the new government including sewage disposal, garbage collection and transit, failed. Four months later, in September 1958, voters approved a narrower plan for improving water quality.

A comprehensive sewer system was built, and all discharges into Lake Washington were eliminated, as well as raw sewage discharge into Puget Sound. Five large plants replaced the 28 old treatment plants.

This massive sewage program,

118 | Chapter 13: The '60s and the Birth of a City

The Owen Blauman collection

This photo from the early 1960s looks north on Island Crest Way. The town of Mercer Island, primarily the downtown area, had a population of between 300 and 400 people; the rest of the Island constituted the city.

paid for mostly by the people of King County, was a pioneering effort, copied by other communities with similar problems. The entire system was operable in 1961, and in the ensuing years Island residents followed reports of decreasing algae and improved visibility.

Metro was achieving the objective of a beautiful blue lake. A 12-year program of area-wide participation enabled the *Reporter* to headline in June 1970: "Lake Clearest in 20 Years."

Learning self-government

The decade was one of growth and progress as residents settled in with the benefits of self-government. The Town Council handled the affairs of the shopping center and the town's 30-plus homes and 28 apartment houses, totaling 835 residents.

The City Council handled the affairs of the rest of the Island from the City Hall in two rented apartment buildings in the Shorewood apartment complex.

In the words of Mayor Peter McTavish in 1969, "We incorporated because county government was downgrading the Island. We are trying to supervise an orderly growth without losing our way of life."

New residents kept arriving. The decade began with an Island population of 12,137; in 1966 there were more than 16,000; at the end of the decade, the population was almost 20,000.

But an economic crisis was causing a change in the community. The Boeing Company slump started in 1969, with layoffs of thousands of employees in all echelons of the company. Many executives, supervisors, engineers and other workers lived on Mercer Island. Many homes bore "For Sale" signs, and many people changed careers in order to stay on the Island.

The readjustment period came at a time when Islanders were learning self-government and developing greater community pride.

By the end of the 1960s, the bitterness that once separated the different factions was dissolving, and consolidation of the town and city seemed inevitable.

1958 The Mercer Island Directory has 3,250 names.

1959 South Mercer Junior High School is built at the south end.

1959 The first MercerFair is held, complete with a Miss Mercer Island contest. Robin Dunden was chosen.

1959 The Island's population is 12,000.

1960 City of Mercer Island is incorporated July 5. Harold Oliver becomes the first mayor of Mercer Island.

1960 St. Monica Catholic Church is built.

1960 MercerView Elementary School opens on the north end of the Island.

1960 The reversible-lane configuration of I-90 is instituted, with three lanes heading westbound in the morning and three lanes heading eastbound in the afternoon.

1961 New post office on Southeast 78th is dedicated in February; it is built for $200,000.

1961 North Mercer Junior High opens in November.

1961 Safeway advertises lamb steaks for 39 cents per pound, eggs at four dozen for $1 and butter for 65 cents per pound.

1961 The city of Mercer Island takes over fire protection and hires professional firefighters.

1962 A new 1,920-square-foot addition to the Mercer Island Library is dedicated, and the deed is presented to the city of Mercer Island, represented by Mayor Tom Barto.

1963 The Rotary Club of Mercer Island is chartered in December.

1963 Ten women establish the Mercer Island Welcome Wagon, an organization dedicated to welcoming new families to the Island. It later became the Mercer Island Women's Club.

Chapter 13: The '60s and the Birth of a City | 119

Bob Bersos

This 1968 photo shows Mercer Island's auxiliary firefighters, trained volunteers who provided on-call service to fight fires and provide emergency service on the Island. Top row, left to right, Roger Kenyon, Joe Martine, Brian Mcferran, Brad Graham, Eric Hurlburt, Ed Langlois, George Tyrell, Bob Saquitne, Curt Johnson. Middle row, left to right, John Ramsey, Al Provost, Bill Barnes, Dick Radke, Bill Shoentrup, Bob Cooper, Bill Green, Roger Wood, Fred Alm, Marv Saquitne. Front row, left to right, Tom Forsyth, Robbie Robinson, Bill Stanger, Joe Roberson, Gordon Stacy, Gordon Macalister, Jim Tyo, Gary Williams, Bruce Young, John Waymire, Harold Tate, Frank Sand, Ed Mckinney, Larry Little, Ken Kander, Cecil Little, Chief Earl Brower.

Neighbors helping each other fight fires

Bob Bersos

For most of Mercer Island's history, fighting fires was done by volunteers.

The Mercer Island Volunteer Fire Department began in 1945, after the creation of Fire District 21.

Islanders from a wide range of careers and backgrounds came together to respond to fire and aid calls. They would gather every Thursday night at the fire station in the triangle lot at 76th Avenue and Southeast 27th for practice drills, first-aid training and equipment maintenance.

Some joined because they loved fighting fires, some because they hoped for a career as a professional firefighter. But they all wanted to help protect their community, and in doing so they forged a strong bond of camaraderie.

An audible alarm sounded at the first sign of a fire, and volunteers would race to the station. The first to arrive got to drive the truck.

It wasn't until 1967 that the Fire Department hired its first full-time professional firefighter. More professionals were added as years went on. But the volunteer (or auxiliary) force was essential to provide for fire safety on the Island.

For years, volunteer firefighters played an active role in setting up a first-aid station during Seafair, and organizing Public Safety Days and other community events.

The auxiliary firefighters were appreciated by Islanders for their community involvement. During the holiday season, they held an annual candy giveaway: for several evenings they drove the decorated, lighted fire truck through the neighborhood streets, playing holiday music and tossing candy to excited children who followed the truck.

Mercer Island Reporter

In the 1970s and 1980s, Islanders raised horses on plots of pastureland such as this one on the "South 40." This 1979 photo shows two girls with a Shetland pony on former Mercer Island School District property that was later developed into The Lakes.

The 1970s and '80s

The young city matures, acquires parks, improves services, opens a community center

As the 1970s began, Mercer Islanders discovered that insular does not mean isolated. The shock of Boeing layoffs; the reality of Metro; the multi-city participation in waste disposal and transit service; the continuing saga of Interstate 90—all made interdependence a necessity.

Town-city merger

At the beginning of the '70s, Mercer Island still had both town and city governments. Pro- and anti-development factions were in head-to-head disagreement, and increasing population caused growth pains for the fledgling city and town.

In 1969, a new state law made it possible for two merging municipalities to assume the indebtedness of the other, and that set up a framework for annexation.

Joint city-town committees had been quietly building bridges between the two entities. When the Town Council requested the town's annexation to the city, the City Council accepted the request by resolution. The plan and contract covered assumption of indebtedness, and town employees were to be retained.

The King County Review Board on Boundaries approved annexation on Feb. 26, 1970. Voters of both municipalities would have to ratify it in May.

It looked like a sure yes vote until the *Mercer Island Reporter* pointed out the problem of voter turnout percentages. In the town, 122 yes votes were needed for annexation. But the number of registered voters was just 160, down from 350 because of the transience of apartment dwellers and the exodus from Boeing layoffs. Scarcely 100 town voters had voted in the November election.

> "The two municipalities ultimately will get together. It is obvious that consolidation is the only way this Island can grow as an integrated unit."
>
> —Norine Martin
> *the town's one and only clerk-treasurer since incorporation, speaking in 1969*

Concerned citizens got to work and formed COIN, the Committee for One Island Now. Two long-time businessmen and property owners, Gar Alm and James Crosby, were chairmen, overseeing a dynamic campaign of doorbelling and voter registration.

Their efforts paid off. On May 19, 1970, voter turnout was more than adequate, affirming the town-city merger. At last it was "One Island Now" and forevermore.

Chapter 14: The 1970s and '80s | 121

"Almost every event discussed, researched, voted upon has had two viewpoints: development or conservation. The first is associated with traditional values of building, improving, and using and is supported by the need for jobs and income. The second, recognizing the limited supply of natural things, urges living with and preserving. Fortunately, few Islanders have been apostles of one and blind to the other. The problem for Island leadership has been to strike a balance between the need for development and the newly-recognized necessity to preserve our natural environment. These conflicting claims on our actions have made for an interesting year, and will make for an interesting future."

- Aubrey Davis

as quoted in the Mercer Island Reporter, *April, 1971*

Mercer Island Reporter

The City Council of 1972-'74, left to right: Robert Norton, Amos Wood, Lissa Wells, Ben Werner, Mayor Aubrey Davis, City Manager Don Hitchman, Marguerite Sutherland, Sherman Diamond and Deputy City Clerk Edie Berry.

Preservation vs. development

The perennial push-pull between the forces of preservation and development—which continues today—moved into high gear in the 1970s.

The first showdown was over the Moss-Ralston Plan, named after the creators of the idea, later known as the Greenbelt Plan. The plan was to set aside all the Island's green areas, especially the ravines, gullies and steep slopes, and put them in the public domain as green areas, never to be built upon. But the voters gave a resounding no to the Greenbelt Plan in 1971.

The decade of the 1970s was marked by an interest in ecology and the environment, and a growing sense of community pride. "The year 1970," wrote Peggy Reynolds in the *Mercer Island Reporter*, "should go down in history as the undevelopment year. It means the first clear break with the American ethic, the assumption that building bigger meant building better, and the more we build the better lives we can construct."

Citizens protested mightily against paving over the north end with I-90, against public buildings and against unbridled growth. Previously, people took for granted "the prospect of filling up the Island with homes and humans where eventually the botanical balance of hillsides must be destroyed by bulldozers," (*Mercer Island Reporter*, Dec. 31, 1970). While the Greenbelt Plan failed in the early 1970s, the Gallagher Hill Greenbelt project passed in the 1980s.

In 1969, a group of citizens formed the Committee to Save Pioneer Park, which worked to preserve the Island's largest woodland park. Proposals to convert part of the park to a golf course were defeated.

Out of these efforts, the Mercer Island Environmental Council emerged, with a mission to "create a more effective voice on issues and matters affecting the quality of the environment on Mercer Island."

Its first undertaking was marshaling public opinion on the redesign of Interstate-90, the 14-lane highway slated to cross the Island. Through the decade the

122 | Chapter 14: The 1970s and '80s |

Opened in 1975 by Mercer Island High School's Committee to Save the Earth, the Mercer Island Recycling Center (left) was one of the first to be certified by the state Department of Ecology. It established Mercer Island as a state leader in recycling and waste reduction.

In the 1960s and 1980s, there were proposals to build a golf course in Pioneer Park, below. They ended when the park was put into the Open Space Conservancy Trust in 1992.

Mercer Island Reporter

group continued to be a watchdog and lobbyist for many city ordinances.

The voices of many people had changed the decade from "undevelopment" to "planned development." The Mercer Island Environmental Council disbanded after the city enacted environmental ordinances.

City government responded to the environmentalist attitude by adopting several ordinances to protect the natural resources and preserve the wooded character of the Island. City Council ordinances regulated private development, protected steep slopes subject to slides and erosion, watercourses, shorelines and trees to a reasonable extent, and required fairly large lots in residential areas.

These protective measures became increasingly necessary as the shortage of building lots led to construction on lots that earlier had been thought unbuildable.

Recycling Center

Construction of the Recycling Center at the corner of Mercerdale Field came long before the general public realized the critical need for reducing waste.

It came about through the pioneering efforts of a small group of Mercer Island High School students, members of the Committee

Honorees at the Mercerversary Celebration in 1985 include, left to right, Anna Matheson, Marienne "Nuky" Fellows and Judy Gellatly. Mayor Fred Jarrett and Mercerversary Committee member James Crosby look on. The new, six-lane I-90 floating bridge opened in 1989, during Jim Horn's tenure as mayor of Mercer Island (right).

Mercer Island Reporter

Mercer Island Reporter

Historic Conestogas lead the parade on the new I-90 on June 7, 1989, in celebration of Washington state's Centennial celebration. Washington was admitted to the Union on Nov. 11, 1889, with the signature of President Benjamin Harrison.

to Save the Earth, led by their longtime adviser Harry Leavitt.

They spent more than three years raising money for the new center, and on opening day, Sept. 15, 1975, Islanders lined up with glass bottles, newspapers and cardboard boxes to recycle. This continued for 35 years.

The Mercer Island Recycling Center was one of the first to be certified by the state Department of Ecology. In 1976, then-Gov. Dan Evans awarded the committee the state's Environmental Excellence Award. Over the years, the center generated considerable revenue for the high school.

In mid-1989, 14 years after the center started, the City Council adopted an Island-wide recycling plan. Starting in October 1989, separated household waste was picked up at Islanders' homes. A drop-off recycling program at Shorewood Apartments was one of the first of its kind in the state.

As participation in the curbside program increased, the need for the recycling center decreased. The school district closed it on Feb. 28, 2010. Mercer Islanders currently divert more than 60 percent of their household waste through the curbside recycling and yard waste programs.

Celebrations

Three big community-wide celebrations during the '70s and '80s marked national, state and local occasions, pulling the community together in a spirit of friendship and fun.

The Bicentennial celebration of 200 years since the nation's founding in 1776 was like one of the old-time all-Island events that involved most residents. The organization began in May 1974 when the City Council named Amos Wood as liaison and Ruth Fricke as chair. The group formed committees, gathered donations and sold a Mercer Island Bicentennial medallion.

The work of the Heritage Committee resulted in the publication of the first local history book, *Mercer Island, the First 100 Years*, by Judy Gellatly.

124 | Chapter 14: The 1970s and '80s |

The central business district in 1971 looking north, with downtown Bellevue at the upper right. Bisecting horizontally is the old I-90. Luther Burbank Park is on the right, the old parental school property having been purchased in 1968 by King County for use as a park. Prominent north-south streets are 78th Avenue Southeast (left) and 80th Avenue Southeast.

Mercer Island Reporter

The Festival Committee pulled out all the stops for a big Memorial Day parade, the biggest ever on the Island, with floats, marching bands, drill teams, military units, mounted paraders, vintage cars and motorcycle stuntmen. The two-hour parade had 72 units, and the celebration included an air show.

On Sunday, July 4, Islanders joined in the nationwide bell ringing at 11 a.m. and churches held special commemorative services. In the evening, a community concert at Luther Burbank Park was followed by a big street dance planned by the Jaycees.

The third part of the festival, on Monday, July 5, was a revival of MercerFair, including a children's parade, races, games with prizes, skydivers, hot-air balloon rides, rocketry, booths, a carnival and music by Dixieland and German bands. The grand finale of the birthday festival was a large fireworks display organized by the Kiwanis Club.

The Horizon Committee presented an idea for a small city park with a plaza and a flagpole suitable for ceremonies and gatherings as well as individual enjoyment. The result was Bicentennial Park, at Southeast 32nd Street and 77th Avenue Southeast, on land contributed jointly by the city and the school district. It was dedicated on July 4, 1976.

In 1985, to celebrate the 25th anniversary of the city's incorporation, Mercer Island threw itself a big community party, dubbed Mercerversary. The Island birthday bash on July 13 and 14, organized by chairman Hunter Simpson, included parades, tennis tournaments, fireworks, concerts, aerial stunts, tours of historic houses and landmarks by bus and boat, and even Frisbee-throwing contests. An auction raised several thousand dollars to create the Mercer Island Community Fund, dedicated to community enhancement.

The first Mercerversary recognized 19 outstanding citizens for their work to enhance the community: Philip and Lola Deane, Aubrey Davis, Ben Werner, George Clarke, Cleve Anschell, Tom and Ginny Barto, Gerry Prince, Alfred Fleury, Anna Matheson, Judy Gellatly, Marienne "Nuky" Fellows, Fay Whitney, Tom Gibbons, Holly Broom, David Stiles, Steven Miller and Kelly Goto.

On July 7 to 9, 1989, about 25,000 people, the largest crowd ever assembled on Mercer Island, participated in the Island's celebration of Washington state's centennial. The theme was "Bridging a Century", the chair of local events was Nan Hutchins.

Mercer Island chose a fitting venue, a "Bash on the Bridge." Many events took place on the old floating bridge, which had been taken out of service a few weeks earlier when traffic was routed to the new floating bridge. Dozens of events were staged on the bridge, ending in a dance and fireworks on Saturday night.

There was an auction to ben-

Poll worker Barbara Blackburn works on cross-stitch during a lull at the polls on an election day in 1989. For decades neighbors caught up with each other at the polling places. In-person voting ended in 2009 when King County went to voting by mail only.

Mercer Island Reporter

efit the Mercer Island Community Fund, a tennis tournament, a fishing derby, a historic bus tour, boat tours, games for kids and much more — all organized and executed by volunteers.

A Sunday-evening concert ended a busy weekend marking the birthday of Washington state.

Organizing the young city

The 1970s and 1980s were maturing years for the young city government and the community as a whole. The city assumed major new responsibilities, strengthened other functions and overcame crippling financial restrictions.

During these decades, the city:

• Negotiated the final I-90 highway design and more than 100 agreements with the state to minimize adverse impacts on the Island.
• Developed the Community Center at Mercer View.
• Organized Youth Services (now Youth and Family Services).
• Purchased additional open space and park lands and made major improvements in the parks system.
• Strengthened police and fire services.
• Acquired and renovated the building at 9611 S.E. 36th Street (formerly Farmers Insurance) to serve as City Hall
• Built maintenance and storage facilities on the 9611 property.
• Enacted basic ordinances governing residential and commercial development to protect the envi-

1962 Mercer Island Presbyterian Church, designed by architect Paul Thiry, is built.

1963 Albert Rossellini cuts the ribbon on Aug. 28 to open the Albert D. Rossellini Memorial Evergreen Point Floating Bridge—the second Lake Washington floating bridge.

1964 Mercer Island citizens pass a bond issue to purchase the "University properties," three 40-acre sections of woodland now called Pioneer Park. The land had been privately owned until 1931, when Mrs. Maude Walker-Ames willed the property to the University of Washington.

1964 Mayfair Department Store opens in Islandia Center. Ship & Shore blouses sell for $5; men's dress shoes are $14.50.

1964 The Town Council passes an ordinance that effectively prevents more gas stations from opening. There are 19 gas stations on the Island.

1965 The Mercer Island Preschool Association holds the first Circus McGurkus.

1965 The Mercer Island Police Department has 15 employees.

1965 Luther Burbank School for Boys is closed.

1966 The Mercer Island School District administration building is constructed.

1967 Ed Pepple becomes the basketball coach at Mercer Island High School.

1967 Mercer Island Visual Arts League holds the first Summer Arts Festival.

1967 The Beautification Committee is formed, funded by business and occupation taxes enacted by the Town Council.

Mercer Island Reporter
A long line of cars at the Texaco station in 1979 shows the effects of the energy crisis on Mercer Island.

Mercer Island Reporter
Mercer Island Youth & Family Services staff in 1988 are, left to right back row: Kirsten Taylor and Nan Henderson; middle row: Louise Haslund, director Peg Morgan, Peggy Hiatt and Mary Kay Morgan; front, Gloria Shigeno. The organization expanded its role from youth services to youth and family services in 1987.

ronment and preserve the woodsy character of the Island.
• Augmented library services run by the Island and formulated plans for replacing the inadequate library building.
• Acquired and consolidated independent water and sewer districts (except for Mercercrest water district).
• Improved roads and the water and sewer systems.
• Developed master plans for major capital facilities to guide future developments.
• Established a program for senior citizens and greatly expanded other recreational and leisure programs.
• Organized the Arts Council and established a Design Commission.
• Adopted a curbside waste-recycling plan.

Community Center

In 1980, the city developed the highly popular Community Center in the then-vacant Mercer View Elementary School, which it leased from the school district.

"The thing was an enormous gamble," said the late Larry Rose in 1994, about his years as city manager. "We didn't have any money. For the first year, we couldn't even pay the school district. The city cobbled together $84,000—an enormous sum in those days—to repair electricity and plumbing before moving in. We went for broke and then held our breath," he said. "It was far more successful than we had ever dared hope for."

The Community Center at Mercer View became the meeting place for the City Council and city boards and commissions and for dozens of groups: Weight Watchers, Trout Unlimited, Kiwanis, Probus, the Historical Society and many more.

It was the center for the senior citizen program and the numerous classes conducted by the city's Parks and Recreation Department. The Mercer Island Arts Council developed a busy art gallery in its halls. Numerous other events, concerts and community celebrations happened there.

> We went for broke and then held our breath.... "It [the community center] was far more successful than we had ever dared hope for."
> —City Manager Larry Rose
> *speaking of the city's decision to lease the old school for a community center*

Mercer Island Reporter
The former Mercer View Elementary School became the Community Center at Mercer View when the city leased the building in 1980. It served as the community center until the new Mercer Island Community and Events Center was built in 2000.

By 1989, about 100,000 people a year attended or participated in activities conducted at the center.

Youth Services

In 1973, a committee of community leaders urged the City Council to better meet the needs of youths on the Island, especially those seeking employment, needing foster homes or requiring counseling after run-ins with the law. The City Council appointed a Youth Services Board (later named the Youth and Family Services Board) to launch and oversee these social service programs, headed by Peg Morgan, who was hired as director in August 1973.

In 1975, Youth Services formally became a city department. In the following years, Morgan organized a staff of counselors and volunteers to help youths with substance abuse, self-esteem and family problems. In cooperation with the school district, the R & R Place was established at Mercer Island High School, serving as a resource and referral program to counsel students and provide information on such subjects as drugs, suicide, depression and AIDS.

Jobline helped about 300 students a year find temporary jobs ranging from babysitting to lawn work to computer operations. The agency started a drug prevention program in 1985 and hired a specialist to help the community fight drugs through such activities as the "Just Say No" program and the annual Walk Against Drugs. A volunteer group called Chemical People also addressed the Island's growing issues with teenage alcohol and substance abuse.

The city had always provided some of the funds for the department, but other sources were essential. Annual fundraising drives in the community raised considerable money, and service clubs, the school district and foundations made important contributions.

A monthly fundraising garage sale operating out of the garage of the original Youth and Family Services building, a little house on Sunset Highway near Island Crest Way, eventually evolved into the Mercer Island Youth and Family Services Thrift Shop. It has grown over the years to be a phenomenally successful venture, raising nearly $1 million a year for MIYFS.

Accent on the Arts

In forming the Arts Council in 1983, the city of Mercer Island took a major step to encourage and promote arts in the community. The Arts Council, a city advisory board made up of volunteers appoiinted by the mayor, sponsored major artistic events and also assisted others in their artistic enterprises.

The Arts Council sought grants from the King County Arts Commission and other sources to supplement funds provided by the city.

The Arts Council sponsored a series of free summer outdoor concerts appealing to every taste, from classical to rock. In 1988, there were 10 such concerts, which drew hundreds of listeners. Many came with picnic suppers, thermos bottles, lawn chairs and blankets to enhance their enjoyment. This was the genesis of the highly successful Mostly Music in the Park summer concert series, which continue to draw thousands of spectators each summer.

For a number of years, the Arts Council also sponsored a winter concert series and a "Community Spotlight" in November, in which a dozen or more groups or individ-

The Winner:

The Island of Mercer, it's true
Like Ireland is greenish in hue
We boast fresh clean air,
Tall trees—but be fair!
Come see it and say "Isle of View."

For nearly 30 years, readers of the *Mercer Island Reporter* enjoyed sketches, illustrations, editorial cartoons—and occasional humorous essays—by longtime Island resident and artist Andrea Lorig. The center sketch includes one of the winning entries in the *Mercer Island Reporter's* annual limerick contest. Old-timers also remember Lorig, as one of the original owners of Island Books & More, where her sketches often appeared in the shop wndow.

Andrea Lorig

Mercer Island Reporter

In the mid-1980s, there were long and sometimes bitter battles over where City Hall should be located: at Mercerdale or the former headquarters of Farmers New World Life. The voters chose the Farmers site by a narrow margin, and the building renovation was completed in 1989. Sharing the ribbon-cutting duties are City Council members, left to right, Hunter Simpson, Elliott Newman, Fred Jarrett, Al Huhs, Mayor Jim Horn, Nan Hutchins and Bob Coe.

uals danced, sang, enacted plays, performed magic and otherwise entertained hundreds of people on a single evening.

The Arts Council's art gallery in the Community Center features rotating art exhibits by local, regional and even nationally known artists. Artwork includes all types of media. A prestigious international poster exhibit attracted widespread acclaim in 1985.

Public Safety

The city consolidated police and fire functions into the Department of Public Safety in 1975, under the direction of Jan Deveny, previously chief of police.

In the Police Division, Mercer Island initiated the CrimeStoppers program in 1982, the second such program in the state. A few years later, King County, Seattle and other neighboring cities followed suit and then worked together in a cooperative effort.

Mercer Island was the first in the state to adopt the DARE (Drug Abuse Resistance Education) program conducted in the local schools by a police officer. The department formed a dive team and a marine patrol unit to increase safety for boating, swimming, and other water-related activities in Lake Washington.

Mercer Island was one of the first cities in the nation to establish a 911 emergency telephone service in 1972. Another decade passed before a countywide service was established.

In the Fire Division, Mercer Island expanded fire prevention, protection and first aid activities. In 1984, it purchased new fire trucks and first-aid vehicles, and trained all fire personnel as emergency medical technicians to enable them to provide quality first aid. They were equipped with heart defibrillators and other state-of-the-art equipment. In 1985, first-aid calls outnumbered fire calls by nearly a three-to-one ratio—747 to 272.

Parks and Open Space

Excellent playfields, spacious parks, and undeveloped open spaces owned by the city contributed significantly to the prized quality of life. Mercer Island acquired much of its parkland and open space in the 1970s and '80s.

The city owned 253 acres of parks and open space in 1989. In addition, King County owned and operated Luther Burbank Park, the 72-acre park on the northeast section of the Island. Luther Burbank had several thousand feet of waterfront and extensive recreational facilities.

Major park acquisitions and developments in subsequent years included the purchase of 17 acres of wooded open space on First Hill in 1979; development of lighted playfields at Island Crest Park and Islander Middle School in 1983; the purchase of seven acres of open space on Gallagher Hill in 1988; and development of several street ends on the western shoreline. In 1983, the city acquired the 12-acre Mercerdale site from the school district after it was declared surplus property.

Bond issues approved by Islanders financed most of the land and park projects, but federal and state funds, which were available for such purposes in the 1970s,

130 | Chapter 14: The 1970s and '80s

This photo, from about 1976, before the giant highway project began to transform the Island, shows Interstate 90 crossing the north end, with one of the Shorewood Apartment buildings above.

Mercer Island Reporter

financed some. Altogether, the voters approved bond issues totaling about $5 million for park acquisitions and improvements.

Other bond proposals for lands and parks failed despite receiving a majority of the votes cast. In those cases, a 60 percent favorable vote was required. A 1976 proposal in the amount of $2.9 million for parks, including a golf course on the South 40, also failed to garner a 60 percent majority.

Later, a proposal for the city to buy some of the surplus school properties, including part of the South 40 and the East Seattle School, failed, as did a proposal for a bike path around the Island.

Land swaps

From the beginning, the City of Mercer Island lacked sufficient land to accommodate its essential facilities. That prompted the city to move quickly in 1979 to acquire an office building and 14 acres of land from the Farmers New World Life Insurance Company. Located at 9611 SE 36th Street, the insurance company land was traded for city land in the central business district, where the company later built its headquarters. The former Farmers building, subsequently known as the 9611 building, was donated to the city.

Land at 9611 was needed for city shops and maintenance facilities, since I-90 construction across the Island was about to displace the previous shops. The 9611 land was virtually the only place on the Island suitable for such a purpose. When that site became available, the city constructed its needed facilities there.

The city also needed a site for a new City Hall. City staff was squeezed into rented space in Shorewood Apartments. Staff members improvised as best they could, using bathtubs and kitchen cabinets for document storage, remodeling a bedroom to serve as a holding cell for prisoners and devising other schemes to get by.

When the 9611 building was acquired, most city officials thought it feasible to remodel and renovate it to serve as City Hall. After more was learned about the condition of the building, some thought it better to build a new building on the Mercerdale site. Toward that end, the 9611 building and land not needed for maintenance were traded to the school district for the 12-acre Mercerdale site adjacent to the central business district in 1983.

1967 The Mercer Island Saddle Club is organized by a handful of dedicated horse enthusiasts.

1967 Sen. George Clarke ends his 22-year tenure on the Mercer Island School Board.

1968 Groveland Park is dedicated.

1969 Camp Tarywood is sold to the Mercer Island School District.

1969 King County purchases the Luther Burbank School and property, which becomes a regional park.

1970 The population of Mercer Island is 19,819; the median home value is $41,500.

1970 The Town of Mercer Island and the City of Mercer Island merge.

1970 Phase one of the Jewish Community Center, with a swimming pool, gym, auditorium, locker rooms, men's health club, nursery school, club rooms, lounge and offices, is built. Phase two is completed in 1981. The name is changed to the Samuel and Althea Jewish Community Center of Greater Seattle in 1982.

1970 Teacher Fran Call starts Cyclemates.

1970 Herzl Congregation merges with Congregation Ner Tamid to become Herzl-Ner Tamid Conservative Congregation and moves to Mercer Island.

1970 Mercer Island United Church of Christ is built.

1970 Islanders vote no on a parks measure known as the Greenbelt Plan, which would have put all remaining green areas, especially gullies, ravines, steep slopes and forests, into the public domain.

1971 Country Village Day School opens in the basement of the Methodist Church.

1970 Sunnybeam School opens in the former Lakeview School.

1972 Mercer Island Free and Accepted Masons of Washington is established.

Chapter 14: The 1970s and '80s | 131

Mercer Island Reporter

I-90 construction was a dusty, noisy part of life during the late 80s and early 90s. This view of "the pit" shows summer construction activity, looking east during July, 1987.

I-90: The trials and triumphs

Roads crossing the north end of the Island began in 1890, to connect C.C. Calkins' resort on the west side waterfront to his home on the northeast corner of the Island.

About 1914 a second east-to-west crossing joined segments of the "boulevard" (now known as North, East, and West Mercer Ways). It was a primitive road. Even as late as the 1930s, Islanders found it easier to row a boat from one landing to another than to struggle with that miserable roadway.

Hence, there was rejoicing in 1930 when another road was completed. The well-paved, road had highway access to the outside world via the East Channel Bridge. The Sunset Highway was likewise greeted with approval in 1940 because it provided a connection to Seattle via the new floating bridge.

By contrast, the next highway proposal in the 1960s for a grandiose expansion of Interstate-90 was met with vehement protests.

That plan called for 14 lanes of concrete and as many as four additional lanes for convenience and access roads. Much of it was to be on 50-foot stilts. In places it would have been wider than a football field is long. The Island essentially would have been cut in two; dozens of homes and business buildings would have been swept from its path; the noise and the smells of the traffic and the ugliness of the elevated monster would have been hard to swallow. Islanders held dozens of protest meetings, wrote critical editorials, and circulated petitions opposing the plans.

> "We don't want to see I-90, we don't want to hear I-90, and we don't want to smell I-90."
>
> **Aubrey Davis, mayor**
> *Expessing the view of the City Council and the volunteer I-90 committee*

Aubrey Davis, mayor of the newly unified city, and Ben Werner, who succeeded him, led the protest. They were strongly supported by successive City Councils and by a volunteer I-90 committee. The protest movement was successful; the State agreed to redesign the project.

Then followed decades of delays. In fact, it was nearly 40 years from preliminary planning to completion of construction. The planning started in the mid-1950s; the first designs were completed in 1963; but major construction did not start until 1982 and was not completed until 1992. Finishing details took a couple of years more.

While the project was stalled, the highway across the Island and the floating bridge became a death trap with its overloading, its hazardous peak-hour reversible lane, and "the bulge," an engineering safety snag. More than 6,200 cars per hour at busy times made the situation a commuter's nightmare.

Local protests over the elevated, 14-lane configuration caused some delay. But, by 1971 the State had redesigned the project, and the authorities of Mercer Island had approved the modified plans, which provided for a 4-2T-4 lane configuration (four westbound lanes, two transit and car pool lanes, and four eastbound lanes). Construction could not proceed, however, because of lawsuits designed to kill the project brought by anti-freeway groups.

Mercer Island Reporter

This view of I-90 looking west in 1987 shows the construction of the on- and off-ramp tunnels for Island Crest Way.

It was not until 1979 that the last suit was settled and the last legal roadblock removed. Monuments to the lawsuits were "ramps to nowhere," overpasses cut off in mid-air in Seattle, which stagnated for over a decade until legal challenges were overcome.

Disputes among neighboring cities over the plans for I-90 caused further delays. In particular, Seattle fought vigorously to scale down the project. Gov. Dan Evans was not willing to give the green light to the project until Seattle, King County, Bellevue, Mercer Island, and the Highway Commission agreed on a plan.

A compromise was reached in 1976 among these authorities, but Mercer Island had to a pay a price. It had to agree to reduce the scope to a 3-2T-3 configuration and thus lose the exclusive Mercer Island lanes. The governor was then willing to proceed, but financial uncertainties and time consumed by yet another redesign delayed major construction until 1982.

The first step was to make the old highway safer. The deadly bulge in the floating bridge was removed and additional lanes added on the Island, making it possible to install jersey barriers while still leaving room for two westbound lanes, two eastbound lanes, and two reversible express lanes in the middle. These improvements sharply decreased the accident rate. Then, work began on the new lanes. It was a gigantic and complicated construction job made even more complex by the necessity of keeping the traffic moving while construction was underway.

It was also a financial behemoth. Stretching from Eastgate to Seattle, a total of 6.9 miles, it cost about $1.5 billion, that is, more than $200 million per mile and nearly $40,000 per lineal foot. It was reputedly the most costly highway construction job underway in the nation.

Why was it so costly? Because it was no ordinary highway construction job. In addition to the eight lanes it included the three-level tunnel through Mount Baker, the floating bridge to the west, and two bridges to the east.

It has long lids both in Seattle and Mercer Island and required an excavated trench 20 to 40 feet deep on the Island. The lids on the Island total more than a half a mile in length. The west side lid in the First Hill area is 2,900 feet long, and constructing it was likened to building two Columbia Towers horizontally end to end.

Excavation for the project involved removal of about 5.5 million cubic yards of dirt from the corridor. The amount of concrete was enough to build a two-lane highway from Mercer Island to the California border.

As the mammoth job of construction went on, Islanders had to put up with the noise and dust, detours and road closures, and, for some, the pain of displaced homes and businesses. But the nuisances of construction would have been markedly worse if the State Department of Transportation had not taken Herculean measures to mitigate the adverse impacts of construction.

> **Constructing the First Hill lid was like building two Columbia Towers horizontally end to end.**

The project added a heavy burden to the work of the City Council and City staff. More than 100 agreements had to be worked out with the State for replacements of water and sewer lines, routing of construction traffic, zoning of state-acquired land, reimbursements to the City for expenses caused by construction activity, and more.

Part of the promise of I-90 was fulfilled in June 1989 when traffic was switched to the westbound lanes. Construction was far from complete, however. The old highway across the Island still had to be ripped out to make room for the new eastbound lanes. There were three more years of heavy construction ahead.

But by the end of the 1980s the result was "some of the most innovative miles of freeway in the country," according to the *Mercer Island Reporter* (May 31, 1989).

The new westbound lanes also were tangible evidence of unprecedented cooperation between highway builders and a community severely impacted by the highway. The enormous project then was meeting or beating time and budget targets.

But that did not settle the site issue. A long and sometimes bitter battle ensued between those who wanted City Hall at 9611 and those who wanted it at Mercerdale. It took an election to settle the issue. The voters chose the 9611 building by a vote of 630 to 596, a margin of just 34 votes.

That action made it necessary for the city to buy the 9611 property back from the school district. In the same election the voters approved by a wider margin the levying of $4,979,000 over the ensuing 20 years to cover the cost of acquiring City Hall and renovating the 9611 building.

Renovation of the 9611 building was completed in early 1989. On moving day in mid-May of that year, staff members found themselves for the first time in adequate and attractive office and police facilities. For the first time also the city had a well-designed room for City Council meetings and meetings of city boards and commissions.

Other city acquisitions of surplus school properties included Secret Park and a building on the southeast corner of Mercerdale, which had formerly been the Mercerdale Island Club and then the Mercer Island Boys & Girls Club. The city turned it into the Mercer Island Youth and Family Services Thrift Shop. In that prominent location the Thrift Shop substantially increased the funds it raises to help finance the Youth and Family Services department.

Mercer Island Reporter
This 1979 photo looks north along 78th Avenue Southeast.

Mercer Island Reporter
Taken in the mid-1970s, this photo looks west up Southeast 27th Street.

Improving finances

In the early years, the city government was financially strapped. Its revenue per capita was one of the lowest in the state, partly because it was a bedroom city lacking heavy industry and large shopping malls to generate substantial sales tax revenues.

A limit on property tax assessments imposed by the state added to its financial difficulties. The lid prevented the city from collecting property taxes in one year greater than 106 percent of the amount collected in the previous year (except for taxes on new construction) unless expressly approved by a majority of the voters. In a period of double-digit inflation, a 6 percent increase was crippling.

Two events provided significant relief. The voters in 1979 approved indexing the tax lid, which allowed collection of much-needed additional property tax revenue. The second relief measure came in 1982 in the form of state sales tax legislation, permitting the city to increase the local sales tax levy.

It also provided for an equalization fund from which the city received state funds to compensate partially for its unusually low sales tax revenue. With this additional financial elbow room, the city was able to provide the services that helped make it a more mature city.

The CBD

The central business district (CBD) was a sore point with Islanders from the beginning—not just because they considered it an eyesore, but because it was deficient in other ways. Not until 1980 did the city have complete jurisdiction

134 | Chapter 14: The 1970s and '80s

Mercer Island Reporter

Crosby Row was the name given to this group of shops on 80th Avenue Southeast at about Southeast 28th Street. James Crosby's gift shop was to the left of this view.

Mercer Island Reporter

This photo from the early 1980s looks north above the central business district. The street on the lower right is 78th Avenue Southeast. The large building in the center is Mercer Island Lumber, which was torn down in 1985.

Mercer Island Reporter

Safeway operated at 76th Avenue Southeast for decades, until it closed in April 1993. The building was leased by Plantscaping for a number of years, then was vacant until it was demolished in 2011 to make way for the Aviara mixed-use development.

over the CBD. During the 1960s, the town was in charge, and during the 1970s a successor organization, the Community Council, had veto power over any city action relating to land use in the CBD.

After 1980, the city tried to find solutions to the CBD's problems, as did numerous members of the business community. Consultants provided advice and citizen groups offered recommendations, but the underlying problems seemed intractable.

Existing businesses served only a fraction of Islanders' needs. There were grocery stores, gas stations, drugstores, barber and beauty shops, and specialty shops, but no department stores, general clothing stores or home-appliance stores. The CBD was stymied, as were many towns elsewhere, by the development

The issue that received the most attention was building heights.

of huge shopping centers nearby. There was not enough local business to support department stores that could serve as magnets for customers for their own establishments and for smaller neighboring shops as well.

The CBD was criticized for not being pedestrian friendly. The stores were so scattered that most customers found it inconvenient to walk from store to store.

On the bright side, efforts to make the CBD more attractive achieved some success. The contrast between the old and the new was vividly described by Peggy Reynolds, editor of the *Mercer Island Reporter*: "The place was a horror of unplanned traffic patterns, garish high signs and wires, and uninterrupted concrete, not to speak of potholes large enough to swallow small animals. Now utilities have been undergrounded and mature sycamores and maples line the streets.

Chapter 14: The 1970s and '80s | 135

Mercer Island Reporter

This 1989 photo looks west across the north end of the central business district, with Island Crest Way in the foreground.

Shrubbery obscures some of the asphalt, design controls have resulted in tasteful new buildings and subtle signings and most of the high signs have come down. While it still has a ways to go, the center is much improved." *(Reporter*, June 28, 1985)

Prompted by councilmember Marguerite Sutherland in the late 1970s, and others in the next decade, the city gradually made improvements in the CBD: colorful flower beds were planted in the median strips; trees were lighted during the winter holidays; flower baskets and banners were hung on light poles in other seasons.

In 1986 and 1987, the city launched a major effort to make progress on CBD problems. It significantly modified design standards for new construction, such as architectural features, plazas, landscaping and fountains. The changes were intended to make the area more pedestrian friendly and improve its general appearance.

By far, the issue that received most attention was building heights. Proposals for eight-story buildings along the

> "Downtown Mercer Island was a horror of unplanned traffic patterns, garish high signs and wires, and uninterrupted concrete, not to speak of potholes large enough to swallow small animals."
>
> - Peggy Reynolds
> *editor of the Mercer Island Reporter*

I-90 corridor provoked considerable community opposition. Islanders were concerned about view blockage, crowding and traffic congestion. Opponents contended that the CBD should give priority to serving the main need of the Island, which was for more retail stores. They argued that such stores usually were housed in low buildings; hence, the Island did not need tall office buildings. Tall buildings would drive up land prices and retail rents, thus making it harder for retailers to survive. they said.

But others argued that the only way to attract investors who could make significant improvements in the CBD was to allow higher buildings. There was also objection to proposals for dividing the CBD into various zones with regard to building heights.

The sharp differences of opinion in the community on these issues were mirrored in the City Council. In late 1987, the council, by a four-to-three vote, imposed a height limitation of two stories (with some technical exceptions) for the entire CBD and rejected proposals that would treat one part of the CBD differently from other parts. Some council members regarded this action as a temporary measure until a better solution could be devised.

The council reconsidered the issue in early 1988 but made no change. Instead, it decided to support Project Renaissance (initially called the Main Street program). It was a joint effort of merchants, city representatives, and other interested citizens to find ways of improving the CBD. The work of Project Renaissance was to come to fruition in the next decade.

Mercer Island Reporter

In this 1982 photo, Mercer Island kids play pinball at the Video Arcade, located on Southeast 76th Avenue and Sunset Highway. At one point during the '80s, there were three video arcades on the Island.

Owen Blauman collection

This photo shows Southeast 24th Street at 76th Avenue Southeast looking east in 1982.

1973 Island Books & More opens.

1974 The Calkins Water Tower burns down.

1974 Temple B'nai Torah opens, in a building designed by architect David Gray.

1974 The Mercer Island Thrift Shop begins, in the garage of the little white brick Youth Services building at the north end.

1975 Mercer Island High School's Committee to Save the Earth opens the Mercer Island Recycling Center in downtown Mercer Island.

1975 Mercer Island Swim Club at Mercerdale closes.

1975 Utilities in the central business district are put underground.

1975 *Ladies Home Journal* names Mercer Island the second most livable suburb in its July 24 issue.

1976 Bicentennial Park is dedicated.

1976 Banks advertise 9 percent loans; median home price is $62,500.

1976 Mercer Island School District population is 5,236.

1977 Temple B'nai Torah is destroyed by arson.

1977 Little Skandia sauna parlor closes after several years of legal difficulties.

1978 Craig Currie becomes superintendent of the Mercer Island School District.

1978 The Welcome Wagon becomes the Mercer Island Women's Club.

1980 Mercer Island Boys & Girls Club moves into the former East Seattle School.

1980 Beth Bland is elected the Island's first woman mayor.

Chapter 14: The 1970s and '80s | 137

Mercerdale Park

Mercer Island Reporter, Judy Leithe
Skateboarder Ryan Healy gets some air in the skateboard park at Mercerdale Park in this 1994 photo. The skateboard facility came about through the City Council's response to petitions for a park from a persistent, well-organized group of teens. At left is the veterans' pergola, installed by the Arts Council to honor veterans of all wars. It has become the centerpiece of the park and the stage for concerts and other activities.

From stump-filled swamp to urban jewel

In the beginning it was a swamp, dotted with tree stumps and referred to as Devil's Hollow by children who played nearby.

Then it was filled and leveled and became prime real estate, bounded by businesses, offices, residences and woods. It was dubbed Mercerdale.

The Mercer Island School District purchased Mercerdale in 1956 to serve as a school site. But enrollment declined and it was not needed for a school.

So for decades it was Mercer Island's empty lot, used mainly for baseball, soccer and Fourth of July fireworks displays. It was a scruffy, unkempt square with rough playfields and lots of potential.

Then the controversies began. The school district proposed changing its zoning from "for public use only" to "commercial" and selling it for private development. The voters objected and the city declined to change its zoning.

From the beginning, city leaders, planners, consultants and citizen groups too numerous to count wanted Mercerdale field developed as a civic center. A federal Economic Development Association grant was sought but not approved. The community was too affluent to qualify, it was said.

A decade passed. The school district traded Mercerdale to the city for the 9611 building on the frontage road of I-90. The city prepared long-range plans for a civic center at Mercerdale. A design competition yielded more detailed proposals and the people were asked for comments. The comments were loud and clear—and mostly negative.

Then plans were curtailed. It was proposed by some that only City Hall be built on Mercerdale. Then the controversy focused not on the need for City Hall but on its location. Should City Hall be located at Mercerdale? Or at the 9611 building? The community was divided, and so was the City Council. An election 1987 narrowly decided the issue, and the 9611 building became City Hall.

Since then, the 12.1-acre Mercerdale Park has become a much-loved, well-used park in downtown Mercer Island, with an open lawn encircled by a paved footpath. The Mercer Island Preschool Association raised money to construct a children's play area in the southeast corner, and a skateboard park attracts teens. What was formerly a swim club and then the home of the Boys & Girls Club became the vibrant Youth and Family Services Thrift Shop.

A Veterans Recognition Project organized by the Arts Council and executed by artist Richard Frombach was dedicated in 2005. This pergola structure provides a popular gathering place and a focal point for Mostly Music in the Park summer concerts and other community events.

For decades the Cat in the Hat was the personification of Circus McGurkus, the Dr. Seuss-inspired annual carnival sponsored by the Mercer Island Preschool Association. Because of licensing issues, the event lives on simply as Circus, one of the longest-running events on the Island.

Mercer Island Reporter

The Ties That Bind

Clubs and organizations are the heart of the community

Even more than 150 years ago on Mercer Island, groups formed for common purposes—to help each other build the community, to lobby for better services, to talk politics, to amuse themselves, to enrich their children and more.

Susan Blake, a longtime Islander who has served on the city council, school board and the historical society, says, "Volunteerism is the backbone of Mercer Island, from its earliest times, when work parties cleared land and built clubhouses to now, when foundations raise funds for worthy causes and help preserve our core values." Some flourished for a time and disappeared, such as the early "improvement clubs," the Badminton Club or the Straw Hat Summer Theatre.

Other organizations survived and have left lasting imprints on the community.

Earliest clubs

On Sept. 19, 1928, women interested in supporting Children's Orthopedic Hospital organized the **Mercer Island Orthopedic Guild,** later renamed the **Children's Hospital Guild.** It was the first such guild on the Eastside. The women would collect clothing for the thrift shop; salvage tin foil, tires and metal for the Melting Pot; hem diapers and linens for the Corner Cupboard Shop; and collect money for the annual penny drive.

But when World War II began, the local guild took on a new project. Warren Upper, an enterprising high school student, had been printing on his home press a list of Island residents and telephone numbers, which he sold to make spending money. When he left for the war, he turned the project over to the Mercer Island Orthopedic Guild.

The guild's first directory, in 1943, contained not only the 200 telephone subscribers but also all of the residents of the Island, regardless of whether they had phones.

The guild has been producing its familiar Mercer Island directory ever since, deriving funds from voluntary contributions for the directory and advertising sales. Since its beginning, the guild has raised millions of dollars for Children's Hospital. Islanders still look forward to guessing what color the directory cover will be each year.

The **Chamber of Commerce**, established in December 1946, grew out of early efforts to incorporate Mercer Island.

According to Al Fleury, the chamber's first secretary, the chamber was primarily to promote incorporation, but even after that effort failed, the chamber continued to further develop the community. It promoted the development of the business center in the pasture and swamp where the current Town Center exists, rather than in East Seattle..

Although it was active and growing — it had 85 members in 1955 — the chamber had no office until the 1980s, when it used a corner of the former Seafirst Bank (now Bank of America). Before that, chamber records were kept in volunteers' homes, or in the trunk of the car of longtime director Delores Erchinger.

In 2012, the office on Southeast 27th Street in the Town Center has become the hub of information for events and happenings on the Island, under longtime director Terry Moreman. The chamber not only promotes Mercer Island as a special place to live, work and play, it also provides business and demographic information and serves as a visitor center.

After the end of World War II, some 30 veterans activated the charter for the **Veterans of Foreign Wars (VFW) Post 5760** on Mercer Island on March 11, 1948. Having "served honorably in the Army, Navy and Marine Corps… in foreign wars of the United States of America," they solidified the relationship between local veterans and the citizens of Mercer Island. In 1966, the post

The May 12, 1949, issue of the *Overlake Outlook* newspaper (above) has a feature on the Mercer Island Orthopedic Guild, which was founded in 1928.

Members of the Veterans of Foreign Wars Post 5760 (center) lead the Summer Celebration parade in 2010. Veterans are, left to right, Bob Harper, Bob Brahm and Gary Winterstein.

Phil Flash, below, longtime member and president of the Mercer Island Historical Society, points to the photo of a ferry on a newly installed educational marker at the former Roanoke ferry dock on the north end of the Island.

Mercer Island Reporter

140 | Chapter 15: The Ties That Bind

Mercer Island Reporter

Runners gather at the starting line in the 1990 Mercer Island Rotary Half Marathon, a major Island event and fundraiser that plows proceeds back into community programs.

Mercer Island Reporter

Left to right, Lions Club veterans Bob Knoll, Sam Lake and Leo Anderson get ready to work in 1995 in the Lions Club's Christmas tree lot, the group's annual fundraiser.

Mercer Island Reporter

Dr. Michael Copass, longtime Islander and legendary developer of the Medic One program, speaks at a Kiwanis Club luncheon in the 1990s.

purchased the Mercer Island Community Club (formerly the Keewaydin Club, built in 1922) and remodeled it extensively, restoring and improving the building and its facilities. The hall is used for VFW activities and rented to other social and community groups. In 2005, the domed pergola at Mercerdale Park, entitled "Standing Strong to Honor the Service of our Veterans," was dedicated to Mercer Island veterans.

After the war

Many key organizations formed in the 1950s and '60s after the post-war boom. In 1954, before there was a city or a town to chronicle, the **Mercer Island Historical Society** was established to preserve the heritage of what members recognized as a very special place. The group collected early memorabilia from Island residents and displayed them on special occasions. As from its beginnings, it continues to host programs on Mercer Island history.

The Historical Society published *Mercer Island, the First 100 Years* in 1977 as a result of activities marking the American Bicentennial; it published a revision of that book, *Mercer Island Heritage,* in 1989. Also in that year, it established a meeting room, office and archive space in a room in the basement of City Hall. Recent efforts, spearheaded by its co-presidents Phil Flash and Susan Blake, include marking historic places on the Island with educational displays or brass markers, and publishing a revised history.

The **Lions Club** was chartered in 1955 to focus on community service and helping those with impaired vision or hearing. For more than 30 years, the Lions Club has sold Christmas trees to support its various philanthropies.

The **Kiwanis Club**, established on the Island in 1960, concen-

Chapter 15: The Ties That Bind | 141

Mercer Island Reporter

Members of the Mercer Island Orthopedic Guild, (l-r) Pat Schaumberg, Celia Burton, Harriet Shrontz and Harriet Wolfe, display the new 1986 directories. Later renamed the Mercer Island Guild of Children's Hospital and Regional Medical Center, the guild has been producing the directory as a fundraiser since 1943.

trates its philanthropic efforts on children and youths. Kiwanians have raised funds from selling fireworks for the Fourth of July, selling shaved ice at Summer Celebration and raising the U.S. flag on national holidays at subscribing Island businesses.

The largest service organization, **Rotary Club**, founded on the Island in 1963, supports youth and social service activities on Mercer Island. For many decades the Rotary Club has recognized two outstanding Mercer Island High School students with its Rotary Girl/Boy of the Month award. The Rotary's biggest annual event is its Half Marathon run and walk, which attracts 4,000 to 5,000 participants and raises funds for colon cancer research and other local projects. One of its goals worldwide is to eradicate polio.

The **Mercer Island Visual Arts League** (MIVAL) was organized in 1961 by a group of Island artists and supporters to promote and encourage artistic endeavors on Mercer Island, stimulate appreciation of the visual arts and sponsor art exhibits and workshops. Its first arts and crafts show was part of the 1963 MercerFair.

In 1967, it founded the Summer Arts Festival, first held in a geodesic dome at the shopping center. That festival grew into the Mercer Island Arts and Crafts Fair, held on the grounds of the Community Center at Mercer View. It became so popular that it outgrew the site and MIVAL's limited cadre of volunteers. By 1990, the Arts and Crafts Fair morphed into Summer Celebration, hosted by the city of Mercer Island. MIVAL continues its involvement in Summer Celebration through its Junior Art Show.

Over the years, MIVAL has sponsored scholarships for high school students, given grants to various organizations and donated art to Mercer Island. In 2010, MIVAL opened a new gallery in the Avellino building on Southeast 78th Street.

In 1963, 10 women started the **Mercer Island Welcome Wagon**, dedicated to welcoming families who had just moved to the Island. The group flourished and increased in membership. In fact, the word was that it was so much fun that women didn't want to leave when they were no longer newcomers. So, in 1981, it morphed into the **Mercer Island Women's Club**, and opened membership to all women living on the Island. Now, with more than 300 members, it's the largest organization on the Island. Its motto is "Friendship Starts Here."

The **Saddle Club** is a vestige of the Island's rural past, when roads were few and horses were the preferred transportation. It was organized in about 1967 by a handful of horse enthusiasts, with dues of $1 per month. Two outdoor rings were surrounded by a simple pole fence.

In 1969, the Saddle Club signed an agreement with the South End Community Club (now known as the Pioneer Park Youth Club) and the Mercer Island Country Club agreeing to the construction of a 20-stall barn. Three years later, they built the barn, cook shack, jump shed/judge's stand. In 1988, with money from donations, the club built an indoor arena and, with recycled concrete from the I-90 project, repaired drainage problems and improved the site. Today it's not uncommon to see teenagers riding their horses on the trails of Pioneer Park or along south Island Crest Way.

The **Mercer Island Community Fund** was born at the Mercerversary celebration of 1985, when the Island pulled out all the stops for a gala party marking the city's 25th birthday. Part of the

142 | Chapter 15: The Ties That Bind

Fran Call: The legend behind the '-mates'

Call her *Miss* Call. Variously described as a drill sergeant, a tough-as-nails teacher and, sometimes, a teddy bear, Fran Call is a Mercer Island treasure, the creator of the storied Cyclemates, Solemates, and Trailmates.

Always an outdoor enthusiast, Call taught history and outdoor fitness to junior high and middle school students on Mercer Island for 26 years. In June 1970 she took a group of students on a two-month-long bicycle trip from Mercer Island to New York City. That was the beginning of the legendary Cyclemates, 13- to 15-year-old students who were "careful, courteous, capable and determined" enough for the challenge of a once-in-a-lifetime trip led by Miss Call.

There was no sag wagon; each cyclist pedaled his or her own gear. They learned to pitch tents, find church basements to sleep in when the weather was bad, buy groceries on a budget, pick up mail at general delivery, repair flat tires and *never* walk up a hill.

Cyclemates II rode from the Island to Washington, D.C., and met President Richard Nixon at the White House. Cyclemates III rode 4,000 miles to Halifax, Nova Scotia. Cyclemates IV rode to historic Williamsburg, Va. in the summer of 1976 to mark the country's bicentennial. And so it went for 22 summers.

When Call retired, in 1993, she began leading 3- to 4-mile walks for seniors in Seattle and suburban neighborhoods. She began with a handful of people; now 40-some Solemates walk with her on Wednesdays from September through May. Call was honored for her contribution to the community with the 2011 Flash Family Inspirational Award. She was named the 2012 Mercer Island Citizen of the Year.

Cyclemates III rode their bikes to Halifax, Nova Scotia, in 1972.

Mercer Island Reporter

Fran Call, above right. Above left, members of Cyclemates III gather 37 years after their memorable cross-country ride. At left, Trailmates is a group of senior hikers who follow Call on twice-monthly hikes. Below are Solemates who go with Call on weekly 3- to 4-mile walks.

Fran Call

Chapter 15: The Ties That Bind | 143

1980 Farmers New World Life breaks ground on the site of a former bowling alley.

1980 The city opens a community center in the old Mercer View Elementary School building, leasing the property from the school district.

1980 Mercer Island's median home price soars to $180,000.

1980 The south end fire station is staffed on a full-time basis.

1981 The Mercer Island Schools Foundation is established.

1981 Opening of the new East Channel Bridge—70 feet high to allow passage of pleasure boats.

1981 The Mercer Island Welcome Wagon changes its name to the Mercer Island Women's Club.

1981 The infamous "bulge" on the I-90 floating bridge is removed in September.

1983 Mercer Crest Elementary School closes due to declining enrollment.

1983 Lynn Oliver, the Island's first female fire chief, is hired.

1984 Mary Wayte wins Olympic gold for swimming, and the Island honors her by renaming the pool for her.

1984 Mercer Island Thrift Shop moves to a building at the edge of Mercerdale Park, formerly the Boys & Girls Club building, and before that Mercerdale Island Club.

1985 Wilma Smith becomes superintendent of Mercer Island schools.

1985 The 11-member Arts Council becomes an official advisory board to the Mercer Island City Council.

1985 A six-story office building, Island Office Plaza, is planned for an empty lot next to Safeway. It is the tallest building on the Island.

Mercer Island Reporter

In 1988, Peter Donaldson, director of Youth Theatre Northwest, and Denis Baskin, chairman of the board, consult about the space at the former North Mercer Junior High, which they turned into the home of YTN.

celebration involved an oral auction, which raised several thousand dollars — what became the seed money for the Mercer Island Community Fund, the brainchild of longtime community activist Lola Deane.

The Community Fund awards grants to support community goals in the areas of social welfare, arts and culture, recreation, health, the environment, education, community development and other charitable needs.

Focus on Youth

Some of the earliest organizations were focused on children. There have been Boy Scout groups on the Island since 1919, and Girl Scouts and Camp Fire since the early '20s.

The matriarch of kid-centered organizations is the **Mercer Island Preschool Association**, founded by Katharine MacGilvra in 1937 as a private volunteer group to enhance the lives of Mercer Island children from newborn through kindergarten. In the 1940s, MIPA started two nursery school programs, established the first cooperative preschool on the Island and was instrumental in bringing kindergarten to Island elementary schools.

MIPA was a strong force in bringing a library to the Island in 1945. Members donated time and talent to create the Mercer Island Children's Park, later named Deane's Children's Park after Lola and Philip Deane. In 2000, MIPA raised much of the money to build, in partnership with the city, the children's playground in Mercerdale Park. MIPA is an affiliate of the state PTA, and has been a fertile training ground for future PTA members and officers.

Its annual events for kids, Circus (formerly Circus McGurkus), Toy Swap and Halloween Party, are legendary, involving armies of volunteers.

The **Mercer Island Boys & Girls Club** opened in 1969 as a small organization housed in the Guild Hall on West Mercer Way and Southeast 27th Street. After a few years, the club moved to a state-owned house located in the site currently occupied by the park-and-ride lot. In 1975, it launched a capital campaign to purchase what is now the Mercer Island Youth and Fam-

144 | Chapter 15: The Ties That Bind

Mercer Island Reporter

Cheryl Falk, above, directs the Mercer Island Children's Choir in this 1980s photo. John Nelson, below, addresses members of the Probus Club of Mercer Island in this 1990s photo in the old Community Center at Mercer View.

ily Services Thrift Shop.

When the club began to outgrow the building, the board began a dialogue with the school district to lease or buy the East Seattle School. It leased the building in 1982, and two years later traded properties with the school district and received a donation of $250,000 from Ann Dulien for the mortgage of the East Seattle School. The historic building served as its headquarters and clubhouse for nearly 30 years. A new gym was added to the building in 1999.

In 2005 the club announced plans to move from the East Seattle School building, which it deemed too old and too small for its purposes. It sold the property in October 2007 to Island resident Michael O'Brien for $6 million.

After a four-year capital campaign and numerous meetings with city officials and neighbors, the club built a new home, PEAK (Providing Empowering Activities for Kids), on school district property at the North Mercer campus near the district's transportation center on 86th Avenue Southeast. The $16 million project opened in July 2010.

With the slogan "A Positive Place for Kids," the club provides sports programs, activities, special events, summer camps and child care for about 2,000 Island school-age children.

The **Mercer Island Children's Choir** was started in 1976 under the direction of Rae Mulholland to train young voices and provide performance experience for girls in the fourth through sixth grades.

Cheryl Falk became the director of the Children's Choir in 1983 and also started Island Sound, for girls ages 13 to 18, in 1990 and later the Prep Choir, for children in second through fourth grades.

Since then, the three choirs comprising Island Choral Experience have touched the lives of thousands of Island youths.

Youth Theatre Northwest began in 1984 and has been at the forefront of providing quality theatre "for kids and by kids." Founded and nurtured by Peter Donaldson, it became known for its enthusiastic performances, dynamic storytelling, high-quality productions and creative opportunities for students.

It found a home in the former North Mercer Junior High building on Southeast 40th Street, and then undertook a major renovation of the facility.

In addition to the performances it mounts, YTN offers a wide range of classes and programs for children ages 3 to 18. Since its beginning, YTN has produced more than 181 plays for more than 150,000 people.

YTN is pondering a new location because of potential school district needs for North Campus.

Leslie Rosen founded the Evergreen Chapter of the **National Charity League** in 1990. The organization of mothers and their daughters in grades 7 through 12 fosters a sense of community responsibility through charitable, cultural and educational endeavors.

The Island's focus on education led to the formation of strong **Parent Teacher Associations (PTAs)** in Island schools. Reflecting the times, the PTAs in the early decades were largely women's groups that put on bake sales to help support the schools.

Today the PTAs are powerful organizations of parents that lobby for legislation in Olympia, provide enrichment programs for students, sponsor parenting classes in the community and purchase equipment and supplies for the schools.

Over the years a number of other organizations for kids have sprung up, such as **Indian Prin-**

Chapter 15: The Ties That Bind | 145

The *Mercer Island Reporter*, the Island's newspaper of record since 1954, has undergone a number of facelifts through the years.

Mercer Island Reporter

Newspapers foster community spirit

It is often said that newspapers are the first draft of history. Newspapers recount the big events and headline news, announce weddings, births, deaths and the myriad events that make up people's lives.

Mercer Island's earliest recorded newspaper was the semimonthly *Mercer Island News,* published by Frank Nolan in the 1910s. A copy dated 1911 was found in the wall of a house being remodeled in the East Seattle area in the '70s. The *Livewire News* was published briefly by George and Hap Lightfoot around 1919. The *Mercer Island Journal* was published around 1927 by south end developer E.M. Greenwood. During the first years of World War II, Jack Cassidy published the *Livewire Mercer Island News*. From 1949 through 1953, a Seattle resident, Wilfred "Jack" Genack, who had a son living on Mercer Island, published the weekly *Mercer Islander*. Jack Genack was a retired Chicago newspaperman who liked "to keep his hand in."

The *Mercer Island Reporter,* today's weekly Mercer Island newspaper, was founded in 1954 by Fred M. Bassetti, father of Seattle architect Fred F. Bassetti. Affectionately called "F.M.B.," Bassetti senior was an Italian immigrant who had published an Italian-language newspaper from a press in Rainier Valley. By the 1950s, most members of Seattle's Italian community preferred to read newspapers in English. To keep his press busy, F.M.B. started several community newspapers; only the *Mercer Island Reporter* survives.

The "office" for the early *Mercer Island Reporter* was a dropbox outside Chick's Shoes in Tabit Square. In the florid style of the era, the newspaper reported in minute detail the news of the day: who attended a ladies' coffee,

> The "office" for the early *Mercer Island Reporter* was a dropbox outside Chick's Shoes in Tabit Square.

the current opinions on incorporation or other issues, who was in town visiting whom, what the bride and wedding party wore at a recent wedding.

F.M.B., who had supported all-Island incorporation, was not to see the new City or Town. He died at 73, in the closing hours of 1960.

In 1961, three Island residents, Sydney Abrams, Alec Bayless and Virginia Barto, pooled $1,200 and bought the Mercer Island Reporter. They converted the tabloid to a broadsheet format, and Barto became the manager.

Immediately, two competitors appeared: the *Mercer Island Observer,* a short-lived publication of the Chamber of Commerce; and the *Mercer Island American,* launched by Bellevue American owners Bruce Helberg and C.B. Lafromboise. In July 1961, the *American* and the *Reporter* merged. The *American* dropped from the flag the next year, but Abrams and Bayless remained on the masthead until 1964. Bayless said he, Abrams and Barto each received $1 for their shares, and retired from the scene.

Mercer Island Reporter editor Dorothy McKnight and later Lee Lathrop published the newspaper until 1967, when Peggy Reynolds became editor and then publisher, a job she held for 18 years. In 1976, Lafromboise and Helberg sold their interest in the Reporter to John McClelland of the Longview Publishing Company.

Under Reynolds' leadership the newspaper grew in circulation and size in the late 1970s and early 1980s. The *Reporter* was a consistent winner in state press association "general excellence" competitions, and garnered numerous citations for news, features, editorials, photography and community service. Longtime editors under Reynolds included Liz Schensted, Sharon Wooten and Teresa Wippel.

In 1986, the Persis Corporation of Honolulu bought Longview Publishing, including the Reporter and the Journal-American. Reynolds left the Reporter and later helped start a short-lived monthly, *Mercer Islander*.

Persis combined the *Reporter*'s business and advertising operation with that of the *Journal-American*, and the increased Eastside advertising gave Mercer Island its largest newspaper ever, despite the loss of many major advertisers to preprinted inserts and direct mail. Liz Enbysk became editor (1986-1988), followed by Virginia Smyth (1988–1992) and then Jane Meyer (Brahm) (1992-2004). The newspaper and its reporters continued to garner numerous awards for journalism excellence.

The *Reporter* changed hands again in 1994, when Persis sold the *King County Journal* (formerly the *Journal American*) and its six weeklies to Horvitz Newspapers, a family-owned newspaper group out of Ohio. When Brahm retired in 2004, she was succeeded by Steve Weigand (2004-2005) and Mary Grady (2005-present).

The decade was the beginning of a difficult time for newspapers all over the country, as the Internet be-

Dave Ekren / Mercer Island Reporter

Mercer Island Reporter staff in 1978: (clockwise from bottom left) Sally York Brown, Linda Floyd, Dave Adams, LaVonne Ekren, Dave Mack, Peggy Reynolds, Carole Wright, Shelley Grimes, Ed Russell, Susan Winike; in the center, Nancy Gould Hilliard and, behind her, Charlotte Steiner. Editor Liz Schensted is not pictured.

gan attracting readers and advertisers away from print media. In 2006, Peter Horvitz, owner and publisher of the *Reporter*, sold his 10-newspaper group to Sound Publications, a subsidiary of a Canadian company, the Black Press Group of Victoria, British Columbia. The newspaper changed from a broadsheet to a tabloid format the following year.

Meanwhile, an online local newspaper, *Patch*, owned and operated by AOL, was introduced on Mercer Island in 2010.

Traditional newspapers, online publications, blogs and other social media are fragmenting the market and competing for readers and viewers, yet people's interest in their community and their need for information continues. Time will tell how the market will evolve.

Chapter 15: The Ties That Bind | 147

Free samples are a treat at the Mercer Island Farmers Market, a popular Sunday happening which began in 2008. It was one of the new initiatives spawned by Island Vision, an organization focusing on sustainabillity.

Joel Wachs

cesses and **Indian Guides,** science clubs and chess clubs, as well as various booster clubs to support various youth activities.

Changing priorities

As the Island has changed, so have its organizations. The creation of the **Senior Foundation of Mercer Island** reflects an aging population, where the average age in 2010 was 47. It supports such things as the adult daycare program, clinics, van transportation, geriatric counseling and social functions. The **Strivers** was started by John Rose and others in 1994 to help senior citizens improve their lives with a healthy diet, exercise and other techniques.

The **Probus Club** of Mercer Island, founded in 1988, is an organization of retired and semiretired business and professional people that meets monthly for fellowship and programs of general interest. Today, with about 250 members, Probus of Mercer Island is one of the largest Probus clubs in the U.S. and has an active year-round schedule of meetings, social events and field trips.

"Going green" has spawned a variety of groups with a focus on preserving the environment and showing citizens how to use less energy, protect and preserve our waters and reduce the use of fossil fuels. The **Mercer Island Open Space Conservancy Trust** was established by ordinance on Feb. 10, 1992, to protect and preserve open-space properties. The 113-acre forest of Pioneer Park is managed by the Conservancy Trust and as such is protected from development in perpetuity.

Friends of Luther Burbank Park is a group dedicated to preserving the beauty of the park and its shorelines and wildlife.

The **Ivy Brigade** is a group of dedicated volunteers who hold regular work parties to pull destructive ivy from the Douglas firs and other trees in Pioneer Park and other Island parks and open spaces.

People interested in achieving sustainability on Mercer Island established **Island Vision** in 2005. They worked with the Planning Commission and City Council to establish sustainability as a core community value in the city's comprehensive plan and partnered with the city in creating the annual Leap for Green sustainability fair.

They joined a consortium of citizens groups in the region focusing on sustainability, and served to incubate the Mercer Island Farmers Market, which started in 2008.

The Island took on a more global focus with the establishment of the **Mercer Island Sister City Association** in 2000, when Mercer Island and Thonon-les-Bains, France, signed an official agreement establishing their relationship as sister cities.

Thonon-les-Bains is a city of about 32,000 on the shores of Lake Geneva in the Haute Savoie region of France.

The Mercer Island Sister City Association sponsors direct student exchanges, with Island students staying in the homes of students in France, and then hosting the French students on Mercer Island the following year. MISCA also organizes adult delegations to Thonon, and hosts events related to French culture, arts, athletics, government and trade.

Mercer Island is a member of Sister Cities International, a global citizen-diplomacy network whose mission is to promote peace through mutual respect, understanding and cooperation — one individual and one community at a time.

The Island has also spawned numerous special-interest groups, such as the **Classical Music Supporters**, the **Mercer Island Radio Operators**, **Special Olympics** and dozens of sports, cultural and arts groups. Support groups deal with disease, age, divorce and loss. Some protect the Island's horses, birds, dogs, raccoons, beavers and others in the plant and animal kingdoms,

In 2012, there were 250 nonprofit organizations on the Island — and no doubt many more that have not incorporated.

They provide a rich resource of people who care about their community and who give their time and talents to enrich life on the Island.

Mercer Island has had a strong interdenominational Clergy Association for decades. This 1978 photo of the seventh annual Thanksgiving Eve service, sponsored by the Mercer Island Interfaith Union, shows, left to right, Rabbi Jacob Singer, Temple B'nai Torah; the Rev. James Fergin, Redeemer Lutheran Church; Rabbi Maurice Pomerantz, Herzl-Ner Tamid; the Rev. Finley Cooper, Emmanuel Episcopal; the Rev. Robert Haertig, MI United Church of Christ; the Rev. Riley Jensen, MI Presbyterian Church; and the Rev. Roger Barnard, MI Baptist Church.

Mercer Island Reporter

Communities of Faith

United in helping the local community and the larger region

In the beginning the joke was that "All Mercer Islanders are Episcopalians."

That's because Emmanuel Episcopal Church was the first religious congregation established on the Island, in 1909, and it remained the only one until 1929. Moreover, for years its Guild Hall building was a community center for the Island, hosting the Island's library, scout meetings, plays and numerous other events and activities.

Emmanuel Episcopal

The earliest days of Emmanuel are recounted in Chapter 5. Its second phase began on Jan. 12, 1956, when the church purchased for $25,000 the five acres that Emmanuel now occupies at 4400 86th Ave. SE. The congregation selected the architectural firm of Waldron & Dietz, and a contract was let for $168,000 for the new church and Christian education building. Groundbreaking for the new church was May 18, 1958. Emmanuel put on a big centennial celebration in the summer of 2010. The current rector is Hunt Priest.

Christian Science

During the 1920s, Christian Science services were held at various homes. Attendance increased, and the Christian Science Society of Mercer Island was organized and chartered in 1929, with 31 charter members. Services were held in the Keewaydin Clubhouse. Later, Sunday school was added. In the fall of 1933, the church purchased a building site on Summit Street (now 70th Avenue Southeast) near Thompson Avenue (now Southeast 24th Street) and members cleared the virgin timber and prepared the site. In December 1933, they held services in the new "little white church," an authentic copy of an early New England colonial church. Today the building, substantially enlarged, belongs to the Mercer Island United Methodist Church. The First Church of Christ, Scientist, is now located at Southeast 47th Street and Island Crest Way.

Holy Trinity Lutheran

Not until 1947 did another church locate on Mercer Island. A minister sent by the Lutheran Board of American Missions to visit every Island family found enough interest to start services in the Keewaydin Clubhouse. Eighty members formally organized Holy Trinity Lutheran Church in January 1948. The group grew, raised money for a building and constructed a small brick church, later used as a chapel, at Southeast 40th Street and

Chapter 16: Communities of Faith | 149

University of Washington

Emmanuel Episcopal Church in 1960.

Mercer Island Reporter

The "little white church" on First Hill first housed the Christian Science church. Mercer Island United Methodist Church held its first service there in 1962.

Mercer Island Reporter

This 1980s photo shows St. Monica School children in the annual Christmas pageant. St. Monica Catholic Church opened in 1960. The interior of the church was remodeled by the Rev. John Bowman in the mid-2000s.

86th Avenue Southeast, on land that had been part of the Lucas farm. They purchased a new parsonage on 86th Avenue Southeast in 1958 for $20,000.

By 1959, the present sanctuary was completed under the Rev. Charles Dion, known as Pastor Chuck. Construction of the education wing began with the rainy-day groundbreaking held on Jan. 19, 1964, and the first Sunday school class was held in the new wing that September. A new atrium project was completed in 1998. The current pastor is the Rev. Deanna Wildermuth.

St. Monica Catholic Church

St. Monica Catholic Church, the largest congregation on the Island, with 1,455 families, occupies 8 acres of land on the highest point on the Island, originally part of the Lucas holdings. The purchase price was $30,000 in 1950. The first Mass was offered in November 1954 in the East Seattle School gymnasium, and the new congregation held services in temporary meeting places in Bellevue and Seattle. By December 1958, the parish had 380 families and a building fund was established.

In June 1959, the land was cleared, and building contracts were signed for a church, a 10-room school and a 10-room convent. The Rev. John Walsh, the first pastor, celebrated the first Mass in the new church a year later, on June 26, 1960.

The school opened in September with 186 students; the 2012 enrollment is about 270.

In 1973, the convent became the permanent rectory after the nuns departed. In 1983, the more than 1,000 families in the parish raised funds for a gift to the whole Island, a carillon, to commemorate the church's 25 years. The Rev. Patrick Freitag became pastor in 2008.

Mercer Island Covenant

In 1949, a small group of Covenant Church members, weary of the trip to Bellevue or Seattle, began meeting in a private home on Mercer Island and conducting Sunday school classes at the VFW Hall (formerly the Keewaydin Clubhouse). Shortly afterward, they erected a small sanctuary on 80th Avenue at Southeast 32nd Street, and in 1967 they called the Rev. Bud Palmberg, who served as pastor for 26 years. The church grew rapidly and in 1974 opened a big, new sanctuary just west of the old building, fronting on Southeast 32nd Street. Subsequently, a parish hall has been added as well, to the south of the former sanctuary. Current pastors are Peter Sung, Jim Jansen and Julie Steel.

United Methodist

The Mercer Island United Methodist Church held its first services on Dec. 9, 1962. Dr. L.L. Dunnington, the first pastor of the new congregation, welcomed 115 people to that service, held in the "little white church" on First Hill, the New-England-style building that had been constructed in 1933 as the early home of the Christian Science Church.

The Fellowship Hall was built and dedicated in 1968. During the late '80s, a larger sanctuary was built and a new parsonage was acquired. The current pastor is the Rev. John Chae.

Mercer Island Baptist

The Baptist Church started on the Island in 1959, and was at first a mission church of the Brooklyn Baptist Church in Seattle. At that time there were 13,000 Island residents and four churches. The Baptist congregation held its first meetings at the Keewaydin Clubhouse. In 1961, the church purchased 3.5 acres of property in the middle of the Island above Island Crest Way.

Donna Palmberg

Mercer Island Covenant Church built its Fireside Chapel (above) on the site currently occupied by the post office. It was later moved to its present location at 3200 78th Ave. SE and a lower floor was placed beneath it, as it appears today.

Mercer Island Reporter

Holy Trinity Lutheran Church, circa 1990.

Mercer Island Reporter

The United Church of Christ (Congregational) was completed in 1969 on a woodsy site at 4500 Island Crest Way.

Chapter 16: Communities of Faith | 151

Mercer Island Reporter

The Church of Jesus Christ of Latter-day Saints, at the corner of Southeast 40th Street and Island Crest Way, built in 1991, is the newest church structure on the Island.

Mercer Island Reporter

Herzl-Ner Tamid, the largest and oldest Conservative Jewish congregation in the Seattle area, was dedicated in 1972.

Mercer Island Reporter

Redeemer Lutheran Church is nestled in the trees along Island Crest Way just north of Pioneer Park.

A cottage on the property served as a makeshift sanctuary until 1964, when a new sanctuary was built, largely with volunteer labor. With a shrinking congregation, the Baptist Church closed in 1991. Only 18 congregants cast ballots to merge the church with Eastside Evergreen Church. It sold the building to Northwest Yeshiva High School.

Presbyterian Church

In November 1951, Presbyterian leadership approved assignment of a church on Mercer Island, and a local group nominated the Rev. Clarence Sinclair as the organizing pastor. Regular worship services and Christian education classes began in October 1952 in space rented at Mercer Crest Elementary School. A formal service of organization was held May 24, 1953; 115 charter members participated. They purchased hymnals and folding chairs, obtained a pianist and organized a choir. A full church school program was set in motion; its growth was vigorous, corresponding to the growth of the Island. Double sessions began in 1955.

After study and negotiation, the site committee purchased a 7-acre tract overlooking Lake Washington, on the hill that was part of the Lucas farm. They retained well-known architect Paul Thiry and in 1956 built a dual-purpose sanctuary and fellowship hall, Christian Education Center, administrative wing and kitchen. They broke ground on July 16, 1961, on the new sanctuary, also designed by Thiry.

"Architecturally, ours is a transparent church," wrote former pastor Riley Jensen. "The clear windows remind us that we are part of the world around us."

In 2000, after numerous meetings with neighbors and a three-year fundraising effort, the church undertook a major remodel and expansion project, adding approximately 20,000 square feet to the church facilities, making it the largest religious facility on the Island. The church is led by co-senior pastors Paul Barrett and Sheri Edwards Dalton.

UCC/Congregational Church

In 1963, the Washington North Idaho Conference, United Church of Christ allocated funds and formed a sponsoring committee for its Mercer Island church. Fifteen Islanders formed the committee and held services in Island Park Elementary School. They called the Rev. Jim Gilliom as the first pastor.

Mercer Island United Church of Christ (Congregational) purchased a parcel of land in the 4500 block of Island Crest Way for a church, which was completed in 1969.

The building, designed by Don Frothingham, a Seattle architect and Island resident, extensively used Northwest materials and took advantage of natural lighting, bringing the trees and sky into the sanctuary. It was designed so the sanctuary could be used for a variety of events; the church makes its space available for rental to nonprofit groups.

Over the years membership has ranged from approximately 250 members to around 100 members. The church has had seven pastors since its inception; the current pastor is the Rev. Mark Travis.

Redeemer Lutheran

Redeemer Lutheran Church began with a worship service Oct. 15, 1961, at the South Mercer Island Club, conducted by its first pastor, the Rev. Bernhard Filbert. The fledgling congregation built church facilities on a 5-acre site on Island Crest Way just north of Pioneer Park. They broke ground on the new facility Dec. 9, 1962, and built a new parsonage in 1964.

Redeemer Lutheran became self-supporting with the sale of excess property in April 1977. Five pastors and three interim pastors have led the congregation since it began. The current interim pastor is the Rev. Eugene Baade. The church is known in the community for its annual "Mostly Live" Nativity scene in front of the church at Christmastime.

Mercer Island Presbyterian Church was designed by well-known architect Paul Thiry.

The "Mostly Live" drive-through Nativity (below) has been an annual Christmas event at Redeemer Lutheran Church for decades.

MI Presbyterian Church
Mercer Island Reporter

Latter-Day Saints

The newest church building on the Island, at the corner of Southeast 40th Avenue and Island Crest Way, houses the Mercer Island ward of the Church of Jesus Christ of Latter-day Saints.

The 10,000-square-foot church includes a chapel that seats 270, several classrooms, and a cultural hall/gymnasium with a portable stage for plays. Local architect Don McDonald of Loschky Marquardt and Nesholm designed it. The first worship service was held there in 1991.

Hope of God Church

Hope of God Church, currently New Hope International Church, opened in the former facility of Temple B'nai Torah, at 9170 SE 64th St., after purchasing the property in 1998. The church held services in English and Thai.

The congregation left the Island in May 2012.

The Jewish Community

The estimated number of Jewish residents on Mercer Island is about 4,300, or 20 percent of the Island's population. That would earn Mercer Island the distinction of having the highest percentage of Jewish residents of any municipality in the state. The

Chapter 16: Communities of Faith | 153

Stroum Jewish Community Center: The J

The Jewish Community Center originated in Seattle in 1949. When its leaders decided to build a new facility at the north end of Mercer Island in 1968, this prompted an influx of Jewish population to the Island. Since then the center has become a focal point of Jewish life on the Island and beyond.

The facility includes an auditorium, fitness center, racquetball courts, indoor running track, gymnasium, indoor swimming pool, children's library, kitchen, classrooms, and meeting rooms. Since its start, "the J" has offered a wide spectrum of activities to the general public, not limited to members of the Jewish faith. It offers programs for all ages in areas of social, cultural, and recreational activities.

In 1978, the JCC launched a campaign for a major expansion to double the size of the building; the groundbreaking for the project took place in 1980. The following year the Holocaust Memorial, with a sculpture by well-known Mercer Island artist Gizel Berman, was installed near the entrance.

But by 1982, a financial crisis arose when the JCC was unable to meet its mortgage and construction loan payments. Prominent Seattle businessman Samuel Stroum stepped up and led a vigorous campaign that raised $4 million to "save" the JCC. Afterwards the facility was named the Sam and Althea Stroum Jewish Community Center of Greater Seattle. The SJCC completed a major renovation of its fitness wing in 1998.

More than 10,000 people pass through the doors of the SJCC on Mercer Island each year, and more than 200 children are enrolled in its infant, toddler, preschool, and kindergarten programs.

Museum of History and Industry

The Stroum Jewish Community Center, pictured here in the 1980s, moved to the Island in 1968. Near the entrance is a sculpture by well-known Mercer Island artist Gizel Berman entitled Lo Tishkach, or "Thou Shall Not Forget," in memory of those who died in the Holocaust.

The gym and other sports facilities make the J a popular gathering place.

SJCC

Parenting classes of all kinds are offered at the facility.

SJCC

Little swimmers get ready for a session in the pool. More than 200 children participate in programs for infants, toddlers, preschoolers, and kindergarteners.

SJCC

154 | Chapter 16: Communities of Faith

Members of the Mercer Island Clergy Association in 1993 include, front row, left to right, Bill Clements, Fred Harder, John Bowman, Jean Davis, John Fellows, and David Jackson. Back row, left to right: Al E. Johnson, Paul Fauske, Woody Carlson, Roy Green, Dale Sewall, and Eldon Toll.

Mercer Island Reporter

Jewish Federation of Greater Seattle estimates a total of 35,000 to 40,000 Jews live in the Puget Sound region.

Temple B'nai Torah

In 1970, a reform Jewish congregation was established north of Pioneer Park, on the east side of Island Crest Way. Temple B'nai Torah bought land and completed its building program by 1974. In 1977, in an act that outraged the community, two vandals set fire to the temple. Rabbi Jacob Singer donned fire gear and rushed into the burning building and saved two Torahs, but the temple was completely destroyed. In two years it was rebuilt.

The congregation increased over the years and soon outgrew the building. In 1998, it sold the building to the Hope of God Church of Seattle and built a new 18,750-square-foot building in Bellevue. In May 1998, more than 500 members of the congregation, led by Rabbi James Mirel, said goodbye to Mercer Island and walked together the 10 miles to their new home in Bellevue.

Herzl-Ner Tamid

In the late 1960s, the Herzl congregation of Seattle and the Ner Tamid congregation of Bellevue merged into the Herzl-Ner Tamid Conservative congregation. In 1969, they started to build a small school on East Mercer Way near the East Channel Bridge. Later, the congregation built a modern school and a sanctuary/social hall complex, which was dedicated in 1972. It has a beautiful leaded-glass window visible from I-90.

Herzl is the largest and oldest Conservative congregation in the Seattle area and the only Conservative congregation in suburban Seattle. It draws its members, about 850 families, from all over the region. The synagogue has a vibrant religious school and adult education program; it also runs a Judaica Shop. Rabbi David Rose followed the founding rabbi, Rabbi Maurice Pomerantz. The current rabbi is Rabbi Jay Rosenbaum.

Shevet Achim

In the late 1980s, South Island Jewish Center, a small congregation of Orthodox Jews, was established at the south end of the Island, headed by Dr. Ze'ev Young. Over time the small congregation became Minyan Mizrach. As it continued to grow, it changed its name to Congregation Shevet Achim and in 2000 relocated to Northwest Yeshiva High School, above Island Crest Way at 5017 90th Ave. SE. Now the "Shul on the Rock" has about 70 families in its congregation, led by Rabbi Yechezkel Kornfeld.

Today, Mercer Island has 11 churches, two synagogues and an active clergy association.

Clergy Association

Nobody knows exactly when the Clergy Association began, but the loosely organized group of church leaders gathers occasionally to discuss matters of mutual concern in the community. The Clergy Association has hosted an annual community-wide Thanksgiving service and a baccalaureate service for graduating high school seniors for many decades. It has worked to foster the climate of tolerance and cooperation among faith communities.

Chapter 16: Communities of Faith | 155

1986 Mercer Island Lumber and Ernst Hardware close.

1987 Mercer Island School District population is 3,172.

1987 The Mercer Island Orthopedic Guild produces its first computerized Mercer Island Directory.

1988 Median purchase price for a single-family home is $220,000.

1988 Eastside Minyan, an Orthodox Jewish community, is established on the Island.

1989 The Bash on the Bridge celebrates the state's centennial the weekend of July 7 to 9.

1989 The new City Hall, formerly Farmers New World Life, is dedicated on June 17.

1989 Ronald McDonald comes to the Island for the opening of McDonald's on August 13.

1989 A jet-noise watchdog group forms.

1989 The Mercer Island Community Fund is established.

1990 The Evergreen Chapter of the National Charity League is established on the Island.

1990 Gas station owners predict a gas shortage; average price per gallon is $1.18.

1990 The Boys & Girls Club builds a new gym at its site, the former East Seattle School.

1990 The Lacey V. Murrow Bridge sinks in a storm on Nov. 25, as it is being refurbished.

1990 The annual Mercer Island Visual Arts League Summer Arts Festival moves to downtown Mercer Island.

1990 Schools Superintendent Wilma Smith retires.

1990 The District Court opens in Mercer Island City Hall.

Mercer Island Reporter

Island churches and synagogues minister to the needy locally and around the world. Above, women of St. Monica Parish cook donated food for weekly meals to feed the hungry in Seattle. Below, Tanya Sylvester and retired Pastor Dale Sewall stand by the bulletin board at MI Presbyterian Church which shows highlights of their 1994 trip to Thailand.

156 | Chapter 16: Communities of Faith

Mercer Island Reporter

In 1990, Islanders gather along Island Crest Way to protest a proposed golf club at Pioneer Park. Ultimately, their efforts resulted in the creation of the Open Space Conservancy Trust, a unique trust created to protect the park from development.

The 1990s

Downtown takes shape, the Island gets more parks, and I-90 construction is finally finished

Mercer Island had barely finished celebrating the opening of a new floating bridge in 1989 with the Bash on the Bridge before it had to mark the loss of the original bridge at the beginning of a new decade. After a week of rain and high winds, the Lacey V. Murrow Bridge broke apart and plunged to the bottom of Lake Washington on Nov. 25, 1990.

The 50-year-old, 1.5-mile-long bridge had been undergoing repairs, and a new twin bridge had been constructed parallel to it to handle the increasing traffic on I-90. Before the Thanksgiving holiday, workers for Traylor Bros., of Indiana, had cut holes into the hollow concrete pontoons to facilitate work. But the holes had not been closed before the weekend, which turned out to be particularly stormy.

When the bridge settled low enough, water poured through the holes and it began to sag. One by one, sections of the bridge broke off and sank in 200 feet of water.

By the end of the day, the largest floating structure in the world, Mercer Island's pride, was gone.

Even after a blue-ribbon panel headed by Aubrey Davis and sev-

Mercer Island Reporter

Mercer Island Park Board members and their families (above) volunteer to clean up Island Crest Park in 1993: (left to right) Katie and Bruce Anderson, Jim Pearman, Austin Kuhns, Joe Tom, and Jeff Kuhns.

Chapter 17: The 1990s | 157

1990 The average home price on Mercer Island is $433,000.

1990 After a four-year battle with neighbors, the city opens Slater Park on a west-side waterfront property willed to the city by Harry and Loretta Slater.

1990 Mercer Island nears its goal of 35 percent recycling.

1992 Northwest Yeshiva High School opens with 45 students, in the facility previously owned by Mercer Island Baptist Church.

1992 Schools Superintendent Corey Wentzell is put on leave in February after a budget shortfall of $758,000 is revealed.

1992 Dick Giger becomes interim superintendent of Mercer Island schools.

1992 Mercer Island High School marching band plays in the Rose Bowl Parade.

1992 Mercer Island's first-ever public boat launch opens in May under the East Channel Bridge overpass.

1992 Paul Allen's multi-acre home construction project takes shape.

1993 The new I-90 bridge is dedicated as the Homer M. Hadley Memorial Bridge, honoring the engineer of the original floating bridge, on July 17.

1993 The $73 million replacement Lacey V. Murrow Bridge opens on September 12.

1993 The Mercer Island Police Department begins a bike patrol.

1993 The City Council approves the One Percent for Art ordinance, dedicating 1 percent of the overall cost of each city project to public art.

1993 The Connection, a storefront office for the Mercer Island Parks and Recreation Department, opens to give the city a presence in downtown Mercer Island.

WSDOT; Seattle Post Intelligencer

While it was shut down for repairs, the Lacey V. Murrow Bridge broke apart and sank in stormy weather on Thanksgiving weekend, Nov. 25, 1990. One day later (below), ocean-going tugs steam into the wind, pulling on cables to keep the new bridge aligned after its anchor cables were severed by sinking sections of the old bridge.

eral forensic engineering firms investigated the disaster, questions remained. A $20 million out-of-court settlement resulted between Traylor and the Washington State Department of Transportation.

It was a decade of big storms. A major snowstorm on Jan. 1, 1997, caused more than 1,000 homes on the Island to lose power and a number of carports to collapse. A week later, seven major mudslides caused more than $1 million in damage. News reports described mud flowing like lava into one south-end home.

A unique land trust

Some of the issues that carried over from previous decades were settled in the 1990s. There had been proposals in 1969 and in 1976 to develop a golf course in a portion of Pioneer Park; they were defeated. A third proposal surfaced in 1990, prompting new debate over the destiny of Pioneer Park.

Overflow crowds attended meetings on the issue during the summer of 1990. On Sept. 12, the City Council decided not to put the golf course issue on the ballot, ending an 18-month effort by a citizens' group called FORE.

The subject of a golf course at Pioneer Park was finally laid to rest in 1992, with the creation of the Mercer Island Open Space Conservancy Trust. The trust was unique in that it was a public trust created by a city, and as of 2013, it was still the only trust of its kind in the state. Placed in the trust, Pioneer Park, a

forest refuge with 6.5 miles of trails, was effectively protected from development in perpetuity—all 113 acres of mostly second-growth forest in its natural state.

Over the next few years, the trust developed a Pioneer Park master plan to provide public access while protecting the future of the park. The seven-person Open Space Conservancy Trust board serves under the City Council and meets monthly.

Pioneer Park was the only public land placed into the Open Space Conservancy Trust until fall 2010, when the City Council placed the 7-acre Engstrom Open Space into the trust. This property adjoining Pioneer Park on the east side above East Mercer Way was donated to the city in 2006 by Margaret and Kenneth Quarles. It is named after Margaret's father, Oscar Engstrom.

Shaping downtown

As I-90 construction across the Island wound down, Mercer Islanders learned how to navigate the new on- and off-ramps and the altered landscape at the north end of the Island. The perennial detours and constant presence of flaggers gradually decreased, and residents began to see the lidded I-90 as an asset.

The city, working with the state Department of Transportation, was figuring out what should go on the 84 acres of land it gained on top of the new, lidded freeway. The DOT began auctioning off "turn-back" property and houses no longer needed for right-of-way, with minimum bids ranging from $45,000 to $145,000.

Mercer Island Reporter

Streets in the Town Center were completely redone in the early 1990s. The two-year, $5.1 million street project was funded by federal and state grants and by the city's street fund. Above, Lillian Martin walks along 78th Avenue Southeast in November 1994, shortly after the new swidewalks, benches, and street lamps were installed.

Chapter 17: The 1990s | 159

1993 Safeway closes in April, after 34 years on the Island.

1993 Jack in the Box customers begin returning in June after E. coli incident.

1993 CHILD (Children's Institute for Learning Differences) School opens in August.

1993 Islanders approve annexing the Mercer Island Library to the King County Library System.

1993 The Planning Commission approves a five-story height limit downtown.

1994 Islander Middle School (formerly South Mercer Junior High) is renovated.

1994 Mercer Island Library installs computers hooked up to the Internet.

1994 The Mercer Island Boys & Girls Club celebrates its 25th year.

1994 A permanent off-leash dog area goes in at Luther Burbank Park.

1994 The Park on the Lid opens.

1994 A Mercer Island man is accused of illegally harvesting the underwater forest off the shore of Mercer Island.

1994 The Island's Adopt-a-Park program begins.

1995 King, Pierce, and Snohomish county voters reject a $6.7 billion regional Sound Transit bus and rail plan in March.

1995 The I-90 Sculpture Garden opens.

1995 This is the worst year ever for house fires on Mercer Island.

1995 After a long fundraising effort, the city purchases the *Primavera* sculpture in the I-90 Sculpture Garden for $35,000.

1995 Carol Gilmour, a popular longtime women's clothing boutique in Island Market Square, closes.

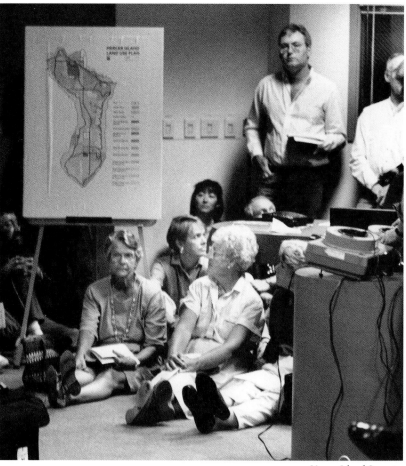

Mercer Island Reporter

Crowded public meetings are the norm when the City tackles thorny land use issues. This 1994 Planning Commission public hearing has standing room only.

A charrette process

Now that there was no more uncertainty about the path of I-90 and most of the construction was over, city planners, developers, and property owners turned their attention to the downtown, which had been languishing for years.

Project Renaissance, under its president Bruce Lorig, was planning how the central business district (CBD) area should develop. In May 1993, the city and Project Renaissance held a five-day charrette, an intensive planning process, bringing together city officials, professional designers, engineers, citizens, interest groups, and business owners to come up with a plan for the downtown. It included a master plan, urban regulations, transportation and parking plan, housing and mixed-use sample projects and financial market feasibility stud-

The state's Growth Management Act stipulated that Mercer Island must accommodate population growth up to 25,000 by 2022.

ies. Metro and Regional Transit Authority (RTA) representatives and engineers also worked on the design of a proposed light-rail station adjacent to the below-grade highway.

It was an intense process in which participants were divided into work groups to tackle specific assignments, using computers, debating options, and drawing on white boards and giant sheets of paper. The idea was that with all the needed information at hand and all the experts and decision makers in the room, they could

160 | Chapter 17: The 1990s

Mercer Island Reporter

Crowds gather at the corner of Mercerdale Park for the lighting of the Christmas tree on the first Friday in December. During the 1990s, it was part of Merchants Munch, organized by the Chamber of Commerce, when shops stayed open late and offered snacks, entertainment, and holiday cheer to the community.

arrive at a good conclusion in a relatively short time.

What they came up with was essentially the road map that guided Town Center development.

One critical aspect of the plan was that it raised allowable building heights in the CBD to a maximum of five stories, and made 78th Avenue Southeast the Island's main street. The goal was to make the downtown area more pedestrian-friendly by locating the buildings along the sidewalks and placing parking behind the buildings. The plan encouraged mixed-use buildings with storefronts or restaurants on the street level and condominiums or apartments in the upper stories.

The plan went hand-in-hand with the statewide Growth Management Act (GMA), passed in 1990 to curb unplanned, uncoordinated growth. The GMA stipulated that, by law, Mercer Island must accommodate up to a population of 25,000 by 2022.

Mercer Island Reporter

A horse-drawn wagon heads west on Southeast 27th Street during Merchants Munch, 1995, the annual holiday event held on the first Friday evening in December.

With most of the Island already zoned and developed with single-family homes, planners decided the only place to funnel growth was in the downtown. They saw development of residential units downtown as a way to comply with the GMA and promote a lively and attractive downtown.

The Town Center Plan garnered

Chapter 17: The 1990s | 161

I-90: A modern marvel

This 1990 aerial photo shows I-90 across Mercer Island looking west.

Mercer Island Reporter

Facts and figures

- The I-90 corridor project was one of the largest, most complex, most expensive and controversial highway construction projects in the world.

- It took 35 years (1957 to 1992) from planning to completion of the 7-mile stretch of roadway.

- The cost of the last 7 miles of I-90 exploded from an $80 million estimate in 1966 to $1.56 billion.

- The final stretch of I-90 cost more than $200 million per mile, or nearly $400,000 per linear foot.

- Ninety percent of the I-90 project was federally funded.

- I-90 was the first freeway project in the state to come under the National Environmental Policy Act of 1969 and be subject to its environmental, social, and economic guidelines.

- The Washington State Department of Transportation (WSDOT) had a staff of 345 for I-90 management.

- One of the biggest challenges of the entire project was getting the work done while keeping traffic flowing on the old roadway.

- For every $1 million committed to the I-90 project, 44 jobs were created.

- The I-90 project involved more than 4,000 workers, the moving of 5.5 million cubic yards of earth, and the use of 53,000 tons of reinforcing steel and 1.1 million cubic yards of concrete.

- The First Hill lid combined tunnel and bridge technology to create the largest structure on Mercer Island, a 3,000-foot three-span bridge. It is 70 feet tall at its highest point.

- It took 2,600 tons of fill material to bury the north and south sides of the lid, in addition to the tons of topsoil that went on top of it.

- So much stainless steel was used in the control room of the I-90 lid that it affected the worldwide price of steel.

- At its peak, 165 electricians were employed to wire the lid's systems.

- There is someone at work in the control room of the I-90 Lid at all times, keeping an eye on traffic.

- Hidden beneath tennis courts and softball fields, there is a honeycomb of long ventilation shafts, workshops for WSDOT, and a control room.

- On peak shifts, up to a dozen people work inside the tunnel, cleaning and maintaining equipment and monitoring the roadway.

- Before the I-90 Lid was finished, Bill Southern, public affairs officer for WSDOT, organized tours for more than 10,000 people. There was worldwide interest in the project.

- Because there were no alternative sites for highway expansion, utility corridors carrying the city of Seattle's water and power had to be moved.

Mercer Island Reporter

Former mayors of Mercer Island Ben Werner, left, and Aubrey Davis spent years negotiating the design of I-90 and the agreement that solo drivers may use the I-90 high occupancy vehicle (HOV) reversible express lanes between downtown Mercer Island and Rainier Avenue South in Seattle. In this 1994 photo, Werner and Davis stand above the new center roadway that just opened.

Concept to concrete, I-90 spans 35 years

1957: The Washington State Department of Highways starts engineering studies for location and design of the I-90 freeway.

1960: Reversible lanes implemented to ease traffic during peak hours.

1963: The I-90 corridor is selected, just to the north of U.S. 10 (known as Sunset Highway) crossing Mercer Island, and is approved by the Federal Highway Administration.

1964: Construction begins on the interchange connecting I-90 with I-5.

1966: Construction begins on the Factoria exchange connecting I-90 with I-405.

1968: A task force commissioned to reevaluate lane requirements recommends a 10-lane facility consisting of four lanes in each direction and two exclusive transit lanes (4-2T-4) in addition to the existing four-lane facility, totaling 14 lanes.

1969: A community outreach program is initiated to provide residents near the project with up-to-date information.

1969: Construction begins on a new East Channel Bridge.

1970: Construction on the East Channel Bridge is halted in response to public concerns over environmental issues and lane arrangements for the entire roadway.

1971: A second design team is formed to redesign I-90 across Mercer Island.

1971: The design team plan is presented: a 4-2-4 lane configuration with center lanes to be reserved for exclusive use of transit.

1971: The 9th U.S. Circuit Court of Appeals grants an injunction against further construction on I-90.

1973: The 9th U.S. Circuit Court of Appeals upholds a previous District Court ruling that the Environmental Impact Statement (EIS) is inadequate.

1974: Gov. Dan Evans appoints a 10-member committee to develop a solution to the I-90 impasse.

1976: Testimony at hearings makes it clear that serious disagreements on I-90 persist among Seattle, Mercer Island, Bellevue, and King County. The governor appoints a two-person mediation team to determine if agreement can be reached.

1976: A memorandum of agreement is signed by Seattle, Mercer Island, Bellevue, King County, and Metro and the highway commission recording a consensus on a basic 3-2T-3 lane arrangement for I-90. To compensate for the loss of Mercer Island–only lanes, Mercer Island negotiates that solo drivers be allowed on the center roadway. between Island Crest Way and Rainier Avenue South.

1977: The final Environmental Impact Statement, incorporating the 3-2T-3 configuration, is filed with the Federal Highway Administration.

1979: Construction resumes on the East Channel Bridge.

1981: Half of the East Channel Bridge opens to traffic. The "bulge," or drawbridge portion of the floating bridge that allowed ships to pass through, is removed.

1983: Construction begins on the interim roadway, walls, tunnel, and lids across Mercer Island. The first pontoon for the bridge is floated through the Ballard Locks. Boring begins on the new Mount Baker tunnel.

1984: The six-lane interim roadway on the Island opens.

1985: Excavation for the new roadway, an average of 30 feet below grade, begins on the Island.

1985: Work begins to add five more lanes on the south side of the East Channel Bridge.

1987: Construction begins on the westbound and center roadways section of the First Hill lid.

1987: Construction costs reach $1 million per day.

1988: The south half of the new East Channel Bridge opens to traffic.

1989: Traffic is switched over from the old roadway to the new floating bridge.

1990: Part of the old I-90 floating bridge, closed for refurbishing, sinks in a Thanksgiving weekend storm.

1991: Fast-track construction replaces most of the pontoon sections of the old bridge.

1992: The eastbound I-90 lanes open, with a two-day celebration and ribbon-cutting ceremony.

164 | Chapter 17: The 1990s

A final section of the floating bridge is moved into place in 1992. The old bridge sank in the Thanksgiving weekend storm of 1990 while it was undergoing repairs.

Washington State Department of Transportation

This 1989 photo shows newly installed landscaping in the Park on the Lid. The city gained acres of property over I-90 to be used as park and recreation areas. After the death of Aubrey Davis in 2013, the park was named for him, honoring the man largely responsible for the configuration of I-90 across the Island.
Mercer Island Reporter

Chapter 17: The 1990s | 165

Mercer Island Reporter

Longtime Island residents Henry and Loretta Slater willed their west-side waterfront property to the city of Mercer Island. It prompted years of controversy, as many neighbors didn't want the property turned onto a park. This photo, from 1987, shows pro-park people putting flowers and signs on the chain-link fence that surrounded the property. Slater Park, in the 2800 block of 60th Avenue Southeast, opened in 1990.

much attention when it was completed in November 1994. It was not without critics, as some people complained that they wanted to be able to drive right up to the front of a store and park, and they didn't want Mercer Island to become "another Factoria."

In fact, the Town Center Plan sat on a shelf for years, waiting for the economic climate to change to make it feasible for developers to invest in Mercer Island.

Improving streets

Meanwhile, there was new disruption downtown. Taking advantage of available state and federal money to help pay for it, the city launched a major downtown street project, with the planning process beginning in 1990. New streets and utilities, sidewalks, street lamps, benches, and lights were installed, in the most expensive public works project undertaken to date by Mercer Island city government.

The ribbon-cutting ceremony in November 1994 marked the end of the two-year project. The cost was $5.1 million, with $2.3 million from a federal grant, $150,000 from the Washington State Department of Transportation, and the remaining $2.6 million from the city's Street Fund.

The project was controversial from the start and suffered a barrage of criticism in letters to the editor and public hearings. Construction delays threatened merchants during the crucial holiday season. Some criticized the narrowing of 78th Avenue Southeast and the inclusion of bike lanes on 77th Avenue Southeast. Walbridge Powell launched a campaign to get people to loiter downtown and use the benches: The Downtown Bench Loiter-In. He protested what he called the extravagance of the benches, which cost $875 each in 1995.

Criticism gradually subsided, and in 1995 council member Elliot Newman predicted the tide would shift further. "I believe that five years from now, people are going to be telling us how great the concept was. So hang in there," he said.

Real estate booms

Real estate values soared throughout the region during the 1990s—and especially on Mercer Island. The Island's high property values were attributable to three things: the completion of I-90, the easy commute to Bellevue and Seattle, and the quality of Mercer Island schools, according to real estate broker John Deely of Coldwell Banker Bain.

The average price for a home on Mercer Island in 1989 was $345,885, and the lowest-priced house that year was $195,000.

Prices jumped 34 percent from 1994 to 1996, when the median sales price was $429,880. With inventory low, the prices kept rising. In February 1997, the average sales price for an Island home was $502,423; a year earlier it was $459,891.

At the end of the decade, in 1999, the most expensive listing on the Island was $9 million and the least expensive was $359,000.

Home demolition burgeoned. More houses were torn down than ever before, to make way for bigger homes. More than 30 homes were demolished in 1999 alone, according to the *Mercer Island Reporter.*

Megahouse issue

With land values so high, builders were constructing homes as big as zoning laws allowed. That led some Islanders to call for the city to change its zoning laws to regulate the size of homes. Terms like "megahouse" and "McMansion" became common parlance, as people struggled with the changing look and character of their neighborhoods.

The older First Hill neighborhood and Mercerwood Shores, the Island's first planned unit-development of the 1940s, were particularly affected, as modest, one-story ramblers were replaced by large, two-story homes built right up to the lot-line setbacks.

The megahouse issue was debated at Planning Commission and City Council meetings starting in 1989. Some people felt the city's proposal to limit home size and bulk was an infringement of an individual's right to develop his property; others urged the council to do more to regulate the construction of large-scale homes.

In March 1991, the City Council voted to modify the Mercer Island Unified Land Development Code to regulate the size and scale of home construction to require compatibility between lot size and house size. It imposed a floor area ratio not to exceed 45 percent of the lot area, and reduced the allowable height of a home from 35 to 30 feet, calculated from the average base elevation. The new development requirement became known as the megahouse ordinance.

Mercer View options

If the big issue of the 1980s was where to put City Hall, in the next decade it was where to locate a community center.

By the early 1990s, the former Mercer View Elementary School was constantly busy as a meeting place. But the building, constructed in 1960 and leased by the city from the school district since 1980, was showing its age and was

Mercer Island Reporter

The Mercer Island Parks and Recreation Department responded to the growing population of senior citizens with increased program offerings. Roy Smith entertains at the senior Thanksgiving potluck in November 1993.

For the first time in decades, deer are spotted on the Island in the early 1990s, presumably having swum over from Bellevue. The city put up Deer Crossing signs along Island Crest Way. City employee Dave Anderson and City Council member Linda Jackman inspect a new sign in 1992. Several deer were accidentally killed along Island Crest, and eventually the deer disappeared on the Island. It wasn't until later, in the mid-2000s, that deer began to be sighted regularly on the Island again.

Mercer Island Reporter

Chapter 17: The 1990s | 167

1995 Starbucks opens Jan. 3 and is only the second one in the country with a drive-through window.

1995 The city eliminates two citizen advisory boards: the Park Board and the Road and Trails Board.

1995 The Connection, the city's downtown community center, closes.

1995 The city buys Mythical Bird, a sculpture by Dudley Carter, for Pioneer Park.

1995 Mercer Island High School establishes a new open-campus policy allowing upper classmen to leave campus; freshmen may not.

1996 Baby bald eagles hatch in two separate nests, the first known active nests on the Island in 25 years.

1996 Town Center is the official name for downtown.

1996 In February, Mercer Island High School basketball coach Ed Pepple chalks up his 600th win.

1996 In foreign language offerings at Mercer Island High School, Chinese is in, German is out.

1996 A ribbon-cutting ceremony marks completion of the $5.1 million street project in the Town Center.

1997 The iconic Mercer Island High School Mushroom is demolished and replaced with the Commons, as part of the school remodel.

1997 Temple B'nai Torah leaves the Island; Hope of God church purchases the former synagogue.

1997 The Mercer Island Schools Foundation achieves its highest fund-raising goal to date: $457,000.

1997 Mercer Island Ski and Cycle is hit by burglars twice over one weekend, with burglars getting away with thousands of dollars' worth of merchandise.

Mercer Island Reporter

Downed trees and resultant power outages are a frequent fact of life during the '80s and '90s, especially on the south end. This 1994 photo looks east on Southeast 68th from Island Crest Way.

costly to maintain.

The school district was watching its enrollment figures carefully, since it needed classroom space in the event of a surge in the student population. In 1992, the school district decided to continue leasing Mercer View, since it didn't appear likely it would be needed as a school. The city signed a lease for three more years.

Meanwhile, ideas swirled about the future of Mercer View. Should the school district retain the property or sell all or part of it—and, if so, to whom? Should the city try to acquire the property and remodel the old building or construct a brand-new community center on the same site? Or should the city build a community center closer to downtown? In February 1994, Tom Weathers was appointed head of a citizens' committee to identify options for Mercer View.

The Connection

To test the idea of a downtown community center and to relieve the crowded Parks and Recreation offices at Mercer View, the city rented an empty storefront space in the old Mercer Island Shopping Center. In 1993, it opened The Connection, a kind of visitors center for the Island, an annex for Parks and Recreation Department activities, and a venue for meetings and events.

The idea was to strengthen the connection between the city and the community and establish a city presence where Islanders shopped and did business.

The experiment was generally viewed as successful, but the city had to close The Connection in November 1995 because rising rental rates were draining city coffers.

Community Center: the big debate

In the spring of 1997, the Ad Hoc Community Center Task Force, led by Mary Ann Flynn and Jim Pearman, was created. Over several months the group studied other community centers and gathered information from Island organizations, current community center users, and various interest groups about what a new community center should be.

By the end of 1997, the City Council approved the task force's recommendations to build a new community center on the Mercer View site. The measure was slated to go on the November 1998 ballot.

Mercer Island Reporter

Islander Flo Harris directs traffic around road work on Southeast 24th Street in 1993. With the Town Center street work, I-90 construction and First Hill road improvements, traffic delays and flaggers on the road were a common occurrence during the 1990s.

In true Mercer Island style, no such change could go without challenge. A citizen group called the Mercer Island Action Forum, led by Sven Goldmanis, sprang up primarily to fight the community center proposal.

Months of lively community discussion and heated debates culminated in a public forum on October 14, 1998, when there was a standing-room-only crowd in the City Council Chambers of the old Mercer View school. The debate focused on the $19.5 million proposal for a new Community Center at Mercer View (CCMV).

Goldmanis and Flynn went head to head debating the issues. Goldmanis, who lived near the CCMV, called the proposed center a Taj Mahal and compared the project to the construction of the Columbia Tower in downtown Seattle. He said the new community center should be primarily a senior center, with some facilities for children. Flynn made the point that a community center should appeal to the entire community. The *Mercer Island Reporter* wrote

Mercer Island Reporter

Laurie McQueen gives a thumbs-up to a motorist as the group she organized protests outside the McCaw Cellular headquarters in Kirkland. They are protesting the construction of cell towers on Mercer Island.

of the forum: "Their strained decorum hinted at an underlying animosity that is turning this into one of the nastiest debates in recent Island memory."

When the vote was taken, the $19.5 million community center proposal was soundly defeated in November 1998, with 66 percent voting against it.

Afterwards, the City Council did little to further a new community center proposal beyond exploring private fundraising.

It wasn't until the next decade that the city finally took over the Mercer View property and a new, more modest community center plan was put forward in 2003 and was finally built in 2005.

Mercer Island Reporter

Top: Everybody loves a deal! People line up at the Mercer Island Youth and Family Services Thrift Shop on a Thursday morning in 1994. Above, the Thrift Shop in 1990, before the building was remodeled and enlarged.

Thrift Shop a gold mine that gives back to the community

It started out in 1973 as a rummage sale to raise some money for the city's fledgling social service agency, Mercer Island Youth Services. The monthly sale was held in the garage of the MIYS office, an old house on Sunset Highway in the path of Interstate 90.

Before long the sale was held once a week, then twice a week. When the agency had to move because of the highway construction, it opened its offices at the Community Center at Mercer View, and the Thrift Shop moved in 1982 to the building at the corner of Mercerdale Park.

That was the genesis of one of the most successful retail operations in Mercer Island's history: the Mercer Island Thrift Shop.

At first the Thrift Shop, operated entirely by volunteers, was open only a few hours per week and generated a few thousand dollars per year. In 2008, the city lifted the conditional-use permit that allowed it to be open only 32 hours per week. Now, with four full-time employees and an army of volunteers and work-study students, it made more than $1.1 million in 2012..

Under the leadership of manager Suzanne Philen, it utilizes the latest merchandising methods to make the shop feel like a boutique. It appeals to bargain hunters from around the region. It sells its rare donations on eBay, and manages a vehicle donation program.

In addition, the shop provides volunteer opportunities, internships, and community placements for youths and young adults.

The Thrift Shop turns donated goods into dollars that go right back into the community to help support the myriad programs of Mercer Island Youth and Family Services. In 2012, the Thrift Shop funded more the 50 percent of the operating budget of MIYFS.

Recycling leader

Recycling is such a way of life for most people in the decades of the 2000s that it's hard to imagine how new and revolutionary the concept once was. Mercer Island was early to embrace the ideas of reducing, reusing, and recycling. In 1990, the city launched an Island-wide recycling effort, and by 1991 it was leading the region in percentage of waste recycled.

The community recycling center, built and operated by Mercer Island High School's club Committee to Save the Earth, was still thriving in the 1990s, even after the city adopted an Island-wide curbside recycling program. In 1990, Shorewood Apartments was the first to launch multifamily recycling in the region. The recycling center was closed in 2009.

Acquiring more parks

Interest in parks escalated during the 1990s, and during the decade the city acquired nearly 800 acres of parkland and open space.

In 1990, the city purchased a 24-acre woodsy ravine along Southeast 53rd Place between Island Crest and East Mercer Way for $3.5 million. The acquisition was funded primarily with proceeds from a 1989 King County parks and open space bond issue and grant funds from the Washington State Interagency Committee for Outdoor Recreation.

The biggest chunk of park land acquired in the 1990s was the Park on the Lid, the land over I-90 that provided about 730 acres of new park area bridging the freeway. It took several years of planning on the part of the city and the Department of Transportation to determine the configuration of the park and its amenities. The state had compensated Mercer Island with these lids for the interstate that cut across the north end of the Island. Throughout 1992, the concrete lid was gradually transformed into a park, with plantings,

170 | Chapter 17: The 1990s

During 1995, the City Council attempted to enact a shoreline ordinance to pull together into one place the varying regulations on the books regarding docks and covered moorage, some of which were not being enforced. More than 300 people packed a council meeting in May to protest it. Finally, the council backed down and relaxed the ordinance, and allowed covered moorage after it had been prohibited since 1979.
Mercer Island Reporter

Mercer Island Reporter
City manager Paul Lanspery, in front, sits with assistant city manager Rich Conrad. Lanspery was city manager from 1986 to 1996, when Conrad was promoted to succeed him. Conrad was first hired by the city in July 1979.

ball fields, tennis courts, picnic areas and jogging paths.

Another bonus from the completion of I-90 was the creation of the city's boat launch under the East Channel Bridge. Although the Island has 16 miles of shoreline, this was the first—and to date only—public boat launch on the Island. It was officially opened by Mayor Elliot Newman on May 9, 1992. The paving of the road and parking lot and the installation of the launching ramp, dock, and landscaping cost $675,000, and was paid for by the state Department of Transportation and the city of Mercer Island.

One of the smallest new parks was the most controversial. In 1985, the waterfront property of Harry and Loretta Slater at 2835 60th Ave. SE was given to the city through their will. They were longtime Island residents, and Harry was the volunteer fire chief for 14 years. The couple probably never imagined that their simple gift to the city would cause such a hullabaloo.

A four-year battle ensued, with neighbors suing the city to prevent the park. Finally, a compromise was reached with the creation of a passive park without a dock, but with four parking stalls, a bench, and a table. Construction began in April 1990, and the park was dedicated in 1991.

In early 1991, the City Council decided to develop Mercerdale Field into a park. The idea was that the 12.7 acres bordering the downtown area would eventually become a town commons, for people of all ages to enjoy. A paved footpath, a plaza, a large lawn, and benches were put in, and over time other amenities were added..

In 1993, a group of teenagers approached the City Council with their desire to have a skateboard park on Mercer Island. Working closely with councilmember Judy Clibborn, they developed a plan, and by March 1994, the City Council approved the construction of a small skateboard park on the west side of Mercerdale.

It was successful and well used by Island teens almost from the very beginning. In December 2001, the City Council approved the expansion of the skateboard park to its present configuration.

Cell towers

With the advent of new communication technology, Islanders embraced cell phones—but not cell towers. According to city permit records, the first cell tower was constructed in 1994.

Not long after that the controversy began over where they could be located, how tall they could be, and whether they pose a health risk.

In early 1995, Northwest Yeshiva High School applied for a permit for a cell tower to be constructed on its property, for which the school would receive rental income from the cellular company. The cell tower went up on the school property in the 5000 block of 90th Avenue Southeast, prompting a furor in the neighborhood and beyond.

For months there were letters to the editor in the *Mercer Island Re-*

Chapter 17: The 1990s | 171

MIPD: Keeping the Island safe

Throughout the 1990s, the Mercer Island Police Department expanded and improved its services to Island residents. The bike team started in 1993 with two oficers, primarily to patrol the Town Center and Park on the Lid areas. In 2012, it had eight officers.

The Marine Patrol, established in 1981, promotes water safety on Lake Washington and provides boating safety education and rescue service. Two full-time employees (a sergeant and a technician) run the unit; 16 officers are trained to operate the boats and respond to emergencies as needed. Mercer Island formerly provided Marine Patrol services to Medina, Hunts Point, and Yarrow Point. As of 2012, it serves Bellevue and Renton in addition to Mercer Island.

During the '90s, the department improved its crime prevention efforts by organizing neighborhood Block Watch parties with the help of volunteers.

It also developed an emergency preparedness plan and hired a full-time emergency management coordinator. It developed a network of trained volunteers and established sites stocked with emergency supplies.

Officer Jennifer Drain (top) shows the inside of a police car to preschoolers from Emmanuel in 1994. Officer Lowell Forsman (middle) moors the Marine Patrol boat at the public boat ramp, which opened in 1992. Bicycle Patrol officer Lance Davenport patrols along 78th Avenue Southeast in 1995.
Mercer Island Reporter

172 | Chapter 17: The 1990s

porter, neighbors circulating petitions against it, and people speaking about it at public meetings. Eventually, the cell tower was relocated along Island Crest Way.

By 1996, five cell towers were on the Island, but none south of Southeast 40th Street. In October that year, the city enacted an ordinance restricting cellular antennas from residential areas.

In 1999, the term "monopole" came into common parlance on the Island. It was the beginning of a three-year fight over a 133-foot Qwest Communications pole near the south-end fire station.

The Planning Commission denied the request for the monopole and would approve only a 70-foot pole. Qwest contested that decision, and the City Council overturned it and gave the OK for the 133-foot pole. A group of Islanders filed an appeal of that decision, and won. Finally, the state court of appeals upheld the Council's decision to allow the monopole, and the tall pole went in.

Over time, perhaps as more and more Islanders began to view cell phones and network coverage as a necessity of life, the brouhaha over cell towers faded. As of the end of 2012, there were nearly 30 cell towers or rooftop poles on the Island.

Greenwood Village

Shortly after Mercer Island's incorporation in 1960, the 12.9-acre tract bordered on two sides by Pioneer Park and on the south by the Mercer Island Country Club was zoned for business. A commercial complex was developed by E.M. Greenwood, who called it Greenwood Village.

In 1961, it was home to Bill Muncy's Thriftway store, Lakeside Mercer Drug, Lawrence's Styling Salon, a Western Auto store, Henry Brothers Barber Shop, Glendale Realty, (John) McKenzies' Chevron Service Station, and a postal station.

By 1975, it held a gasoline station, a vacant building and two single-story buildings housing an expanded QFC supermarket and a Seafirst Bank branch, Lakeside Mercer Drugs, and Clampitt's Cleaners. Various enterprises—other than the grocery, drugstore and limited neighborhood services—were tried and failed.

When owner E.M. Greenwood proposed an apartment development there in 1975, the city's design commission, "responding to howls from neighboring homeowners, declined to recommend any change in the zoning," according to Peggy Reynolds in a special to the *The Seattle Times*.

In 1984, Greenwood's estate sold his land to QFC, which had operated the supermarket since 1969. QFC improved trails and landscaping, and in 1986 proposed to sell most of its land for a 122-apartment "senior citizen" development. Again, neighborhood outcry killed the concept.

In 1997, the long-debated question of housing at QFC Village was settled by the City Council's decision to allow 18 new homes on 8 acres of the property zoned for commercial uses. The homes would be modest in size, compared to Mercer Island standards.

Now, 15 years later, there's a more upbeat ambiance to the south-end center, despite the losses of banks, cleaners, postal station and other services.

A well-attended Starbucks hub,

In 1996, Gary Lewis and John O'Shea purchased Greenwood Village and began a three-phase redevelopment: constructing new homes, building a storage facility, and renovating commercial buildings.

Mercer Island Reporter

four restaurants, medical offices, Rite Aid, a complex of storage units, and other service shops have been added to the QFC and Chevron anchors. South-end QFC was named the favorite grocery store on the Island in the Mercer Island Reporter online blog in 2012.

Millennium's end

The 1990s—with the completion of I-90, the construction of the new floating bridge, the downtown redevelopment plan, the new fire station, and the new library—was a decade that shaped the way Mercer Island looks today.

Reflecting on the end of the millennium, the *Mercer Island Reporter* wrote:

"The story of the millennium? The real Island history is made up of concrete and asphalt, rebar and retaining walls—the stuff of roads and bridges. That's because most of the big events in Mercer Island's history have centered on transportation. It's not surprising, since this is an island, and getting on or off of it has always been a major focus.

"Bridges and roads are the Island's lifeline. Transportation has been the vehicle for Island transformation from an uninhabited forest in the heart of Lake Washington to a residential suburb 10 minutes from Seattle."

Enduring enterprises

A few retail shops on Mercer Island have endured for generations. These three family-owned businesses have deep roots in the community and are thriving still.

Mercer Island Reporter

ISLAND BOOKS: Island Books Etc. was founded in 1973 by Lola Deane, nurse, entrepreneur, and wife of well-known Island pediatrician Dr. Phil Deane. The "Etc.," which referred to the pottery, crafts, and macrame the shops sold in addition to books, was dropped in the succeeding decade. Deane sold the business to friends Fam Bayless, Marjory Wilkens, and Elinor MacDonald in 1980. Roger Page started working at the store in 1984, then bought it in 1991. In the 1986 photo above (left to right): Roger Page, Fam Bayless, Marjory Wilkens, and Elinor MacDonald. Island Books is the Eastside's oldest independent bookstore.

Mercer Island Reporter

CHICK'S SHOES & SERVICE: His name is Charles Joseph Tabit Jr., but everyone knows him as Chick. He's the patriarch of Chick's Shoes & Service in Tabit Square, the family business he founded in 1949 on land purchased as a summer home. He follows in the footsteps of his father, Chick Sr., who operated a shoe repair shop at the foot of Queen Anne Hill in Seattle for 40 years. Now Chick Jr. has handed the business to his son, Chris Tabit, and grandson, C.J. Tabit.

Earl Payne

MERCER ISLAND FLORIST: In 1957, Earl Payne and his wife, Anne, took over the former Brown's Florist located just north of the QFC. They changed the name to Mercer Island Florist in 1961. In 1964, the business moved to 2728 78th Ave. SE where it remained until it was displaced by the Town Center development and moved to its current location at 3006 78th Ave. SE. This photo, from 1966, shows the Paynes, at left, with their employees. Among them (second from right) is Shirley Larson, who worked for Payne for 20 years before buying the business from him in 1986. Her daughter, Diane, helped out as part-time bookkeeper, then took over the business when her mother retired in 1997.

Street art at your feet

If you're walking around the Town Center and you don't look down, you might be missing art at your feet that will tell you something about the Island's history. It's part of the improvements added downtown when the streets were redone between 1992 and 1994.

"The art plan for the redevelopment of Mercer Island's downtown drew upon the historical origins of the Island and contemporary expressions of the Island's character," said T. Ellen Sollod, the artist who developed the art plan for downtown. "Rather than proposing large-scale independent artworks, an emphasis on artworks integrated into the functional landscape was recommended."

Bronze sidewalk inlays

1. Where: At the corner of Southeast 27th Street and 77th Avenue Southeast

What: *History of Transport/Conveyance by Time* is a circular inlay about 36 inches in diameter. The Island's connection to Seattle is a critical aspect of its history. This depicts a series of concentric circles representing various means of transportation/communication, with the outermost ring the cell phone.

2. Where: On 77th Avenue Southeast, north of Albertson's

What: *(In)Visible Histories* is a 16-by-25-inch map of the Island, which includes symbols for orienteering and a key, providing a quick insight into the history of the Island. It points out the sunken forests offshore, the skid road where logging on the Island occurred, and the early dairy farms, among others.

3. Where: On the west side of 78th Avenue Southeast and Southeast 32nd Street

What: Two bronze, inlaid milk bottles, recalling the days when dairy farms, such as the Person farm and the Lucas farm, operated on the Island.

4. Where: On the northeast corner of Southeast 30th Street and 78th Avenue Southeast

What: A casting of a draft horse shoe, recalling the horses used in skidding logs to the lake when the Island was logged between 1880 and 1900.

Tree grates

There are three different tree grate designs. The simplest is the salmon design, used along 78th Avenue Southeast Along Southeast 27th Street, *Bird in Hand* incorporates a stanza from a W.H. Auden poem.

'O do you imagine,' said fearer to farer,
That dusk will delay on your path to the pass,
Your diligent looking discover the lacking
Your footsteps feel from granite to grass?

Along 77th Avenue Southeast between Southeast 27th and Southeast 30th, the design is entitled *Enviable Isle*. By walking along four adjacent tree grates you can read the entire poem, *Enviable Isle* by Herman Melville:

Through storms you reach them and from storms are free.
Afar descried, the foremost drear in hue,
But, nearer, green; and, on the marge, the sea
Makes thunder low and mist of rainbow dew.

But, inland,—where the sleep that folds the hills
A dreamier sleep, the trance of God instills,—
On uplands hazed, in wandering airs aswoon,
Slow-swaying palms salute love's cypress tree.

Adown in vale where pebble runlets croon
A song to lull all sorrow and all glee.
Sweet-fern and moss in many a glade are here,
Where, strown in flocks, what cheek-flushed myriads lie
Dimpling in dream, unconscious slumberers mere,
While billows endless round the beaches die.

Street names

The original names of some of the Town Center streets are inlaid in bronze at the intersections along 77th and 78th avenues from Southeast 32nd north to Southeast 27th Street. King County replaced the original street names with numbers during the 1930s as part of a Works Progress Administration project.

So, the Island's main street, 78th Avenue, is Gilpin Street; 77th is Helen; Southeast 27th is Cable; Southeast 28th is Tallman; Southeast 29th is Summit; Southeast 30th is Treen; and Southeast 32nd is Proctor Street.

Mercer Island Reporter

Bronze milk bottles in the sidewalk on the west side of 78th Avenue Southeast and Southeast 32nd Street recall the Person dairy farm and the Island's rural past.

Business comings and goings in the 1990s

Here is a list of some openings and closings of Island shops and businesses during the decade. Some both opened and closed between 1990 and 2000.

OPENINGS/CHANGES

Walgreens opens in space formerly occupied by Ernst, Pay 'n Save, PayLess, Boardwalk Motors
Cucina Presto
Noah's Bagels
Island Cats
Mercer Nails
Royal Florist
World Martial Arts
Purified Water To Go
Thai Kitchen
Continental Bank
Cascade Frames
The Porch gift shop
Jet City Java
Cindy's Nails
Q Nails
Denise's Parrot Place
Alpine Chiropractic
Pon Proem
Espresso Sam's
Louise Matzke Gallery
French Pastry Place
Caffe Italia
Taco Loco opens where Jack in the Box was
Orkin Plantscaping
Riley's gift shop sold; becomes Addison's
The Tennis Shop
Mercer Island Auto Spa
Club Emerald
Johansen's Meats
Tony Maroni's
Mama Reuben's becomes Rene's Restaurant
Thai on Mercer
Subito's opens, changes to Cafe Italia then Sirocco
Mercer Island Auto Supply
Finders
Tangerine becomes Deane's Island Café, then Bourbon Street Café, then Panda Inn
Pat's Cards & Gifts becomes Confetti
Baskin Robbins
Last Tango consignment shop
Ooby's Boutique
Island Treasures
My Travel Agency
Subway
Teriyaki USA
La Fiesta Mexican Restaurant changes to Mi Pueblo
Studio 904
Café Mercer View
Arjuna women's boutique
Happy Hounds dog grooming

Wickerware
Homespun Crafters' Mall
Swan's Jewelry
Tully's
Quality Food Center (north end)
Club Emerald
Hollywood Video opens in former Pizza Hut space
Island Beads & More
Chris Francisco Jewelers
Boardwalk Motors
Bruegger's Bagels
Starbucks
Mercer Island Ski and Cycle
Seven Star
My Travel Agency

CLOSINGS

Alexander & Astin Florist
Addison's Gift Store
Carol Gilmour Women's Clothing
John Dunney Real Estate closes after 72 years
Rene's Restaurant
78th Street Café
Miller's Miracles
Island Prescriptions closes after 30 years
Royal Florist
Emmy's Attic
Tolles Gallery closes after 27 years
Essentially You Spa
Look's Pharmacy closes after nearly 50 years.
Pay 'n Save
The Staircase women's shop closes after 25 years
Kent Jewelry
Ralston Studio
Safeway
Thriftway
PayLess
Mercer Island Cyclery
Travel Professionals
Ashley's Toys
Mercer Island Equipment Rentals
Deane's Island Café
Island Auto Supply
Confetti Cards & Gifts
Island Candy and Gifts
Louise Matzke Gallery
Bourbon Street Café
Shaffer Systems Computers
Davidson's Art Gallery
Jack in the Box
Homespun Crafters Mall
Senff's Fine Jewelry

Raccoons have adapted well to metro living. Problems arise when people feed the raccoons or leave food outside, leading them to lose their fear of humans and become more aggressive around people and pets.

Duke Coonrad

Wild Things in the 'Hood

Sharing this Island home with four-footed and winged creatures

For the past 120 years at least, the evolving human-wildlife ecosystem has been a tricky tango. As we both fight for dominion/survival, we can wreak havoc on each other's habitats.

They rifle through our garbage, confront our pets, eat our landscaping, peck holes in our rafters, and roll up new-laid sod to get at grubs. Crows can bring with them West Nile virus, and raccoons and rodents may have rabies.

We put bombs down their tunnels, hire pest and animal control to reduce their numbers, and other such tactics. On the other hand, we've grown wildlife-friendly backyards, and created a city ordinance that prohibits building around eagles' nests.

From the early days, our animal kingdom attracted the Indians to hunt, fish, and trap the abundant wildlife in a forested land surrounded by water. Since the 1940s, when land development began in earnest here, stories of pesky deer and the occasional bear abound. In the early 1950s, Virginia Nygren, then principal of Mercer Crest Elementary, locked down the school until King County sheriff's deputies could clear the premises of a reported bear in the area. More recently, scat akin to bear's was discovered in Luther Burbank Park.

Since the development of the Island, we've seen local extinction of some species (western pond turtle, Chinese pheasant), increases in others (American crow, raccoons, squirrels, rodents), more or less consistent presence in others (deer on and off).

Our most abundant critters include Pacific tree frogs, crows, rodents, raccoons and squirrels, in addition to domesticated dogs and cats. The recent return of deer and increased numbers of raccoons may be a result of more construction in East King County.

Raccoons. Mercer Island had them "pre-bridges" and throughout its development, but never as many as today (2012). Here we are rife with garbage, pet food left outdoors and other food sources. Raccoons can reach populations of up to one territory per three square blocks, with up to 20 den sites in the territory, adding up to potentially hundreds of raccoons on the Island. Everyone has their favorite "little bandit" story of raccoons rolling up new sod for grubs, nesting in their chimneys, coming in through pet doors and rifling through kitchens, or parading their new kits—balls of fluff—in backyards for show-and-tell in June.

Deer. The Island was a favor-

Chapter 18: Wild Things in the 'Hood | 177

After having disappeared for decades, deer are back on the Island. This black-tailed deer visited the yard of Carrie Bell on First Hill in May 2012, when she took the photo. The buck bedded down for the night in the soft mulch.

Carrie Bell

ite hunting ground in the pre-development years. Post-1940, black-tailed deer were more abundant than today, but hunting kept them in check. They dwindled to near nonexistence until the mid-2000s, when "reoccupation" occurred, as surrounding suburbia removed much of their habitat. The Island's greenbelts, lack of predator pressure and delicious gardens are still a draw. Deer easily swim across the East Channel.

Bears. Bear make occasional appearances, as can be determined from scat finds, but generally stick to wooded land farther east.

Rodents. Many native rodents associated with lowlands (bushy-tailed woodrat, mountain beaver, Douglas squirrel, flying squirrel, various voles, Townsend's chipmunk and such) were here pre-development, along with non-native rodents such as the Norway rat and black rat. The non-native eastern gray squirrel is seen throughout Mercer Island.

Beavers. A couple of beaver lodges are known to exist on the Island today, on the north end of Luther Burbank Park and on the westside waterfront.

Bats. Bats were prevalent on the Island in the 1940s, but logging and removal of dead trees reduced their numbers.

Coyotes. In 1940, Mercer Island had only a few. Coyote are good swimmers, so they likely started to show more of a presence on the Island sometime in the 1950s to 1970s.

Fish. About 30 species of fish live in Lake Washington. The most plentiful species are chinook, coho and sockeye salmon, plus trout, longfin smelt, large and smallmouth bass and yellow perch.

Birds

The Audubon Society's annual bird count on Mercer Island shows bird species decreased from 66 species in 2010 to 53 in 2011, yet there were notable sightings of trumpeter swans, barred owls, common loons, ruddy ducks and a hermit thrush, the first in a long time.

Of special note was a decrease in Canada geese and adult bald eagles, from 11 to 6, and an increase in cormorants.

Eagles. There are three known bald eagle territories on Mercer Island (this includes a number of alternate nests associated with the same territory, which is why the city shows six nests but not six pairs, as multiple nests are associated with the same territorial pairs).

The city's development regulations protect bald eagle nests and their nearby perch trees from construction or removal of vegetation within 400 to 800 feet, among other stipulations. Since eagles are territorial and there's only so much space they can occupy on the Island, their population hasn't fluctuated much over the decades.

Crows. There are 400 to 800 crows on the Island at any one time, many of whom can be seen at dusk flying to their roosts near University of Washington's Bothell campus, according to John Marzluff, professor of forest sciences at University of Washington. The winter count for crows that nest in local Island roosts is lower than in the past.

Herons. Herons have been noted in the Luther Burbank wetlands and along the shoreline of the north end of the Island, although this bird is not very common on the shores of the Island.

Pioneer Park— *a unique urban preserve*

The largest park on the Island, with 120 acres of urban forest, Pioneer Park is the last large piece of Mercer Island that reminds us of what the Island was like long ago.

The property was privately owned until 1931, when Maud Walker-Ames willed it to the University of Washington.

Like the rest of the Island, it had been logged of its virgin timber before the turn of the century; most of the park's tallest trees today are second-growth cedar, Douglas fir and hemlock.

Shortly after Mercer Island incorporated into a city in 1960, the citizens learned that the land, referred to as "the University properties," was for sale. In 1964, they passed a bond issue to purchase the property.

Since then there have been several attempts to turn a portion of the park into a golf course. Citizens organized to save the park, and the City Council voted to put the issue of development of the park to rest once and for all by creating the Mercer Island Open Space Conservancy Trust in 1992. The park was put under the ownership of the trust, to be protected from development in perpetuity. The Open Space Conservancy Trust Board continues to maintain, oversee and protect the park.

Some facts about the park from *Pioneer Park: A Natural History*:
- Pioneer Park consists of three 40-acre parcels of woodlands on the northwest, northeast and southeast corners of the intersection of Island Crest Way and Southeast 68th Street.
- The northeast quadrant has the most variation in topography and plant life. It has the steepest slopes, on the sides of the ravine.
- The park has four forested habitat types: conifer forest, conifer/deciduous mixed forest, riparian forest and landscaped forest.
- There are more than 112 species of flowering plants, ferns, trees and shrubs in Pioneer Park.
- Birders have compiled a species list of up to 74 birds found in Pioneer Park.
- The great horned owl, barred owl, western screech owl and hawks such as Cooper's hawk, sharp-shinned hawk and red-tailed hawk nest successfully in the interior of Pioneer Park.
- The park is home to a wide variety of small mammals, amphibians and insects.

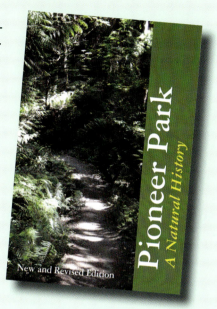

Pioneer Park: A Natural History was published in 2012 by the Farrington Foundation for the city of Mercer Island.

Cohabiting with Island flora, fauna

Frances Wood, local bird expert, addresses our human-wildlife connections in her 2009 column in the *Mercer Island Reporter*:

"The bald eagles that nest on the Island and soar majestically over our heads have re-populated the Puget Sound region because we humans acted and banned the use of DDT back in the 1950s.

"Great-horned owls fill the still night air on fall evenings with their soft 'hoo, hoo-hoo, hoo, hoo,' in the cadence of, 'Who's awake, me too.' We might well change our cadence to: 'Thanks for trees, save more,' reminding us to preserve trees in our parks and neighborhoods.

"Song sparrows also belt out their springtime song in Luther Burbank Park, in part, because the city has established restoration projects to preserve the natural habitat. The mini-musicians will continue to sing and nest in the low shrubs as long as we all keep dogs on leash at the park.

"Mallards mutter through the winter on Ellis Pond, showing their iridescent green heads and curly tail feathers. They are sustained by healthy weeds and insects (and the occasional bread crumbs) because we limit our use of pesticides and herbicides in surrounding gardens.

"Juncos, chickadees and towhees visit our seed feeders and bring joy to us on housebound days. They feed and nest on the native species we planted in our gardens. Mercer Island hosts all five Western Washington woodpecker species, here because we have preserved larger dead trees and snags in Pioneer Park, other green spaces and backyards."

City of Mercer Island

Aerial photos of Mercer Island in 1939 (left) and 1999 (right) show the development the Island underwent in 60 years.

180 | Chapter 18: Wild Things in the 'Hood

Chad Coleman / Mercer Island Reporter

This photo looks west across the First Hill neighborhood of Mercer Island. While known for its expensive real estate, the Island has homes ranging from mansions to modest cabins, and even a yacht-turned-house on the waterfront near Clarke Beach.

Neighborhoods of 'The Rock'

Island neighborhoods still have their distinctive characteristics

Life on "The Rock" is not as homogeneous as stereotypes suggest. Residents live in pencil-shaped homes in forested ravines; in sprawling waterfront spreads; in modest 1950 moderns; in apartments, condos, townhomes and assisted-living complexes. Some are extremely wealthy, others live on moderate to assisted incomes, and all levels in between.

According to the 2010 census, there were 22,699 Islanders in 9,930 dwellings; about one-third live in the most populous census tract: 243, the northwest portion of Mercer Island, where the majority of apartments and condos are. The tract's population increase from 6,477 in 2000 to 7,225 in 2010 reflected eight new multi-story complexes in the Town Center, a trend expected to continue.

About 72 percent of Islanders own housing; 28 percent rent. The median home sale price was $859,500 in 2012. Average rents: $1,500 and way up.

Bob Ewing

The farmhouse of the Person dairy farm on First Hill was originally surrounded by pasture. The home, remodeled through the years, is at 3049 68th Ave. S.E.

In 2010, the mean age of the Island was 49, with approximately 6,000 under 18; 9,000 between 20-55; and 7,700 over age 55. Racial diversity increased from predominantly white to 16 percent Asian, 2.8 percent Hispanic, 1.2 percent black, and traces of others.

While the Island's unique neighborhoods remain, the federal government no longer defines us by them.

Rather, Mercer Island is sliced into five geographic portions: Tract 243, the northwest; Tract 244, the northeast; Tract 245 the north-midland; Tract 246.01, the south midland; and Tract 246.02, the southernmost tip.

Here's how they translate from yesteryear.

TRACT 243

From North Mercer Way to Southeast 40th Street, and 60th Avenue Southeast to Island Crest Way; 7,255 living in 3,294 households, 60 percent owner-occupied, 40 percent rented in 2010. The neighborhoods:

East Seattle

The Island's first west-side settlement was home to the first church, the elaborate C.C. Calkins resort of the 1890s, library, post office, store and restaurant. None remain.

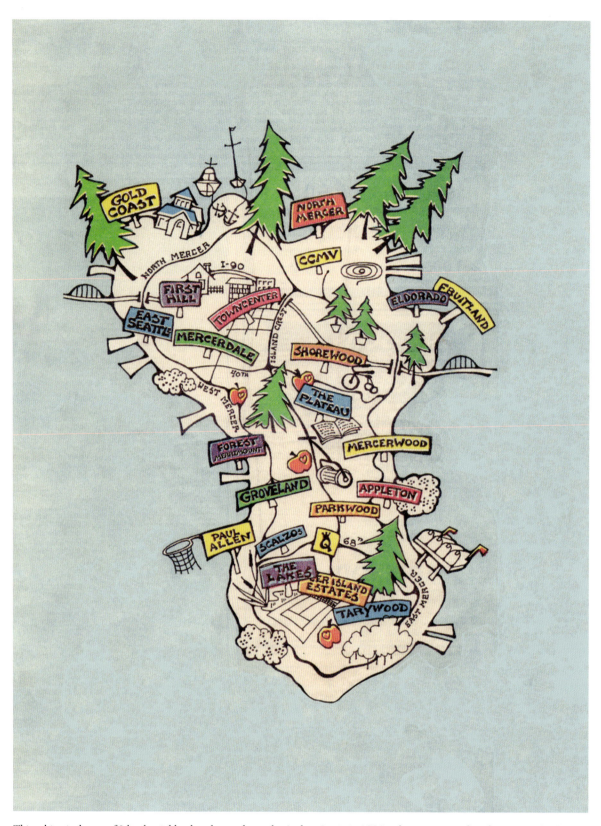
This whimsical map of Island neighborhoods was drawn by Andrea Lorig in 1994, when it appeared in the *Mercer Island Reporter*.

Mercer Island Historical Society

This home at the corner of 60th Avenue Southeast and Southeast 28th Street was built in 1910. It is across the street from Calkins Landing, which was maintained for years by Boyd Burchard before the city took over street-end maintenance.

Mercer Island Historical Society

This East Seattle home at 6119 SE 28th St. has been lovingly restored by owners Richard and Jeanne Bayley.

Mercer Island Historical Society

The D.B. McMahon family built this home at 2740 W. Mercer Way in 1910. Known as "The Castle," it was next to the East Seattle water tower, which burned down in 1975.

Only the street-end parks at Calkins, Proctor, Franklin and Garfield landings mark the once-bustling ferry docks. The small summer places have been recast as more upscale homes.

The former East Seattle School, later home to the Mercer Island Boys & Girls Club, now is privately owned. East Seattle streets were built in a grid pattern, with alleyways, a tradition disdained in the 1960s and '70s when newer Island neighborhoods were developed. Today, "New Urbanists" champion the grid pattern and say alleys make for more neighborliness. Sixtieth Avenue Southeast became East Seattle's new waterfront after the lake was lowered in 1914.

The Gold Coast

The early settlers used the Roanoke Inn and Keewaydin Club (VFW Hall) as social and political hubs. They still do. This Roanoke area also was known as McGilvra. Faben Point, named after Capt. Vince Faben, and the stretch of waterfront homes to the north of the bridge, made up our first "Gold Coast." The late Hunter Simpson lived here in a historic brick home. He and his neighbors, who were most impacted by freeway construction, fought the I-90 battles.

First Hill

The new I-90 Park on the Lid and bike paths added cachet to the Island's hippest neighborhood. Young families could now commute by bicycle to downtown Seattle or the University District, carrying on the quasi-bohemian spirit of the 1950s, when some hitched rides on the bridge to avoid paying the toll. It is home of First Hill Park and the early "little white church."

Town Center

Dramatic changes in Mercer Island's downtown, beginning in 2004, created mixed-use developments with an increased number

Chapter 19: Our Neighborhoods | 183

Jane Meyer Brahm

This East Seattle home on 61st Avenue Southeast, built circa 1910, was the home of Andy and Susan Anderson.

Mercer Island Historical Society

This ad from *The Seattle Times* in the 1930s shows property on the Island for $275 per acre.

Jane Meyer Brahm

This Tudor home in the 4300 block of East Mercer Way was built in the 1920s by Arthur Loveless, Seattle architect well-known for his Tudor revivalist designs.

of apartment and condo dwellers, close to public transit, parks and trails, shopping and services. What began as a muddy, stump-littered field called "The Flats" has become the most populous neighborhood on the Island. By 2023, light rail also will stop here.

Mercerdale

The homes are modest 1950s and 1960s suburban style. A few were built in the 1970s, and a smattering since. Mercerdale's mix of families with no children, some with children, empty nesters, senior citizens, immigrants and others give it a diverse mix.

The neighborhood was built around the Mercerdale Island Club, with a swimming pool (now gone) and clubhouse, which became the Boys & Girls Club, and now is the Youth & Family Services Thrift Shop. Mercerdale Park is used for community events and sits next to the seasonal Sunday Farmers Market. Throughout the years the open space was envisioned as a community center, a city hall, athletic fields or fire station, but it has remained the Island's "Central Park." To the west is Hillside Park; to the south is Homestead Field.

North Mercer

Also called Beaumont, this area is home to Luther Burbank Park, the community center and some families raising the fourth generation here. Waterfront homes have not changed hands as often as elsewhere. Longtime residents point down the shoreline and name the families who have lived in the same place since the 1950s and '60s.

The earliest home still standing was built by William Guitteau on five acres in 1889. The house, owned for many years by the Martine family, was dubbed Crestfallen Manor; it is now owned by Marcus and Kirsten Ward.

184 | Chapter 19: Our Neighborhoods

Possibly Mercer Island's oldest dwelling, this home at 8240 SE 26th St. was built on five acres of land sold by C.C. Calkins to William Guitteau in 1889.

Mercer Island Historical Society

Jane Brahm

This waterfront home in the Fruitland neighborhood was the home of Anna and John Boettiger in the mid-1940s. Anna was the eldest child and only daughter of Franklin Delano Roosevelt and Eleanor Roosevelt. John Boettiger was publisher of the *Seattle Post-Intelligencer;* Anna was women's page editor at the PI from 1936 to 1943. Their son, John Jr., born in 1939, attended East Seattle School, accompanied by a Secret Service guard. It is said that when FDR and Eleanor came to visit on Mercer Island, the Secret Service set up a guard station near the Boettiger home. Archived footage of old movies shows the Boettiger family waterskiing in front of the house, with little but woods on the lake shore.

TRACT 244

From 84th Avenue Southeast along North Mercer Way to East Mercer Way and up Southeast 40th Street; 2,885 people in 1,360 households, 470 owner-occupied, 890 rented. The neighborhoods:

El Dorado/Fruitland

This neighborhood, between I-90 and the northeast shore, is one of the Island's best-kept secrets. A small street-end park marks an old ferry landing. The nearby path paralleling I-90 is the hottest bicycling throughway, shared by intrepid walkers. Bruce Leven's "Garage Mahal" with his 20 collector cars, and his waterfront home at Fruitland landing, are its showpieces. The former home of FDR's daughter, Anna Roosevelt Boettiger, is nearby. The El Dorado Beach Club is a close-knit group that shares waterfront.

Upper Shorewood

It's said that everyone on the Island has lived in Shorewood Apartments at some time. It's Mercer Island's temporary and affordable housing just off I-90. There's a tie between the apartment complex and the neighborhood just south. Children from Shorewood walk along these streets on their way to school, adopting them as their own.

The homeowners and apartment dwellers range from retirees to young professionals without children and young families or single parents. The per capita income here is the Island's lowest.

Covenant Shores

Also known as Fortuna, this area's 12 acres and 10 buildings were purchased from Shorewood in 1970 by the Covenant Church and

Chapter 19: Our Neighborhoods | 185

Roy Ellingsen

In 1949, Betty Ekrem Ellingsen bought the top section of the USS *Manzanita,* saving it from the scrap heap. She had it barged from Ballard and pulled onto the family's Mercer Island waterfront property, where it was used as a guesthouse. This photo, taken in 1964, shows Betty Ellingsen, right, and her sister, Dorothy Fulcher. When Lillian Tao bought the property in 2006, she wanted to continue to preserve the historic boat-turned-house, which can be seen from the water on the southeast tip of the Island.

Mercer Island Patch

This home sold for $13.25 million in November 2012. The seven-bedroom, eight-bath, 13,560-square-foot home is at 4131 Boulevard Place.

Covenant Shores

The historic Fortuna Lodge, on the left, once a dance hall and party place, is now the dining hall of Covenant Shores Retirement Community on the north end of the Island.

now house more than 300 senior citizens. The old Fortuna Lodge was converted to the dining facility.

Homes around the Stroum Jewish Community Center, Herzl-Ner Tamid, City Hall, Gallagher Hill, the public boat launch under the East Channel Bridge and Barnabie Point, site of the first Island school, are other parts of this tract.

TRACT 245

From West Mercer Way to East Mercer Way, and from Southeast 40th Street to Southeast 53rd Street; population 4,595 in 1,659 households, 1497 owner occupied, 162 rented. The neighborhoods:

Mercerwood Shores

On this eastern hillside, the first of the post-World War II tract developments in the 1950s, each of the ramblers had great views. Mercerwood was then considered the neighborhood for the Island's upper crust.

Today, it's typical, or even modest, by Island standards. Covenants have lapsed, and large homes are beginning to replace the older ramblers originally designed to protect views.

The Mercerwood Shore Club includes a swimming pool and tennis courts for its members. The club was developed on the site of an old Lutheran home for unwed mothers. Traffic on Mercerwood Drive, a convenient shortcut for eastbound commuters, is a pet peeve of the development.

East Mercer

A hairpin curve track of road winds from the Stroum Jewish Community Center to Island Point, dotted with homes in deep ravines and long access roads to the waterfront. Drivers and cyclists and brave walkers share serpentine East Mercer Way. Residents endure the drive, frequent power outages from falling trees and year-round shade to live in one of the Island's unique natural settings.

186 | Chapter 19: Our Neighborhoods

Jane Meyer Brahm

The late Huston Riley grew up in this home on North Mercer Way, where he lived with his wife, Charlotte, until his death in 2010. His parents, Seattle architect Howard Riley and his wife, Etta, bought the property in 1910 before the lake was lowered. They built the home in 1915.

Early settlers clustered along the shore, socialized at the docks where supply boats stopped and exchanged ideas on entertainment and fresh water sources. From those social beginnings sprang the Mercer Island Beach Club, at the far end of East Mercer Way, and Avalon Park, nearby.

Appleton

Mercer Island's first eastside settlement was where Charles Olds built a one-room cabin plus loft, up from a waterfront stream. In November of 1885, the family loaded its possessions, including a goat, onto a barge at Leschi and towed it by rowboat around the north end of the Island and down the East Channel to the claim. The following spring Olds cleared more land and planted 12 acres with apples. He named it Appleton. A few original apple trees remain.

Today a plaque at Appleton Lane marks the early settlement. Some old cabins and newer luxury homes are down narrow, winding streets. Over the years, debates arose over who should maintain those streets—the homeowners or the city.

Forest Avenue

A stretch overlooking the westside water (an extension to Merrimount) has been besieged with drainage problems, landslides and disputes over views and tree cutting, all of which have unified the neighbors. More than half the homes were built before 1969; new building has occurred since then on even steeper lots. Off its shore is an underwater forest, perhaps how it got its name.

The Plateau

Geographically, this is Mercer Island's largest neighborhood, where lies the high school, the school district offices, the old North Mercer Junior High campus, the city's fresh-water reservoir, historic Ellis Pond and Hollerbach Park. The Presbyterian, Lutheran, Episcopal, Catholic and Mormon churches are here as well. Many homes, built in the 1950s, are of suburban ranch-style architecture.

TRACT 246.01

From West Mercer Way to East Mercer Way and Southeast 53rd Place to Southeast 72nd Street; 3,662 population in 1,247 households, 1,181 owned, 66 rented. The neighborhoods:

Scalzo Scar

Residents generally have grown fond of the name Scalzo Scar, which began as outrage in the early '60s, when the Thomas Scalzo Development Co. clear-cut the forest to build this tract of homes. The reaction led to Mercer Island's land-clearing ordinance, the first of its kind in Washington. By the 1990s, it looked like a verdant empty-nester neighborhood—more than seven adults for every school-age child or teen. The first residents raised their families together, shared youth sports and school activities, and hosted neighborhood sleepovers. Politically, they worked together to slow traffic, sharing the cost of intersection islands.

Parkwood

Known for its meticulous landscaping, Parkwood also sports forts and treehouses in the woods that border three sides of the neighborhood: Southeast 53rd Place Open Space, Pioneer Park and Island Crest Park. After the homes were built in the late 1960s, this was a bustling family community. At one time in the 1970s, a family with eight children lived across the street from a family with nine kids.

In the 1980s, the neighborhood children left home, but by the mid-90s young families were starting to return. By 1994, there were more than four adults for each child. Neighbors are joined by legal covenants and restrictions in the deeds to their property. They must agree to pay for lighting and open space.

Paul Allen Estate

This multi-acre, multiple-home complex along Shore Lane also boasts docks, a helipad, a basketball gym and accessory buildings in the 6500 block of West Mercer Way.

Jane Meyer Brahm

Old and new on Faben Point: This 1940 home (top), owned by the late Hunter Simpson, was designed by Elizabeth Ayer, the first female graduate of the University of Washington architecture program, and the first registered female architect in the state of Washington. Just feet away (right) is an ultra-modern home designed by Eric Cobb.

Paul Allen built his mega-estate in the 1990s with remarkably few complaints from the Shore Lane neighbors. Of course, this is Mercer Island's wealthiest neighborhood. Median household income is skewed by the reporting limits on the census forms.

The waterfront homes are mostly isolated down private roads. In the early 1900s, real estate wasn't in such high demand on this southwest shore, when one promoter tried to rope in buyers by posting a "Grocery Store" sign on the shore — which turned out to be bogus.

Groveland

This area was founded as a summer Bible camp built in the 1920s. A handful of remodeled, expanded cabins still exist, mixed in with waterfront mansions. This is home to Mercer Island's only significant one-way streets.

In 1965, the city bought the church camp property and opened Groveland Beach Park. In the summer, neighborhood children spend their days at the beach and in the off-season they play basketball in the beach parking lot.

Homes around Deane's Children's Park, Island Park School and two quadrants of Pioneer Park also are in this tract.

TRACT 246.02

The southernmost tip, from Southeast 68th Street to South Point and Lakeview Highlands; 4,302 people in 1,549 households, 1,466

Mercer Island Reporter

Chris Briggs, a framing foreman for William E. Buchan Inc., works on one of the many houses under construction in The Lakes in 1989. The Lakes was the last large housing development on the Island.

owned, 83 rented. The neighborhoods:

Mercer Island Estates and Island Point

These neighborhoods have been geographic and demographic twins since the late '80s. Most of the homes here were built in the late 1960s and early '70s.

Young families enjoy proximity to Lakeridge and Island Park elementary schools and Islander Middle School. Level streets are good for bike riding. A higher percentage of residents here are school-age, compared to other neighborhoods.

Mercer Island Country Club, a first-rate tennis and swimming facility, is its anchor.

Homes in Mercer Island Estates are generally older and more modest than other south-end homes. These neighborhoods enjoy proximity to the south-end QFC Village, Sunnybeam School and the Mercer Island Saddle Club. Another quadrant of Pioneer Park offers trails for the horses.

Tarywood

Bald eagles maintain a nest in the top branches of a tree in the midst of this southeast Island neighborhood, blending nature with the grand homes that were developed in the 1980s, just south of Southeast 69th Street, east off Island Crest Way.

During the Great Depression, vagrants camped in the thick forests here, and by 1933, the Girl Scout Council established Camp Tarywood, with a lodge, tent platforms and cabins, which in the 1940s became a Brownie camp.

The school district bought the property in 1969, sold the beach area to the city for Mabel Clarke Park, and established the high school Humanities Block program at Tarywood. Declining enrollment forced the district to sell the land in the early 1980s and move humanities back to the main campus.

The Lakes and its neighbors

The president of this neighborhood association of 100 homes in The Lakes called this a "typical, all-American neighborhood" in the 1990s.

Built in the mid-1980s, it was derisively called a "typical, California-style development." The Buchan brothers (John and Bill) transformed a swampy property into a land o' (man-made) lakes, with beautiful landscaping, amenities and covenants that forbade fences.

Prior to development, the school district owned this land, a thick woods known as the South 40.

Halloween is famous here. Children arrive from all around to trick-or-treat. Because the homes are closely spaced, kids can ring more doorbells per hour, and the treats are tops.

This census block is one of the wealthiest on the Island, housing professionals and executives from large companies.

Chapter 19: Our Neighborhoods | 189

Midcentury Modern on Mercer Island

For decades home demolition was a growth industry on the Island, with lots being scraped for the construction of ever-bigger homes covering the property from lot line to lot line. Many Islanders of the new millennium are seeking to preserve hundreds of the modest-size "retro-kitsch" midcentury modern (MCM) homes that have survived five decades and more.

These ramblers and dramatic hillside hangers play to the sustainable sensibilities of new-age citizens, who also appreciate using modern materials, angles, natural light and green building techniques.

Of Mercer Island's 9,000-some households, hundreds of MCMs survive today, conceived between the 1930s and 1980s by such renowned Pacific Northwest architects as Paul Hayden Kirk (the Evans House, 1956), Wendell Harper Lovett (Scofield House, 1976), Gene Zema (the Lupton home, 1961), Ralph Anderson (the Stroum house), Elizabeth Ayers (the Davis house), as well as Nina Menon and Al Bumgardner and others who created practical houses for contemporary living..

In this genre on the institutional side were buildings by Fred Bassetti, who designed Lakeview Elementary School (1954) and Mercer Island High School (1958); Paul Thiry, who designed the Mercer Island Presbyterian Church (1961); and Larry Waldron, who, in the late 1950s designed Emmanuel Episcopal Church with angular spires. Don

Chadbourne + Doss

Located on the west side, this house is a reconstruction by Chadbourne + Doss of one of architect Fred Bassetti's earliest designs, built in 1962.

This renovated midcentury modern home originally designed by Paul Hayden Kirk is on the north end of the Island.

Frothingham designed the Congregational Church (1969), using all Northwest materials and natural lighting, and bringing the trees outside the windows into the thoughts of parishioners.

The Island's first planned unit development of 105-plus homes with a clubhouse on the eastern slopes, was platted from 1953 to 1966. Russell C. Emrich and his wife, Helen L. Ackerson Emrich (the heiress of the Ackerson Park property), began the development process of Mercerwood Shore Club in 1954.

Other partners joined in: Eva Crowder, Darwin and Esther Pitz, V.V. Brice and Hugh Benton Jr. in 1956; Fredrick and Leona Tennant Slyfield in 1958. By 1963 and 1966, Linn Emrich, son of Russell Emrich, had power of attorney for the project, under the umbrella of the Western Development Co. Mercerwood Shore Club began with fairly restrictive covenants:

"We had 25-foot setbacks, ridgeline (height) restrictions and the covenants called for windows on only one side of structures to protect neighbors' views and privacies," says Chuck O'Brien, who built his home from 1954 to 1957. The association and its covenants have long since vanished and megahomes now crowd the curved hillside streets once designed for California-style ramblers, many with a view of the lake.

The current trend is "recasting" MCMs—ramblers sprout angular upper levels featuring steel and glass, skylights and modern materials to integrate inside with outside.

"Taking an existing home and improving it is very satisfying," says longtime Island resident and architect Jerry Gropp, who specializes in modern design and adaptation. "Our own home, originally designed by University of Washington architecture classmate Hawley Dudley, was a 'tear-down,' which we saved from the demolition crew. We've completely rebuilt it as well as restored the half-acre garden."

Matt Brashears

The gym at Mercer Island High School is lined with the banners of teams going back to the 1960s.

The Sporting Life

Athletics and fitness are important to Islanders young and old

The Island is surrounded by water, so it's no surprise that the lake has been the sporting field for many Islanders. Old-timers reminisce about growing up near the shoreline, learning to swim, row and sail at an early age. It was common to hear of people swimming from Mercer Island to Bellevue or Seattle.

In her account of growing up in the late 1880s and early 1900s, Florence Guitteau Storey wrote that, as a small child, "Father taught me to handle both boats (sailboat and rowboat). Once I rowed all the way by myself to Leschi Park and back, and often Ollie [her sister] and I rowed Mother to call on ladies in East Seattle."

Island Olympians

It seems natural that several of Mercer Island's Olympic athletes have earned their medals in water sports.

The first Olympic medal won by an Islander was in rowing, when Carl Lovsted was part of the University of Washington men's crew team that won the bronze medal in the 1952 Olympics in Helsinki. That same year, Peter Kennedy and his sister, Karol, won silver in pairs figure skating in the Winter Olympics in Oslo.

Nancy Ramey (Lethcoe) was the first Island-grown athlete to gain national and international attention in swimming. At 16 she won the silver medal in the 100-meter butterfly in the 1956 Summer Olympics in Melbourne, Australia. She set a world record in the 100- and 200-meter butterfly in 1958 and won six national titles.

In sailing, the Buchan name is legendary, for both racing and boat building. Bill Sr. (William Earl) won 11 medals at the Star World Championships and won his class in the Swiftsure Classic four times. He and his son, Bill Jr. (William Carl), each won gold medals in the 1984 Olympics in

Mary Wayte (Bradburne) wears her Olympic gold medal and displays the proclamation given in her honor by King County. She won the gold in the 200-meter freestyle swimming event at the 1984 Olympics.

Mercer Island Reporter

Chapter 20: The Sporting Life | 191

Mercer Island High School basketball coach Ed Pepple is surrounded by jubilant players as the team wins its first state title, in 1985. Pepple is the winningest high school basketball coach in state history.

Mercer Island Reporter

Ed Pepple: A legend in basketball coaching

In 1967, a decade after the high school opened, Ed Pepple was hired to take over the boys' basketball program. His impact was felt immediately.

"My first dinner party, I got into it with an assistant football coach," Pepple told the Mercer Island Reporter in 2009. The high school football team had just lost a heartbreaker, and the coaches blamed it on "Mercer Island-itis." The term was widely used at the high school to describe its struggling sports programs.

"I blamed it on the negative attitude that was constantly being reinforced," said Pepple. "Kids will try to meet your expectations; you have to set the bar high."

The bar went to great heights under Pepple. He believed that a team should work as a unit and no one player was bigger than the team. He required his players to wear maroon blazers and short hair—with no exceptions. He strictly enforced his tough rules.

During his 42 years at the high school Pepple accrued more wins than any other coach in the history of Washington state high school competition, regardless of the sport. At the time of his retirement, his 952 wins—880 with the Islanders—totaled 300 more than the next closest high school basketball coach in the state.

Part of Pepple's success was his Little Dribblers program, which taught kids the game beginning in elementary school, and in which the older players were mentors to the younger ones.

Pepple's teams won state titles in 1985, 1993, 1997 and 1999, won 22 division titles and finished second in state four times.

But it was the state title game in 1981 that became legend. With the score 65-64, a last-second shot by opponents Shadle Park went through the net. To many, including those at the scorer's table, the shot clearly occurred after the game was over. The Mercer Island team rushed the floor to celebrate their apparent victory. But Shadle Park was given the bucket and the state championship trophy. Most spectators vehemently questioned whether the ball left the player's hand before the final horn. Shadle Park was given the victory even after Mercer Island had been directed by an official to cut down the net.

Despite all the success of the boys' basketball team, there is only one retired jersey. Chris Kampe, the captain of the infamous 1981 team, died of cancer in 1993. The school honored the former student by retiring his number; his jersey still hangs in the gym.

Pepple's teams, on average, sent two players a year to play in college. Quin Snyder, who led the Islanders to their first state title, played on three Final Four teams for Duke University and went on to coach at a Division I college. He was an assistant coach for the Philadelphia 76ers in 2010 and 2011, and for the Los Angeles Lakers in 2012. For 2013 he accepted a coaching position at CSKV basketball club in Moscow, Russia. Snyder is one of Pepple's most successful players. Steve Hawes and Petur Gudmundsson went on to have extensive careers in the National Basketball Association.

Pepple had his only losing season as the Islanders head coach in 2006; he retired in 2009. He has been inducted into nine Halls of Fame, including the Naismith Memorial Basketball Hall of Fame in Springfield, Mass. A display in the National Basketball Hall of Fame features the Islander high school basketball program. In 2012, the Mercer Island High School basketball court was dedicated to Ed and Shirley Pepple.

Ed Pepple's basketball tradition lives on in his grandson, Matt Logie, who is head basketball coach at Whitworth University.

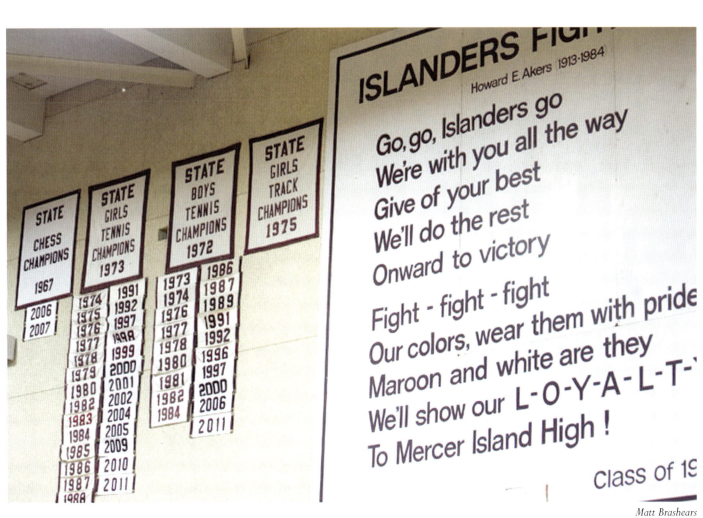

Matt Brashears

The walls of the Mercer Island High School gym are decked with maroon-and-white banners for championship wins in the many high school sports. The fight song banner above right is from the MIHS class of 1988.

Los Angeles, Bill Sr. in the Star class, and Bill Jr. in the Flying Dutchman class.

The best-known Olympian from Mercer Island is Mary Wayte (Bradburne), who swam with the Chinook Aquatic Club and Mercer Island High School before joining the 1984 and 1988 Olympic teams. She won the gold medal in the 1984 Olympics in Los Angeles in the 200-meter freestyle.

She also earned gold by swimming the preliminary heat for the winning 400-meter freestyle relay team. Wayte won two individual NCAA national titles in the 100-yard freestyle and the 400-yard individual medley in 1985. She went on to swim for the University of Florida. The Mercer Island swimming pool is named in her honor.

In the 1972 Olympics in Munich, West Germany, Islander Jeff Bannister competed in the decathlon. The most recent Olympian is Scott Driggers, who competed on the men's handball team in Seoul, Korea, in 1988. A 1981 MIHS grad, Driggers played football and basketball for the Islanders, and played both sports at Colorado College.

Over the decades, Mercer Island has spawned a diversity of sports and been a trailblazer in such arenas as basketball, water polo, lacrosse and marathoning, among others.

Many Islanders got their start in swimming and tennis at one of the three private clubs on the Island: Mercer Island Beach Club, Mercerwood Shore Club and Mercer Island Country Club. These clubs played an important role in athletics on the Island, resulting in dominant teams at Mercer Island High School.

Little League baseball, football and soccer, and Little Dribblers basketball also have thriving feeder programs.

Swimming

The Mary Wayte Pool has been the home of some of the greatest

Mercer Island Reporter

Christi Dorsey keeps her eye on the ball in this 1985 photo. The Mercer Island High School girls' tennis team has won 26 state titles since 1973.

Chapter 20: The Sporting Life | 193

Mercer Island Sports Figures

Don Bennett, who lost a leg in an accident in 1972, was the first amputee to climb Mount Rainier. He continued to ski and climb and do all the sports he loved. He started the American Amputee Soccer Association.

Steve Bunin, MIHS class of 1992, is an ESPN commentator as of 2012.

Brayden Billbe, MIHS class of 2003, played professional basketball in Europe and Japan.

Michael Blue, MIHS class of 1978, was champion in his age group in the 2010 Ironman Triathlon World Championships in Kona, Hawaii, finishing in 9 hours, 44 minutes and 19 seconds. He placed second in 2011. He has competed 12 times in the October event.

Trish Bostrom, in the pre-Title IX days, challenged the University of Washington to play on the men's tennis team. She won the right and went on to win an NCAA title, and was ranked as high as fifth in the world in doubles in 1978. A career highlight was a mixed-doubles team victory over a team with Billie Jean King at Wimbledon in 1977.

Fred Brown "Downtown Freddie" played 13 seasons in the NBA, all with the Seattle SuperSonics. He was selected to the NBA All-Star Game in 1976 and was captain of the Sonics' NBA championship team in 1978-1979. He holds the team's record for points in a regular season game (58), points in a playoff game (45) and steals in a game (10).

Bill Buchan (William Earl) and his son, **William Carl Buchan**, won gold medals in sailing in the 1984 Olympics.

Frank Ceteznik, former MIHS girls' swimming coach, was named National Coach of the Year in 1989.

Michael Chang, former professional tennis player, won the 1989 French Open. The International Tennis Hall of Fame member was the youngest-ever male player to win a Grand Slam singles title, at the age of 17.

Scott Didrickson played basketball for the University of Washington Huskies, then was assistant basketball coach at Colorado State, Oregon State and Gonzaga before becoming assistant coach for University of New Mexico.

Kevin Durant played basketball for the Seattle SuperSonics and now plays for the Oklahoma City Thunder.

Grant Farmer, MIHS class of 1994, played basketball at Williams College, then was a coach at Williams and at Washington and Lee University before becoming assistant coach at the University of New Mexico.

Adrian Hanauer is a minority owner and general manager of Seattle Sounders FC; as a student at Mercer Island High School, he made the varsity soccer team as a freshman.

Steve Hawes, MIHS grad, played professional basketball for the Houston Rockets, Portland Trailblazers, Atlanta Hawks and Seattle Supersonics.

Mike Holmgren was former Seattle Seahawks head coach.

Paul Jackson, MIHS wrestling coach for 27 years, guided four wrestlers to individual state titles.

Keith Jarrett and **Logan Gee** swam around the Island's perimeter in 2002.

Mark Jerue played nine years in the National Football League, with the New York Jets and the Los Angeles Rams.

Kasey Keller is a former goalkeeper for the Seattle Sounders FC.

Peter and Karol Kennedy, brother and sister, won silver medals in pairs figure skating in the 1952 Winter Olympics in Oslo, Norway.

David Kirtman, MIHS class of 2001, played college football for the USC Trojans, and played for the Seattle Seahawks, San Diego Chargers, San Francisco 49ers and New Orleans Saints.

Rashard Lewis, NBA forward, played for the Seattle Sonics for nine years.

Jeff Lindquist, MIHS class of 2012, was one of only five football players in the state named a "blue chip" recruit by *The Seattle Times*. He plays for the University of Washington Huskies.

Carl Lovsted was on the crew team that won a bronze medal in the 1952 Olympics.

Jamien and Justin McCullum, MIHS grads and sons of Seattle Seahawks receiver **Sam McCullum**, both played college football for the Stanford Cardinal. Justin played professional football for the Carolina Panthers.

Bill Muncey, winning unlimited hydroplane boat racer, died when his hydroplane flipped over in Acapulco in1981.

Dick Nicholl, former MIHS football coach, became the winningest coach in high school football in the state of Washington when he won his 137th game in 2001.

Jack Patera was the first head coach of the Seattle Seahawks, 1976 to 1982; 35-59-0 record.

Steve Penny is president and CEO of USA Gymnastics, and is responsible for the overall management of the national governing body of USA Gymnastics program.

Ed Pepple, longtime Mercer Island High School boys basketball coach, is the winningest high school coach in the state of Washington.

Owen Pochman, MIHS class of 1995, played football for the New York Giants in 2001 and the San Francisco 49ers in 2003.

Nancy Ramey (Lethcoe) won a silver medal in the 100-meter butterfly in the 1956 Summer Olympics. in Melbourne, Australia.

Blair Rasmussen played basketball for the Denver Nuggets and the Atlanta Hawks.

Bill Russell, NBA Hall of Famer, won 11 championships with the Boston Celtics. He also won five Most Valuable Player awards and was a 12-time All-Star.

Kazuhiro Sasaki was a relief pitcher for the Seattle Mariners, 2000-2003.

Sarah Shulman, MIHS grad, was named by *Inside Triathlon* magazine as an All-American athlete for 2004.

Quin Snyder, MIHS '85, is assistant coach for CSKA in Moscow, Russia. He was assistant coach for the Los Angeles Lakers, headed player development for the 76ers, was head coach of the Austin Toros from 2007-2010, and head coach at University of Missouri from 1999-2006. He was assistant coach at his alma mater, Duke, from 1993-1999, and assistant coach of the Los Angeles Clippers from 1992-1993.

Mark Stewart, former Island resident, was a linebacker at the University of Washington from 1979-1982, then for the Minnesota Vikings for two years. He was assistant football coach at Mercer Island High School for a time.

David Wainhouse, former professional baseball player, pitched for seven seasons in major league baseball. He played for the Montreal Expos, Seattle Mariners, Pittsburgh Pirates, Colorado Rockies and St. Louis Cardinals.

Mary Wayte (Bradburne) won the gold medal in the women's 200-meter freestyle at the 1984 Summer Olympics in Los Angeles.

Eric Wedge is a manager of the Seattle Mariners, as of 2012.

Sean White, MIHS class of 1999, is a Seattle Mariners pitcher as of 2012; he also played for the Boston Red Sox.

Jim Zorn, quarterback for the Seattle Seahawks during their first seven seasons, is the Seahawks quarterback coach as of 2012.

Matt Brashears

Mercer Island High School has won the state academic championship in numerous sports over the years. The Scholastic Awards Program recognizes the team with the highest grade point average among all Washington high schools in their enrollment classification.

swimmers and coaches in the state. Frank Ceteznik and Jeff Lowell helped guide the high school program during the past 40 years, along with local club coaches who helped shape the talent.

Ceteznik coached for 25 years, winning seven consecutive girls' state titles during the 1990s. In 1995, the girls won the national championship. Ceteznik coached 28 individual state champions, 13 relay champions and 167 All-American swimmers throughout his career. In 1989, he was recognized as the National Coach of the Year. One of his top swimmers, Megan Oesting, still holds the 4A state meet record in the 50-meter freestyle, which she set in 1990.

On the boys' side, former Islander Andy Lloyd holds the state swim record for the 200 individual medley, which he set in 1988. One of the most decorated swimmers in Islander history is Sean Sussex, who was an All-American swimmer at the University of Southern California. Sussex holds the 3A state meet record in the 50-meter freestyle and 100-meter freestyle. Sussex was also part of the 2003 state-title team that produced a national record in the 200-meter freestyle relay.

The Islander boys again set a state record in 2009 in the 400-meter freestyle relay. Under coach Jeff Lowell, the team won the state title in swimming in five of 11 seasons. Altogether, the boys' and girls' swim teams have won 17 state titles.

Tennis

Islander tennis has been a winning enterprise, a dynasty developed over decades. Island kids have played together since they were very young—usually at one of the private clubs—and come to the high school having already developed excellent skills.

The girls' team won 26 state titles from 1973 to 2012, many of them under the leadership of the late Joyce Hedlund, head coach for 15 years. Geoff Mills laid the foundation for both the world-class boys' and girls' programs. He and coach Mark Frisby led boys' teams to 19 state titles.

Basketball

Prior to 1967, much of the local sporting life centered around the lake and water sports—boating, waterskiing and swimming—along with tennis, horsemanship and a smattering of high school sports. But that year, Ed Pepple took over the Mercer Island High School boys' basketball program and began building it into a powerhouse—from the ground up.

His Little Dribblers program groomed youths and paired them with the already skilled players. Its all-star teams won five national tournaments in Loveland, Texas, from 1971 to 2001. The 12-year-old teams stayed with families there and enjoyed Western life. His traveling teams visited Australia, Europe and all across the U.S. to play the best teams possible. Pepple also ran summer camps and clinics to hone skills year-round.

During Pepple's 42-year tenure, his teams helped put Mercer Island High School sports on the map, and packed the gyms for basketball games. The boys' high school basketball team won four state titles, in 1985, 1993, 1997 and 1999. They

Mercer Island Reporter

The Mercer Island High school girls swim team celebrates their state championship in 1993, with coaches Bob Harshbarger, left, and Frank Ceteznik, right.

Mercer Island Reporter

Wrestling coach Paul Jackson watches a pair of team members in this 1993 photo. Jackson was Mercer Island High School's wrestling coach for 27 years.

Mercer Island's Northwest Yeshiva High School made history in 2010 when it became the first Orthodox Jewish school to send a basketball team to the state tournament. The girls' squad became the first team in state history to forfeit a state tournament game that same year, as it conflicted with days of religious fasting.

Football

Dick Nicholl was Mercer Island High School head football coach for 28 years, from 1979 to 2006. In 2002, he had the most wins of any football coach in KingCo league history. He guided the 1976 Islander team to the state title and was inducted into the Washington State Football Coaches Hall of Fame in 2004, the Pro Athlete Outreach Coaches' Wall of Honor in 2007 and the Pacific Northwest Hall of Fame in 2009.

In 1986, Mercer Island set a new KingCo record by allowing only nine points to be scored against the undefeated team during the entire nine-game regular season. Nicholl also guided the 1988 Islander team to the state semifinals.

Greg Mahoney had one of the best individual games in the history of the Mercer Island High School football program, running for more than 350 yards and six touchdowns in a 2006 game against Seattle Prep. Doubling as the team's place kicker, Mahoney set a school record for points scored in a game by one player.

Jeff Lindquist rewrote the Mercer Island record book at the quarterback position in 2012, when he was one of the top-rated high school quarterbacks in the nation. He committed to play for the University of Washington Huskies.

Mercer Island High School has produced many college players. Mark Jerue (1978 grad), Owen Pochman (1995 grad) and David Kirtman (2001 grad) all went on to play in the National Football League.

won 22 division titles and finished second in state four times.

Pepple's teams, on average, sent two players a year to play at the college level, and several players went on to play as professionals. Two players, Steve Hawes and Petur Gudmundsson, went on to careers in the National Basketball Association, and another, Quin Snyder, went on to coach at a Division I college and in the NBA. Pepple may have been proudest that both his sons, Terry and Kyle, played on his teams and helped coach — as well as his grandson, Matt Logie.

Chapter 20: The Sporting Life | 197

MI High School Sports Hall of Fame

Athletes are selected by their coaches to enter the Mercer Island High School Hall of Fame a minimum of five years after graduation, taking into account not only their high school career, but also college and/or professional participation in the sport.

Baseball
1961 Dennis Keating
1961 Jerry Stubs
1970 Jim Webster
1972 Rob Kraft
1973 Tracy Harris
1980 Mark Field
1985 David Wainhouse
1997 Bryan Brown
2003 Justin Waldie

Boys' Basketball
1958 Bill Hanson
1959 Paul Crutchfield
1961 Dennis Keating
1964 John Nebel
1968 Steve Hawes
1970 Jeff Hawes
1972 Steve Biehn
1972 Greg Jack
1974 Doug Gribble
1977 Petur Gudmundsson
1979 Paul Bain
1982 Albert Moscatel
1982 Kyle Pepple
1985 Brian Schwabe
1985 Quin Snyder
1987 Brock Wortman
1987 Eric Brady
1987 John Gilliland
1989 Grant Tracy
1989 Travis DeCure
1991 Scott Didrickson
1992 Fred Brown Jr.
1993 Grant Farmer
1995 Terrik Brown
1996 Jamal Hill
1997 Bryan Brown
1997 Jamien McCullum
1997 Diron Mobley
1999 Tyler Besecker
1999 Josh Fisher
1999 Matt Logie
1999 Elliot Prasse-Freeman
2000 Gavin Cree
2001 Justin McCullum
2002 Kevin Tempest
2003 Brayden Billbe
2003 Brandon Burmeister
2003 Justin Waldie
2004 Michael Gottlieb

2005 Brandon Fellows
2007 Trevor Fulp
1961-1980 Mel Light (coach)
1967-2009 Ed Pepple (coach)

Girls' Basketball
1975 Barb Berry
1992 Dena Dey
1999 Lexie Richards
2000 Nicole Kelleher
2001 Courtney Reimers
2001 Julie Rindlaub
2003 Beth Richards Christofferson
2003 Allison Stewart
2004 Rita Dierdorff
2005 Lynne Tempest

Cross-country
1961 Karl Weiser
1984 Cattie Fox
1984 Claudia Crawford
1986 Stephan Nelson
1991 Chris Hillyer
1992 Jola Prock
1997 Donnie Fellows
2000 Darienne Dey
2000 Nicole Kelleher
2004 Sarah McFadden
2005 Jean Lashchever
2005 Brandon Fellows
2005 Brian Govier

Football
1961 Dennis Keating
1962 Darren Hostvedt
1963 Don Hazen
1969 Jeff Apostolou
1970 Jim Webster
1978 Mark Jerue
1978 George Winterscheid
1979 Paul Schwabe
1980 Bruce Kroon
1981 Ed Katz
1982 Tony Grossi
1982 Mike Neklason
1983 Dale Bathun
1986 Peter Bailey
1986 Jeff Johnson
1987 Reed Pangborn
1988 Sam Davidson
1989 Geoff Evans

1990 Jon Braman
1990 Nick Morris
1991 Chris Nicholl
1992 Gary Shavey
1993 Matt Hale
1995 Owen Pochman
1996 Jamal Hill
1997 Jamien McCullum
1998 Ben Mahdavi
1999 Justin Peterson
2001 David Kirtman
2001 Justin McCullum
2001 Alex Sirianni
2003 Brandon Burmeister
2004 Michael Gottlieb
2005 Jessse Johnson
2005 Chris Taylor
2007 Greg Mahony
1974-2007 Dick Nicholl (coach)

Boys' Golf
1978 Gordon Graybeal

Gymnastics
2006 Kelsey Ingram

Boys' Lacrosse
2007 Greg Mahoney

Girls' Soccer
1992 Dena Dey
1999 Lexie Richards
2000 Darienne Dey
2000 Nicole Kelleher
2003 Beth Richards Christofferson
2005 Maddie O'Meara
2005 Lynne Tempest

Boys' Soccer
1978 Scott Gibson
1980 Jean-Daniel Ballet
1982 Matt Smith
1987 Matt Gavin
1988 Chris Bauer
1997 Dalibor Snyder
2002 Duke Biggers
2005 Brian Govier

Girls' Softball
2003 Allison Stewart
2004 Rita Dierdorff

198 | Chapter 20: The Sporting Life

Boys' Swimming
1966 Nick LeClerq
1981 John Bryant
1988 Andy Lloyd
1990 Tom Campbell
1998 Jeff Guyman
1999 Timmy Chung
2003 Sean Sussex
1974-1978 Frank Ceteznik (coach)

Girls' Swimming
1958 Nancy Ramey
1977 Cyndi McCullum
1978 Cathy Wilson
1981 Marci Ballard
1983 Mary Wayte
1984 Loretta Soffe
1985 Tammy Nedel
1987 Shelley Farmer
1987 Jennie Cameron
1989 Carrie Reed Mackay
1990 Megan Oesting
1996 Jennifer Strasburger
1998 Michelle Harper
1999 Jane Humphries
2000 Ashleigh Jacobs
2003 Annika Giesbrecht (diving)
2006 Kelsey Ingram
1974-1978 Frank Ceteznik (coach)

Boys' Tennis
1971 Brian Adams
1971 Rob Bradshaw
1974 Dave Larson
1974 Dave Maeser
1974 Dave Rumph
1977 Tom Segers
1979 Steve Winterbauer
1982 Andy Winterbauer
1984 Rick Hodge
1987 Matt Zisette
1989 Chet Crile
1992 Tim Gottesman
1997 Dalibor Snyder
2007 Chris Bailey
2007 Trevor Fulp
1961-1995 Geoff Mills (coach)
1991-2009 Joyce Hedlund (coach)

Girls' Tennis
1978 Leslie Tobin
1980 Terri Agee
1982 Lori Brillhart
1982 Erin Majury
1985 Mindy Mounger
1985 Wendy Gross
1987 Cindy Olejar
1988 Shelly Keller

Mercer Island Repoter
Quin Snyder carries the state championship trophy in 1985, the first state title won by the Mercer Island High School basketball team.

1989 Liz Allen
1989 April Appel
1993 Erin Gowen
1998 Allison Rindlaub
1999 Katie Cunha
2001 Lindsey Adams
2004 Stephanie Hammond
1991-2009 Joyce Hedlund (coach)

Track and Field
1961 Karl Weiser
1962 Darren Hostvedt
1963 Bart Barto
1963 Tom Harmon
1965 Steve Hoover
1969 Bob Glaze
1969 Mark Wooden
1970 Sam LeClerq
1971 Chris Cole
1976 Jeff Johnson
1976 Dick Pangallo
1976 Steve Vargha
1977 Peter Dawson
1978 Kathy Wilson
1980 Annie Barrett
1980 Missy Nelson
1982 Tauni Sanchez
1984 Meagan Dewey
1986 Stephen Nelson
1991 Brook Lorenzen
1992 Dena Dey
1996 Jamal Hill

1997 Donnie Fellows
1999 Justin Peterson
2000 Darienne Dey
2000 Nicole Kelleher
2000 Susan Rindlaub
2001 David Kirkman
2001 Justin McCullum
2001 Courtney Reimers
2003 Brandon Burmeister
2004 Michael Gottlieb
2004 Sarah McFadden
2005 Brandon Fellows
2005 Brian Govier
2005 Jean Lashchever
2005 Maddie O'Meara
1961-1980 Mel Light (coach)

Volleyball
1981 Marilyn Hopkins
1984 Shelly Birch
1989 Hayley Lorenzen
2000 Allison Campbell
2000 Susan Rindlaub McKay
2001 Courtney Reimers
2001 Julia Rindlaub
2003 Allison Stewart
1961-1980 Mel Light (coach)

Wrestling
1968 Kim Giard
1979 Jeff Wilson
1981 Ed Katz
1981 Todd Cassan
1982 Mike Neklason
1984 Pat Joseph
1986 Jim Nicholl
1987 Barry Bunin
1990 Brad Smith
1990 Jay Jackson
1990 Brad Smith
1998 Ben Mahdavi
2000 Darienne Dey
2005 Jesse Johnson
2005 Jean Lashchever
1977-1999 Paul Jackson (coach)
2001-2005 Paul Jackson (coach)

Boys' Water Polo
1998 Jeff Guyman
2002 Kevin Tempest
2003 Sean Sussex
2006 Kyle Sterling

Girls' Water Polo
1999 Jane Humphries
2000 Allison Campbell

Chapter 20: The Sporting Life | 199

Mercer Island Reporter

Competitors in the 8-and-under boys' 100-meter relay wait as their team does laps during a meet between Mercer Island Country Club and Mercer Island Beach Club in 1995. The private clubs have always played an important role in recreation and athletics for Island families.

Wrestling

Paul Jackson was a big part of the Islander football team for nearly 22 years as an assistant coach. But it was his 27 years as the school's wrestling coach that defined his career. Jackson guided four wrestlers to individual state titles, including his son, Jay Jackson, who later was captain of the Stanford wrestling team and earned All-American in the National Olympic Trials; Jeff Wilson, who was a two-time state champion and a College All-American at Stanford; Ben Mahdavi, who was an outstanding linebacker at UW; and Trevor Howard.

The Mercer Island High School wrestling team won six division titles. Kim Giard was the school's first state champion, in 1961; the most recent winner of a state wrestling title was Blake Johnson, in 2012. Coach Jackson was inducted into the Washington State Wrestling Coaches Hall of Fame in 2008.

One of the most impressive Mercer Island High School wrestlers was a female. Jean Laschever is one of the only girls in the history of Washington state high school athletics to compete in a male-dominated sport and letter all four years. Laschever, who went on to wrestle in college, is one of the only Islander athletes to letter in all 12 seasons of her high school career.

Lacrosse/Water polo

Two of the newest varsity sports programs at Mercer Island High School have also achieved impres-

Mercer Island Reporter

Edie Marshall guides her horse over a jump in a performance at the Mercer Island Saddle Club in 1988. The Saddle Club has long been the hub of equestrian activity.

sive results. The boys' lacrosse program is one of the best in the state, under the tutelage of head coach Ian O'Hearn. The Islander boys have won five state titles, in 2001, 2004, 2005, 2006 and 2011, and produced major-league lacrosse players Greg Mahoney and Chris Taylor. The girls' lacrosse team were 2001 state champs.

Mercer Island High School dominates in water polo for both the boys' and girls' teams. The boys' teams,

Jay Kim, left, and Sunny Yoo, both members of the Mercer Island Martial Arts Academy, practice their moves to get ready for a competition in this 1989 photo. Over the years, there's been a strong interest in martial arts, tae kwon do and similar sports.

Mercer Island Reporter

under coach Jeff Lowell, have won 11 state titles since 1997, while the girls have won eight state titles during the same time.

Baseball

Mercer Island Little League baseball, which began in the 1950s, and the next-step Babe Ruth program segued to Island high school teams, once coached by Bernie Averill, son of Earl, a Hall of Famer. But it wasn't until 2009 that Mercer Island Little League went high profile as the fifth squad from Washington to win the Northwest Region and the eighth overall from the state to advance to the Little League World Series in Williamsport since 1957.

In 2011, the U-11 all-star team won the state title. The 2012 MI Little League team of 12-year-old boys were runners-up in the Northwest Regional Division for the World Series. They powerhoused their way through 12 consecutive games but were finally beaten by the Gresham, Ore., team.

Mercer Island had joined American Little League play in 2006, spearheaded by Brian Emanuels and the Boys & Girls Club

Mercer Island produced two Major League baseball players: Dave Wainhouse and Sean White. Wainhouse played seven years in the majors, while, as of 2012, White continues in the majors after three seasons. One of the legendary high school teams played in 1972, after which Rob Kraft and the late Steve Stillwell were drafted by the Seattle Rainiers minor-league team.

Other MIHS sports

Other sports at MIHS include cross-country, golf, soccer, volleyball, gymnastics, softball, and track and field, as well as cheerleading and drill team. The school has long been known for its consistently high number of scholar athletes, who not only excel in sports, but also maintain a high grade point average.

Community events

Island athletics goes far beyond the high school. One of the biggest annual events on the Island every March is the Mercer Island Rotary Half Marathon. The event marked its 40th year in 2012, and has grown from a mere 19 participants its first year to nearly 5,000 in 2012. Hundreds of volunteers help with the variety of events: half marathon, 10K, 5K and a kids' dash for ages 12 and under. In recent years the proceeds have gone to colon cancer research and prevention, and other local projects of the Mercer Island Rotary Club.

Escape from the Rock, the annual Mercer Island triathlon, celebrated its 16th year in 2012. Held in September, the event includes a half-mile swim off Luther Burbank Park, a 12-mile bike ride out and back on the closed express lanes of I-90, and a 2.5-mile run on Mercer Island.

Staying fit

Islanders who want to stay fit and have fun while exercising or playing on a team can find many choices on the Island. The private clubs—Mercer Island Country Club, Mercer Island Beach Club, Mercerwood Shore Club and Stroum Jewish Community Center—provide a broad range of sporting opportunities. Mary Wayte Pool offers swimming for all ages and is the home of Mercer Island High School aquatic sports.

The Mercer Island Parks and Recreation Department offers a wide variety of sports and activities for all ages, including martial arts, walking and cycling groups, and exercise and conditioning programs. Due to the rising use of the Island's parks and ballfields, the Ballfield User Group was established in 1991 to help regulate facilities, policies and scheduling.

Mercer Island Reporter

A bicyclist wends his way on an autumn day on the Park on the Lid. The Island has become a destination spot for bicyclists.

A member of the Rockers, Mercer Island's senior-league softball team, is about to make a catch. The team has been playing for more than 30 years.

Mercer Island Reporter

202 | Chapter 20: The Sporting Life

Jane Meyer Brahm

Retired artist Adah Edwards renders Mercer Island in a primitive style on wooden bowls, baskets, stools, note cards and other gift items.

2000 to the Future

A sea change for the Island community

As the new decade opened, Mercer Island's Town Center began its Pygmalian transformation. The economy was booming, optimism was high and building activity was picking up. In January 2000 Alan Merkle was voted mayor, taking the helm of a city that was quiet, stable and in the black.

The state's Growth Management Act of 1990 stipulated that Mercer Island must eventually absorb a population increase to 25,000. Rather than increase density by rezoning single-family neighborhoods, Mercer Island chose higher density in its Town Center, allowing construction of buildings up to five stories (with an additional story for certain amenities) and encouraging apartments and condominiums.

These goals were part of the city's Comprehensive Plan in 1994, but it took nearly a decade before property owners and developers had confidence enough in the economy to begin construction. Finally the street project was finished, the infrastructure was in place and the economy was booming.

Town Center changes

By 2002, Mercer Island was no longer the sleepy burg it had been for decades. As many as six multistory building projects were on the drawing boards all at once.

The first mixed-use project was **Avellino Apartments**, just south of the QFC. It includes 23 apartments and 2,600 square feet of retail and office space.

Across the street came **Newell Court**, in the former location of the Jack in the Box. It includes 2,542 square feet of retail space and 40 apartments in a three-story building.

Dwarfing those buildings was the five-story, mixed-use project

The Town Center Plan was completed in 1994, but it took nearly a decade before any development occurred.

Island Square, approved by the Design Commission in 2001. The largest downtown project to date (2012), it consists of five buildings totaling 252,000 square feet over a two-level parking structure with 500 parking stalls. It was owned by Islander Steve Cohn and was built by SECO Development, with 210 apartments and 40,000 square feet of retail/business space.

Not long after, demolition began on the old, low-slung buildings on the northwest corner of Southeast 27th Street and 77th Avenue Southeast. A new mixed-use project, **The Mercer**, developed by Dollar Development owner James Cassan, consists of three

Chapter 21: 2000 to the Present | 203

This photo depicts least four trees topped by vandals at the Park on the Lid in 1995. Trimming trees on public property for views was just one of the myriad tree-related issues the City Council considered.

Mercer Island Reporter

Tussle over trees: property rights advocates vs. environmentalists

A few issues that had simmered in the late '90s bubbled up in the new decade. One was the debate on trees.

It began in July 1999, when the City Council appointed the Tree and Natural Resources Task Force to shape the Island's vision for trees in the Comprehensive Plan. After working for months with little public interest, the task force found its work under fire as over-regulation of private property, just weeks before its recommendation was to be adopted. The recommendation was ultimately rejected by the City Council.

Meanwhile, many criticized the city's existing tree regulations, since they became clearer after the city collected all of its tree-related regulations into one document.

In September 2000, the council had a chance to make the ordinance less restrictive by amending parts the public complained about during meetings—mainly a tree replacement ratio and the requirement to set aside money for replacement trees. The ordinance did not regulate private property, with the exception of property located in "critical areas"—that is, steep slopes, wetlands and watercourses.

Rather than taking a piecemeal approach, the City Council decided to rewrite the entire ordinance. They began in January 2001, using a draft written by council members Dan Grausz and El Jahncke as a starting point. They were attempting to strike a balance between tree protection and private property rights—but they struck a nerve with many Islanders.

There was concern about loss of the Island's tree canopy and changes in the essential character of Mercer Island. The debate about trees brought out property rights advocates and environmentalists, old-timers and new residents, developers and preservationists, "tree huggers" and people who wanted to regain lost views. It seemed that everyone had an opinion about trees.

After several revisions, in May the council sent the draft ordinance to the Planning Commission for its opinion, since they couldn't agree whether to include provisions regulating private non-critical-area property or allowing people to prune public trees to improve their views.

Public comments were divided, but leaned against regulating trees on private property. A majority was against allowing pruning of public trees for views.

The Planning Commission recommended against regulation of flat-lot private property or private pruning of public trees for views. But the council went against that recommendation and, on a 4-3 vote, passed an ordinance that included more private property regulation and allowed view pruning on public land.

It was a stunning turn of events. And it fomented so much discord that south-end citizen Ira Appelman launched a referendum campaign to either repeal the new ordinance or put it on the ballot for a vote. The campaign collected more than 3,800 signatures, far surpassing the 2,450 needed. It was the first—and, as of 2013, only—successful referendum in Mercer Island's history. The City Council repealed the ordinance on July 31, 2001.

In January 2002, the City Council approved a tree ordinance that was very similar to the draft approved by the Planning Commission the year before. The tree issue was finally put to rest—at least temporarily.

This aerial photo, left, taken in about 2000, looks north from Mercerdale Park to Lake Washington. The park-and-ride lot, below, was expanded in 2008. From the day it reopened, it has been full most days. It is the most heavily used park-and-ride lot in the county, according to the Puget Sound Regional Council.
Mercer Island Reporter

five-story buildings with 210 apartments and 18,000 square feet of retail and office space. The Mercer's second phase is expected to be completed by fall 2013, adding 85 units and more retail space, giving it the distinction of being the largest Town Center residence as of 2013.

The sliver of property in front of The Mercer, occupied for years by Simba's Auto Service, was sold to Starbucks. A lawsuit filed by Dollar Development claimed that Starbucks' planned drive-through would cause pollution affecting The Mercer's apartment dwellers. Starbucks prevailed and constructed its ski-lodge-type coffeehouse, with outdoor seating.

A small dry cleaner next to Tully's on 78th Avenue Southeast was demolished and the **7800 Plaza Condos** were built, which had 24 units in 27,000 square feet of residential space.

In April 2007, the Sunset Chevron and Foodmart, Cleaners Plus 1 and Coldwell Banker Bain offices (property formerly owned by Steve Cohn) were demolished to make way for the construction of the **77 Central** complex. Opened in July 2009, the project has more than 150 apartments and 25,000 square feet of ground-floor retail space, with HSBC Bank as its anchor tenant.

In 2008, **Aljoya**, an upscale retirement home built by ERA Living on the property formerly occupied by Denny's and Haruko's Restaurant, opened. The five-story development fronts the Outdoor Sculpture Garden and includes 114 independent and assisted-living units, 24,800 square feet of resident amenities and a restaurant, Lilly's, that is open to the public.

In 2012, on the site of the old Safeway on 76th Avenue Southeast, the six-level, mixed-use **Aviara** began taking shape, with 163 apartments above, seven to nine retail/restaurant spaces on the ground floor and 300 underground parking spaces.

The Hudesman Center, on 76th Avenue Southeast, which housed True Value Hardware, The Islander Pub and other businesses, was purchased in 2012 by The Legacy Group

1997 Mercer Island High School goes from a AAAA to a AAA school after sports league reorganization and declining enrollment.

1997 Iggy, the iguana in Mr. Oaklief's science room at Islander Middle School, makes national news for pulling the school's fire alarm.

1998 The school board bans possession of tobacco on school property for anyone under 18.

1998 The Mercer Island Marching Band marches in cardboard boxes at a football game in October to demonstrate the need for new uniforms.

1998 Mercer Island makes the news with a cover story in *The New York Times* about alledged racism in the MI Police Department and endemic harassment of minorities. In the end, the story is the result of one man's vendetta against the MIPD.

1998 The death of 12-year-old Islander Middle School student Kristine Kastner due to a severe allergic reaction to peanuts in a cookie eventually leads to a law in Washington state, the Kristine Kastner Act, allowing emergency medical technicians to administer lifesaving epinephrine.

1998 The Mercer Island School District celebrates the completion of the $37.5 million renovation of Mercer Island High School.

1998 In November, voters reject a $19.5 million bond issue to build a new community center.

1999 The French American School of Puget Sound opens in September.

1999 Paula Butterfield is named Mercer Island school superintendent.

1999 The Gateway Project, a tableau with silhouette figures and a Mercer Island marker, is dedicated in October.

1999 The new $2.9 million north-end fire station is completed in June. The two-story, 16,400-square-foot station is more than double the size of the old one.

Primavera, a sculpture by Roslyn Mazzilli at corner of Southeast 27th Street and 80th Avenue Southeast, is the anchor of the Outdoor Sculpture Gallery.

Mercer Island Reporter

and the Keeler family of Mercer Island. A mixed-use development, named **Legacy Mercer Island**, is planned.

With more than 1,000 new housing units added to the mix within 11 years, some citizens feared excessive traffic, parking problems and crime. However, after the detours and construction dust settled, the city's biennial survey showed that most Islanders accepted their new niche of pedestrian-oriented urban living, with lots of nearby walking paths, transit, restaurants, shops and services.

Parking and traffic

The city had its work cut out to adjust to parking demands. Parking in the Town Center became the council's top priority in 2001. The park-and-ride lot was overflowing, as were downtown and north-end neighborhood streets.

After numerous meetings with north-end neighbors, the council adopted an ordinance to restrict all-day parking near the park-and-ride. Parking permits were issued, and only residents with permits could park on certain public streets in the north-end neighborhoods. In addition, on-street parking from 7 a.m. to 9 a.m. was not allowed without a permit, thus relieving the Town Center parking pressure.

At the same time, the city changed the parking requirements for new developments. Previously, downtown property owners were required to provide parking spaces based on the square footage of their property, without distinction as to types of businesses with high-demand parking. The new parking ordinance required developers to account for types of uses and activities.

The first downtown traffic lights, at Southeast 27th Street and 77th and 78th Avenues Southeast, were installed in January 2012,

After much debate, Island Crest Way was reconfigured on its southern end in 2012—the "road diet"—to reduce it from four to three lanes, for safer driving.

City of Mercer Island

The new Community Center at Mercer View—later renamed the Mercer Island Community and Events Center—opened with a big, two-day celebration in December 2005.

A new transportation and traffic challenge emerged in 2012, when the tolling of the SR 520 bridge diverted thousands of motorists to drive I-90 instead. Commute time across the Island is jammed.

The state is considering tolling I-90 across Mercer Island as well, which could add several thousands of dollars to motorists' daily commuting costs. That decision is expected by the end of 2015.

More changes

As demolition and construction continued to change the face of the downtown, the disruption hit a peak in 2005, as Town Center projects converged with construction of the new Community Center at Mercer View, only a few blocks away.

The economic downturn that began with the banking crisis of 2007-2008 also eventually affected the Town Center.

By 2012, Finders gift shop had closed after decades, as did several tenants of The Mercer, such as Cellar 46 wine shop and restaurant, Dooz hair salon for children and Quiznos.

New mixed-use projects had been able to rent their apartments, but it was harder to rent their ground-floor spaces. Some developers complained that the city's requirements were onerous for a specific mix of retail and other businesses on the ground floor of new developments.

By the middle of 2012, the City Council was considering relaxing its Town Center regulations to help fill empty storefronts.

After the 2007-2012 recession depressed activity in the Town Center, positive signs emerged. Freshy's Seafood revamped the former Windle's 76 gas station at 76th Avenue Southeast, close to the site of Hap Lightfoot's pioneer-days store.

The Sunday Farmers Market, which began in 2007, injected lively activity into the downtown during the growing season, and the Mercer Island Thrift Shop began grossing more than $1 million a year in sales.

Some Island merchants also began selling spirits in 2012 after the state discontinued its sales. Liquor sales were up 3 percent after this privatization.

At last, a new community center

After the resounding defeat of the community center bond issue in 1998, community soul-searching ensued. Public and private groups discussed possible shared use of facilities to benefit all residents—the community center, the school district, the Boys & Girls Club, the Stroum Jewish Community Center and the French American School of Puget Sound.

Meanwhile, city planners again explored whether to remodel the former Mercer View School that had been serving as a community center, construct a brand-new building, or form a public-private partnership for a community center elsewhere.

The question was put to rest in 2003, when the city took ownership of the Mercer View property, paying the remaining $2.4 million on the property to the Mercer Island School District.

Planners pared down the design and costs to demolish the old Mercer View building and construct a new community center on the same site. The $13.1 million, 42,000-square-foot building designed by Miller Hull was the biggest and most complex capital improvement project in the city of

Chapter 21: 2000 to the Present | *207*

1999 Joanne Peterson files a suit to close the Roanoke Inn, claiming it's illegal and a neighborhood nuisance.

1999 The city and local businesses get ready for Y2K, fearing business disruptions, food shortages, electricity blackouts, etc. The anticipated problems didn't materialize.

2000 The population is 22,036.

2000 Superintendent Paula Butterfield suddenly resigns from the school district after only seven months on the job, taking with her a settlement of $197,000.

2000 Mercer Island mayor Alan Merkle and Jean Denais, mayor of Thonon-les-Bains, France, sign the official agreement establishing a sister-city relationship between the two cities.

2001 The Nisqually earthquake, registering 6.8 on the Richter scale, rattles Puget Sound on Feb. 28. Mercer Island suffers minor damage.

2001 A 133-foot cell tower is erected at the south-end fire station.

2001 The city's largest-ever downtown project, Island Square, receives Design Commission approval.

2001 The state Supreme Court refuses to hear John and Joanne Peterson's lawsuit against the city and the Roanoke Inn, ending years of legal maneuvering to close the tavern.

2001 Denny's closes after 25 years on the Island.

2001 The Mercer Island Preschool Association marks the 30th anniversary of Toy Swap.

2001 The city launches the E-Gov interactive Web site.

2001 Shorewood Heights completes a $20 million project renovating 500 apartments and constructing two new 39-unit buildings.

2001 School enrollment is down by 121 students, the first decline in more than 10 years.

Mercer Island Reporter

For decades, Youth Theatre Northwest has been located on the north campus or "megablock" of school district property, in a building that was once North Mercer Junior High School. The future location of YTN is uncertain, as it will have to move when the megablock is redeveloped.

Mercer Island Reporter

Mary Wayte Pool, built in 1973, is a public pool that is also home to the aquatics programs of Mercer Island High School. It is owned by the school district, subsidized by the city of Mercer Island and operated by Olympic Cascade Aquatics. The future of the aging facility is uncertain, pending decisions on the development of the megablock property.

Mercer Island's history.

What's more, the city built it without going to the taxpayers on a bond issue. The city borrowed less than $3 million for the project; the rest came from the city's capital reserve budget, which had profited from the hot economy.

A party commemorated the old Mercer View School and honored its teachers and students. The building was demolished in 2004 and construction began on the new center.

Three preschools there were relocated: Patti's Play Center to Emmanuel Episcopal Church, and Little Acorn and Pixie Hill to the North Mercer campus. The offices of Mercer Island Youth and Family Services and the

Ray Kaltenbach

Camille Chrysler, above, high-kicks in the Summer Celebration parade in 2006. She and Mercerart have participated in all but one Summer Celebration parade. Above right, Chrysler and her husband, Ray Kaltenbach, break ground on the new Mercerart dance studio in 1978. At right, the first SeaGals dance team in 1977, directed by Chrysler.

Mercerart: Still dancing after all these years

Camille Chrysler and her husband, Ray Kaltenbach, have engaged more than 6,000 youths—two-thirds from Mercer Island—in the performing arts over their 53-year run. Their enterprise, Mercerart, began as a private conservatory of music, dance and drama, but soon became focused on Chrysler's forté: dance. (She trained under Ray Bolger for tap, Merce Cunningham and Martha Graham for modern, Russian ballet teachers Balanchine and Preobajinkska.)

From the first of her students' performances at the VFW Hall in 1958 to Mercerart's 50th commemorative recital at Carco Park in 2008, she has shepherded Island protégés to the Radio City Rockettes, Martha Graham Dance, the Chamber Dance Company, Joffrey Ballet, Broadway and Las Vegas stages. Dance training inspired others to become physical therapists, physicians and teachers of the next generation of dancers.

Mercerart began in the studio of their First Hill home, where Kaltenbach built Chrysler a floating floor and mirrored walls—until it was bumped by I-90. When they moved to the Calkins Homestead nearby, it too was scratched for an on-ramp. Next, Kaltenbach built a stand-alone studio in 1978, which, within a decade, was usurped by the park-and-ride lot. Since 1987, Chrysler has taught in her studio above Oh! Chocolate, a safe distance from I-90, she hopes.

It's never been about place anyway, she insists. She has trouped students through Britain, Europe, Africa, San Francisco (50th trip in 2010), New York and other stages afar to give them a taste of dance and life. They've performed in scores of parades, often accompanied by Kaltenbach's show Corvettes, and annually at the VFW Hall, an homage to where it all began.

Other highlights:

• Directing the first Seahawks Sea Gals dance team—which included Islanders Nan and Celeste Barnett, Paris Brown, Ann Bullis, Diane Eng, Susan Gresia, Anita and Lynn Italiane, Albeny Jinka, Mary Ann Lamb, Laurie Manlowe and Kim Santee—in 1977.

• Dancing with her students on the "old" I-90 bridge before it sank in 1990.

• Choreographing the first Mercer Island Children's Theater production and other high school musicals; performing a concert with University of Washington's 21-piece jazz ensemble; running summer dance camps, a children's chorus, and charity lessons and performances.

• Teaching kids to be "thinkers, survivors and nice people—as important as any dance form," Chrysler insists.

At age 70-something, Chrysler's still kicking high over her head, and performing, with the aid of bionic body parts installed by Dr. Charles Peterson, a longtime friend. Kaltenbach counts her having done 3 million pliés through it all, and she's filled more than 100 journals about her dance career.

In 2008, thanks to the passage of a $12 million bond issue for park improvement at Luther Burbank Park, the popular off-leash dog park was redone. In addition, 1,500 feet of adjacent shoreline were restored and improved.

Mercer Island Reporter

2002 An 111th-hour deal with Northwest Center, a regional organization for developmentally disabled people, keeps Mary Wayte pool open.

2002 School Superintendent Bill Keim resigns.

2003 The city of Mercer Island takes over Luther Burbank Park from King County.

2003 St. Monica and Islander Middle School become part of KING5 SchoolNet, a network of weather stations located at schools.

2003 The city takes ownership of the MercerView property it rented since 1980.

2003 The Bounce, a teen cybercafe, for which the City Council approved $35,000, closes after four months.

2003 Mercer Island pulls out of the Cascade Water Alliance and contracts with Seattle to provide water.

2003 Kerri Kinkman Lang, QFC bookkeeper, wins a $19 million lottery with a ticket she bought at a Safeway near her home.

Mercer Island Parks and Recreation Department moved to the brick building at Luther Burbank Park.

The grand opening of the new Community Center at Mercer View was held in December 2005, with a two-day celebration including tours, music, free activities and a festive dinner. Dignitaries from Mercer Island's sister city, Thonon-les-Bains, France, inaugurated the CCMV's first art exhibition, a collection of 70 antique engravings of the Thonon region.

From the beginning, the community embraced its center; usage increased, as did its hours of operation. By 2010, the five-year birthday of the community center, it supported a broad range of recreational, cultural, health and educational opportunities.

To better market the site as a venue for regional events, the City Council voted in 2011 to change its name to the Mercer Island Community and Events Center.

The city built the new community center without going to the taxpayers on a bond issue.

Mary Wayte Pool

The future of Mary Wayte Pool came to the fore in the 2000s, as the aging pool changed hands twice.

The public pool was constructed with King County Forward Thrust bond funds on land leased from the Mercer Island School District. Inaugural events on Oct. 14, 1973, included a ribbon cutting accompanied by the pouring of a pitcher of water from the Olympic pool in Munich, where the Games were held the year before.

First dubbed Mercer Island Pool, it was renamed in honor of Mercer Island five-time Olympic champion Mary Wayte (Bradburne) in 1984.

King County operated and maintained it until the early 2000s, when the county began divesting itself of its pool operations. The future of the pool was in question until February 2003, when the

Chad Coleman / Mercer Island Reporter

Ellis Pond is covered with ice in December 2008. Neighbors who live near the pond celebrated its 30-year "birthday" in 2004. It was the commemoration of the city's purchase of property around the pond, establishing a 5-acre park.

nonprofit organization Northwest Center stepped forward to operate it. The county transferred its leasehold interests in the pool to the Northwest Center.

Recognizing the importance of the pool as a community asset, the Mercer Island City Council voted to subsidize the pool for $100,000 per year. In 2008, by a narrow vote, the council cut the city funding by $20,000 per year, to "wean" the Northwest Center from the subsidy. A barrage of criticism followed the decision. The next year, the council restored the funding.

Islanders use the public pool for lap swimming, lessons, water aerobics and open swimming, and it's heavily used by the award-winning Mercer Island High School swim teams.

Eventually, in spite of the subsidy and a number of changes in its operations, Northwest Center lost money on the pool operation and ended its agreement with the school district by the end of 2010.

With the Luther Burbank transfer, the city gained a 77-acre park with three-quarters of a mile of prime Lake Washington waterfront.

Again, the future of the facility was in question.

The city and the school district began talks about the feasibility of building a new pool elsewhere on the Island, partnering with the Stroum Jewish Community Center on a newly expanded pool at its facility, or participating with nearby cities on a new, regional aquatics center. But as yet, nothing has come of those ideas.

At the 11th hour, the school district found another operator for the pool, Olympic Cascade Aquatics, an association of aquatics coaches with deep roots on the Island. The school district, the city and Olympic Cascade Aquatics signed an agreement in 2011 that keeps the pool open and takes care of its maintenance for the near future.

More parks

Mercer Island parks got a big boost in 2002 when King County began divesting itself of properties in incorporated areas. King County transferred ownership of the 77-acre Luther Burbank Park to the city of Mercer Island on Dec. 9, 2002.

The city took it over on Jan. 1, 2003, and gained a jewel of a park with three-quarters of a mile of Lake Washington waterfront, tennis courts, amphitheater, gas plant, administration building, swimming beach, dock, large children's play area, off-leash area for dogs, and picnic and barbecue areas. In addition, large areas of the park have been left undeveloped to foster a variety of wildlife and natural habitat.

With the acquisition of the park

2003 The city approves the design for a pergola memorial to honor veterans at Mercerdale Park.

2003 Goodwill closes its last collection station on Mercer Island in May.

2003 Mercer Island PeaceMakers organizes to oppose a war in Iraq.

2004 After 40 years, local dispatching is eliminated; police and fire communications are routed through Kirkland and Bellevue.

2005 Mercer Island Municipal Court opens with Wayne Stewart, former city attorney, as its first Judge.

2005 Herzl-Ner Tamid synagogue celebrates its centennial.

2006 Margaret and Kenneth Quarles transfer title to the city for 7 acres of land adjacent to Pioneer Park, called the Engstrom Open Space.

2006 The Mercer Island High School marching band marches in the Rose Bowl Parade on Jan. 1.

2006 Island home prices reach a new high, with average sale price of $1.3 million, up 12 percent from the previous year.

2006 District enrollments are forecast to continue to decline, creating problems for future school funding.

2006 Mercer Island Boys & Girls Club hires former pro basketball player Blair Rasmussen as its director.

2006 Permit records show a record number of homes are demolished to be replaced by new ones.

2006 The Mercer Island High School chess team wins its first state championship in 39 years.

2006 Cost of gas is $3 per gallon.

2006 Islander Jessica Epstein wins $26,000 on the *Jeopardy* television show.

Mercer Island Reporter
Generations of Island children have played on the iconic dragon at Deane's Childrens Park, above. This park is named in honor of Dr. Phil and Lola Deane, who led the effort in the 1980s to acquire and develop the park.
At left, a girl swings in the park. Every year since 2008, Mercer Island has been recognized by the national nonprofit KaBOOM! as a Playful City USA. KaBOOM!, an organization dedicated to promoting healthy activity for children, selected Mercer Island as one of 213 cities for its continuing dedication to play.

came assumption of the maintenance costs—not insignificant, since Luther Burbank had been somewhat neglected in the years prior to the property transfer. The city began the Luther Burbank Master Plan visioning process in 2004, with input from hundreds of citizens and groups such as ball field users and Friends of Luther Burbank Park, organized in 1988. The city adopted the Luther Burbank Park Master Plan in 2006, to guide its improvements in the next 20 years.

In 2008, Islanders voted on two park measures: a $12 million bond issue for park improvements to Luther Burbank Park and ball field repairs; and an annual maintenance levy, to continue upkeep of Luther Burbank Park. Both measures received majority vote, but the bond issue failed because it lacked the supermajority needed to pass.

In 2008, the muddy, makeshift off-leash dog park in Luther Burbank got a much-needed makeover. The adjacent shoreline, overrun with invasive blackberry bushes, also was renovated from Calkins Point to the docks. The $1.3 million project restored and improved 1,500 feet of shoreline that included six beach access areas.

In this decade, the acquisition of the Engstrom Open Space also added to the city's green space. Margaret and Kenneth Quarles sold 7 acres of their land adjacent to Pioneer Park to the city for a fraction of its market value in 2006.

The Quarles also transferred

Another Mercerversary, celebrating Mercer Island's 50th anniversary as a city

Mercer Island Reporter
Longtime residents John Davis and Ruth Mary Close, above, are honored at the festivities. At left, city manager Rich Conrad lights candles as Mayor Jim Pearman and his daughters, Charlotte, left, and Julia, look on.

Mercer Island Reporter
Then-councilman (and subsequent mayor) Bruce Bassett helps Mercer Island Chamber director Terry Moreman with preparations, right. Above are longtime Islanders Lynn and Joe Lightfoot. Joe is the son of George Lightfoot, known as "the Father of the Floating Bridge."

A young community honors its past

It was a big birthday party July 18, 2010, for Mercer Island, a Mercerversary. This was the second, celebrating the Island's 50th anniversary of incorporation. The first Mercerversary was held in July, 1985, marking the city's 25th anniversary.

The festivities at Mercerdale Park were complete with a big birthday cake and a live concert by the Nowhere Men, a Beatles tribute band. Speeches, a historic recap by Linda Jackman and the dedication of a tree and a special bench marked the community milestone.

The Mercerversary effort was led by Terry Pottmeyer and Susan Kaplan, co-chairs, with a committee that included Amber Britten, Mary Jo Bruckner, Terry Moreman and Kirsten Taylor.

In the weeks prior to the event, the community read in the *Mercer Island Reporter* articles on historic places and pioneer families by Kris Kelsay. A website, www.mi50.org, collected the names of Islanders who had lived on the Island 50 years or more, and recorded some of their stories.

2007 The city puts in a permanent well at Rotary Park to supply Islanders with water in an emergency.

2007 Since school was cancelled for eight days due to storms, Mercer Island High School seniors had to return to school after graduation, a first in more than a decade.

2007 The Island's only motel, the Travelodge, closes in September after 50 years in business.

2007 The former East Seattle School building is sold by the Boys & Girls Club to Islanders Michael and Billi Jo O'Brien for $6 million.

2008 The City Council approves the use of tasers by Mercer Island police.

2008 A roving homeless encampment, Tent City 4, comes to Mercer Island for three months.

2008 Dick Nicholl retires after 33 years as head football coach of Mercer Island High School.

2008 The City Council formally ends the state's longest-running DARE drug and alcohol prevention program.

2008 The first farmers market is held in downtown Mercer Island.

2008 The dog park at Luther Burbank Park gets a makeover.

2008 The City Council begins televising its meetings on Channel 21 in July.

2008 Dredging of Lake Washington begins the sewer lakeline project.

2009 Social networking sweeps the Island—Twitter, Facebook, blogs, online news, texting. A new cell tower is approved with ease, unlike in years past.

2009 Islanders host the first Round the Rock paddle surfing competition.

2009 The city decides to narrow Island Crest Way from four lanes to three, setting off a years-long controversy over the "road diet."

Mercer Island Reporter

After years of hearings and appeals, the Mercer Island Boys & Girls Club's PEAK facility finally opened in June 2009 on the school district's "megablock" property on 86th Avenue Southeast.

Mercer Island Reporter

In 2011, as mandated by the state of Washington, the City Council began working on revising the city's Shoreline Management Plan, the set of regulations regarding beaches, bulkheads and docks along the shoreline. It was slated for adoption in 2013.

1.57 acres in the 6500 block of East Mercer Way to the city in 2002. Deed restrictions stipulate that the land be used only for parks and recreation.

The original 10-acre parcel off East Mercer Way was purchased in 1925 as the Engstrom's summer home. Margaret Engstrom Quarles fondly remembered spending summers on the Island, when she would ride horseback over "an old, rickety bridge" to get the horse shoed in Bellevue, and walk six miles to Roanoke Dock to meet her ferry-commuting father.

In 2004, neighbors around Ellis Park Pond celebrated the pond's 30-year "birthday." It had been three decades since the city purchased 12 lots around the pond for $86,700 to establish the 5-acre park, keeping it from being developed into a housing development.

Now, boardwalks cross the marshes and wetland ecosystem, and neighbors take pride in and take care of the pond and the park.

The PEAK saga

Beginning in 1982, the Mercer Island Boys & Girls Club oc-

214 | Chapter 21: 2000 to the Present

Due in large part to the lobbying efforts of citizen activist Myra Lupton, the city of Mercer Island began offering a sailing camp for kids at Luther Burbank Park in 2008. Here six boats in the "handkerchief fleet" catch the wind.

Mercer Island Reporter

cupied the former East Seattle School. From about 2000 on, the club's board struggled with what do to about the aging structure, built in 1914.

But as early as 2003, an idea surfaced to sell the East Seattle property and build a new Boys & Girls Club on the school district's "megablock" property, adjacent to Crest Learning Center. The club began fundraising and sold the West Mercer Way property to Island resident Michael O'Brien to help pay for the project.

Called PEAK, (a Positive Place for Enrichment, Education, Activities, Athletics, Kinship and Community), the three-story, 41,000-square-foot youth sports and teen center was controversial from the start.

Neighbors protested that the project was out of scale with the neighborhood and would exacerbate existing traffic, noise and parking problems. But supporters pointed to the lack of gym space on the Island and the need for a safe place for teens to congregate.

PEAK— A Positive Place for enrichment, education athletics, kinship and community

PEAK was built with public and private support. The school district leased the land to the Boys & Girls Club for 20 years, and contributed $1 million. The city of Mercer Island contributed $1 million. The balance of funding came from private donations, according to Blair Rasmussen, then director of the Boys & Girls Club.

It took nearly six years for the project to wend its way through various hearings and legal appeals. The conditional use permit for the facility was granted in November 2008, with several conditions and a requirement that the Boys & Girls Club and the school district sign a shared parking agreement and a coordinated scheduling system.

The $15 million project finally broke ground in June 2009 and had its grand opening in August 2010. PEAK has a field house with three high-school size basketball courts, a multipurpose room, a tech and learning center, game room, child-care rooms and office space. The Boys & Girls Club's PEAK facility serves about 2,000 children and is fully scheduled every weekday from early morning until 10 p.m.

Tent City

The roving Eastside homeless encampment called Tent City 4 came to Mercer Island in August 2008. And while it stayed on the Island only three months, it brought many more months of collective soul-searching, angst and legal wrangling.

After discussing the idea for more than a year, the Mercer Island Clergy Association unanimously agreed to invite Tent City 4 to the Island. In anticipation, city staff created a draft temporary-use permit based on advice from other host communities and from SHARE/WHEEL, the homeless advocacy group.

A group called Mercer Island Citizens for Fair Process filed a

Mercer Island Reporter

In December, 2008, a big snowstorm hit the region, dumping several inches of snow. On Mercer Island, a number of businesses were closed for days and school was canceled for the two days before the holiday break. Sledders took to the hills and Islanders got out their snow boots and cross-country skis to travel their neighborhoods. Many homes were without power for days.

2009 Ed Pepple, the state's winningest boys' high school basketball coach, retires after 42 years at Mercer Island High School.

2009 The Mercer Island Recycling Center closes.

2009 Mercer Island 11- to 12-year-old Little Leaguers compete at the Little League World Series in Williamsport, Pa.

2009 After a 30-plus-year career as an elected official, Fred Jarrett is tapped to be deputy King County executive.

2010 The city's biggest-ever public works project, the $24.2 million replacement of a portion of the sewer lake line, is completed, on time and $2 million under budget.

2010 Grand opening of PEAK, the new Boys & Girls Club facility.

2010 Mercer Island celebrates the 50th anniversary of its incorporation.

2010 After 50 years as a broadsheet newspaper, the *Mercer Island Reporter* goes back to its original tabloid format.

2010 Members of Emmanuel Episcopal Church celebrate its centennial year.

lawsuit to prevent the camp from opening on the Island. But in July 2008, a Superior Court judge denied the group's request to grant an injunction against the encampment, and Tent City 4 opened on Aug. 4, 2008, on Southeast 24th Street adjacent to Mercer Island United Methodist Church. Citizens for Fair Process went on to file but lose more lawsuits and appeals.

The camp, with a population of about 100, stayed through October; its quiet departure was in stark contrast to the noisy controversy at its arrival. Mercer Island Police reported nine arrests related to Tent City, five of which were for outstanding warrants.

Afterward, the city conducted a post mortem process with Island residents and representatives of all parties involved to evaluate Tent City 4. In the two years afterward, the city worked on a temporary encampment ordinance.

The City Council approved the ordinance by a 5-2 vote on Feb. 1, 2010, but not without disagreement. Some people felt the ordinance was too restrictive and discouraged future homeless groups from coming to the Island.

The following year, the council voted against reconsidering the ordinance, opting instead to evaluate it if and when another encampment wishes to come to the Island. At the end of 2012, Mercer Island Presbyterian Church was considering hosting one.

Lindell lawsuit

A messy controversy in the city involving allegations of sexual harassment, workplace impropriety and retribution began in 2008 after the firing of deputy city manager and former city attorney Londi Lindell. She sued the city, claiming that she was fired in retaliation for complaining that her boss, city manager Rich Conrad, ignored sexual harassment and inappropriate behavior that she alleged was occurring in city offices.

The lawsuit also named as defendants then Mayor Jim Pearman, councilman El Jahncke and city finance director Chip Corder.

The complicated case dragged on for more than three years, distracting the City Council and staff and polarizing the community. Ultimately the city was ordered to pay a penalty of $90,000 for violations of the Public Records Act, and the city's insurance carrier decided to settle the lawsuit for $1 million. Neither side admitted to any wrongdoing.

It was an unsatisfactory ending to an unsavory chapter in

216 | Chapter 21: 2000 to the Present

Chad Coleman / Mercer Island Reporter

In 2011 to comply with state requirements, the City Council began updating its Shoreline Master Plan, which regulates development along all watercourses and shorelines. Mercer Island has only a few undeveloped waterfront lots and is ringed with some 700 docks. The city's SMP must be approved by the state Department of Ecology.

the Island's history. "I'm very disappointed. I wanted our day in court," then-Mayor Pearman said. Lindell and the city issued a joint statement saying "both sides recognized that it was time to put this behind them and move forward." Lindell was hired by the City of North Bend in 2012 as its city administrator.

City projects

Replacing a worn-out sewer line is a big project for any city. But when the sewer line is underwater, yards offshore from multimillion-dollar homes and in a sensitive marine environment, it is a massive, costly and complex challenge.

After years of planning, feasibility studies, environmental review, permit approvals and design, Mercer Island undertook the largest public works project in the city's history.

Islanders became accustomed to seeing giant cranes offshore near the I-90 high-rise during the summers of 2009 and 2010.

The $24 million sewer lake line project replaced existing sewer pipe on a 2-mile stretch off the Island's northwest shore and built a new, 50-foot-deep pump station under I-90 to replace an existing old pump station. The project included reconnecting 40 sewer lateral lines serving 80 waterfront homes.

By all accounts the project was a big success—it was completed one year early and $2 million under budget.

In August, 2012, voters approved a $5.2 million bond issue to build a larger and improved fire station to replace the 50-year-old one at the south end of the Island. The measure included purchase a new rescue truck in 2013. This project and the sewer project will raise taxes through 2021.

Boom, then bust

In the early 2000s, the real estate market began to skyrocket throughout the Puget Sound region, but few places more so than on Mercer Island. In a December 2002 survey of the real estate market conducted by CNN and *Money* magazine, Mercer Island ranked as the fifth most expensive in the country behind Wellesley, Mass.; Darien, Conn.; Lake Forest, Ill.; and Danville, Calif.

The average Island home cost $750,000 in 2002, which was nearly twice the 1992 average of $398,400. By 2012 it was $862,500, a less dramatic increase during a decade of recession.

"Location, location, location," the mantra of real estate value, figured as an ever more important draw for Mercer Island, as growth on the Eastside and changing commute patterns led to an increase in traffic on I-90.

By 2006, Island home prices had reached a new high, while the num-

Chapter 21: 2000 to the Present | 217

2010 Mercer Island High School grad Franklin Page sets a new Guinness World Record for texting: 35.54 seconds to type 160 characters into a touch-screen mobile phone.

2010 The city's emergency well at Rotary Park is completed.

2011 Finders Gift Shop closes after decades on the Island.

2011 City Council approves a new emergency transport ordinance.

2011 The Mercer Island High School marching band marches in London's New Year's Day parade.

2011 Island volunteers build places for learning, growing, meditating: Kesher Garden at Stroum Jewish Community Center, a learning garden at the library and a labyrinth at Emmanuel Episcopal Church.

2011 The City Council completes a months-long process to submit the Shoreline Management Plan to the state.

2012 The Mercer Island High School marching band appears in the Rose Bowl Parade in Pasadena, Calif.

2012 With the appointment of Tana Senn, the City Council has three women on the council for the first time in history. They are Senn, Jane Meyer Brahm and Debbie Bertlin.

2012 The first traffic lights are placed in the Town Center in January.

2012 The repaving of most of Island Crest Way, and restriping it from four lanes to three, is completed in September.

2012 The city enacts an ordinance forbidding smoking in its parks.

2012 Vicki Puckett is the new principal at Mercer Island High School, the fifth in 10 years.

Jane Meyer Brahm

In the winter of 2012, an installation of three topiary deer entitled Gazing was placed on the sloping hillside of the Park on the Lid near Southeast 24th Street and 76th Avenue Southeast. Spearheaded by the Arts Council, the project was paid for from the One Percent for the Arts Fund.

ber of homes on the market had declined. The average sale price was $1.13 million, up 12 percent from 2005, according to the Northwest Multiple Listing Service.

But soon the national economic downturn—the Great Recession beginning in 2007—had its effects on Mercer Island as on everywhere else in the country. People were paying higher prices for everything from electricity to food; the city sent out three times the usual number of past-due utility bills in 2008; gas topped $4 per gallon in 2011.

As home values fell, the number of short sales and foreclosures was up, and fewer homes sold for lower prices. The median home price fell to $685,000 from $1 million plus in 2008.

Unemployment was rising, spending was down, applications for assistance at Mercer Island's Youth and Family Services were up and the Mercer Island post office cut routes.

One indicator of vitality, the number of building permits issued on Mercer Island, went from a 10-year high of 476 in 2007 to its low of 297 in 2009, just two years later.

With projected revenues declining as a result of the sluggish economy, the city began trimming its budget each biennium, beginning in 2008.

In its 2011-2012 budget, the city reduced general fund expenditures by more than $2.3 million per year, cutting staff and trimming programs. The city opted not to fund the popular Summer Celebration fireworks and some Parks and Recreation programs, but instead to rely on donations from the community. "Doing more with less" became the mantra in the city as departments struggled to maintain services with dwindling resources and, occasionally, increased demand.

By the end of 2012, there were signs that the real estate market was beginning to improve. A total of 259 homes sold on Mercer Island in 2012, up 14 percent from the previous year. The median sale price was $862,500, up 3 percent from the previous year

Sustainability

Mercer Island has been a regional leader in resource conser-

218 | Chapter 21: 2000 to the Present

City of Mercer Island

vation, with strong recycling and water conservation programs, storm water quality improvements, invasive species removal and others. In this decade the city launched a program to reduce energy use in all city facilities and completed an emergency well project at Rotary Park, which will supply clean water to Islanders in the event of a community-wide emergency.

Several grassroots sustainability-related organizations sprang up during the decade. Among them were Island Vision, a group of citizens and leaders interested in creating the conditions for sustainability on the Island. One of its vanguard events is the annual Leap for Green. Transition Initiative Mercer Island (TIMI) launched a time bank, an on-line database thorough which participants provide a skill to a member in exchange for a needed skill from another member.

Electric car-charging stations began turning up along the I-90 corridor in 2012, at City Hall, the Community and Events Center and the PEAK building, as more drivers moved to hybrids or electric cars.

The school district was involved in sustainability efforts as well. Student Harry Bolson was in the media spotlight in 2010 for

Mercer Island Reporter

Emmanuel Episcopal Church, the oldest faith community on the Island, installed a labyrinth on its property in 2012.

producing the district's first sustainability demonstration project: solar panels to power Mercer Island High School's store and marketing department.

In 2012, the mayor appointed a citizen sustainability task force to develop policies directing the city's actions and priorities in the future. The goal is to meet the needs of today without adversely affecting the needs of future generations. The City Council approved the hiring of a part-time sustainability coordinator to guide this effort.

During 2012, the city partnered with Puget Sound Energy on the Green Power Challenge to win a $30,000 solar panel installation on the community center if a goal of green power sign-ups was met.

The road ahead

Land-use and property issues are important in any community, but nowhere more so than on an island, where boundaries are defined and land is limited. The push and pull between developers and

Chapter 21: 2000 to the Present | 219

2012 Bruce Bassett is elected mayor of Mercer Island.

2012 A new U.S. Census Bureau report lists Mercer Island as the wealthiest city in Washington state, with a median family income of $146,476.

2012 15,261 Islanders vote in the general election—87.3 percent of its 17,490 registered voters (slightly shy of the 2008 high-water mark of 87.8 percent and higher than the King County average of 83.5 percent).

2012 Islanders vote by 60 percent to reject the school district's $196 million bond measure for school facilities.

2012 Islander John Urquhart becomes King County sheriff.

2012 The school district adds two more portable classrooms, at a cost of $100,000 each, bringing the total to 28.

2012 Superintendent Gary Plano and head of Island Vision Lucia Pirzio-Biroli, receive King County's Earth Heroes at School award.

2012 The City Council votes to televise its study sessions.

2012 The Senior Foundation of Mercer Island receives the 2012 Award for Public Trust from Aging Services of Washington.

2012 Mercer Island meets its goal in Puget Sound Energy's Green Power Challenge: 650 households sign up for green energy. The city receives $30,000 toward solar panels at the community center.

2012 Noel Treat, former Seattle Schools assistant superintendent, is hired as Mercer Island assistant city manager.

2012 The school district and city reach an agreement for school board meetings to be held in the council chambers so they can be televised.

Mercer Island Reporter
Mercer Islanders at play: top, teens swimming at Luther Burbank Park; middle, sailing lessons offered by the Parks and Recreation Department at Luther Burbank Park; bottom, the All Island Track Meet among the three elementary schools in 2010.

Doonesbury ©2007 G. B. Trudeau. Reprinted with permission of Universal Uclick. All rights reserved

Mercer Island made it onto the national cartoon scene when this *Doonesbury* cartoon appeared March 12, 2007, in 1,300 newspapers across the United States.

preservationists that's been part of the Island's history since its beginning will no doubt continue and increase.

Light rail, scheduled to begin crossing the Island in about 2024, will be a major factor. It will bring more shoppers and diners to add to the vitality of the Town Center, but it also will bring increased traffic, parking issues and pressure for taller buildings downtown.

The possible of tolling on I-90 will have a major impact on the daily lives of Islanders, as well as on employers and employees and property values.

The school district's need to build least one new school in the near future to begin to address the issue of overcrowded classrooms is a big issue for Mercer Islanders. Beyond that, the community needs to formulate a plan for rebuilding and/or renovating all of the other school buildings.

An increasing focus of the city's capital funding will be the city's infrastructure, the aging sewer and water lines and storm water utilities that were put into place in the 1950s and '60s.

Future focus

What will Mercer Island be like in the future?

It's safe to say that in 2040, a generation away, the Island's population will be higher and the Town Center density greater. Islanders will have become accustomed to taking the lightrail trains in the center roadway of I-90, and whether or not tolling on I-90 comes to pass, they will have become accustomed to paying more for transportation infrastructure.

The school district will have built another school and completed major construction of new facilities—whatever they will be.

Property values and home prices will continue to increase with Mercer Island's value as a sylvan refuge.

The words of John Dunney, Mercer Island's first real estate broker, spoken in 1947, will be truer than ever: "I am convinced that the Island will become the most desirable residential district near Seattle. Mercer Island is 4,000 acres of evergreen playground forever set apart from the smoke, bustle and noise of the city ready for people who value good things to build good homes. Mercer Island has, indeed, a bright future."

Crystal ball views

To get a longer look at the future, here are some prognostications from various points of view:

• "Sometime in the next 30 years I see the seeds planted by a few new merchants and local groups such as the farmer's market slowly growing into a varied, useful, entertaining retail core. There will be tolls on the bridge and a growing desire to connect to those close to you.

"Local will trump more and bigger. There will be a theater, a great grocery store, seven coffee shops, children's toy shop and a little place with Italian food and wine. We will nurture our own style. Island style vs. Seattle or Eastside style. People will envy us."

—Roger Page,
owner of Island Books

• "Mercer Island will continue to rely on timely and professional-level services for medical, rescue and fire emergencies. We'll see increased forms of regionalization in the service, and call volumes will likely escalate as increased density occurs in the Town Center. Citizens will continue to demand more from public services, and there will be continued pressure on reducing the dependence on property tax as the primary revenue for local government."

—Chris Tubbs,
Mercer Island fire chief

• "There will always be a presence of organized faith on Mercer Island, and it will be more expansive and inclusive. We'll have integration of an online presence. Our community will expand its boundaries to include people of the Muslim, Buddhist and Hindu faiths, even if we don't have an edifice for each of them. Perhaps we'll have a community worship cen-

Chapter 21: 2000 to the Present | 221

The *Gateway* sculpture forms the west end of the Outdoor Sculpture Gallery that runs along Sunset Highway south of I-90, between 77th Avenue Southeast and 80th Avenue Southeast.

Jane Meyer Brahm

ter, a shared space. There will be a sharing of outreach of each faith to the community, whether it's hosting a homeless encampment, gathering food and funds for the needy or holding food drives for disaster relief."

—Kristen Jamerson,
head of the Mercer Island
Clergy Association

• "In the future our officers will be flying around in their George Jetson police interceptors, utilizing truth extractors when interviewing suspects, and employing mind-reading technology to predict crimes before they happen! How about that?"

—Ed Holmes,
Mercer Island police chief

• "The public library will be a concept more than a place. Library buildings will be used in different way and services will be provided beyond the building and virtually. The library as a catalyst or civic engagement will facilitate learning and growth for people of all ages."

— Bill Ptacek, director
King County Library System

• "Autonomous vehicles or self-driving cars will have a huge impact on our transportation expectations and options in the coming years. We know that the 'last mile' is a very difficult problem to solve in transportation, especially in a suburban community like Mercer Island. Autonomous vehicles solve that problem in a way that doesn't require more parking spaces.

"We'll call up the car as we would a taxi. It'll deliver us to our destination or a public transit stop; then it will continue to its next assignment, or it may find its way to a nearby electric charging station to recharge while awaiting another assignment.

"Roads will be safer. We'll need fewer cars. Parking will be moved away from our most congested locations."

— Bruce Bassett,
mayor of Mercer Island

• "There will be more people over age 65 than under 18. Being an elder will become in vogue; wisdom will be appreciated and much sought after.

"More families will live together multigenerationally. Em-

Mercer Island has, indeed, a bright future."

—John Dunney,
in 1947
Mercer Island's first real estate broker

ployers will finally see the value in hiring older workers because they have better interpersonal skills, less absenteeism and less turnover. Mercer Island will become a retirement destination. Look out, Phoenix!"

—Betsy Zuber,
geriatric specialist,
city of Mercer Island.

• "Mercer Island is a very precious place that has managed to protect itself from some very bad development ideas—and that needs to be continued.

Mercer Islanders have always been passionate about their community. There's a reason for the passion: they are intelligent, economically successful people—everybody, the whole town. They're participants. You have to expect participation in a place like Mercer Island. We're usually pretty lucky because our leaders are usually successful, well-informed people who don't need to make a career out of it.

Mercer Island is different from the suburbs and the downtown. It is a unique jewel. While generations will change, we need to make sure new generations will want to continue to preserve it.

—the late Aubrey Davis
former mayor, civil servant

222 | Chapter 21: 2000 to the Present

Then and Now

Mercer Island Reporter

This 1979 photo, looking north along 78th Avenue Southeast, shows the list of businesses that were in the complex now known as Rite Aid Plaza. Jack in the Box, Alm's Drugs and Mayfair Market are in the background.

Matt Brashears

Today, looking north from 78th Avenue Southeast and Southeast 32nd Street. The downtown was transformed in the early 1990s, with new streets, utilities, sidewalks, street lamps and benches.

Chapter 22: Then and Now | 223

Then and Now

Mercer Island Reporter

This is a lineup of cars waiting for gas at the Standard station at Island Crest Way and Southeast 28th Street during the energy crisis of the late 1970s. In 1970, the average price of a gallon of gas was about 36 cents; by 1980 it was about $1.20, according to the *The Seattle Times*.

Matt Brashears

Today this intersection has a traffic light. On the right is Island Crest Way looking south; on the left are the backs of the signs for the westbound I-90 on-ramp. Southeast 28th Street continues toward the left up the hill often referred to as Snake Hill.

Mercer Island Reporter

This is the intersection of 76th Avenue Southeast, at left, and Southeast 24th Street in the 1980s. On the right is Mercer Island Care Center; Jim Windle's Union 76 gas station, now home to Freshy's Seafood, is on the left. Safeway is beyond the trees in the middle.

Matt Brashears

The same view today shows Aljoya, a retirement community, on the left and Island Corporate Center on the right.

Chapter 22: Then and Now | 225

Then and Now

Mercer Island Reporter

This 1976 photo looks north on 78th Avenue Southeast from the intersection at Southeast 30th Street.

Matt Brashears

This view in spring 2012, from the same spot, shows the effects of undergrounding utilities and the ordinance regulating large overhead signage on businesses.

Mercer Island Reporter

This photo from 1990 looks west across the parking lot at Southeast 27th Street and 77th Avenue Southeast. For many years, Mama Reuben's deli occupied the storefront on the far right. The Tangerine Restaurant is on the left, in the building also formerly occupied by Carsten & Humphreys television and electronics store. The white building on the right is the rear of the Travelodge.

Matt Brashears

From the same location, this 2012 photo looks west at The Mercer from across 77th Avenue Southeast, just north of Southeast 27th Street.

Chapter 22: Then and Now | 227

Then and Now

Mercer Island Reporter

This 1992 photo shows the Paul Allen project, the largest single-family project in the history of the Island. During construction, workers were bused in to keep down traffic at the site, off West Mercer Way in the 6400 block (down Shore Lane and Southeast 77th Street).

David Dykstra

The 9.6-acre Paul Allen complex today, with the catamaran *Dragonfly*, also a floating helicopter pad, moored in front. The property has the highest assessed value on the Island: $137 million in 2010.

Ted Heaton

This photo shows the iconic Mercer Island High School "Mushroom" during its construction in the late 1950s. The building not only served as the lunchroom and gathering place for students, but was where numerous dances, proms and tolos were held through the years.

Matt Brashears

The Mushroom was demolished in 1997 and replaced with the Mercer Island High School Commons, part of the extensive renovation of the high school completed in 1998.

Mercer Island Reporter

This photo was taken looking west from 77th Avenue Southeast a few months before the Travelodge closed in September 2007. At the far right is Denny's. The postcard above shows the Travelodge in its heyday during the '50s and '60s.

Matt Brashears

Today, in this view from the same spot, Aljoya occupies the site where Denny's and part of the Travelodge used to be.

230 | Chapter 22: Then and Now

Phil Flash

This photo, taken in 2002, shows the intersection of Southeast 27th Street and 77th Avenue Southeast, looking to the northwest. The building with the distinctive roof housed the Tangerine Restaurant for years.

Matt Brashears

This is the same view in 2012, the year the first traffic lights were installed in the Town Center.

Chapter 22: Then and Now | 231

Then and Now

Mercer Island Reporter

This photo looks to the southeast at about Southeast 29th Street, with 80th Avenue Southeast in the foreground. The lot on the left is where the James Crosby complex of stores once stood. Seafirst Bank was later built on the site. On the far right are the Landmark condominiums.

Matt Brashears

Today Bank of America occupies the former Seafirst site, and trees line the street. The Landmark condos are still there, hidden behind the trees.

232 | *Chapter 22: Then and Now*

Appendix

Bibliography

Cone, Molly and Howard Droker, Jacqueline Williams. *Family of Strangers. Building a Jewish Community in Washington State.* Seattle: Washington state Jewish Historical Society, 2003.

Davis, Jeff and All Eufrasio. *Weird Washington Your Travel Guide to Washington's Local Legends and Best-Kept Secrets.* New York, NY: Sterling Publishing Co., 2008.

Dykstra, David. *Lake Washington 130 Homes.* Mercer Island, WA: Hundred Homes Publishing, 2009.

Eastside Heritage Center. *Lake Washington: The East Side.* Charleston, SC: Arcadia Publishing, 2006.

Kelsay, Kris. *Walk! Mercer Island: The Insiders Guide to Walking on Mercer Island.* Mercer Island, WA: Walk Mercer Island, 2009

McDonald, Lucille. *The Lake Washington Story: A Pictorial History.* Seattle, WA: Superior Publishing Company, 1979.

Mercer Island Parks & Recreation Department. *Pioneer Park: A Natural History.* Mercer Island, WA: City of Mercer Island, Washington, 2012.

Olsen, Jack. *Charmer: The True Story of a Ladies' Man and His Victims.* New York: Avon Books, 1995.

Pierce, J. Kingston. *Eccentric Seattle.* Pullman, WA: Washington State University Press, 2003.

Norlen, Paul. *Swedish Seattle.* Charleston, S.C.: Arcadia Publishing, 2007

Sale, Roger. *Seattle, Past to Present.* Seattle, WA: University of Washington Press, 1976.

Seattle Chamber of Commerce Record, 1914

Stein, Alan J. and the HistoryLink Staff. *Bellevue Timeline: The story of Washington's Leading Edge City from Homesteads to High Rises, 1863-2003.* Bellevue Wa: City of Bellevue, 2004

The Seattle Times. *A Hidden Past: An Exploration of Eastside History.* Seattle, WA: The Seattle Times, 2000.

Welch, Bob. *Bellevue and the New Eastside: A Contemporary Portrait.* Chatsworth, CA: Windsor Publications, Inc., 1989.

Wright, Mary C. *More Voices, New Stories: King County, Washington's First 150 Years.* Seattle, WA: Pacific Northwest Historians Guild, 2002.

Mercer Island Reporter

Spiderlike, a worker navigates a web of rebar in the mid-1990s during the construction of the I-90 lid across Mercer Island.

Mercer Island Census Data, 2010

Total population:	22,699
Ethnicity:	78% Caucasian
	16% Asian or Pacific Islander
	1.3% African American
	4% who identified themselves as being of two or more races
Sex:	Males - 48.7%; 11,046
	Females - 51.3%; 11,653
Median age:	46
Total households:	9,109
Registered voters:	16,624
Voted in November, 2010:	13,000
Single-family residences:	7,011
Multi-family residences:	2,435
Household income average :	$172,973
Mean housing value:	$1.0 million
Total land area:	4,034 acres
	6.2 square miles
Position:	47.56 degrees north of the equator and 122.23 degrees west of the prime meridian
Parks and open space:	475 acres
Largest park:	120 acres, with 6.6 miles of trails
Top property taxpayers:	Paul Allen (assessed valuation $137 million)
	Shorewood Heights Apartments
	Island Square
	The Mercer
	77 Central
People in jobs on the Island:	7,000 (approximately)
Largest employers :	Farmer's New World Life
	Mercer Island School District
	City of Mercer Island

(Sources: The 2010 U.S. Census, the City of Mercer Island)

Mercer Island Reporter

This photo, taken in 1987, shows downtown Mercer Island looking toward the north. The big building in the foreground is Mercer Island Lumber. The street in the right corner is 78th Avenue S.E.

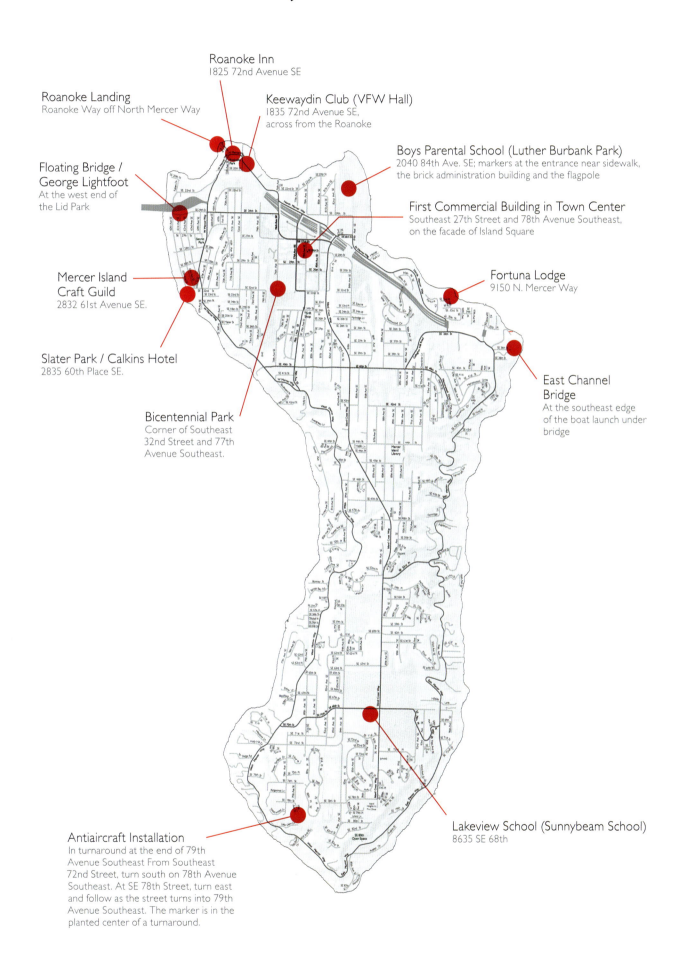

Appendix | 235

Mercer Island Mayors, City Council

Town Mayors
Henry Borgendale 1960 – 1962
Irv E. Totten 1962 – 1964
Joseph Lightfoot 1964 – 1968
Art Burton 1968 – 1970

City Mayors
Harold Oliver 1960–1962
Tom Barto 1962 – 1964
John Day 1964 – 1966
Cleve Anschell 1966 – 1967
Peter McTavish 1967 – 1969
Aubrey Davis 1969 – 1973
Ben Werner 1974 – 1979
Beth Bland 1980 – 1983
Fred Jarrett 1984 – 1987
Jim Horn 1988 – 1989
Elliot Newman 1989 – 1993
Judy Clibborn 1994 – 1997
Gordy Edberg 1998 – 1999
Alan Merkle 2000 – 2005
Bryan Cairns 2006 – 2007
Jim Pearman 2008 – 2011
Bruce Bassett 2012 —

City Council members
Harold Oliver 1960 – 1962
Mark Kirchner 1960 – 1962
Sheila LeClercq 1960 – 1967
Daniel Riviera 1960 – 1969
Al Fleury 1960 – 1962
Jesse Wilkins 1960 – 1962
Tom Barto 1960 – 1967
John Day 1962 – 1972
Cleve Anschell 1962 – 1969; 1988 – 1988
N.E. Boyce 1962 – 1964
Clarence Howell 1962 – 1964
Frederick C. Peterson 1964 – 1967
Sam Fry 1962 – 1966
Peter McTavish 1966 – 1972
Ben Werner 1967 – 1988
Aubrey Davis 1967 – 1978
Amos Wood 1968 – 1977
Sherman Diamond 1969 – 1973
Lissa Wells 1969 – 1973
Bob Norton 1972 – 1975
Marguerite Sutherland 1972 – 1979
Grant Beck 1973 – 1977
Jim Radcliffe 1973 – 1977
Gordon Rasmussen 1978 – 1981
William Stewart 1978 – 1981
Beth Bland (Winn) 1978 – 1985
Major Elfendahl 1982 – 1985
Verne Lewis 1978 – 1987
Jim Horn 1976 – 1989

Fred Jarrett 1980 – 1995
Fred O. May 1981 – 1985
Al Huhs 1985 – 1993
Nan Hutchins 1985 – 1989
Hunter Simpson 1985 – 1989
Elliot Newman 1988 – 1995
Robert Coe 1988 – 1991
Jim Hale 1992 – 1995
Linda Jackman 1990 – 1997
Judy Clibborn 1990 – 2001
Gordy Edberg 1992 – 1999
David Clancy 1994 – 1999
John Nelson 1996 – 1999
Peter Orser 1996 – 1999
Mike Wensman 1996 – 1996
Alan Merkle 1997 – 2005
Bryan Cairns 1998 – 2007
Susan Blake 1999 – 2003
El Jahncke 2000 – 2011
Dan Grausz 2000 –
Sven Goldmanis 2000 – 2007
Jim Pearman 2002 – 2011
Steve Litzow 2004 – 2010
Mike Grady 2006 — 2013
Bruce Bassett 2008 —
Mike Cero 2008 —
Jane Meyer Brahm 2011 —
Debbie Bertlin 2012 —
Tana Senn 2012 —

City Managers
Donald Hitchman 1961–1975
Larry Rose 1975 –1986
Paul Lanspery 1986 – 1996
Rich Conrad 1996 – 2013

Police Chiefs
James Skaggs 1961 – 1974
Jan Deveny 1974 – 2003
Ron Elsoe 2003 – 2006
Ed Holmes 2006 –

Fire Chiefs
Earl Brower 1962 –1972
Cecil Little 1972 –1978
Rick Smith 1978 – 1980
John Schwarts 1980 – 1982
Lynn Oliver 1983 – 1992
Al Provost 1994 – 2001
Walt Mauldin 2001 – 2008
Chris Tubbs 2008 –

Diane Oliver

Mercer Island's first mayor, Harold J. Oliver, and his wife, Dorothy, in 1960. Oliver was also istrumental in founding the Mercer Island Beach Club and was the club's first president.

School Superintendents

Robert Studebaker 1955 - 1967
Charles Murray 1967-1968
Paul Avery 1968-1971
Charles Miller 1971- 1975
Craig Currie 1978 -1985
Wilma Smith 1985 -1990
Corey Wentzell 1990 -1992
Dick Giger 1992 -1999
Paula Butterfield 1999 - 2000
Bill Keim 2000 - 2002
Paul Sjunnesen 2002 - 2003
Cyndy Simms 2003 - 2007
Gary Plano 2007 - present

Mercer Island School District Board of Directors

J.P. Green 1941 – 1944
Terrell Holloway 1941 – 1945
Erwin Moorehead 1941 – 1946
F. Troxell Beers 1941 – 1947
R.G. Owens 1941 – 1944
Harold Cameron 1944 - 1945
Tom Cockran 1944 – 1947
Lowell Kuebler 1945 – 1949
*George Clarke 1946 – 1967
Milton Link 1946 – 1956
Harold Olson 1948 – 1952
Ruth Prosser 1948 – 1955
Richard Anderson 1949 - 1951
John Stenhouse 1951 – 1958
Don Ide 1952 –1954
Harold Oliver 1954 – 1958
**

*John Davis 1956 – 1965
Sheila LeClercq 1955 – 1957
*H.E. Machenheimer 1958 – 1962
*Howard Standsbury 1958 – 1967
*Howard Bayley 1960 – 1969
Robert Campbell 1962 – 1963
Robert E. Johnson 1963 - 1967
*H. Martin Smith 1965 – 1969
Robert Johnson 1966 - 1967
*Raymond Haman 1968 - 1972
*Tom Barto 1967 –1970
*Robert Paine 1967 – 1971
*John Lackland 1969 – 1972
*John Steding 1969 – 1972
*Harold Fardal 1971 – 1980
*Mary Shelton 1971 – 1973
*Robert Jensen 1971 – 1977
*Myra Franklin 1972 – 1977
*Susan Blake 1972 – 1984

*Robert Boyle 1973 – 1984
Cleveland Anschell 1977 – 1985
*Gretchen Ilgenfritz 1977 – 1985
*Virginia Deforest 1980 – 1987
*Tina Cohen 1984 – 1991
*Mary Anne Knoll 1984 – 1991
Paul Dendy 1985 – 1989
*Liz Warner 1985 – 1992
Rod Hearne 1986 – 1991
*Nancy Clancy 1989 – 1992
*Boyd VanderHouwen 1990 – 1995
*Laurie Koehler 1991 – 1999
Veronica Meneses-Swift 1991 – 1992
Chick Hodge 1991 – 1993
Hilton Smith 1991 – 1993
*Susan Kaplan 1992 – 2003
John Oesting 1993 - 1998
El Jahncke 1993 – 1997
Brenda Paull 1997 – 2003
*Terry Pottmeyer 1997 – 2000
Dirk van der Burch 1997 – 2001
Fred Jarrett 1999 – 2000
Rand Ginn 2000 – 2001
Deborah Boeck 2000 - 2001
*Carrie George 2001- 2005
*John Fry 2001 - 2005
Ken Glass 2001-2003
*Pat Braman 2003 --
*Lisa Eggers 2003 – 2011
*Leslie Farrell 2003 - 2009
*Adair Dingle 2005 --
John DeVleming 2005 - 2009
*Janet Frohnmayer 2007 --
David Myerson 2010 --
Brian Emanuels 2011 --

* also served as board president
** early information not available prior to 1960

Superintendent Dick Giger addresses the crowd at the rededication of Island Park Elementary School. All three elementary schools were remodeled extensively in 1995 and reopened for the start of school in September, 1996.

Mercer Island Reporter

Appendix | 237

Mercer Island Notables
(An Incomplete List of) Well-Known Islanders

Maria Frank Abrams, *artist, painter*

Paul Allen, *co-founder of Microsoft, CEO of Vulcan*

Fred Bassetti, *award-winning architect, contributor to the regional approach to modern architecture from the 1940s to 1990s*

Howard Behar, *Starbucks executive*

Gizel Berman, *Holocaust survivor and sculptor*

Steve Berman, *plaintiff's lawyer for high-profile class-action cases such as the Valdez oil spill and the landmark tobacco settlement*

Meeghan Black, *TV newscaster and host of KING 5 TV's Evening Magazine*

Frank A. Blethen, *publisher and CEO of The Seattle Times*

Dr. John Bonica, *world expert and pioneer in the field of pain management, founder of the Department of Anesthesia at University of Washington*

Phil Borges, *author and photographer*

Anna Roosevelt Boettiger, *daughter of Franklin and Eleanor Roosevelt, who worked at the Seattle Post Intelligencer from 1936 to 1943*

Dr. Ernie Burgess, *orthopedic surgeon and creator of the "Seattle foot" prosthesis*

Dave Cohn, *longtime restaurateur and founder of Consolidated Restaurants*

Phil Condit, *chairman and CEO of Boeing from 1996 to 2003*

Dr. Michael Copass, *founder of Medic One and Airlift Northwest*

Marianne Craft Norton, *ERA activist, leader in state women's organizations*

Kurt Beecher Dammeier, *owner of Beecher's Handmade Cheese and Bennett's Pure Food Bistro*

Aubrey Davis, *health-care reformer, public transportation advocate, politician, civil servant, businessman, inventor, environmentalist*

Father A. Homer Demopulos, *longtime rector/priest of St. Demetrios Greek Orthodox Church*

Stanley Ann Dunham, *President Barack Obama's mother*

Jean Stanislaw Enerson, *television news anchor and reporter for KING-TV Seattle*

Ben B. Ehrlichman *investment banker and developer who played a key role in the commercial and civic life of the Puget Sound region from the 1920s through the 1960s*

Tim Firnstahl, *longtime Seattle restaurateur*

O.W. Fisher, *member of the dynasty that founded Fisher Flour, Fisher Communications*

William Fix, *former CEO of the Bon Marche*

Henry Friedman, *Holocaust survivor, author and founder of the Washington State Holocaust Education Resource Center*

Sue Gilbert, *Rockefeller heiress, documentary filmmaker*

Lillian Goon Dip, *1920s classical Chinese and classical ballet dancer, UW graduate in education; daughter of Chinese labor contractor, consul and Seattle pioneer Goon Dip*

Budd Gould, *founder of the Anthony's restaurants*

Karolyn Grimes, *actress who played "Zuzu" in the movie It's A Wonderful Life*

Dr. James W. Haviland, *founder of the world's first outpatient kidney dialysis center*

Sam Israel, *real estate mogul and founder of the Samis Foundation*

Daniel Lorenz Johnson, *social activist and artist*

Tex Johnston, *Boeing test pilot best remembered for performing a barnstormer-style barrel roll of a Boeing 367-80 (Boeing 707 prototype) over Lake Washington in August 1955*

Dr. Robert N. Joyner Jr., *one of Seattle's first African-American physicians. When he began his family practice in Seattle in 1949, he was one of only four black doctors in Seattle.*

Stanley Kramer, *film director and one-time teacher at the University of Washington*

Paul Allen

Dr. John Bonica

Aubrey Davis

Stanley Ann Dunham

Jean Enerson

238 | Appendix

Mercer Island Notables

Sharon Kramis, cookbook author and restaurant consultant
Veronica Lake, film actress and pin-up model from the 1940s
Daniel Lapin, rabbi, commentator and radio personality
Howard Lincoln, CEO of Nintendo, CEO of the Seattle Mariners
Bruce Lorig, longtime developer, creator of Smart Communities in the Northwest
Hummie Mann, Grammy-winning composer
Paul Maritz, former Microsoft senior executive
Dave Matthews, musician and leader of the Dave Matthews Band
H.W. McCurdy, shipbuilder, bridge builder and supporter of maritime research and collecting; his firm built the Lake Washington floating bridge (1940) and the Hood Canal Bridge (1961)
Joel McHale, TV star, host of The Soup, star of Community, movie actor
Mick McHugh, longtime Seattle restaurateur
"Brakeman Bill" McLain, TV personality on KTNT (later KSTW) Channel 11 kids' show
Michael Medved, radio talk show host, author, film critic
Alan Mulally, former Boeing executive, CEO of the Ford Motor Company
Bob Newman, KIRO TV personality; "Gertrude" and foil to JP Patches, kids' show entertainer
Assunta Ng, founder and publisher of the Seattle Chinese Post and Northwest Asian Weekly newspapers
Marni Nixon, soprano and opera singer best known for being the voice in such movie musicals as The King and I, My Fair Lady, West Side Story and many others
Nordstrom family, Bruce, Blake, Peter, Erik and Fran, principals of the Nordstrom stores
Greg Palmer, author, TV and radio commentator, playwright
Annie (Cancelmi) Parisse, actress; TV shows include As the World Turns and Law & Order
Ruth Prins, kids' TV personality Wunda Wunda on KING-TV, drama teacher
Fred Radke and Gina Funes, Seattle-area entertainers—he a trumpet player and band leader, she a singer
H.B. Radke, band leader and trumpeter, son of Fred Radke and Gina Funes
Rick Robertson, "RR" from the BJ Shea show on KISW radio, Seattle
Dave Ross, longtime radio show host on KIRO Radio, Seattle-area actor
Ethan Sandler, writer and actor
Dr. Bernice Cohen Sachs, pioneering woman physician who practiced psychiatry and psychosomatic medicine at Group Health Cooperative for 48 years
Clayton L. Scott, one of the region's best-known aviators, for whom Renton Municipal Airport was renamed
Frank Schrontz, former president and CEO of Boeing
Brad Silverberg, named PC Magazine's Person of the Year in 1995 for his leadership of Windows 95; owner of venture capital firm Ignition
Hunter Simpson, philanthropist and former CEO of Physio-Control.
Barbara Hiscock Stenson, the first woman TV news anchor in the Pacific Northwest
T. Mark Stover, celebrity dog psychologist and trainer who was murdered in 2009
Sam Stroum, self-made businessman and philanthropist
John Urquart, King County sheriff
Allen Vizzutti, renowned trumpeter, composer and music educator
Dennis Waldron, developer of the Cinnabon chain of bakeries, with the late Ray Lindstrom of Mercer Island
Harry Wappler, KIRO TV meteorologist, weatherman and Episcopal priest
Esther Williams, competitive swimmer and Hollywood actress from the 1940s and '50s
Peter Daniel Young, animal rights activist, author

Joel McHale

Alan Mulally

Dave Ross

Samuel Stroum

Esther Williams

Mercer Island Citizens of the Year

Criteria for Selection

· *Honoree should be someone unrecognized for his/her contributions but is obvious to everyone as a good choice.*

· *Should be someone who has given service to the community either on Mercer Island or in the broader community in such a way as to reflect on Mercer Island.*

· *Every attempt to de-politicize the nominee and their efforts in the community should be taken, but politics should not exclude a good candidate.*

· *The nominations are taken at the annual Council retreat. If no one person is an obvious choice, it is better to have no choice than a wrong choice.*

· *An attempt is made to recognize someone who has given a broad base of community service but has not been recognized in a lot of ways.*

· *No elected official in office or known to be candidate for elective office may receive the award (added 3/2001).*

1990

Barbara Swier, *for organizing the daffodil bulb planting in Mercer Island's Central Business District.*

Phil Flash, *for organizing volunteer litter patrol alongside the roads, playing Santa at the Merchant's Munch, leading the Historical Society and participating in other community activities.*

1991

John Nelson, *a founding member and president of the Arts Council, Youth and Family Services Board; active in local and regional Rotary Clubs; all-school track meet volunteer, Community Fund board member and auctioneer; Mercerversary activist, City Council member from 1994 to 1998..*

1992

Dr. Floyd Short, *cardiologist, initiated the first firefighter EMT defibrillation program in the world, on Mercer Island. He continued for 20 years to train firefighters to become emergency medical technicians.*

1993

Anna Matheson, *active in development of the Council on Aging, Meals on Wheels, volunteer transportation for seniors, and other senior support activities.*

Delores Erchinger, *volunteer extraordinaire for the Chamber of Commerce, Council on Aging, and MI Historical Society.*

1994

Pam Eakes, *activist and founder of Mothers Against Violence in America (MAVIA), who created a school-based group called Students Against Violence Everywhere (SAVE).*

1995

John Steding, *posthumously recognized for years of service to community and schools by keeping statistics for sports at Mercer Island High School.*

1996

Fay Whitney, *for 20 years of service to seniors and youth, including volunteering on Blossoms and Burgers, the Council on Aging, Meals on Wheels, MI Thrift Shop, and working with teens at Crest Learning Center.*

1996 *No award given*

1997

Pat Braman, *teacher, union activist, longtime school board member, and member of the Community Network of Mid-East King County, formed to address increasing youth violence and teen pregnancy.*

1998

The Clergy Association, *for advocating affordable housing, culminating in the purchase of Ellsworth House in 1999 and developing a chaplain support group for the Public Safety Department. Members included: Bill Clements, Woody Carlson, Paul Fauske, Wynton Dunford, David Rose, Lisa Gelber, Richard Johnson, John Bowman, Carla Berkedal, Randal Gardner, Jack Olive, Eric Newberg, Jeff Holland, Michael Bush, Frederic Harder, Susan Price, Dale Sewall, Jean Davis, John Fellows, Kimbrough Besheer, and Marlow Schoop.*

1999

Aircraft Noise Abatement Committee, *with more than 260 members, opposed changes proposed by the Federal Aviation Administration that would have caused increased aircraft noise over Mercer Island. Members were: Ira Appelman, Charlie Barb, Jim Gilchrist, Carol Heltzel, Tom Heltzel, Lorelei Herres, Tom Hildebrandt, Elizabeth Huber, Francoise Martin , Maxine Misselwitz, Ted Misselwitz, Phil Ohringer, Fran Ohringer, Kevin Peck, Sue Stewart, Nick Vedder.*

2000

Don Cohen, *for his decade of service on the Mercer Island Planning Commission and chairing it four years, overseeing land-use legislation including the Mercer Island Comprehensive Plan, Critical Lands Ordinance, Mega-House Ordinance and the Unified Land Development Code.*

2001

Eugene Ferguson, *for his 25 years as Band Director and long-time music educator, introducing music into the lives of thousands of Mercer Island students, and bringing acclaim to MISD's superior music programs.*

2002

Jan Deveny, *in recognition of his 28 years as Mercer Island's Public Safety Director. His 40-year career included*

Mercer Island Citizens of the Year

presidency of the Washington Association of Sheriffs and Police Chiefs, activity in the International Association of Chiefs of Police, support of Special Olympics and co-founding of the Washington Law Enforcement Torch Run.

2003

Myra Lupton, retired teacher, active in the League of Women Voters and other civic groups; she was an independent citizen presence at school board and council meetings. She promoted the "Handkerchief Fleet" program of small rented sailboats at Luther Burbank.

2004

Aubrey Davis, godfather of Puget Sound transportation and protector of MI lifestyle when I-90 expanded across the Island, for six decades of public service, including Mercer Island City Council, two terms as mayor, leadership in regional office of the U.S. Department of Transportation, federal Urban Mass Transit Administration, Group Health Board of Trustees, the Washington State Transportation Commission, the Citizens' Oversight Panel Monitoring Sound Transit, and more.

2005

Ben Wolfe Mercer Island School District administrator from 1963-1992, was vice principal of North Mercer Junior High in charge of discipline. He mediated between students and police with wit, earning the title of "Captain Wolfe from the North Precinct." His last stint was Director of Maintenance Operations for the schools. He was a member of the City's Police and Fire Disability Board for 15 years, many as chair.

2006

Margaret and Kenneth Quarles for their contribution of seven acres of open space west of East Mercer Way and adjacent to Pioneer Park to the City of Mercer Island to preserve it for park and recreation.

2007

Dr. Jim Trombold, Seahawks team physician and Rotarian, a community activist, environmentalist and defender of Mercer Island parks. He was president of MI Rotary, chair of its Planet Earth committee, and helped expand support for its half-marathon to raise money for colon cancer awareness. He fought to preserve and improve Mercerdale Park, establish a native garden and set up a display of crosses at the park by Vietnam Veterans against the war in Iraq.

2008

Mercer Island Farmers Market organizers and volunteers, who brought together "farms, family, friends, fresh food, and fun." The Sunday market at Mercerdale Park supports sustainable agriculture. Founders include Callie Ridolfi, Peter Donaldson, Steve Bryan, Ellen Miller Wolfe, Lucia Pirzio-

Biroli, Bert Loosmore, Jason King, Jonathan Harrington, Mark Aggar.

2009

Susan Kaplan and Terry Pottmeyer, active in PTA at every level, from Preschool Association to Mercer Island High School. Both were board members and presidents of Mercer Island Schools Foundation, Mercer Island School Board and Mercer Island Community Fund. They were members of the Committee for Mercer Island Public Schools (CIMPS) and the committee to raise money for new band uniforms. Both were involved in the MIYFS Foundation and the Giving from the Heart Breakfast. They co-chaired the Mercerversary 50 Committee in 2010, a community-wide anniversary celebrating Mercer Island as a city.

2010 No award given

2011

Dr. Michael Copass, neurologist and legend in the emergency services world, was a founding father of Medic One and the founder of Airlift Northwest. He was head of Harborview Medical Center's Emergency Services and director of its paramedic program. The fact that a person's chances of surviving a heart attack in Seattle are the best in the nation is largely due to Copass.

2012

Fran Call, taught at North Mercer Junior High and Islander Middle School for 26 years, creating the legendary Outdoor Fitness class. For 22 consecutive summers, she took groups of middle school students—Cyclemates—on cross-country bicycle trips, traveling thousands of miles with only their bicycle packs and no sag wagon. After retiring from teaching, she started Solemates and Trailmates, popular walking and hiking groups for people over 55.

City of Mercer Island Distinguished Service Award

This award, established by the City Council in 2010, honors residents who provide ongoing leadership and service to the Mercer Island community.

2010 **Marguerite Sutherland**
Jim Horn

2011 **Jane Meyer Brahm**
Alan Merkle

Lawmakers, Judges

Ida Ballasiotes, state representative 1993-2002

Charles Burdell, Jr., former King County Superior Court Judge

Mary Brucker, former King County Superior Court Judge

Regina Cahan, King County Superior Court judge

Sen. George Clarke, state representative 1966-1971; state senator 1971-1985

Judy Clibborn, MI City Council, MI mayor, state representative 2003-present

Barbara Durham, District Court judge, state Supreme Court justice

Harley Hoppe, King County Tax Assessor, 1971-1983

Jim Horn, MI City Council, state representative 1998-1996; state senator 1988-2004

Fred Jarrett, MI City Council, mayor, state representative 2001-2008; state senator 1996-2004; deputy King County executive 2010-present

Steve Litzow, MI City Council, state senator 2010-present

Fred May, MI City Council member, state representative 1984-1992

James Noe, former King County Superior Court Judge

William Polk, former state representative, state Speaker of the House

Carol Schapira, King County Superior Court judge

Jack Scholfield, former King County Superior Court judge

Samuel Steiner, one of the nation's longest-standing bankruptcy judges

Wayne Stewart, Mercer Island Municipal Court judge

Anthony Wartnik, King County Superior Court judge

Robert Winsor, former King County Superior Court judge

Mercer Island authors

Greg Asimakoupoulos	Judy Gellatly	Galen Longstreth	Reed Parsley
Nassim Assefi	Grady Gratt	Meg Lippert	Jack Prelutsky
Paul Barlin	Julie Hearne	Wendy Liu	Ted Rand
Earl Bell	Brian Herbert	Alison Johnston Lohrey	Gloria Rand
Lynne Bragg	Frank Herbert	Jim Lynch	Marjorie Reynolds
Suzanne Brahm	J.A. Jance	Elliott Marple	Thelma Ritchie
Fran Davidson	Alison Johnston	Julian May	Lorne Rubis
Kurt Dammeier	Shiro Kashiba	Joe McDonald	Andrew Schorr
Candace Dempsey	Kris Kelsay	Fred Mednick	Michael W. Sherer
Merle Dowd	Diane Kinman	Clare Hodgson Meeker	Ben Sherman
Mary Anne Earl	Dr. Susan Kleiner	Fred Milkie, Jr.	Mary Ann Simonetti
Bruce Freguson	Aida Kouyoumjian	Linda Morgan	Christine Widman
Henry Friedman	Sharon Kramis	Susan Morrison	

Chad Coleman/Mercer Island Reporter

This 2010 photo shows the eastern highrises of the I-90 bridges. Below the bridge are cranes and other equipment working on the sewer lakeline project that was completed in 2012.

Infamous Islanders

Frederick Darren Berg, the 49-year-old founder and executive officer of Meridian Group, is serving an 18-year term in prison for stealing more than $100 million from investors in his company's mortgage funds. He ran the elaborate Ponzi scheme between 2003 and 2010. Prosecutors say Berg spent tens of millions on a ritzy lifestyle, including a waterfront home on the north end of the Island, two yachts and two jets. He was sentenced in 2012.

Frederick Darren Berg

Indle Gifford King, Jr. was found guilty in 2002 of first-degree murder for the strangulation death of his Russian mail-order bride. Anastasia King, 20, disappeared in September 2000 after returning with her husband from a trip to Kyrgystan. Her body was found three months later in a shallow grave on the Tulalip Indian Reservation near Marysville. King, 40 at the time of the trial, never admitted guilt but said he "absolutely fully" accepted the jury's verdict. He is serving his sentence of 28 years and 11 months for murder and witness tampering.

Indle Gifford King, Jr.

Stephen Long is currently serving a 21-year sentence for the murder of his wife, Elvira, in their Mercer Island home. He claimed she had run away and abandoned him and their 18-month-old child in 1993. But the FBI and police suspected otherwise; eventually he was arrested in Canada in 1996, when he was apparently planning to flee. He led authorities to the site along I-90 east of North Bend where he dumped the body of his wife, whose death was caused by strangulation. In March 1997, Long pleaded guilty to second degree murder for killing his wife, entering an Alford plea to avoid a trial. It was the first murder conviction in Mercer Island history.

Stephen Long

Martin Pang, a Mercer Island High School graduate, confessed to setting the huge fire which destroyed his parents' business, Mary Pang Food Products, a frozen food plant and warehouse at 811 7th Ave. S. in Seattle

Four Seattle firefighters lost their lives in the incident on Jan. 5, 1995, the most devastating fire in the history of the Seattle Fire Department. Pang was arrested in Rio de Janeiro on March 16, and two years later he was sentenced to 35 years in prison.

Martin Pang

George Russell, a 1976 dropout from Mercer Island High School, is the first person ever tried as a serial killer in King County. He went from a fast-talking burglar and petty thief on Mercer Island to committing more serious crimes, and, eventually, murder. In the summer of 1990, he raped and killed three women whom he had met in Bellevue bars, in what King County prosecutors described as three of "the most heinous and depraved crimes in the history of our state." He is serving a life sentence.

George Russell

(Sources: The Mercer Island Reporter, Seattle Times, Seattle Post-Intelligencer)

The Mercer Island Thrift Shop is a spectacularly successful resource for the community. It brings in about $1 million per year that goes to fund the social services programs of Mercer Island Youth and Family Services.

Jane Brahm

Mercer Island Historical Society board

Mercer Island Historical Society

Back row, left to right: Sally York Brown, Ed Rice, Susan Botkin Blake, Rand Ginn, Michael Wright, Tove Winkler Lund, Virginia Anderson. Front row: Dick Decker, Phil Flash, Kisi Goode, Bob Lewis.

Book project editorial committee

Mercer Island Historical Society

Back row, left to right: Sally York Brown, Miriam Bulmer, Jane Meyer Brahm, Nancy Gould Hilliard. Front row: Susan Botkin Blake, Dick Decker, Laurie McHale, Phil Flash.

Marketing committee

Mercer Island Historical Society

Left to right: Sally York Brown, Kris Kelsay, Rand Ginn, Terry Moreman, Roger Page.

Index

Aberle, Dr. John, 110
Abrams, Maria Frank, 238
Abrams, Sydney, 146–47
Ackerson, S. Louise, 104
Adams, Dave, 147
Aircraft Noise Abatement Committee, 240
Allen, Paul, 187–88, 234, 238
All Island Band Night, 61
All Island Track Meet, 220
Allview Heights Good Roads Association District 8, 44
Allview Heights School, 20, 48–49, 50, 52, 53, 114
Alm, Fred, 120
Alm, Gar, 103, 107, 121
Alm's drug store, 103
Anderson, Andy, 184
Anderson, Betsy, 89
Anderson, Bruce, 157
Anderson, C.M., 43
Anderson, Dave, 167
Anderson, John, 24, 37, 39, 40, 82, 90
Anderson, Katie, 157
Anderson, Leo, 141
Anderson, Richard (Dick), 101–3, 237]
Anderson, Susan, 184
Anderson, Virginia, 244
Anderson family, 89
annexation, 113
Anschell, Cleveland (Cleve), 117, 125, 236, 237
antiaircraft site, 93, 235
Appelman, Ira, 204
Appleton, 21, 23, 24, 187
architecture and architects, 190
artifacts, 13
Arts and Crafts Fair, 142
Arts Council, 127, 128, 130
Art's Food Center, 103
Auguston, Knute, 88
Aura family, 87
authors, 242
Avalon Park, 90
Averill, Bernie, 201
Avery, Paul, 237

Baade, Eugene, 153
Badminton Club, 34
Baker, William, 77
Balches, 73
band, 8–9, 58, 61, 63
Bannister, Jeff, 193
Baptist Church, 151–52
Barnabie Point, 22, 41
Barnabie School, 49, 52, 53
Barnard, Roger, 149
Barnes, Bill, 120
Barnett, Celeste, 209
Barnett, Nan, 209

Barrett, Paul, 152
Barto, Tom, 114, 117, 125, 236, 237
Barto, Virginia (Ginny), 125, 146–47
baseball, 198, 201
basketball, 8, 192, 196, 198
Baskin, Denis, 144
Bassett, Bruce, 213, 222, 236
Bassetti, Fred F., 54, 190, 238
Bassetti, Fred M., 146
bats, 178
Bayless, Alec, 146–47
Bayless, Fam, 174
Bayley, Howard, 237
Bayley, Jeanne, 183
Bayley, Richard, 183
Beach Club, 46, 85, 89, 200, 236
bears, 177, 178
beavers, 178
Beck, Grant, 236

Now Open

Roanoke Inn

Mercer Island

Located in beautiful surroundings but a short distance from the ferry landing, Roanoke Inn offers an ideal place for all-year residence. Only a half-hour from downtown by ferry and Yesler Cable. Frequent service.

Room and Two Meals Daily
$55 Per Month

Dinner for auto parties served at 6:30 p. m. week days at 85 cents per plate. Special dinner 4 p. m. Sunday, $1.05. Phone Beacon 2593 for reservations or information.

Roanoke Inn

George McGuire, LeRoy Moore, Proprietors.
Beacon 2593

A 1923 newspaper ad for the Roanoke Inn, Mercer Island's oldest business, highlights it as a place to live year round.

Beddow, Ralph, 69
beer boat, 84
Beers, F. Troxell, 237
Behar, Howard, 238
Bennett, Don, 194
Benotho, 85, 90
Berg, Frederick Darren, 243
Berman, Gizel, 154, 238
Berman, Steve, 238
Berry, Edie, 122
Bertlin, Debbie, 236
Bice, Bill, 72
Bicentennial, 124–25
Bicentennial Park, 125, 235

bicycling, 202
Bigliardi, Matthew Paul, 34
Billbe, Brayden, 194
bird species, 178, 179
Black, Meghan, 238
Black, Vickie, 56
Blackburn, Barbara, 126
Blake, Susan Botkin, 139, 141, 236, 237, 244
Bland Winn, Beth, 236
Bleakney, Jan, 68
Blethen, C.B., 100
Blethen, Frank A., 238
Blue, Michael, 194
Boeck, Deborah, 237
Boettiger, Anna Roosevelt, 185, 238
Boettiger, John, 185
Boettiger, John Jr., 185
Bolson, Harry, 219
bonds, 130–31
Bonica, John, 238
bootleggers, 91
Bordeau, Toni, 56
Borgendale, Henry, 107, 113, 236
Borges, Phil, 238
Bostrom, Trish, 194
Bowman, John, 150, 155
Boyce, N.E., 117, 236
Boyd, Harold, 101, 103
Boyd Building, 30
Boyle, Robert, 237
Boys & Girls Club, 49, 57, 144–45, 214–15
Boys Parental School. *See* Luther Burbank School and Luther Burbank Parental School for Boys
Bradley, Bruce, 110
Braeburn, Mary Wayte, 191, 193, 195, 210
Brahm, Bob, 140
Brahm, Jane Meyer, 147, 236, 241, 244
Braman, Pat, 47, 237, 240
Brazier, Dorothy Brant, 40
Breakfast of Champions, 57
Briarwood, 22
bridges, 46
Briggs, Chris, 189
Britten, Amber, 213
Broman, Sherry Savage, 55
Broom, Holly, 125
Brower, Earl, 120, 236
Brown, Beriah, 20
Brown, Fred, 194
Brown, J.B., 29, 73–74, 91, 101–2, 106
Brown, Paris, 209
Brown, Sally York, 147, 244
Bruckner, Mary Jo, 213
Buchan, Bill (William Carl) Jr., 191, 193, 194
Buchan, Bill (William Earl) Sr., 189, 191, 193, 194

Index | 245

Buchan, John, 189
buildings, 203, 205–07
Bullis, Ann, 209
Bullitt, Dorothy Stimson, 71
Bunin, Steve, 194
Burchard, Boyd, 183
Burgess, Ernie, 238
Burton, Art, 236
Burton, Celia, 142
business district, 101–3, 108, 235. *See also* Central Business District; Town Center
businesses, 176, 203, 205–07
bus service, 46, 105
Butterfield, Paula, 65–66, 237

Cairns, Bryan, 236
Calkins, C.C. (Charles Cicero), 25–28, 30, 48
Calkins, Nellie, 26–27
Calkins, Ruby, 26–27
Calkins Hotel, 25–28, 30, 77, 235
Calkins Landing, 29, 48
Call, Fran, 143
Callahan, Tom, 101
Cameron, Harold, 237
Campbell, Robert, 237
Camp Tarywood, 131, 189
Cancelmi Parisse, Annie, 239
Canterbury Candy Company, 29
Carlson, Woody, 155
Cassidy, Jack, 94, 146
"Castle," the, 30, 34, 183
C.C. Calkins, 25–26, 27, 37
Cedarhurst, 22
cell towers, 169, 171, 173
census data (2010), 234
centennial, state, 125–26
Center Island Club, 105
Central Business District, 30, 125, 134–36, 160–61, 166. *See also* business district; Town Center
Cero, Mike, 236
Ceteznik, Frank, 194, 196, 197
Chae, John, 151
Chamber of Commerce, 103, 108, 116, 117–18, 140, 146
Chang, Michael, 194
cheerleaders, 9, 62
Chemical People, 128
Chick's Shoes & Service, 146, 174
CHILD (Children's Institute for Learning Differences) School, 68
Children's Choir, 145
Children's Educational Foundation, 104
Children's Hospital Guild, 139, 140, 142
Children's Park, 144
Christian Science Church, 149, 150, 151
Chrysler, Camille, 209
Church of Jesus Christ of Latter-day Saints, 152, 153
churches and synagogues, 149–56. *See also individual entries*
Circus McGurkus, 139, 144
citizens of the year, 240–41
City Council, 112–13, 116–17, 119, 122,

124, 127, 136; members, 236
city government, 90, 126–27. *See also* City Council; city managers; mayors
City Hall, 34, 130, 131, 134, 138
city managers, 236
City of Mercer Island, 111–13, 116–17, 121
City University, 57
civil defense, 93–94, 107
Clancy, David, 236
Clancy, Nancy, 61, 237
Claringbould, Charles, 52
Clarke, George, 125, 237
Clarke (Mabel) Park, 189
Clarke family, 73
Classical Music Supporters, 57, 148
Clements, Bill, 155
Clergy Association, 149, 155, 215, 240
Clibborn, Judy, 171, 236
Clise, Charles, 82, 105, 109
Close, Ruth Mary, 213
clubs and organizations, 139–42, 145, 148. *See also individual entries*
Cockran, Tom, 237
Coe, Robert (Bob), 110, 130, 236
Cohen, Don, 240
Cohen, Tina, 237
Cohn, Dave, 238
Cohn, Steve, 203, 205
Colman, Clarissa, 48
Committee for Mercer Island Public Schools, 54
Committee for One Island Now, 121
Committee to Save Pioneer Park, 122
Committee to Save the Earth, 123–24, 170
Commons, the, 54
Community Center at Mercer View, 57, 127–28, 130, 145, 168–69, 207–08, 210
Community Club, 31, 41, 43, 45, 46, 114. *See also* Keewaydin Clubhouse; VFW Hall
Community Fund, 142, 144
Condit, Phil, 238
Congregational Church (United Church of Christ), 151, 153, 190
Connection, The, 168
Conrad, Rich, 171, 213, 216, 236
Contract High School, 57
Cooper, Bob, 120
Cooper, Finley, 149
Cooperative Water Association, 31
Co-op Preschool, 34
Copass, Michael, 141, 238, 241
Corder, Chip, 216
Country Village Day School, 57, 68
Covenant Church, 151
Covenant Shores, 82, 109, 185–86. *See also* Shorewood Apartments
coyotes, 178
Craft Guild, 78, 235
Craft Norton, Marianne, 238
Crest Learning Center, 53
CrimeStoppers, 130
Crosby, James, 102, 106, 108, 121, 124
Crosby Row, 135

Croshaw's Food Store, 103
cross-country team, 198
crows, 178
Crystal Springs Water Company, 31
Currie, Craig, 237
Curry, Stephanie, 60
Cyclemates, 143

dairy farms, 32–33, 69, 70, 71, 111, 181
Dalton, Sheri Edwards, 152
Dammeier, Kurt Beecher, 238
DARE (Drug Abuse Resistance Education), 130
Davenport, Lance, 172
Davidson, Herbert, 103, 110
Davidson, Sam, 110
Davis, Aubrey, 122, 125, 132, 157, 163, 165, 222, 236, 238, 241
Davis, Jean, 155
Davis, John, 213, 237
Dawn, 30, 34, 35, 37, 39–40
Day, John, 117, 236
Deane, Lola, 125, 142, 144, 174, 212
Deane, Philip (Phil), 110, 125, 144, 174, 212
Deane's Children's Park, 144, 212
Decker, Dick, 244
Deely, John, 166
deer, 94, 103, 167, 177–78
Deforest, Virginia, 237
Delgado, Michael, 58
Dellino, Pam, 68
demographics in 2012, 181, 234
Demopulos, A. Homer, 238
Dendy, Paul, 237
Depression, 91–93
development, 122–23, 203, 205–07
Deveny, Jan, 130, 236, 240–41
Devil's Hollow, 73
DeVleming, John, 237
Diamond, Sherman, 114, 122, 236
Didrickson, Scott, 194
Dingle, Adair, 237
Dion, Charles, 150
Dip, Lillian Goon, 238
Distinguished Service Award, 241
docks, ferry, 38, 39, 108, 183; map, 42. *See also individual entries*
doctors, 110
Donaldson, Peter, 62, 144, 145
Doonesbury, 221
Dorsey, Christi, 193
Douglas, Mary, 104
Drain, Jennifer, 172
Driggers, Scott, 193
ducks, 179
Dulien, Ann, 145
Dunden, Robin, 108
Dunden home, 29
Dunham, Stanley Ann, 109, 238
Dunn, Ernie, 110
Dunney, John, 75, 77, 94, 101–2, 113, 221
Dunnington, L.L., 151
Durant, Kevin, 194
Duwamish Tribe, 13, 15

246 | Index

eagles, 178, 179
Eakes, Pam, 240
earthquakes, 15
East Channel Bridge, 2–3, 41, 77, 93, 164, 235, 248. *See also* I-90
Easter, Jenna Lee, 73–74
East Mercer Way, 186–87
East Seattle, 13, 25–28, 29–34, 48, 69–70, 181, 183, 184
East Seattle Dock, 30, 32, 35
East Seattle Grocery, 29, 30
East Seattle School, 23, 48, 49, 50, 51, 52, 53, 54, 55, 57, 94, 131, 144–45, 150, 183, 214–15. *See also* Boys & Girls Club; PEAK
East Seattle Water System, 69
Edberg, Gordy, 236
Eddy, Howard, 103, 110
Eddy, Roger, 110
Edwards, Adah, 203
Eggers, Lisa, 237
Ehrlichman, Ben B., 238
Ekren, LaVonne, 147
El Dorado Beach Club, 108, 185
Elfendahl, Major, 236
Ellingsen, Betty Ekrem, 186
Ellingsen, Ken, 111
Ellingsen, Roy, 111
Elliot, Virginia Ogden, 31, 39, 40, 73
Ellis Pond, 211, 214
Elsoe, Ron, 236
Emmanuel Episcopal Church, 30, 33–34, 114, 149, 150, 190, 219
Emanuels, Brian, 201, 237
Emrich, Russell C., 104
employers, largest, 234
Enbysk, Liz, 147
energy crisis, 127
Enerson, Jean Stanislaw, 238
Eng, Diane, 209
Engstrom, Oscar, 159
Engstrom Open Space, 159, 212, 214
Engstrom Quarles, Margaret, 212

Environmental Council, 122–23
Erchinger, Delores, 140, 240
Escape from the Rock, 201
Esther Marion Shop, 116
ethnicity, 234

Faben, Vince, 183
Faben Point, 93, 183, 188, 250
Falk, Cheryl, 145
Fardal, Harold, 237
Farmer, Grant, 194
Farmers New World Life, 234
farming, 31–33
farmers market, 10, 148, 241
Farrell, Leslie, 237
Farrill, Dorothy, 72
Fauske, Paul, 155
Fellows, John, 155
Fellows, Marienne "Nuky," 124, 125
Fergin, James, 149
Ferguson, Eugene, 58, 240
Ferncroft, 13
ferries, 22, 29, 37–42, 69–70. *See also* steamers; *individual entries*
ferry docks, 38, 39, 108, 183; map, 42. *See also individual entries*
Filbert, Bernhard, 153
Fine Arts Advisory Committee, 60–61
fire chiefs, 236
fire department, 107, 120, 130
firefighting, 94, 120
Firnstahl, Tim, 238
First Hill, 130, 133, 181, 183
fish, 178
Fisher, O.W., 238
Fix, William, 238
Flake, Dr. Charles, 110
Flash, Phil, 140, 141, 240, 244
Flats, The, 73–74, 101, 184
Fleury, Alfred (Al), 90, 91, 92, 125, 140, 236
floating bridge(s), 2–3, 93, 95–100, 101,

105, 124, 132–33, 157–58, 164–65, 235. *See also* I-90
Floating Bridge Inn, 118
Flood, Frank, 83
Flood's Dock, 105
Floyd, Linda, 147
Flynn, Mary Ann, 168
folklore, 13
football team, 197, 198
Fordyce's Standard Supply, 101
Forest Avenue, 187
Forsman, Lowell, 172
Forsyth, Tom, 120
Fortuna, 185–86
Fortuna, 37, 38, 41, 69, 82
Fortuna Lodge, 109, 186, 235
Fortuna Park, 41, 82, 105
Fox, Bernie, 68
Franklin, Myra, 237
Franklin Dock, 71
Freeman, May, 86
Freitag, Patrick, 150
French American School of Puget Sound, 68
Fricke, Ruth, 124
Friedman, Henry, 238
Friends of Luther Burbank Park, 148
Friends of the Mercer Island Library, 115
Frink, Steven, 107
Frisby, Mark, 196
Frohnmayer, Janet, 237
Frothingham, Don, 153
Fruehauf, Charles, 33, 35
Fruitland, 185
Fry, John, 237
Fry, Sam, 236
Fulcher, Dorothy, 186
Funes, Gina, 239
Furness, Lucy, 84
future, 221–22

Gallagher Hill, 130

The entrance to Mercer Island High School in 1966.

Owen Blauman collection

Gallagher Hill Road and Greenbelt, 93, 122
Garden Club, 94
Garkins, Mrs., 28
Garrison, Henry (Harry) Lee, 24
Garrison, Harry Jr., 24, 73
Garrison, Myrta, 23, 24, 73
Garrison Luckenbill, Alla May Olds, 21, 22–23, 24, 48, 114
Gee, Logan, 194
Gellatly, Judy, 124, 125
Genack, Wilfred "Jack," 146
George, Carrie, 237
Gerber, Georgia, 115
Giard, Kim, 200
Gibbons, Tom, 125
Giger, Dick, 64, 237
Gilbert, Charles (Charlie), 38, 40, 70
Gilbert, Frank, 39–40
Gilbert, Sue, 238
Gilbert, William, 40
Gilbertson, Eva, 110
Gilliom, Jim, 153
Ginn, Rand, 237, 244
Glass, Ken, 237
Glazounow, Thelma Rydeen, 84, 85
Goedecke, Arne, 108
Gold Coast, 183
Goldmanis, Sven, 169, 236
golf, 198
golf course(s), proposed, 46, 84, 116, 122, 123, 157, 158–59
Goode, Kisi, 244
Good Roads Association District 8, 44
Goon Dip, Lillian, 238
Goto, Kelly, 125
Gould, Budd, 238
Gould Hilliard, Nancy, 147, 244
Grady, Mary, 147
Grady, Mike, 236
Graham, Brad, 120
Grausz, Dan, 204, 236
Green, Bill, 120
Green, J.P., 237
Green, Mr., 72
Green, Roy, 155
Green, William, 107
Greenbelt Plan, 122
Greenwood, E.M., 116, 146, 173
Greenwood Village, 173
Gregg, Carol, 57
Gregory family, 87
Gresia, Susan, 209
Grimes, Karolyn, 238
Grimes, Shelley, 147
grocery boat, 84
Gropp, Jerry, 190
Groveland, 86, 89, 93, 188
Grubstake, 29, 39
Gudmundsson, Petur, 192, 197
Guild Hall, 29, 33–34, 52, 113, 144, 149
Guitteau, William Putnam, 26, 184

Guitteau Storey, Florence, 17, 27, 48, 191
Guthrie, Alice, 56
gymnastics, 198

Haag, Alex, 86
Hadley, Eleanor, 99
Hadley, Homer, 96, 99
Haertig, Robert, 149
Hagg, Alvin, 86
Hagg, Arnie, 86
Hagg, Bert, 86
Hale, Jim, 236
Hallgren, Howard, 31
Hall of Fame, Sports, 198–99
Haman, Raymond, 237
Hanaeuer, Adrian, 194
Hap's Service Station, 74, 76, 77, 91, 101
Harder, Fred, 155
Harper, Bob, 140
Harris, Flo, 169
Harris family, 89
Harrison, Benjamin, 21, 26
Harshbarger, Bob, 197
Haslund, Louise, 127
Haviland, James W., 238
Hawes, Steve, 192, 194, 197
Hawkins, Harry, 7
Healy, Ryan, 138
Hearne, Rod, 237
Hedlund, Joyce, 196
Helberg, Bruce, 146
Hemions, 73
Henderson, Nan, 127
herons, 178
Herzl-Ner Tamid, 152, 155
Hesse's Restaurant, 118
Hiatt, Peggy, 127
Hicks, Laura, 49
Higdays, 73
high school. *See* Mercer Island High School
Highsmith, Paul, 66
Hilliard, Nancy Gould, 147, 244
Hillman, C.D., 84
Hilton, Thomas A., 33
Hiscock Stenson, Barbara, 239
Historical Society, 74, 93, 141; markers, 235
Hitchman, Donald (Don), 116, 122, 236
Hodge, Chick, 237
Holland, Andrea, 83
Holloway, Terrell, 237
Holmes, Ed, 65, 222, 236
Holmgren, Mike, 194
Holy Trinity Lutheran Church, 69, 149–50, 151
Homecoming, 62, 63
Homer M. Hadley Memorial Bridge. *See* floating bridge
Homestead Field, 69, 70, 71, 73
Hope of God Church, 153, 155
Horn, Jim, 130, 236, 241
Horton, C.H., 43
Horvitz, Peter, 147
Howard, Trevor, 200
Howell, Clarence, 236

This 1981 photos shows the old and new spans of the East Channel Bridge.

Owen Blauman collection

Howell, Red, 117
households, total, 234
Huffmans, 84
Huhs, Al, 130, 236
Humanities Block, 55, 131, 189
Hurlburt, Eric, 120
Hutchins, Nan, 125, 130, 236

I-90, 2–3, 122–23, 124, 125, 132–33, 162–65. *See also* floating bridge(s)
Ide, Don, 237
Ilgenfritz, Gretchen, 237
incorporation, 103, 106, 111–19
Indian Princesses and Indian Guides, 145
Industrial School, 77
infamous Islanders, 243
Interfaith Union, 149
Island Books, 129, 174
Island Choral Experience, 145
Island Crest Park, 130, 157
Island Crest Way, 105
Islander Middle School, 52, 53, 57, 60, 65, 67, 68. *See also* Mercer Island Junior High School
Island Market Square, 103
Island Park Elementary School, 52, 53, 55, 58, 59, 60, 62, 237
Island Point, 189
Island Sound, 145
Island Square, 101, 234
Island Vision, 148, 219
Israel, Sam, 238
Issaquah, 38
Italiane, Anita, 209
Italiane, Lynn, 209
Ivy Brigade, 148

Jackman, Linda, 167, 213, 236
Jackson, David, 155
Jackson, Jay, 200
Jackson, Paul, 194, 197, 200
Jahncke, El, 204, 216, 236, 237
Jamerson, Kristen, 221
James Crosby gift shop, 106, 108. *See also* Crosby, James
Jansen, Jim, 151
Jaquette, Bill, 110
Jarrett, Fred, 124, 130, 236, 237
Jarrett, Keith, 194
Jensen, Riley, 149, 152
Jensen, Robert, 237
Jerue, Mark, 194, 197
Jewish community, 153–55
Jewish Community Center, 11, 154
Jinka, Albeny, 209
Jobline, 128
jobs on Island, 234
John Dunney Trail, 75
John Graham Report, 117
John L. Scott Real Estate, 110
Johnson, Al E., 155
Johnson, Curt, 120
Johnson, Daniel Lorenz, 238
Johnson family, 87
Johnson, Robert, 237

Johnson, Robert E., 237
Johnston, Blake, 200
Johnston, Tex, 238
John Walter Ackerson Home, 104
Joyner, Robert N. Jr., 238
judges, 242
junior high. *See* Islander Middle School; Mercer Island Junior High; North Mercer Island Junior High; South Mercer Junior High

Kaltenbach, Ray, 209
Kampe, Chris, 192
Kander, Ken, 120
Kaplan, Susan, 213, 237, 241
Karl, Laura, 57
kayaking, 5
Keewaydin Club, 45–46, 93
Keewaydin Clubhouse, 43, 45, 75, 149, 151, 235. *See also* Mercer Island Community Club; VFW Hall
Keim, Bill, 66, 237
Keller, Kasey, 194
Kellogg, Gardner, 28
Kelsay, Kris, 213, 244
Kelsey, Henry E., 22, 47–48
Kennedy, Karol, 191, 194
Kennedy, Peter, 191, 194
Kenyon, Roger, 120
Kettering, Harry, 110
Kim, Jay, 201
King, Indle Gifford Jr., 243
King County Library System, 114–15
Kirchner, Mark, 236
Kirtman, David, 194, 197
Kiwanis Club, 117, 125, 141–42
Knoll, Bob, 141
Knoll, Mary Anne, 237
Koehler, Laurie, 237
Kornfeld, Yechezkel, 155
Kraft, Rob, 201
Kramer, Stanley, 238
Kramis, Sharon, 239
Kristoferson, August, 71, 73
Kristoferson farm, 69, 70
Kuebler, Lowell, 237
Kuhns, Austin, 157
Kuhns, Jeff, 157
Kummen, John, 59

Lacey V. Murrow Bridge. *See* floating bridge(s); I-90
Lackland, John, 237
lacrosse, 198, 200
Ladies Auxiliary, 46
Laframboise, C.B., 146
Lake Washington: cleaning, 118–19; lowering, 15, 70; naming, 16
Lake, Sam, 141
Lake, Veronica, 239
Lakeridge Elementary School, 52, 53, 55, 58, 59, 60, 65, 106
Lakes, The, 5, 56, 121, 189
Lakeview Highlands, 90
Lakeview School, 46, 49, 50, 51, 52, 53,

54, 84–85, 89, 90, 93, 106, 190, 235. *See also* Sunnybeam School
Lamb, Mary Ann, 209
land area/acreage, total, 234
land swaps, 131, 134
Landis, Charley, 107
landslides, 15
Langlois, Ed, 120
Lanspery, Paul, 171, 236
Lapin, Daniel, 239
Larson, Clarance, 70
Larson, Diane, 174
Larson, Shirley, 174
Laschever, Jean, 200
Lathrop, Lee, 147
Lavender, Mrs. Geoffrey, 114
lawmakers, 242
Lawrence White's Hair Styling Salon, 103
Lawson, Eugene, 27
Leap for Green, 148, 219
Leavitt, Harry, 124
LeClerq, Sheila, 117, 236, 237
Leiser, J.J., 28
Leschi, 40
Leven, Bruce, 185
Lewis, Bob, 244
Lewis, Gary, 173
Lewis, Rashard, 195
Lewis, Verne, 236
library, 20, 34, 114–15
Lid, 133, 163, 165, 204, 218, 233. *See also* Park on the Lid
light rail, 219, 221
Lightfoot, Elsie Person, 29, 32
Lightfoot, Ewart, 76
Lightfoot, Frederick (Fred), 76, 102
Lightfoot, George, 29, 30, 76, 93, 95–96, 146, 235
Lightfoot, Hap, 29, 30, 74, 146. *See also* Hap's Service Station
Lightfoot, Joseph (Joe), 213, 236
Lightfoot, Lynn, 213
Lightfoot, Mary, 76
Lightfoot family, 102
Lightfoot grocery store, 76, 77
Lincoln, Howard, 239
Lind, John, 110
Lindell, Londi, 216
Lindquist, Jeff, 195, 197
Lindquist, Tarry, 58
Link, Milton, 237
Lions Club, 108, 141
Lions Club Beach, 106
Lions Club camp, 85, 88–89
Little, Cecil, 120, 236
Little, Larry, 120
Little League, 201
Litzow, Steve, 236
Livewire News, 146
Lloyd, Andy, 196
Loewenheim, Irene, 100
logging, 17
Logie, Matt, 192, 197
Long, Stephen, 243
Look's Drug Store/Pharmacy, 103, 110
Lorig, Andrea, 129

Index | 249

Lorig, Bruce, 160, 239
Loveless, Arthur, 184
Lovsted, Carl, 191, 195
Lowell, Jeff, 196, 201*L.T. Haas*, 38
Lucas, Eugene, 71
Lucas, Gene, 71
Lucas, Joseph, 71
Lucas, Josephine Pachoud, 70, 71, 73
Lucas, Marie Blanche, 69, 70, 71
Lucas farm, 69, 70, 71, 73, 150
Luckenbill, Alla May Olds Garrison, 21, 22–23, 24, 48, 114
Luckenbill, George, 23, 24
lumber yard, 135; Mercer Island Lumber Company, 91, 234; Moore's Lumber Yard, 77, 101, 102
Lund, Tove Winkler, 244
Lupton, Myra, 215, 241
Luther Burbank Park, 26, 79, 125, 130, 148, 210, 211–12, 215, 220, 235
Luther Burbank School and Luther Burbank Parental School for Boys, 27, 34, 77, 79–82, 235
Lutheran Church (Redeemer), 152, 153

Mabel Clarke Park, 189
Macalister, Gordon, 120
MacDonald, Elinor, 174
MacGilvra, Katharine, 144
Machenheimer, H. E., 237
Mack, Dave, 147
MacMahon, Theresa, 114
Mahdavi, Ben, 200
Mahoney, Greg, 197, 198, 200
mail delivery, 35. *See also* post office
Malakoff, Jenifer, 57
Mandelkorn, Ted, 110
Manlowe, Laurie, 209

Mann, Hummie, 239
Manzanita, USS, 186
map(s): aerial, 180; circa 1890, 19; circa 1909, 18; East Seattle, 32; Historical Society markers, 235; historic sites and early streets, 36; neighborhoods, 182; steamboat routes, 42
Maple Lane, 108
Marine Patrol, 172
Maritz, Paul, 239
martial arts, 201
Martin, Clarence D., 96, 97, 98, 100
Martin, Lillian, 159
Martin, Norine, 117
Martine, Joe, 120
Martine family, 184
Matthews, Dave, 239
Mary Wayte Pool, 67, 68, 193, 208, 210–11
Matheson, Anna, 124, 125, 240
Mauldin, Walt, 236
May, Fred O., 236
mayors, 236
McClelland, John, 147
McCullum, Jamien, 195
McCullum, Justin, 195
McCullum, Sam, 195
McCurdy, H.W., 239
McDonald, Lucille, 13
Mcferran, Brian, 120
McGilvra, 69, 183
McGilvra, Gordon, 69
McGilvra Improvement Club, 44–45, 74
McGilvra School, 49, 52, 53, 74, 77
McGowan, Joby, 67
McGuire, George, 69, 72
McHale, Joel, 239
McHale, Laurie, 244
McHugh, Mick, 239

Mckinney, Ed, 120
McKnight, Dorothy, 147
McMahon, D.B., 30
McMahon, Edward, 20
McMahon family, 183
McMahon, Theresa Schmid, 19, 20, 22
McLain, "Brakeman Bill," 239
McQueen, Laurie, 169
McTavish, Peter, 119, 236
meat boat, 84
Medved, Michael, 239
Meerscheidt, August, 31
megahouses, 167
Meneses-Swift, Veronica, 237
Mercer, 38
Mercer, Aaron, 14, 16
Mercer, Asa, 14, 16
Mercer, Nancy, 14
Mercer, Thomas, 14, 16, 23
Mercerart, 209
Mercer Crest Elementary School, 52, 53, 54, 55, 57
Mercerdale, 73, 130, 131, 184
Mercerdale Park, 57, 69, 138, 161, 171, 184
MercerFair, 108, 117–18, 125, 142
Mercer Island American, 146
Mercer Island Country Club, 142, 200
Mercer Islander, 146, 147
Mercer Island Estates, 189
Mercer Island Florist, 174
Mercer Island High School, 51, 53, 54, 55, 56, 58, 59, 60, 63, 64, 65, 66, 67, 68, 123–24 190, 247; marching band, 8–9, 63; Sports Hall of Fame, 198–99
Mercer Island Journal, 146
Mercer Island Junior High, 52. *See also* Islander Middle School
Mercer Island Lumber Company, 92, 234

Owen Blauman collection

An early view of Faben Point, on the northwest tip of Mercer Island.

Mercer Island News, 43, 44, 94, 146
Mercer Island Observer, 146
Mercer Island Parental School, 77, 80
Mercer Island Radio Operators, 148
Mercer Island Reporter, 65, 71, 73, 75, 90, 129, 146–47
Mercer Island Shopping Center, 101, 103
Mercer Island Stenographic Services, 116
Mercer Island Travel, 116
Mercer Island Visual Arts League, 142
Mercer Island Women's Club, 142
Mercer Park Medical-Dental Center, 110
Mercerversary, 124, 125, 213
Mercer View Elementary School, 52, 53, 54, 55, 57, 128, 167–68. *See also* Community Center at Mercer View
Mercerwood, 102
Mercerwood Shore Club, 104, 186, 190
Mercerwood Shores, 186
Merchants Munch, 161
Merkle, Alan, 236, 241
Merritt, William, 110
Methodist Church, 151
Metrathon, 60, 63
Metro, 118–19
Meyer, Carol, 68
Meyer, Charles, 33
Meyer Brahm, Jane, 147, 236, 241, 244
midcentury modern homes, 190
middle school. *See* Islander Middle School; Mercer Island Junior High; North Mercer Island Junior High; South Mercer Junior High
Miles, Jimmy, 39
Miller, Charles, 237
Miller, George, 22
Miller, Steven, 125
Mills, Geoff, 196
Minyan Mizrach, 155
Mirel, James, 155
Miss Mercer Island, 108, 117–18
Mobilgas station, 103
Moore, William, 107
Moorehead, Erwin, 237
Moore's Lumber Yard, 77, 101, 102
Moreman, Terry, 140, 213, 244
Morgan, Mary Kay, 127
Morgan, Peg, 127, 128
Moss, Millicent, 100
movies, 74
Mulally, Alan, 239
Mulally, Mandy, 60
Mulholland, Rae, 145
Muncey, Bill, 109, 195
Murray, Charles, 237
Murray, Dr., 27
Murrow, Edward, 100
Murrow, Lacey, 96, 99, 100
"Mushroom," the, 54, 55, 64
Myerson, David, 237
Myre, Jessica, 60

name of island, 14, 16
Naomi, 46
National Charity League, 145
neighborhoods, 181–89

Nelson, John, 145, 236, 240
Nelson, Roy, 86
Newell, Cicero, 27, 77
Newman, Bob, 239
Newman, Elliot, 99, 130, 166, 236
newspapers, 146–47. *See also individual entries*
Ng, Assunta, 239
Nicholl, Dick, 195, 197
Nielsen, Frederik (Fred) S., 35
9611 Building, 57, 131, 134
Niquette, Glen, 111–12
Nixon, Marni, 239
Nolan, Frank, 146
Nordstrom, Blake, 239
Nordstrom, Bruce, 239
Nordstrom, Erik, 239
Nordstrom, Fran, 239
Nordstrom, Peter, 239
North Campus, 54, 57, 68
north end, 69–82
North End Community Club, 94, 103
North Mercer, 184
North Mercer Island Junior High, 52, 53, 54, 55, 57
North Mercer Junior High campus, 144, 145
North Mercer Way, 73, 82
North Star Lodge, 86
Northwest Children's Academy, 57
Northwest Yeshiva High School, 68, 152, 155, 171, 197
Norton, Bob, 236
Norton, Robert (Bob), 122, 236
Norton, Marianne Craft, 238
notables, 238–39. *See also* citizens of the year
Nugent, Ormand C., 114
Nygren, Virginia, 52, 177

Obama, Barack, 109
O'Brien, Chuck, 190
O'Brien, Michael, 145, 215
Oesting, John, 237
Oesting, Megan, 196
Ogden Elliot, Virginia, 31, 39, 40, 73
Ogden, Ray Jr., 114
Ogden family, 73
O'Hearn, Ian
Olden, Dan, 27
Olds, Agnes, 21, 23, 47
Olds, Charles, 21, 22, 23, 24, 47, 187
Olds, David, 21, 22, 23, 24
Olds Garrison Luckenbill, Alla May, 21, 22–23, 24, 48, 114
Oliver, Dorothy, 236
Oliver, Harold, 89, 116, 117, 236, 237
Oliver, Lynn, 236
Olson, Dorothy, 116
Olson, Harold, 237
Olson family, 86
Olympians, 191
Open Space Conservancy Trust, 123, 148, 157, 158–59, 179
Orser, Peter, 236
Orthopedic Guild, 139, 142

O'Shea, John, 173
Oshiro, Cathy, 57
Outdoor Sculpture Gallery, 222
Owens, R.G., 237
owls, 179

Pachoud Lucas, Josephine, 70, 71, 73
Page, Roger, 174, 221, 244
Paine, Robert, 237
Palmberg, Bud, 151
Palmer, Greg, 239
Pang, Martin, 243
Parent Teacher Student Association (PTA), 54–55, 60, 144, 145
Parental School Dock, 41
Parisse, Annie Cancelmi, 239
Park, Carolyn, 114
park-and-ride lot, 205
parking, 206–07
Parkinson, John, 25
Park on the Lid, 165, 170–71, 204, 218
parks, 106, 130–31, 170–71, 211, 234. *See also individual entries*
Parkwood, 187
Patch, 147
Patera, Jack, 195
Paul Allen Estate, 187–88
Paull, Brenda, 237
Paxson, Chauncey "Chip," 110
Payne, Anne, 174
Payne, Earl, 174
PEAK (Providing Empowering Activities for Kids), 145, 214–15
pea patch, 11
Pearman, Charlotte, 213
Pearman, Jim, 157, 168, 213, 216, 236
Pearman, Julia, 213
Peggy Greene's Dance Studio, 29
Penny, Steve, 195
Pepple, Ed, 192, 195
Pepple, Kyle, 197
Pepple, Shirley, 192
Pepple, Terry, 197
pergola, 138, 141
Person, August, 32
Person, Elsie Lightfoot, 29, 32
Person, Ernest (Ernie), 17, 32, 33, 113
Person, Esther, 32
Person, Harold, 32
Person, Helena Olivia Bjorkland, 31–32
Person, Richard, 32
Person, Robert, 32
Person, Swan, 31–32, 33, 35, 91
Person dairy farm, 32–33, 71, 111, 175, 181
Peterson, Charles, 209
Peterson, Frederick C., 236
Peterson, John, 28, 33
Philen, Suzanne, 170
Phone-a-Thon, 57
Pierce, J. Kingston, 27
Pioneer Park, 4, 83, 122, 123, 148, 157, 158–59, 179
Pioneer Park Youth Club, 142
Plano, Gary, 67, 237
Plateau, The, 187

Index | 251

Pleasant Hour Club, 46
Pochman, Owen, 195, 197
police chiefs, 236
police department, 106, 108, 130, 172
Pomerantz, Maurice, 149, 155
population: in 1930s–40s, 91; in 1950s, 105, 106; post-World War II, 101; in 2010, 181, 234
post office, 30 103. *See also* mail delivery
Potter, Tom, 54
Pottmeyer, Terry, 66, 213, 237, 241
Powell, Walbridge, 166
Prelutsky, Jack, 6
Presbyterian Church, 152, 153, 156
Preschool Association, 55, 106, 114, 138, 139, 144
preservation, 122–23
Priest, Hunt, 149
Prince, George N., 112
Prince, Gerry, 125
Prins, Ruth, 239
Privet Academy, 68
Probus Club, 145, 148
Proctor, Ellen, 20–21, 23
Proctor, Gardiner, 20–21, 23, 25
Proctor's Landing, 30
Project Renaissance, 136, 160–61, 166
property taxes, 134
Prosser, Ruth, 237
Provost, Al, 120, 236
Ptacek, Bill, 222
Public Safety, Department of, 130. *See also* fire department; police department
Public Works Administration, 96

QFC, 173
Quarles, Kenneth, 159, 212, 241
Quarles, Margaret Engstrom, 159, 212, 241

raccoons, 177
Radcliffe, Jim, 236
Radke, Dick, 120
Radke, Fred, 65, 239
Radke, H.B., 239
Ramey Lethcoe, Nancy, 191, 195
Ramsey, John, 120
Rand, Martha, 79
Rand, Ted, 79
Rand, Willis, 77, 79
R & R Place, 128
Rasmussen, Blair, 195, 215
Rasmussen, Gordon, 236
Reagan, Nancy, 59
real estate, 166, 217–18; mean housing value, 234
recreation council, 106
recycling, 170
Recycling Center, 123–24, 170
Redeemer Lutheran Church, 152, 153
Reeck, Edwin, 72
Reeck, Hal, 72
Reeck, Laura, 72
religions, 149–56

Renshaw, Maureen, 56
Reynolds, Peggy, 90, 122, 135, 147, 173
rezoning, 108, 111, 116
Rice, Ed, 244
Richards, Virginia, 34
Riley, Charlotte, 187
Riley, Etta, 187
Riley, Howard, 187
Riley, Huston, 74, 77, 187
Risch, Otto, 105
Riviera, Daniel, 236
roads, 74, 103, 105. *See also* streets; *individual entries*
roads associations, 43–44
Roanoke Dock/Landing, 30, 35, 37, 69, 70, 72, 74, 75, 140, 235
Roanoke grocery store, 72, 74, 77
Roanoke Inn/Tavern, 72, 91, 101, 235, 245
Roanoke Park, 95
Roanoke Transportation Company, 46
Roberson, Joe, 120
Robertson, Rick, 239
Robinson, Robbie, 120
Rochester, Nelson, 107
Rochester's Garage, 41, 91, 94, 101, 107
rodents, 178
Roosevelt Boettiger, Anna, 185, 238
Rooster Tail, The, 109
Rose, David, 155
Rose, John, 148
Rose, Larry, 127, 128, 236
Rosen, Leslie, 145
Rosenbaum, Jay, 155
Ross, Dave, 239
Rotary Club, 7, 142
Rotary Half Marathon, 7, 141, 142, 201
rowers, 12
Russell, Bill, 195
Russell, Ed, 147
Russell, George, 243
Rydeen, Hank, 84, 85
Rydeen, Martha, 84
Rydeen, Robert, 84, 85

Sachs, Bernice Cohen, 239
Saddle Club, 117, 142
Safeway, 135, 225
sailing, 4, 215, 220
St. Monica Catholic Church, 150, 156
St. Monica Parish School, 68
Sammamish Tribe, 14
Sand, Frank, 120
Sandell, Frank, 30
Sandin, Frank, 41, 70
Sandin, Mimi, 70–71
Sandler, Ethan, 239
Santee, Kim, 209
Saquitne, Bob, 120
Saquitne, Marv, 120
Sasaki, Kazuhiro, 195
Sauer, Wendy, 60
Scalzo Scar, 187
Scates, Sheila, 68
Schaumberg, Pat, 142
Schensted, Liz, 147

Schmid, Caroline, 19–20
Schmid, Conrad, 19–20
Schmid, Ida Dreyer, 19–20
Schmid, Sarah, 19
Schmid, Theresa, 19, 20, 22. *See* McMahon, Theresa Schmid
Schmid, Victor, 19–20
Schmid, Vitus, 19–20, 114
school bonds, 61, 64, 65, 67–68
school curriculum, 65, 66, 67
School District, 47, 234; board of directors, 237. *See also* schools
school enrollment, 66, 67
schools, 6, 47–68, 221; excellence of, 67. *See also individual entries*
Schools Foundation, 57
school superintendents, 237. *See also individual entries*
Schrontz, Frank, 239
Schwarts, John, 236
Schwarz, Connie, 116
Schwarz, Phil, 116
Science and Technology Education Programs (STEP), 63
Scott, Clayton L., 239
Sea Shore Lakefront Garden of Eden, 84
Seattle-First National Bank, 116
Seattle Sanitarium, 27, 28
Secret Park, 48, 49, 57, 134
Senior Foundation of Mercer Island, 148
Senn, Tana, 236
settlers, 19–24
Sewall, Dale, 155, 156
sewer system, 118–19, 217
Shell station, 76
Shelton, Mary, 237
Shevet Achim, 155
Shigeno, Gloria, 127
Shoentrup, Bill, 120
Shoreline Management Plan/Master Plan, 214, 217
shoreline ordinance, 171
Shorewood Apartments, 52, 82, 105, 109, 113, 119, 124, 170, 185. *See also* Covenant Shores; Shorewood Heights; Shorewood, Upper
Shorewood Heights, 109, 234. *See also* Covenant Shores; Shorewood Apartments
Shorewood, Upper, 185. *See also* Shorewood Apartments
Short, Floyd, 240
Shrontz, Harriet, 142
Shulman, Sarah, 195
sidewalk inlays, 175
Silverberg, Brad, 239
Simms, Cyndy, 66, 67, 237
Simpson, Hunter, 125, 130, 183, 188, 236, 239
Sinclair, Clarence, 152
Singer, Jacob, 149, 155
Sister City Association, 148
Sjunnesen, Paul, 237
Skaggs, James, 236
skateboard park, 138, 171
Skinner, Dr. Al, 110
Slater, Henry (Harry), 78, 107, 114, 166, 171

252 | Index

Mercer Island Historical Society
This 1960 photo looks east above the old Highway 10. The beginnings of the Town Center are in the center of the photo.

Slater, Loretta, 14, 166, 171
Slater Park, 171, 235
Smith, Doug, 101–3
Smith, Hilton, 237
Smith, H. Martin, 237
Smith, Larry, 59
Smith, Rick, 236
Smith, Roy, 167
Smith, Wilma, 61, 237
Smyth, Virginia, 147
Snyder, Quin, 192, 195, 197, 199
soccer, 198
softball, 198, 202
Solemates, 143
Sollod, T. Ellen, 175
Solomon, Mrs. Elias, 114
South 40/Forty, 57, 121, 131
south end, 83–89, 90, 105
South End Club/Community Club/ Improvement Club, 41, 46, 49, 54, 89, 103, 105–6, 116, 142
South End Shopping Center, 116
South Mercer Island Club, 105, 108
South Mercer Junior High, 52, 55, 56, 57, 106

Southern, Bill, 163
Special Olympics, 148
Speed's Garage, 76
sports, 191–202; figures, 194–95; Hall of Fame, 198–99
Stacy, Gordon, 120
Standard Supply Store, 29, 72, 84
Standsbury, Howard, 237
Stanger, Bill, 120
Stanislaw Enerson, Jean, 238
Starbucks, 102, 205
steamers, 24, 25–26, 37–42. *See also* ferries; *individual entries*
Steding, John, 237, 240
Steel, Julie, 151
Steiner, Charlotte, 147
Stenhouse, John, 237
Stenson, Barbara Hiscock, 239
Stevenson, Lewis, 68
Stewart, Hope D., 49
Stewart, Mark, 195
Stewart, William, 236
Stiles, David, 125
Stillwell, Steve, 201
Stimson, W.J., 71

Stocker, Karen, 59
Storey, Florence Guitteau, 17, 27, 48, 191
storms, 158, 216
Stover, T. Mark, 239
Strand, Dr. Norman, 110
Straw Hat Summer Theatre, 34
street(s); art, 175; names, 92–93; numbering, 92–93
Strivers, 148
Stroud, Carl, 110
Stroum, Sam, 239
Stroum Jewish Community Center, 11, 154
Stuart, Barclay, 104
Studebaker, Robert, 55, 237
Summer Arts Festival, 142
Summer Celebration, 10, 142, 209
Sung, Peter, 151
Sunnybeam School, 49, 50, 51, 52, 89, 90, 106, 235. *See also* Lakeview School
Sunset Highway, 82
Sussex, Sean, 196
sustainability, 218–19
Sutherland, Marguerite, 122, 136, 236,

Index | 253

241

Swarts, Dorothy, 24
Swier, Barbara, 240
swimming, 193, 196, 199
Sylvester, Tanya, 156
synagogues and churches, 149–56. See also individual entries

Tabit, C.J., 174
Tabit, Chick (Charles Joseph) Jr., 103, 174
Tabit, Chick Sr., 174
Tabit, Chris, 174
Tabit family, 102
Tabit Square, 103
Tao, Lillian, 186
Tarywood, 55, 56, 57, 88, 189
Tarywood Estates, 55, 88
Tate, Harold, 120
taxpayers, largest property, 234
Taylor, Chris, 200
Taylor, Kirsten, 127, 213
Temple B'nai Torah, 153, 155
tennis, 196, 199
Tent City, 215–16
Thompson, Albert, 79
Thonon-les-Bains, 148
thrift shop, 128, 134, 138, 144, 170, 207, 243
Thuau, Eric, 68
time bank, 219
Todd, John N., 46
Toll, Eldon, 155
toll(s), 221; removal, 105
Tom, Joe, 157
Totten, Irv E., 236
Town Center, 159, 160–61, 166, 175, 183–84, 203, 205–07, 235. See also business district; Central Business District
Town Council, 113, 117, 119
Town of Mercer Island, 111–13, 117, 119, 121
track and field, 199
tracts: Tract 243, 181, 183–84; Tract 244, 185–86; Tract 245, 186–87; Tract 246.01, 187–88; Tract 246.02, 188–89
Tradewell, 108
traffic, 206–07
Trail, John Dunney, 75
Trailmates, 143
Transition Initiative Mercer Island, 219
transportation, 37–42, 45. See also individual entries
Travis, Mark, 153
tree grates, 175
tree ordinance, 204
Triton, 35, 41
Trombold, Jim, 241
Tubbs, Chris, 221, 236
Tyo, Jim, 120
Tyrell, George, 120

United Church of Christ, 151, 153

United Methodist, 151
Urquart, John, 239

Valdez, 46
van der Burch, Dirk, 237
VanderHouwen, Boyd, 237
Vasten, 38
Veterans of Foreign Wars (VFW), 140–41
VFW Hall, 43, 45, 151, 235. See also Keewaydin Clubhouse; Mercer Island Community Club
video arcade, 137
Vinals, 73
Visual Arts Advisory Committee, 60–61. See also Fine Arts Advisory Committee
Vizzutti, Allen, 239
Vogel, Joshua, 93
volleyball, 199

Wainhouse, David, 195, 201
Waldron, Dennis, 239
Walker-Ames, Maud, 179
Wallace, Kay, 56
Wallace, Shantell, 83
Walsh, John, 150
Wappler, Harry, 239
Ward, Kristen, 184
Ward, Marcus, 184
Warner, Liz, 61, 237
Wasson farm, 93
water polo, 199, 200–01
water system, 30–31; south end, 86
water tower, East Seattle, 30–31
Waymire, John, 120
Wayte Bradburn, Mary, 191, 193, 195, 210
Weathers, Lindy, 57
Weathers, Tom, 168
Wedge, Eric, 195
Weigand, Steve, 147
Weinman, Richard, 57
Welch, Mary Margaret, 58
Welcome Wagon, 142
Wells, Lissa, 122, 236
Wensman, Mike, 236
Wentzell, Corey, 61, 237
Wenzler, John, 19
Werner, Ben, 59, 122, 125, 132, 163, 236
West Mercer Elementary School, 52, 53, 55, 59, 60
Westerlund, Trina, 68
Wheeler, Sue, 56
Whipple, Teresa, 147
White, Lawrence, 103
White, Mrs. Al, 114
White, Sean, 195, 201
Whitney, Fay, 125, 240
Wildermuth, Deanna, 150
wildlife, 177–79
Wilhite family, 89
Wilhite, John, 86
Wilkens, Marjory, 174
Wilkins, Jesse, 114, 236
Williams, Esther, 239

Williams, Gary, 120
Wilson, Jeff, 200
Winike, Susan, 147
Winkler Lund, Tove, 244
Winn, Beth Bland, 236
Winterscheid, Muriel, 99
Winterstein, Gary, 140
Wolfe, Ben, 241
Wolfe, Harriet, 142
Wolff, Marianne, 57
Wolter, Dr. David, 110
Women's Guild, 33
Wood, Amos, 94, 122, 124, 236
Wood, Frances, 179
Wood, Roger, 120
Woolley, Janice, 110
Wooten, Sharon, 147
Workman, August, 32
Works Progress Administration, 92–93, 96
World War II, 93–94
wrestling, 197, 199, 200–01
Wright, Carole, 147
Wright, Michael, 244

Yellow Wood Academy, 68
Yesler, Henry, 21
Yoo, Sunny, 201
York Brown, Sally, 147
Young, Bruce, 120
Young, Peter Daniel, 239
Young, Ze'ev, 155
Youth and Family Services, 62, 127, 128, 170, 208. See also thrift shop
Youth Theatre Northwest, 54, 57, 144, 145, 208

Zanner, Dr. Von, 110
Zickuhr, Donna, 66
zoning, 136, 167
Zorn, Jim, 195
Zuber, Betsy, 222

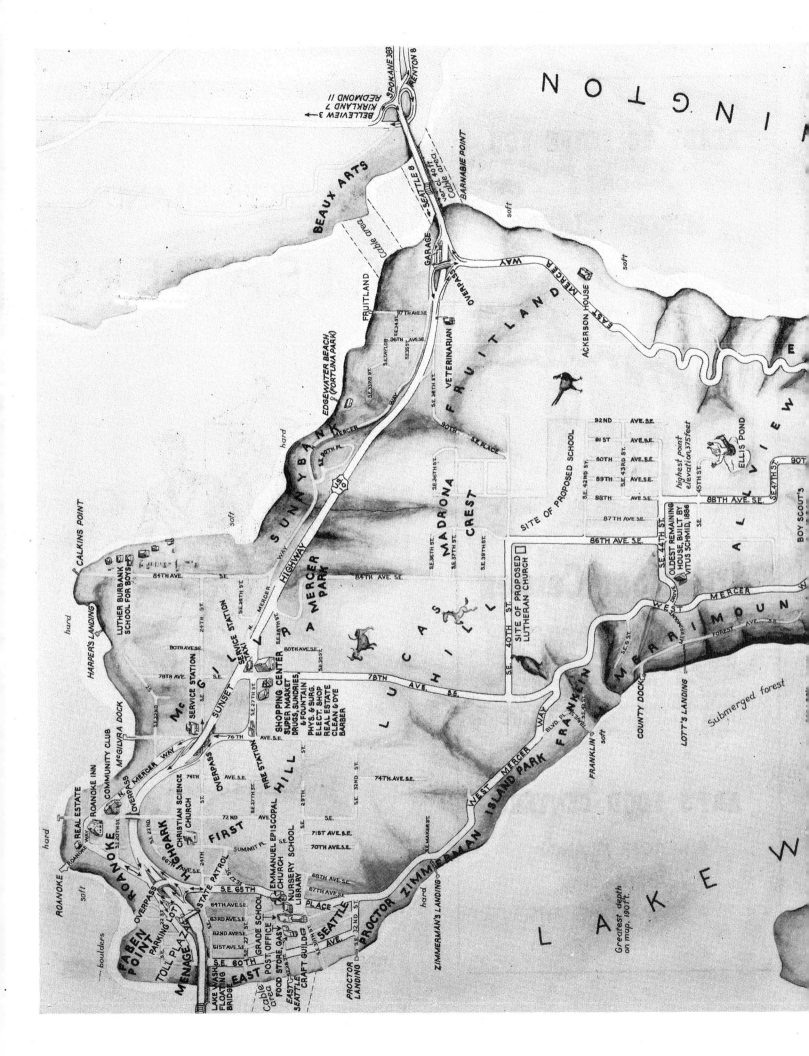